THE MEANS

of world evangelization:

MISSIOLOGICAL EDUCATION

at the
Fuller School of World Mission

edited by Alvin Martin

Preliminary Edition

William Carey Library

533 HERMOSA STREET • SOUTH PASADENA, CALIF. 91030

International Standard Book Number   0-87808-143-7
Library of Congress Catalog Number   74-9185

In accord with some of the most recent thinking in the
academic press, the William Carey Library is pleased to
present this scholarly book which has been prepared from
an author-edited and author-prepared camera-ready manuscript.

Published by the William Carey Library
533 Hermosa Street
South Pasadena, California 91030
Telephone 213-799-4559

PRINTED IN THE UNITED STATES OF AMERICA

Contents

955 15

Contents in Detail

foreword

In September, 1965, the <u>School of World Mission</u> opened
its doors. Three years earlier at the biennial meeting of the <u>Association of Professors of Missions</u>, the
keynote speaker painted a dark picture:

> We in the field of missions are lost sheep,
> scattered among the folds of history, the-
> ology, comparative religions, and education,
> wander from the theological field to the
> practical field and back again...We proclaim
> in our lectures that the world mission is the
> central task of the church, yet we have all
> too often allowed it to become peripheral in
> our curriculum (Dunstan, 1962:1). [1]

No one challenged this serious charge. All agreed
that the typical professor of missions in the average
American Seminary was a muddled soul, uncertain of his
objectives and priorities, and ineffective when it came
to recruiting his students for missionary service.

In this address, a very jaundiced eye was also cast
in the direction of the average seminary dean. He
was described as "dry-eyed" and "secretly glad to do
the obsequies for these wandering animals," since in
his judgment professors of missions were nothing less
than messy creatures that "threaten to contaminate the
pure heritage of the theological flock." All this just
twelve years ago!

Today, however, the situation is significantly different, particularly within the evangelical wing of the
Church. Not that professors of missions are relaxed
people, secure in their calling.   Professor O. G.
Myklebust in his comprehensive two-volume <u>Study of
Missions in Theological Education</u> (1955) has reminded
them too vividly of the fate of most of their illus-
trious predecessors!

What professor of missions has not traced the abysmal failure of Alexander Duff (1806-1878) to make missions theologically respectable at New College, Edinburgh. And he was the 19th century's and India's most distinguished missionary educator! Who has not been sobered at the limited success of Gustav Warneck (1834-1910) in creating and sustaining a scholarly approach to missions that was acceptable to the European Theological Establishment. And he was the "Father of the Protestant Science of Missions." The record of the past cannot but cast a gray pall over the most self-confident would-be missiologist.

Nonetheless, something has happened during the past decade. In the judgment of the School of World Mission faculty, a "new thing" has come to pass in the field of missiology. And its locus is right here at Fuller. God be praised--a new day may be dawning for that troublesome intruder, the professor of missions! Not that missiology has at long last achieved academic respectability in the eyes of the theologians! But, hopefully, we believe that a corner has been turned.

What is this new thing? When Dr. McGavran was approached about coming to Fuller he was intensely interested, because this meant that he was being given a green light to head a new and autonomous School of World Mission. He saw in this invitation the possibility of launching an entirely new discipline--MISSIOLOGY.

No longer would there be the possibility of shunting into the elective category or eliminating altogether those courses in the seminary curriculum that are related to the worldwide mission Christ gave his Church. Now it would be possible to build a faculty that would concentrate their energies in investigating the dynamics of church growth throughout the world.

This handbook describes the present level of curriculum development and research approaches of the School of World Mission. It seeks to describe what the SWM Faculty mean when they speak of MISSIOLOGY. As you examine the course descriptions and note the way in which research and writing objectives are made central to all degree programs, you will find that missiology is neither theology nor history, neither anthropology nor sociology, neither the study of comparative religions nor ecumenics. It is not even the sum total of these fields of study. It is rather their dynamic interaction

when intimately related to those actual situations facing missionaries and national church leaders as they
seek to advance the Christian movement throughout the
world.

Previously, the professor who sought to teach missions
invariably emphasized the one component in which he had
acquired special training and expertise. Indeed, to
mingle among our peers at a gathering of the Association
of Professors of Missions is to find men who call training in mission training in ecumenics, or in linguistics,
or in comparative religions, or in Church-Mission relations, or in communication, depending on their background
and interest. We have heard of a professor in a noted
School of Missions--since defunct--who said that his task
was to teach anthropology "without caring whether anyone
was ever converted to Christ or not."

So then, once the actual missionary task was made
central to the curriculum of an autonomous School of
World Mission--once it was agreed that the SWM Faculty
make top priority the propagation of the Gospel to all
peoples and the incorporation of converts into the Church
of Jesus Christ--then it became possible to harness the
various academic components together and form a stable
discipline in its own right.

This School was not established to provide training
in a variety of missionary subjects. Rather its objective is to assist mid-career missionaries and national
church leaders in surmounting all the barriers that
separate the peoples of our generation from Jesus Christ.
It specializes in training them to become more effective
in multiplying churches.

On this basis the School was launched. And God has
been good to us during these past nine years. To date,
545 have been enrolled. By June 1974 it is anticipated
that 44 will have received the M.A. in Missions, 85 the
M.A. in Missiology and 28 the Doctor of Missiology.

These three degrees differ in their academic requirements whether an undergraduate degree (B.A. or equivalent)
or an additional degree in theology (M.Div. or equivalent).
They also differ in the extent in which they probe the
theoretical components of missiology and relate them to
the actual church situation being researched. They have
been deliberately designed for the mid-career missionary

and national church leader who has spent at least three
years in significant cross-cultural communication of the
Christian faith, generally validated by a demonstrated
ability in a second language.

We would underscore what has already been stated: The
faculty is not content to teach courses. Our basic commitment to the Great Commission means that a central
faculty function is to guide the reading and stimulate
the reflection of each degree candidate. Indeed, this
mentorship program takes more time per week than any
other single activity. Each faculty member works with
at least ten degree candidates. Inasmuch as these
missionaries and national church leaders serve diverse
segments of the human race, it is only through wide
reading and deliberate grappling with their particular
Gospel communication problems that they can be truly
made more effective in the ministry to which God has
called them. Field problems are analyzed and workable
solutions are sought. The writing and defending of a
thesis or dissertation climaxes this study. The overall thrust of our M.A. programs and the professional
doctorate is to heighten the candidate's effectiveness
in the field situation to which he has been called.

When the School of World Mission has produced at least
1000 separate researches of actual church growth situations
throughout the world, it will be in a position to affirm
with authority a measure of understanding of the complexity of the unfinished task facing the Church in our
day.

Arthur F. Glasser, Dean

May 2, 1974

---

1. J. Leslie Dunstan, What is the Justification for
   a Chair of Missions? Paper presented on June 12,
   1962 at the Sixth Biennial Meeting of the Association
   of Professors of Missions at Trinity College, Toronto,
   Canada.

Introduction

*"It is a light thing that thou shouldst raise up
the tribes of Jacob and restore the remnant of
Israel. I will give you as a light to the Gentiles
that my salvation may reach to the ends of the earth."*
-Isa. 49:6

This introduction will comment on the way in which
this entire volume is itself introductory to both the
means and the end of world evangelization. The very
definition of missiology is that it is the study of the
mission of world evangelization. Missiology is preemin-
ently the scholarly discipline underlying the task of
world evangelization.

By way of introduction, then, let us first consider
what to many is an enigma: "Can or should missiology
be developed as a scholarly discipline?" Then, "What,
if developed, can this discipline do for world evangelization?"

This document itself is very preliminary in format
and content. But, insofar as it attempts to represent
the structure of a new scholarly discipline, it is preliminary in a different sense. If it is the discipline
of missiology you are trying to visualize as you page
through this book, it will be very much like looking
through the hole in a plyboard wall at a construction
site: what you will see is a building in the process
of going up. The foundations are laid; workmen are
swarming around; a new entity is being created. It will
be a while yet before the approaches to the building are
covered with grass, the furniture is moved in, the walls
decorated, and routine office force, maintenance and
clean-up crews replace the construction gangs that now
dominate the scene.

To be sure, the scholarly functions to be performed
in this brand new building will not themselves be brand
new. Those functions are even now going on elsewhere,

or the construction of a building would not be necessary
to house them. But other people in nearby, long-estab-
lished buildings may be disturbed at the noise and the
racket of the construction of this new one. The scholarly fields of the other people are settled worlds of rou-
tinized performances. To them the new building may simply be a nuisance, and will be until the construction
period is over. Only then will it be clear for all to
see that a building outwardly similar to the others is
now under construction.

This only provides a vague analogy to the present status of missiology as a discipline "under construction,"
in the immediate neighborhood of other well-established
disciplines. When a building is being built, for example, when does it actually become a building? When the
major frame is up? When all the lights are turned on?
When the furniture is moved in? When all the functions
to be performed are fully laid out in a coherent organization?

These are the questions that besiege missiologists today. Is missiology yet a discipline? If not, at what
point will it become one? What does it take to become a
discipline? Is there room for such a discipline? Before
discussing directly the contribution of this book to the
ordeal of the birth and development of a new discipline,
let us leave the world of inanimate analogies and take
up a social analogy.

What does it take for a new sport to come into existence? Let's imagine a group of soccer players on a university campus talking to the president of the university
about the formation of an intercollegiate soccer team.
The president is naturally pained by this new burden on
his time. The university has already gone to great
lengths to establish outstanding teams in the well-known
sports. They have an outstanding team in football.
They have an outstanding basketball team. They have an
outstanding intercollegiate water polo team. Their
track team has done an outstanding job in competition.
Their funds are stretched thin. Somehow not all sports
pay their way. And who ever heard of soccer? Under the
circumstances it would be very reasonable for the president to urge these would-be soccer players to go back to
the major sports in which most of them had played before
and eventually become distinguished there. Why not?

The facts are that missiology is like a soccer tradition that not only looks to many like a cross between

football, basketball, and hockey, but perhaps, to people
more familiar with these other sports, soccer may actually seem to be an unfortunate and undesirable perversion.
Indeed, so many people are unfamiliar with the sixty-year
history of missiology as a formal field of study that in
even discussing the field those of us involved in it constantly find ourselves accommodating in various ways to
the vocabulary of outsiders. For example, we often talk
as if missiology is (what it only appears to be) an "interdisciplinary" field.

This book clearly indicates, as does Tippett's article (See Sec. II, pages 3 and 4) that missiology certainly does relate to a number of other fields insofar as present-day missiologists have, for the most part, been
trained in the disciplines of these related fields. The
work of missiology, descriptively speaking, may appear
interdisciplinary: Alan Tippett was disciplined in anthropology, Charles Kraft in linguistics, Arthur Glasser
in theology, etc. All of the School of World Mission
faculty members are bringing to the construction site of
this new field skills and insights which they have originally gained in other disciplines. This compares to a
soccer team built out of track stars, football players,
etc. If this were all that were ever to happen, missiology would always be an interdisciplinary activity in the
strictest sense of the words. But missiology already has
a discipline of its own, as this volume clearly shows.
What will it take to confirm itself as an academic discipline? The answer is simple to conceive; more difficult
to accomplish.

Scholarly disciplines are born almost every day. In
a technical sense, a discipline exists the moment a group
of scholars agrees to study the same thing together and
develops the capability of perpetuating their community
over the years. Not all disciplines are well-known. Not
all disciplines make the grade in all circles. Take
theology, for example. After the radical disestablish-
ment of religion following the American Revolution, it
took 150 years for theology as a scholarly discipline to
gain any significant re-entry into major university life.
But in fact this does not mean it fell short of being a
scholarly discipline. Now at last the "Th.D." terminology
is being changed to "Ph.D." all over the country--at the
suggestion of the AATS--precisely because what long already was a scholarly discipline is finally becoming acceptable in a University tradition which for a long time
could not see how theology could be respectable.

So you might say missiology is a discipline, but is
not yet respected as such. In this vein, it is hoped
that the American Society of Missiology--already with
more than 500 charter members (Protestant, Evangelical,
and Roman Catholic) and more than 3,000 subscribers to
its journal, Missiology, (see page 481 for details)--
will soon be a member of the Council on the Study of Religion and join the other recognized scholarly societies
in the field of religion which are already members. That
will help.

Most important to missiology is the development and
the perpetuation of its community of professional missiological scholars. It is by no means desirable that all
missiologists be migrants from other fields, even neighboring fields. It is highly necessary that somewhere
(besides Union Theological Seminary in New York)[1] it be
possible to get a first-class education for professorship
in missiology under a discipline that is released from
the full requirements in any one of the neighboring
fields, and is thus allowed to make a blend that will be
superior to the outlines of any one of the related disciplines. The dean of an engineering school put it this
way: as the new field of materials science developed,
the early faculty consisted of men with Ph.D.'s in phy-
sics, chemistry, metallurgy, and so on, but the discipline of materials science was never well established until they replaced most of the "outsiders" with men who
had Ph.D.'s in the new field itself.

In an important sense, this volume is, therefore, a
demonstration of the new mix in which people can and must
be trained, in order for the best professors of missiology to emerge--better balanced than those who come out of
or stay in a single, related discipline. Glancing through
the book, the reader will readily see that the new discipline is still in many ways under construction; but it
is a building, and it will better serve world evangelization when it is further along. This brings us to our
second question: "What can this discipline do for world
evangelization?"

Now that we have given logical reasons why missiology
can and must become a discipline in its own right, we
must give practical reasons why there is justification
for the title of this book to speak of missiology as a
means of world evangelization.

First of all, we may freely grant that to be "academic" does not necessarily lead to being practical. On

the other hand, it is a striking historical fact that in the last 130 years, the entire older university tradition has undergone a colossal transformation. Once it was indeed quite "academic" and greatly distant from the issues of everyday life. With the advent of the scientific era, engineering and technology have more and more interpenetrated the very structure of the university, so that today the majority of all graduate students in America are studying in "applied" fields rather than in the older fields of knowledge that were mainly pursued for the sake of discussion about discussion.

Just one example: most of the buildings in history have been built without benefit of academic knowledge, pure or applied. Massive cathedrals, famous bridges, breathtaking pyramids, etc. were simply produced by daring, ingenious builders. Building as an activity was too mundane, too practical to warrant academic attention. As recently as 40 years ago, engineering schools were struggling into existence and their faculties contained very few men with advanced degrees, none of those degrees in any field of engineering. Today the major advances in, say, structural engineering are the product of academic faculties. The same is true in the biological and human sciences. Speech pathology has arisen, as a discipline, from nothing in one generation. Forty years ago, you could have assembled all the books on the subject for $200. Today there are 35,000 speech pathologists, and the necessary basic library would cost $100,000--most of the books produced by Ph.D.'s in speech pathology, the discipline that formerly did not exist.

So in missions. Some of the most outstanding attempts to break through to the non-Christian peoples of the world have in the distant past been launched on the basis of the shrewd, sanctified judgment of leaders out on the front lines. Until this century, the systematic thinkers who developed written strategies were relatively rare. Only a few names come to mind: Raymond Lull, Prince Henry the Navigator, Cardinal Brancati, Justinian Welz, William Carey, Alexander Duff, Henry Venn, Rufus Anderson, Hudson Taylor, Gustav Warneck, etc. Perhaps a dozen more. It is still possible for a school to acquire all the books relevant to missiology (beyond those in established related fields) for a few thousand dollars.

Tragic, is it not, that world evangelization, the activity most deserving of disciplined study and planning, would be the last receiving the benefit of such study. But the picture is now rapidly changing. In nine short

years in the Fuller School of World Mission alone, over
500 mature missionaries and national leaders have done
missiological studies. The book distribution center related to the William Carey Library--the Church Growth
Book Club--is now distributing more than 60,000 missiological books a year, mainly to field workers. Many other
schools all around the world are acknowledging the need
for missiology departments and perspectives. We could
name a dozen were there space. Furthermore, mission
agencies that have, over a period of years, poured millions of dollars into situations with no visible results
are beginning now to check to make sure that at least
someone has done his homework--ransacked all related
scholarly disciplines, analyzed all the factors in the
specific situation, sought parallels in similar circumstances elsewhere, deliberately tried new strategies.
It would be safe to say that every $500 spent in missiol-
ogical research will modify the use of $100,000 on the
field.

The purely human impact of missiology is also impressive. Yesterday I talked to a man whose full-time assignment is to do career consultation with missionaries (of
several boards) who are about to come home on furlough.
He said he was in Ethiopia shortly after the departure
of a missiologist whose greatest expertise is in the area
of Oceania. Missionaries were still exclaiming that the
missiologist after only a few weeks there had pointed out
things which had never dawned on them in all their years
of service. Many a discouraged missionary has had, as
it were, scales removed from his eyes, and his whole
attitude toward the future modified through exposure to
missiological studies.

Missiological study centers across the world must provide the strategic brainstorming of fresh approaches to
long-unsolved problems. Three great bastions that have
not yet responded to Christ--Chinese, Hindu, Muslim--con-
stitute 83% of the non-Christians in the entire non-Western world, each with at least a half billion people, yet
only a tiny fraction of all the world's missionary efforts
are effectively focused on these three fields (see pp.
505-518). Recent studies provide radically new approaches
to all three fields (Chinese, see Liao,on page 274; Hindu,
see Subbamma,on page 275 ; Muslim, see page 509).

But these are only tiny beginnings. The task before
us, missiologically speaking, ranges from the "pure" ethnotheological   considerations to the "applied" concerns
of practical methodology. Missiology is not the only

means of world evangelization. The task requires missiological research centers on the one hand, and missiologically trained field leaders on the other, both working in coordination with missiologically alert agencies of mission whose own research departments are like the R&D divisions of major industries that are closely in touch with the corresponding academic divisions of the university world. Other human tasks far less profound in complexity or significance daily profit from disciplined study. Why cannot we develop a similar use of disciplined study for a task presently involving more than 100,000 professional workers with 2,000 years of experience to draw from? It is hoped that even this volume, in very preliminary form, will contribute to that end. Those of us involved in the structure described in these pages earnestly hope that this display of what we are actually doing will not be thought of as a boast, much less a norm, but rather a plea for interaction and constructive discussion, which alone can enhance and confirm the new discipline of missiology.

Ralph D. Winter

---

[1]Outside of the United States (as with soccer) there are many more possibilities. Research doctoral studies in missiology are available at Heidelberg, Tübingen, Münster, Freiburg, Louvain, and at the Pontifical Gregorian University in Rome. These programs are generally, as at Union, based on the presence of a single missiologist. While the Fuller School of World Mission has six full-time faculty members, the present doctoral program is not considered a teaching doctorate. The Ph.D. program contemplated requires field experience as well as six academic years of study, including the usual three-year B.D. or M.Div. degree. This constitutes one more year than the present D.Miss. program.

1. GENERAL INFORMATION

PURPOSE OF THE ACADEMIC MANUAL

This collation of course outlines of the 1972-74 curriculum of the School of World Mission and Institute of Church Growth of Fuller Theological Seminary is the first attempt to meet the need for an SWM Academic Manual. The manual has been compiled to achieve the following objectives, which were articulated by the Dean, Arthur F. Glasser in a July 3, 1973 memo to SWM Faculty and in the SWM Alumni news, summer, 1973:

1. We desire to standardize within our school the course syllabi and bring them all to a high level of completeness and quality.

2. We feel that such a project will be good for our own self-understanding. (It provides the necessary data base for a further evaluation of the curriculum, and possible consolidation or greater coordination of some courses.)

3. SWM associates should have access to what is involved in each course, ... along with comprehensive questions and other such materials.

4. We desire to share such a compilation of courses with institutions with which we are exploring the possibility of future association on a franchise or other basis.

5. We need a comprehensive directory of SWM associates.

6. We should provide coordinated SWM guidelines for field and library research, thesis writing, archival use, graphics and visual aid possibilities and all SWM theses abstracts. The suggested manual will make the following information available to research associates, satellite and associate schools:

   a. List of SWM theses and dissertations;
   b. List of general textbooks plus a bibliography for each course.

7. We should provide basic information concerning the CHURCH GROWTH BULLETIN, CHURCH GROWTH BOOK CLUB, MISSIOLOGY and the AMERICAN SOCIETY OF MISSIOLOGY.

Fuller Theological Seminary Statement of Faith

A FOUNDATION OF FAITH IN A CHANGING WORLD

Doctrinally the institution stands for the fundamentals of the faith as taught in Holy Scripture and handed down by the Church. Consistent with this purpose, the faculty and trustees of the Seminary acknowledge the creeds of the early church and the confessions of the Protestant communions to which they severally belong. Under God, and subject to Biblical authority, they also bear concerted witness to the following articles, to which they subscribe, and which they hold to be essential to their ministry.

I. God has revealed Himself to be the living and true God, perfect in love and righteous in all His ways; one in essence, existing eternally in the three persons of the Trinity: Father, Son and Holy Spirit.

II. God, who discloses Himself to mankind through His creation, has savingly spoken in the words and events of redemptive history. This history is fulfilled in Jesus Christ, the incarnate Word, who is made known to us by the Holy Spirit in sacred Scripture.

III. Scripture is an essential part and trustworthy record of this divine self-disclosure. All the books of the Old and New Testaments, given by divine inspiration, are the written Word of God, the only infallible rule of faith and practice. They are to be interpreted according to their context and purpose and in reverent obedience to the Lord who speaks through them in living power.

IV. God, by His Word and for His glory, freely created the world of nothing. He made man in His own image, as the crown of creation, that man might have fellowship with Him. Tempted by Satan, man rebelled against God. Being estranged from his Maker, yet responsible to Him, he became subject to divine wrath, inwardly depraved and, apart from grace, incapable of returning to God.

V. The only Mediator between God and man is Christ Jesus our Lord, God's eternal Son, who, being conceived by the Holy Spirit and born of the Virgin Mary, fully shared and fulfilled our humanity in a life of perfect obedience. By His death in our stead, He revealed the divine love and upheld divine justice, removing our guilt and reconciling us to God. Having redeemed us from sin, the third day He rose bodily from the grave, victorious over death and the powers of darkness. He ascended into heaven where, God's right hand, He intercedes for His people and rules as Lord over all.

VI. The Holy Spirit, through the proclamation of the Gospel, renews our hearts, persuading us to repent of our sins and confess Jesus as Lord. By the same Spirit we are led to trust in divine mercy, whereby we are forgiven all our sins, justified by faith alone through the merit of Christ our Savior, and granted the free gift of eternal life.

God graciously adopts us into His
family and enables us to call Him Father. As
 are led by the Spirit, we grow in the
knowledge of the Lord, freely keeping His
commandments and endeavoring so to live
the world that men see our good works
and glorify our Father who is in heaven.

. God by His Word and Spirit creates
one holy catholic and apostolic Church,
calling sinful men out of the whole human
race into the fellowship of Christ's Body. By
 same Word and Spirit, He guides and
preserves for eternity that new, redeemed
humanity, which, being formed in every
culture, is spiritually one with the people
 God in all ages.

IX.   The Church is summoned by Christ to
offer acceptable worship to God and to serve
Him by preaching the Gospel and making
disciples of all nations, by tending the flock
through the ministry of the Word and
sacraments and through daily pastoral care,
by striving for social justice and by relieving
human distress and need.

X.   God's redemptive purpose will be
consummated by the return of Christ to raise
the dead, to judge all men according to the
deeds done in the body, and to establish
His glorious kingdom. The wicked shall
be separated from God's presence, but the
righteous, in glorious bodies, shall live and
reign with Him forever. Then shall the eager
expectation of the creation be fulfilled and
the whole earth shall proclaim the glory of
God who makes all things new.

5

ller Theological Seminary   135 North Oakland Avenue   Pasadena, California 91101

school of world mission
and institute of church growth

higher education for missionaries-its character and purpose

Nothing is more important in providing higher education for missionaries than a correct assessment of whether the enterprise of missions is beginning or ending. The School of World Mission at Fuller believes that we stand at the beginning of the missionary task. Everything that has gone before in a hundred and seventy-five years of modern missions is introduction. Except in the primitive populations, there has been little "discipling of the peoples" (Matthew 28:19). The great populations of earth — Marxists, Hindus, Buddhists, Moslems, Secularists, Animists and nominal born Christians — have yet to accept Jesus Christ as Lord and Savior. God calls Christians today to vast, protracted and intelligent labor to make Jesus Christ known, loved and believed throughout the world. As evidence of his call, God grants remarkable responsiveness in many populations. The main task in missions lies ahead. Christians correctly plan to give their lives to "bring about obedience to the faith among all the Gentiles" (Romans 1:5 *RSV*).

At the same time Christian mission is being carried on in the midst of a tremendous revolution affecting every aspect of human life. The guidelines and assumptions under which our fathers sent out missionaries have been swept away. Christian mission today has radically new ground on which to operate: advances in knowledge, changed political alignments, hugely increased control of nature, rise of churches in Asia, Africa and Latin America, lessening ecclesiastical competition and hatred, rising religious relativism, battle for brotherhood and vastly accelerated secularization of life. Education for mission must prepare men to propagate the Christian faith in this new world being born.

Christian mission carried out in this changing world has an unchanging Lord and an unchanging mandate. Jesus Christ is the same yesterday, today and forever. The mission is his, not ours. He remains in charge. Since Jesus Christ is the eternal Son, consubstantial and co-eternal with the Father and the Holy Spirit, and since no man comes to the Father but by him, therefore, propagating the gospel to the ends of the earth by the multiplication of believers and churches is the supreme and controlling purpose of the Christian mission to the world.

In the course of mission, the Church will and should do many good things. The fruits of the Christian life will inevitably bless and heal humanity. Forms of society more pleasing to God will certainly be produced. Deliberate effort toward these good ends is also a part of Christian mission, but must never be substituted for propagating the faith. Proclaiming Christ as God and Savior and persuading men to become his disciples and responsible members of his Church must remain a chief and irreplaceable purpose of Christian mission. Education for mission operates, therefore, in a changing periphery with an unchanging center.

As he "brings about obedience to the faith among men of all nations" (Romans 1:5 *KJ*), the missionary needs light from many disciplines: history, anthropology, sociology, theory of mission, the biblical base of mission, apologetics (knowledge of and approach to non-Christian religions), the world Church (sometimes called ecumenics) and urgent matters such as evangelism, training the ministry and the indigenous church. These are all therefore, properly part of education for mission.

Career missionaries should know the whole sweep of **missions**. The School of World Mission aims to make them competent in the field to which they have given their lives. Graduates of the School of World Mission and Institute of Church Growth ll be qualified to serve effectively in many tasks which missionaries are assigned — front line ɔrkers, district superintendents, field directors, ecutive secretaries and faculty members in theoȝical training schools at home and abroad.

Two main types of missionary education exist:) preparing missionary candidates under appoint-ent for their first plunge into a strange new cul-ɾe and language and (2) giving career missionaries ɪ furlough advanced education in missions. The hool of World Mission considers the latter — ɪining career missionaries — its chief task and ɪns its program to that end. Boards have exten-e recruiting and training programs for candidates ading toward the field. Seminaries have courses missions for their students. Career missionaries ⱦking higher education in missions are poorly served existing institutions. **Advanced education in mis-ɪn is**, therefore, the area in which the School of ɔrld Mission specializes.

Christian mission is a vast body of knowledge d the educated missionary should see it in total. presenting this corpus of learning through lec-ɾes, courses of study and readings, two dangers ⱦ avoided: a frozen intellectual regimen removed ɔm the fast-moving contemporary scene and a ɪorgasbord of "hot" transient emphases. Ad-ɪced education must be validated by advanced ɟrees in missions; yet the degree program must ɲain flexible enough to equip God's men and ɔmen to meet the rapidly changing conditions of ⱦ modern world.

The School of World Mission and Institute of ɪurch Growth emphasizes research. World mission ɜes a curious fact — knowledge of how churches ɔw is extremely limited. Though the discipling the nations is a chief and continuing goal of ɾistian mission, not much is known about how ⱦn and their societies are, in fact, discipled. In most ɪds some churches have broken through to great ɔwth, but these instances are shut away in lin-ɪstic, geographic and denominational compart-ⱦnts. Few books have been published on the sub-t of church growth, and they have enjoyed only

tiny circulation. Membership increase is a central function of mission, yet world mission has no clear-inghouse for knowledge about it, no place dedicated to its research and no center where missionaries and nationals can learn the many ways in which churches grow in particular populations of mankind. This disastrous vacuum in knowledge and training facilities handicaps the entire missionary enterprise.

To meet this need, therefore, the School of World Mission and Institute of Church Growth em-phasizes research in church growth as an integral part of the educational process. The approach to higher education for missionaries places much em-phasis on discovering and teaching truth concerning the spread of churches.

facilities and costs

The offices of the School of World Mission are located in downtown Pasadena at 135 N. Oakland Avenue. In common with the Seminary's other graduate schools, it uses the classrooms, bookstore, refectory and the McAlister Library with its more than 118,000 volumes of theology, missions and related disciplines.

Men's and women's dormitories at the Seminary house single persons for eight to nine dollars a week. In some nearby communities such as Glendale and Altadena apartments available to missionaries on furlough provide suitable living quarters at reason-able cost. Furnished apartments or houses in the Pasadena area are available at commercial rates varying from $80 to $250 a month.

The refectory provides meals at $15 per five-day week for one person. For missionaries not covered with insurance by their own boards, acci-dent, sickness and hospital insurance costs $51 per year for one person and $264 for a married student and his family.

Tuition is $42.00 per quarter hour. Any student needing grant-in-aid may apply to the dean of the School of World Mission, stating his situation.

Typing of final copy of M.A. thesis or D.Miss. dissertation may cost $100 and up.

school of world mission
and institute of church growth

international overseas edition 1974-1976 catalog

admission

The School of World Mission and Institute of Church Growth admits students conditionally to three degree programs and to special courses designed for missionaries. Upon successful completion of at least one quarter of satisfactory work and upon the approval of the faculty, the student is advanced to degree candidacy.

Those entering the master of arts in missions program must normally hold an undergraduate degree (B.A. or equivalent); for the master of arts in missiology program, an additional degree in theology (B.D., M.Div. or equivalent) with a B standard of work; and for the doctor of missiology program, the same theology degree (B.D., M.Div. or equivalent) or about three years of other graduate work, with a B plus standard of work. In addition, all candidates must give evidence of several years in significant cross-cultural communication of the Christian faith, generally to be validated by a demonstrated ability in a second language.

Missionaries on furlough may enroll in special courses or a non-degree program for one, two or three quarters. Those coming for only one quarter are advised to come in the fall. The fall quarter contains core courses which are foundational for the work done in the other two quarters.

research and tuition fellowships

Several research and tuition fellowships are available for nationals holding responsible positions in their churches. In addition, the School of World Mission seeks to assist missionary associates with grants-in-aid when funds are available. Where private resources are not available it is expected that the board or church under which a person serves will contribute to living expenses. Occasionally research fellowships are granted to doctoral candidates who find they must enlarge their data base by additional field research after completing their first year of study at the School of World Mission.

Applications for all fellowships should be made by July 1, preceding matriculation.

the curriculum

In a wider sense, the curriculum consists of a combination of course work, reading and directed research tailored to fit the individual missionary's problems and opportunities. In a narrower sense, the curriculum consists of courses of study which develop a part of one of the following eight major branches of learning and together make up the discipline of missiology. 700 courses are in the corresponding areas but are considered doctoral level

  I. Theory and Theology of Missions (courses 610-619)

  II. Apologetics of the Christian Mission vis á vis non-Christian religions (620-629)

  III. Mission Across Cultures—anthropology, sociology, world revolution, secularism, urbanization (630-639)

  IV. Techniques, Organization and Methods in Mission (640-649)

  V. History of Missions and Church Expansion (650-659)

  VI. Church Growth (660-669)

  VII. The World Church—ecumenics (670-679)

  VIII. Biblical Studies and Theology

Great emphasis is placed on reading. Students at the graduate level are expected to glean the essence of many men's contributions to mission through books. The function of the teacher is to guide, stimulate and provide supplementary summaries of knowledge particularly germane to the situation in each man's field. Missionaries come from such varied segments of the world's vast population that only through wide reading in their field can they become truly educated.

Great emphasis is also placed on working out viable solutions to the special problems each missionary faces in communicating the gospel. He analyzes these problems and through reading, research and counsel, works out solutions. Research seminars thus form a significant portion of the curriculum. Experience has shown these to be most productive of creative thinking.

any given quarter, courses will be selected from
ong the following, depending upon the avail-
lity of faculty and composition of the anticipated
dent body. Typical offerings of the fall and
nter quarters, outlined at the close of the course
scriptions, show what may be expected.

). THEOLOGY OF MISSION I. A comprehensive
dy of the Old Testament as preparation for the Chris-
mission, focusing particular attention on the cultural
erative, Israel and the nations, the Kingdom of God,
gious encounter and the missionary awakenings of
laism during the inter-testamental period. 2 hours
sser

. THEOLOGY OF MISSION II. A comprehensive
dy of the New Testament as revelation of the Christian
sion, focusing particular attention on the evangelistic
ndate, Jesus and the nations, the Kingdom of God,
stolic understanding of mission and the missionary
dience of the Church in the apostolic age. 2 hours
sser

. THEOLOGY OF MISSION III. An evaluation of
development of missiological thought down through
history of the Church until the International Mission-
Council-World Council of Churches merger at New
hi in 1961, with particular attention given to the writ-
of Orthodox, Roman Catholic and Continental Prot-
nt missiologists. 2 hours   Glasser

. THEOLOGY OF MISSIONS TODAY. A study of
mission of the Church interpreted in terms of the
at Commission, in the light of the contemporary
ld-wide struggle for brotherhood, justice and equality,
revolution of rising expectations, and the growing
ralism of most societies with particular attention given
British and American missiologists, the World Council
Churches since 1961, the Wheaton and Frankfurt
larations. 2 hours   McGavran

(714). THEOLOGY OF RELIGIOUS ENCOUNTER.
investigation of the relation between Revelation and
stianity in the context of elenctic missionary encounter
men of other faiths, or no religious allegiance. Par-
lar attention will be given to Roman Catholic and
testant theologians throughout the 20th century. 2/3
rs Glasser

. ANIMISM AND CHURCH GROWTH I. The basic
ures of the animistic view of life common to the masses
sia, Africa, Oceania and Latin America, and its bearing
he acceptance of the gospel and the spread of the in-
nous church. 2 hours   Tippett

. ANIMISM AND CHURCH GROWTH II. Christian
sion in confrontation with persons and institutions of
nistic society — witchcraft, sorcery, possession, sham-
m, priesthoods, prophetic movements. 2 hours
ett

624. HINDUISM AND APPROACH TO HINDUS. A
systematic presentation of both philosophic and popular
Hinduism, its doctrinal base and social structure. Approaches to Hindus which have multiplied churches among
them. Secularism as an outcome of Christian mission. 2
hours McGavran

630. ANTHROPOLOGY AND MISSION I. What anthropology offers the missionary in his task of discipling
the nations and avoiding cultural barriers to the redemptive work of the Holy Spirit, and patterns of culture within which the Christian operates. 2 hours   Kraft

631. ANTHROPOLOGY AND MISSION II. The cross-
cultural communication of the gospel and directed culture
change, with particular attention to the diffusion, acceptance or rejection of the supracultural message of the
Scriptures. 2 hours   Kraft

634 (734). URBAN ANTHROPOLOGY. A seminar for
interaction. Cross-cultural urban and industrial studies of
places open for evangelism today, the character of religious
encounter, sociological and economic factors, methodological procedures for investigating the possibilities of
church planting. 2/3 hours Tippett

636. FUNDAMENTALS OF LANGUAGE LEARNING.
The study and practice of techniques of language learning.
Insights of modern linguistics are employed to assist the
learner in developing his understanding of and ability to
go about language learning and/or improving competence
in a language he already knows. 2 hours   Kraft

637. LINGUISTICS AND MISSION. An introduction
to the study of language ranging from its form and function
to the field of applied linguistics and with particular reference to illiteracy, Bible translation and exegesis, and church
growth. 2 hours Cotterell and faculty

640. RESEARCH METHODS. An introductory study
designed to equip the missionary working in alien cultures
to discern truly and describe exactly the structures of
society and Church, personality conflicts and human environment, customs and beliefs. Techniques of interviewing, observing and documenting. 2 hours Tippett

642. TRAINING THE MINISTRY-LAY AND ORDAINED.
Training lay and ordained ministers to obtain development of the Church and extension of the faith. Theological, historical, cultural and practical factors in designing right kinds of training for radically different contexts,
particularly extension programs. 2 hours Winter

643. TEE WORKSHOP. Seminar designed for researchers
to present case studies of their field situations. Usually
involves determining the validity or effectiveness of a
residential or TEE program. Researcher presents a paper
about Theological Education by Extension which is
discussed in class. Designed to be of practical use in problem solving. 2 hours Winter

644. PROGRAMMED INSTRUCTION. Fundamentals of programming demonstrate use of P I materials in a TEE program. A production workshop where P I frames can be written, rewritten and tested. 2 hours *Winter*

651. THE HISTORICAL DEVELOPMENT OF THE CHRISTIAN MOVEMENT. A brief analysis of the growth dynamics of the Christian movement, from its roots in the Abrahamic covenant to its fruits in the age of Billy Graham and its prospects by the year 2000. Emphasis on the period beginning with World War I, the indigenization of world Christianity, the new mission agencies and new rules for old ones, the structure and function of missions today. 2 hours *Winter*

652. THE EMERGENCE OF THE WESTERN CHRISTIAN TRADITION. A more detailed geographical, cultural and structural analysis of the expansion of Christianity prior to 1914, emphasizing the Western, Roman tradition and the peoples involved: the Jews, the Greeks, the Romans, the Celts, the Goths, the Vikings, the Muslims, the rebel Christians. 2 hours *Winter*

653. PROJECT SEMINAR IN THE CHRISTIAN MOVEMENT. Any element of special interest in courses 651 and 652 may be pursued by individuals in a seminar context whether by presentation of a paper or some other type of research project. 2 hours *Winter*

654 (754). HISTORY OF EVANGELICAL AWAKENINGS Detailed study of the revivals and awakenings in Eurica and Africasia which have been the dynamic behind much missionary expansion and social improvement. 2/3 hours *Orr*

660. PRINCIPLES AND PROCEDURES IN CHURCH GROWTH I. A brief survey of the theological, psychological and statistical obstructions to church growth arising from within the missionary movement; sociological structures of the societies which are the ground of church multiplication, and procedures which cause stagnation, acceleration, introversion and expansion. 2 hours *McGavran and Wagner*

661. PRINCIPLES AND PROCEDURES IN CHURCH GROWTH II. Individual conversion and people movements, leadership training, indigenous principles, mobility, theological rigidity, involvement, psychological road blocks to growth, the revolution and the Church. 2 hours *McGavran and Wagner*

666 (766). STRATEGY OF MISSIONS. Investigates ways in which a sound theory and theology of mission is being put into effect by missions and churches. What missionary structures, ministerial training, patterns of church growth and advanced education for missionaries best serve the unchanging mandate. 2/3 hours *Wagner*

667. CASE STUDIES IN CURRENT CHURCH HISTORY. Systematic study of denominations in Asia, Africa and Latin America from their beginning to the present, with special attention to the spiritual and en-

vironmental factors contributing (1) to healthy expansion, and (2) to slow growth or arrested developm In various terms attention will be paid to China, Poly Korea, New Guinea, Ethiopia, Batakland, the Philippi West Africa, Brazil, Orissa, Mexico and Latin America hours *Faculty*

690 (790). RESEARCH. Guidance provided to ir vidual missionaries or small groups pressing forward w research on their own problems in mission. Special att tion paid to problems assigned to a missionary by his church or mission.[1] Hours as arranged *Faculty*

691 (791). READING AND CONFERENCE. Rea report and discussion designed to cover areas of speci terest or those in which the student is weak. Hours as ranged *Faculty*

692a, b. CHURCH GROWTH RESEARCH AND WRITING. An analysis of research methodology for the planning construction of the thesis or dissertation, resources in Los Angeles area, appraising source materials, note tak and documentation organization of materials with par ticular attention given to graphs of growth during the winter quarter. 692a offered fall quarter and 692b wi quarter. Both are required for degree candidates. 1 ho *Glasser and faculty*

693 (793). SPECIAL PROJECTS. In connection one of the eight branches of the discipline, graduate s dents under faculty guidance pursue an investigation substance. Hours as arranged *Faculty*

695 (795). FIELD RESEARCH IN PROPAGATIN THE GOSPEL. Directed research abroad, in accorda with plans and programs worked out and approved du residence at SWM-ICG, probing some aspect of missio which cannot be known from lectures and books. Pre requisites required. Hours as arranged *Faculty*

713. MODERN THEOLOGIES OF MISSION. Sur the recent Evangelical, Ecumenical and Roman Ca theologies of mission. 3 hours *Glasser*

720. ANIMISTIC BASES OF THE GREAT RELIGI Study of the animistic substructures of the religion o common people of Buddhist, Hindu, Islamic, Confuc Shinto lands, with special bearing on the relevance of evangelistic methods and on conversion to Christianit 3 hours *Tippett*

730. CHRISTIANITY AND CULTURE I. Explore cultural concomitants of divine-human interaction. T dealt with include man and culture, God and culture, tion and culture, the witness and culture and the peo God and culture. Attention is given to the developme a perspective of Christian truth that combines the ins of theology with those of anthropology. 3 hours *Kr*

---

[1]690 (790) may be used for credit in any section of curriculum I to VIII for special work or for thesis.

CHRISTANITY AND CULTURE II. Explores
in each non-Christian heritage is cultural and may be
d over into the Church and what must be altered or
ated. The extensive debate between Hinduism and
tianity illustrates the problem. 3 hours *McGavran*

CULTURE PERSONALITY AND THE GOSPEL.
ination of cross-cultural studies in psychological
opology, interactions of culture and the thought, emo-
and actions of individuals, the resulting culture pat-
and configurations and the bearing of these on church
ing and growth. 3 hours *Kraft*

CONVERSION WITH A MINIMUM OF DISLOCA-
. Analysis of the anthropological, theological and
ological factors relating to conversion, with focus on
guishing cultural from supracultural elements, so tha
onaries may encourage conversion truly Christian,
ulturally appropriate. 3 hours *Kraft*

ANTHROPOLOGICAL THEORY. Historical devel-
nt of encounters in anthropological theory as it bears
ch matters as the conceptualization of culture, social
ture, innovation and social change, primitive religion,
re and personality, diffusion, function, stress situa-
and how this theory relates to missiological princi-
nd techniques in cross-cultural religious processes,
al and directed. 3 hours *Tippett*

ETHNOLINGUISTICS. A study of the interrela-
hips between language and culture. Topics covered in-
Bible translation, discovery of a culture's values
gh the study of its folklore and mythology, language
sition, bilingualism and indigenous hymnology. 3
Kraft

ANTHROPOLOGICAL BASIS OF LEADERSHIP.
dy of leadership in different societies, the significance
tus, roles, authority and decision-making patterns in
e and changing societies, the nature and function of
tion, the justification of directed change, what these
epts mean for the church-planter, and for meeting the
al needs of an indigenous church at its different his-
periods. 3 hours *Tippett*

INDIGENEITY Explores the nature of the rela-
hip of churches to their surrounding cultures and the
ssion of churchness in culture. Models of indigeneity
eveloped and a variety of mission and independent
hes evaluated in terms of their approximation to the
3 hours *Kraft*

MISSIONS AND SOCIAL CHANGE. The reciprocal
t of missions and changing world conditions with
al emphasis on urbanization, secularization and
tion movements in The Third World. 3 hours *Wagner*

core course schedules

The following courses are considered core curriculum and are required of all degree candidates
during their first year in residence. They are
foundational to School of World Mission comprehensive examinations given in the spring quarter.

masters level

610/611. THEOLOGY OF MISSION. 4 hours *Glasser*

622/623. ANIMISM AND CHURCH GROWTH. 4 hours
Tippett

630/631. ANTHROPOLOGY AND MISSION. 4 hours
Kraft

651/652. HISTORICAL DEVELOPMENT OF THE
CHRISTIAN TRADITION. 4 hours *Winter*

660/661. PRINCIPLES AND PROCEDURES OF CHURCH
GROWTH. 4 hours *McGavran*

692a/b. CHURCH GROWTH RESEARCH AND WRITING.
2 hours *Glasser*

doctoral level

Doctoral candidates must choose 8 of the following core courses, at least one under each faculty
member.

713. MODERN THEOLOGIES OF MISSION. 3 hours
Glasser

770. HERMENEUTICS-ECCLESIOLOGY-ECUMENICS
AND MISSION. 3 hours *Glasser*

730. CHRISTIANITY AND CULTURE I. 3 hours *Kraft*

737. INDIGENEITY. 3 hours *Kraft*

731. CHRISTIANITY AND CULTURE II. 3 hours
McGavran

760. ADVANCED CHURCH GROWTH. 3 hours *McGavran*

734. ANTHROPOLOGICAL THEORY. 3 hours *Tippett*

736. ANTHROPOLOGICAL BASIS OF LEADERSHIP.
3 hours *Tippett*

738. MISSIONS AND SOCIAL CHANGE. 3 hours *Wagner*

666/766. STRATEGY OF MISSIONS. 3 hours *Wagner*

756. THE CHURCH GROWTH MOVEMENT IN HIS-
TORICAL PERSPECTIVE. 3 hours *Winter*

767. CURRENT CHURCH HISTORY. 3 hours *Winter*

740. COMMUNICATION, MASS MEDIA AND CHURCH GROWTH. The role of communications in initial evangelism, in the development of people movements and in church planting and continuing missions. The actual and potential contributions of the modern media. 3 hours *Winter*

756. THE CHURCH GROWTH MOVEMENT IN HISTORICAL PERSPECTIVE. The key books and articles of the Church Growth movement are surveyed and analyzed to familiarize the doctoral candidate with the documents and their relation to the historical context and their continuing role in the movement. 3 hours *Winter*

760. ADVANCED CHURCH GROWTH. Current theological, methodological and ethnic considerations bearing on growth and non-growth are studied. A typology of younger churches is set forth. 660, 661 are prerequisite. 3 hours *McGavran*

761. THE PATTERNS OF CHURCH GROWTH. Typical growth patterns of non-western churches. Histories of denominations in process of formation, focusing o the social contexts, graphs of growth and potential for further communication of a vital Christian faith. 3 hours *Winter*

767. CURRENT CHURCH HISTORY. Case studies ir current church history involving denominations, churc and missions in the Third World, Europe and North America. Special attention on spiritual and environme factors in growing and non-growing movements. 3 hou *Winter*

770. HERMENEUTICS, ECCLESIOLOGY, ECU-MENICS AND MISSION. The interrelation of contem patterns of biblical interpretation, the Church's understanding of herself and ecumenical theology and pract and their impact on Great Commission missions. 3 hou *Glasser*

12

faculty

school of world mission

ARTHUR F. GLASSER, C.E. Cornell University, B.D. Faith Seminary, S.T.M. Union Seminary, D.l Covenant College and Seminary, *Dean and Associate Professor of Theology, Mission and E Asian Studies.*

DONALD A. McGAVRAN, B.A., D.D. Butler University, B.D. Yale Divinity School, M.A. College Missions, Ph.D. Columbia University, D.Litt. Phillips University, *Dean Emeritus and Senior Profes of Mission, Church Growth and South Asian Studies.*

ALAN R. TIPPETT, L.Th. Melbourne College of Divinity, M.A. American University, Ph.D. Univ sity of Oregon, *Professor of Anthropology and Oceanic Studies.*

RALPH D. WINTER, B.S. California Institute of Technology, M.A. American University, Ph.D. Corr University, B.D. Princeton Seminary, *Professor of the Historical Development of the Christiar Movement.*

CHARLES H. KRAFT, B.A. Wheaton College, Ph.D. Hartford Seminary Foundation, B.D. Ashlar Seminary, *Associate Professor of Anthropology and African Studies.*

C. PETER WAGNER, B.S. Rutgers University, B.D., M.A. (Missiology) Fuller Theological Seminar Th.M. Princeton Theological Seminary, *Associate Professor of Church Growth and Latin Americ Studies.*

visiting professors

J. EDWIN ORR, M.A. Northwestern University, Th.D. Northern Baptist Seminary, D.Phil. Oxford University, D.Theol. Serampore University, D.D. University of South Africa, Ed.D. University • California at Los Angeles, *Resource Professor in Church History.*

DAVID B. BARRETT, B.A., M.A., B.D. Cambridge University, S.T.M. Union Seminary, Ph.D., Coluﬆ University.

JAMES H. EMERY, B.Mech.E. University of Louisville, B.D. Princeton Theological Seminary, M Hartford Seminary Foundation.

F. PETER COTTERELL, B.S.C. University of London, B.D. Spurgeon's College, Ph.D. School of Orien & African Studies, University of London.

ster of arts in cross-cultural ministry *(for missionary candidates)*

School of Theology offers a two-year Master of Arts program with a concentration cross-cultural ministry. Each person, in consultation with the director of the M.A. gram and a faculty member from the area of specialization, proposes his own riculum considering his previous educational background, his personal objectives the requirements of a particular program.

s area of concentration is designed specifically for men and women who wish to pare for a ministry in a cross-cultural setting. A missions concentration has been structed by the faculty of the School of World Mission to equip missionary candi- es and others who will put their theological training to work in another culture.

Master of Arts   Suggested Curriculum for Cross-Cultural Ministry

Fall	Winter	Spring
ndations for Ministry M10	Old Testament 126	Old Testament 126
tematic Theology T21	Systematic Theology T23	Systematic Theology T32
rch History T22	Church Growth 383	Anthropology and Mission 384
ical Theology and Mission	Communications P11 or Elective	NT Theology B13
Theology B31	New Testament B12 or Biblical Elective	New Testament B23 or Biblical Elective
orical Development of the istian Movement 385	Strategy of Missions 386	History of Evangelical Awakenings 387
guage Learning 388	Area Studies 389	Non-Christian Religions 390
tive	Church History T31	Elective

(See School of Theology catalog for details and course descriptions.)

Master of Divinity   Suggested Curriculum for Cross-Cultural Ministry

From its inception graduates of the School of Theology have made a significant contribution to the world-wide expansion of the Christian movement. In keeping with this tradition, the School of Theology in partnership with the School of World Mission is offering a new Master of Divinity concentration in cross-cultural ministry. It is designed for missionary candidates, as well as for those men and women concerned to serve Christ in cross-cultural ministry, whether in the Western world or in Africa, Asia and Latin America.

Fall	Winter	Spring
Foundations for Ministry M10	Hermeneutics B11	NT Theology B13
Greek 10	Philosophical Presuppositions T12	Church History T13
	Communications P11	Anthropology and Mission 384
	Church Growth Principles and Procedures 383	Field Education 306
Church History T22	New Testament B12	New Testament B23
Hebrew 15	OT Pentateuch B21	OT Prophets B22
or Hebrew 18; Biblical Theology and Mission 382; and Language Learning 388	Christian Ethics T33	Introduction to Theology T11
	Homiletics M12	Field Education 306
Systematic Theology T21	Systematic Theology T23	Systematic Theology T21
NT Theology B31	Church History T31	Unity of the Bible B33
OT Writings B32	Strategy of Missions 386	History of Evangelical Awakenings 387
Historical Development of the Christian Movement 385	Area Studies 389	Non-Christian Religions 390

missions

380, 381. MISSIONARY INTERNSHIP. Inaugurated in 1962, this internship program has proved to be a worthwhile and stimulating venture for students who expect to be missionaries. The purpose of the program is to cooperate with various missionary agencies in opening doors of foreign service on an intern basis for students between their junior and middler or middler and senior years.

Students desiring to receive academic credit for this year of internship in foreign missions are required to take a four-hour reading course (380) under the missions faculty preparatory to going overseas. During this course they receive some direction for the substantial term paper to be written as a result of their internship. Four hours of credit are also granted for the paper, to be submitted to the mission faculty five weeks after the beginning of the fall quarter upon return. This paper (381) is to fulfill, in writing, goals set during the preparatory course.

The following 13 courses are recommended for students in the M.A. or M.Div. programs who see training in theology and missions in preparation f a ministry in another culture.

382. BIBLICAL THEOLOGY AND MISSION. A com prehensive review of those perspectives in the Scriptures which bear on the preparation for and early beginnings the Christian mission, with particular reference to the cultural imperative, Israel and the nations, the Kingdom of God, religious encounter, the Great Commission, Jesus and the nations, the apostolic understanding of mi sion and the missionary obedience of the Early Church. *Glasser*

383. CHURCH GROWTH PRINCIPLES AND PROCE DURES. A comprehensive survey of current obstacles church growth; the sociological structures of the societi which are the ground of church multiplication with part cular attention to indigenous principles, people moveme leadership training and the removal of psychological roa blocks to the growth of the Church. *McGavran*

. CHRISTIANITY AND CULTURE I: ANTHRO-
LOGY. A Christian approach to the basic concepts of
hropology: culture, social structure, the influence of
ture on the individual, the influence of the individual
culture, culture change, cultural pathology and revital-
ion and the opportunities for Christianity and Christ-
s to operate in terms of cultural reality. Illustrations
applications will be developed from American culture,
n-western cultures and the cultures of the Bible. *Kraft*

. THE HISTORICAL DEVELOPMENT OF THE
RISTIAN MOVEMENT. An analysis of the growth
namics of the Christian movement from Pentecost to
present with particular attention to the early evan-
ization of Europe, the geographical, cultural and struc-
al factors behind the Reformation, the delayed emer-
ce of Protestantism as a missionary force and the con-
nporary theological indigenization of world Christianity.
3 *Winter*

. STRATEGY OF MISSIONS. The systematic study
what contemporary changes in governments, social
tems and economic orders mean to the carrying out of
Great Commission. What missionary structures, minis-
al training, patterns of church growth and in-service
ining for missionaries best serve the unchanging man-
e, with particular reference to the phenomenon of
rd World mission agencies. *Wagner*

7. HISTORY OF EVANGELICAL AWAKENINGS.
analysis of the pattern of revivals and awakenings that
e significantly influenced the expansion of the Christ-
movement throughout its history. W74 *Orr*

. LANGUAGE LEARNING. The study and prac-
 of techniques of language learning. Insights of modern
guistics will be employed to enlarge the student's under-
nding of and ability to learn a language and/or to im-
ve his competence in a language he already knows.
aft

. AREA STUDIES. A directed research course in
ich the student will be introduced to the historical,
tural, political and ecclesiastical components of the
ntry in which he hopes to serve. By arrangement with
 SWM faculty member whose area responsibility in-
des that country.

390. NON-CHRISTIAN RELIGIONS. A directed research course in which the student will be introduced to
the religious situation in the country where he hopes to
serve, with particular focus on religious encounter in the
missionary sense. By arrangement with the SWM faculty
member whose specialty is this particular non-Christian
religion.

391. CHRISTIANITY AND CULTURE II: CHRISTIAN
ETHNOTHEOLOGY. Prerequisite: Christianity and Culture I. An anthropological approach to Christian theology:
the influence of culture on theologizing, the effects of culture on the perception of Christian truth, the Bible in cross-
cultural perceptive, Bible translation, conversion, the
Church and the communication of Christianity cross-
culturally. Illustrations and applications will be developed
from American culture, non-western cultures and the cultures of the Bible. *Kraft*

392. BIBLE TRANSLATION. Prerequisite: Christianity
and Culture I. An introduction to the basic theories and
principles of Bible translation. Evaluation of specific Bible
translations. The understandings developed will focus on
both the linguistic and the cultural concomitants of the
translation process. Designed for both prospective missionaries and for those whose primary task will be to
communicate the biblical message in North America.
Kraft

393. CONVERSION TO CHRIST. Prerequisites: Christianity and Culture I, II. An approach that investigates
theological, psychological and cultural facets of the process and attempts to develop a comprehensive understanding of (1) God's part, (2) man's part and (3) the continuing
divine-human interaction in which conversion to Christ
issues. *Kraft*

394. THE CHURCH IN CROSS-CULTURAL PERSPEC-
TIVE. Prerequisites: Christianity and Culture I, II. An
approach to the understanding of Christian churchness that
investigates both the theological and the cultural facets of
the problem. A basic assumption is that a church cannot
be theologically healthy if it is sociologically ill. The concept of indigeneity will be examined and redefined. *Kraft*

general information

application for admission

An application form is included in the back of this catalog. A form also can be obtained from the office of the registrar. This should be completed and filed with the registrar as early as possible in the academic year prior to matriculation. Along with the completed forms the applicant must (1) submit three photographs of himself (approximately 2½"x2½" close-up of head and shoulders), (2) have transcripts from all colleges he has attended sent directly to the registrar's office, and (3) enclose the application fee of $10.00 (non-refundable)

Qualified individuals of any ethnic background, culture or national origin are encouraged to apply.

notification of acceptance

As soon as possible after an application file is completed, it will be reviewed by the admissions committee. In all cases, applicants should be notified of the action of the committee within one month after the file is completed. Within 30 days of notification of acceptance, the student must pay the matriculation fee which will be applied against his tuition. Payment of this fee places a student in position to make request for scholarship aid and lists his name with the director of student employment and housing. His name also will be put on the mailing list to receive bulletins and other information from the Seminary. Failure to pay this fee within the stated time cancels the student's acceptance notice so that vacancies may be filled from waiting applicants.

foreign students

As a general rule, foreign students with dependents will be considered for admission at Fuller Seminary only if some responsible Christian organization in their homeland specifically commits itself either (1) to guarantee the support and care of the dependents at home during the student's entire stay abroad, or (2) to provide round-trip transportation and the entire support for the dependents if they are to accompany the student to the Seminary.

Every foreign applicant is required to take an examination to determine his ability to use the English language. The cost of this examination is $13.00. Of this amount, $3.00 must be sent with the $10.00 application fee and the remaining $10.00 is to be paid to the examiner at the time the examination is administered.

All foreign applicants must submit, with their applications, a catalog of the school from which they received their baccalaureate degree (B.A. or B.S.). The Th.B. is not considered adequate for admission to Fuller Seminary.

Students from outside the continental limits of America are received for study under the J visa.

room and board

Single students rooming on campus during the regular school year are required to contract for board. Meals are served in the refectory Monday through Friday. Minimal kitchen facilities are available in the residence halls for weekend meals. Meal tickets or single meals may be purchased by anyone.

orientation

The course of study at Fuller Seminary begins with orientation, held during registration week of the fall quarter. The activities of orientation are integrated into the structure of the fall quarter classes to the extent that class work for new students actually begins on the Monday of registration week. The orientation program introduces the student to Seminary life and theological training and provides an experience of Christian community.

ular fees[1]

<table>
<tr><td>•lication non-refundable</td><td>$</td><td>10.00</td></tr>
<tr><td>nscript Evaluation[2]</td><td></td><td>5.00</td></tr>
<tr><td>riculation applies against tuition;
•on-refundable</td><td></td><td></td></tr>
<tr><td>Theology, Missions</td><td></td><td>50.00</td></tr>
<tr><td>•sychology</td><td></td><td>150.00</td></tr>
<tr><td>ology Tuition for degree candidates,
•pecial students or auditors</td><td></td><td>1973-74</td></tr>
<tr><td>M.Div.* M.A.* D.Min. (In-sequence)
•er course</td><td></td><td>128.00</td></tr>
<tr><td>h.M.[3] per course</td><td></td><td>168.00</td></tr>
<tr><td>Continuation fee per year;
non-refundable</td><td></td><td>250.00</td></tr>
<tr><td>).Min. (In-ministry)[4] per quarter</td><td></td><td>512.00</td></tr>
<tr><td>Continuation fee per year;
non-refundable</td><td></td><td>250.00</td></tr>
<tr><td>h.D.[5] per year; non-refundable</td><td></td><td>1,940.00</td></tr>
<tr><td>Continuation fee per year;
non-refundable</td><td></td><td>250.00</td></tr>
<tr><td>External Reader Fee (second year)</td><td></td><td>300.00</td></tr>
<tr><td>ummer Language Program, per
quarter</td><td></td><td>384.00</td></tr>
<tr><td>udit fees per course; non-refundable</td><td></td><td>128.00</td></tr>
<tr><td>ions Tuition for degree candidates,
•ecial students or auditors</td><td></td><td>1973-74</td></tr>
<tr><td>1.A. per quarter hour:
Missions, Missiology</td><td></td><td>42.00</td></tr>
<tr><td>•.Miss. per quarter hour</td><td></td><td>42.00</td></tr>
<tr><td>udit fees per quarter hour;
non-refundable</td><td></td><td>42.00</td></tr>
<tr><td>hology Tuition</td><td></td><td>1973-74</td></tr>
<tr><td>uition per year (includes summer
session, Greek)</td><td></td><td>2,400.00[6]</td></tr>
<tr><td>•ecial Student Fee (per unit)</td><td></td><td>70.00</td></tr>
<tr><td>•ff-Campus Tuition, for students
completing the Ph.D. dissertation
(per year)</td><td></td><td>365.00</td></tr>
<tr><td>osts incidental to program an-
nouncing dissertation defense
to be underwritten by the
student</td><td></td><td>22.50</td></tr>
<tr><td>•ent Activities per year</td><td></td><td>24.00</td></tr>
<tr><td>guage Laboratory per unit</td><td></td><td>1.00</td></tr>
<tr><td>Student Orientation
heology, Missions</td><td></td><td>16.00</td></tr>
<tr><td>sychology</td><td></td><td>20.00</td></tr>
<tr><td>•ent Activities — Grant in Aid Program</td><td></td><td>10.00</td></tr>
</table>

Graduation Fees:

<table>
<tr><td>M.Div. and other Master's includes
rental of cap and gown, printed announce-
ments, diploma and miscellaneous gradua-
tion expenses</td><td></td><td>45.00</td></tr>
<tr><td>Doctor's includes rental of cap and gown,
printed announcements, diploma and
miscellaneous graduation expenses</td><td></td><td>50.00</td></tr>
<tr><td>Thesis Binding</td><td>each</td><td>7.50</td></tr>
<tr><td>Microfilming Fee</td><td></td><td>27.50</td></tr>
<tr><td>Accident, Sickness and Hospital
Insurance[7]</td><td></td><td></td></tr>
<tr><td>Single per year</td><td></td><td>51.00</td></tr>
<tr><td>Married per year[8]</td><td></td><td>264.00</td></tr>
</table>

17

special fees

<table>
<tr><td>Late Examination Fee</td><td>$</td><td>10.00</td></tr>
<tr><td>Late Registration</td><td></td><td>5.00-9.00</td></tr>
<tr><td>Program Change</td><td></td><td>3.00</td></tr>
<tr><td>Removal of Incomplete</td><td></td><td>3.00</td></tr>
<tr><td>Parking per month</td><td></td><td>$1.25</td></tr>
<tr><td>Severance Fee for students with-
drawing first week of classes</td><td></td><td>61.00</td></tr>
</table>

---

[1] The Seminary reserves the right to change rates when fluctuations in costs make this necessary.

[2] Chargeable only when no formal application is submitted.

[3] Tuition charged on per-course basis for 11 courses. Continuation fee (non-refundable) commences one year after student has paid for 11 courses at Th.M. tuition, at the beginning of that quarter and will be charged on an annual basis.

[4] One full year (or two half-years) at full tuition. Continuation fee (non-refundable) charged after one full year until degree is awarded.

[5] Two years at full tuition. Continuation fee (non-refundable) until degree is awarded.

[6] In instances where a student withdraws, there is no refund of tuition for that particular quarter. An assessment of $250.00 is made for withdrawal in the fall quarter adjusted to $125.00 for withdrawal in the winter quarter. There is no assessment made for withdrawal in the spring quarter.

[7] Not required where student has existing insurance with approximately comparable coverage.

[8] Optional for the wife and children.

* Academically qualified spouse whose mate is a full time student in any degree program may enroll in M.Div. or M.A. program for one-fourth tuition rate.

annual expense estimate

	Single	Married
Tuition *for three*	$1,536.00-	$1,536.00-
quarters	2,400.00[1]	2,400.00[1]
Student Housing	335.00[2]	1,200.00[3]
Average		
Food Service	525.00[2]	varies
Accident, Sickness	51.00	264.00[4]
& Hospital Insurance		
Books	200.00-	200.00-
Estimate	350.00	350.00
Student Activities	24.00	24.00
New Student	16.00-20.00	32.00
Orientation		
Overnight Parking	22.50	
dormitory students		
only		

18

deferred payment plan

This plan is available for those not able to pay the total charges at the time of registration. A $3.00 service fee allows the individual to pay one-third at registration and the balance in two equal installments during the quarter. Where the student neglects making the installment payment, as agreed upon in advance, an additional $4.00 service fee is added to the account. Student accounts not paid in full by the end of the quarter may result in no opportunity to take the finals and in no credit or grade for the subjects taken.

refunds

For theology and mission courses dropped between registration and the end of the first week of classes, tuition refund is 100%; for those dropped the second week of classes, the refund is 75%; for those dropped the third week of classes, the refund is 50%; for those dropped the fourth week of classes the refund is 25%. No refund is made on courses dropped after the fourth week.

The refund policy for the twelve-week summer session in Greek and Hebrew are the same as the refund policy for the regular school year (stated in the first paragraph). For the eight-week summer sessions in Greek and Hebrew there is a 100% refund if the course is dropped during the first four days, a 75% refund during the next four days; and a 50% refund for the next four days; and a 25% refund for the next four class days. No refund will be made thereafter.

financial aid

Fuller Theological Seminary is committed to the policy that no worthy student should be left in a position of financial need without the school first having done everything possible for him.

Through employment, long and short term loans, and grants the Seminary seeks to alleviate financial need. Before grants are considered, it is expected that a student will provide a reasonable part of the total amount required to meet expenses by accepting employment and/or a loan. Any student desiring a loan or a grant is required to complete the proper forms for student aid, which include a detailed copy of his estimated budget for the year. These forms may be obtained from the office of the dean of students.

The Seminary provides help in finding employment. Field work appointments are often remunerative, and there are numerous secular employment opportunities in the area. In accepting employment however, it is understood that the student will not exceed the number of hours commensurate with the demands of his academic load, family responsibilities, etc. A student whose financial situation makes it imperative for him to obtain secular or church employment for more than 20 hours per week must reduce his academic load accordingly.

In many instances the parents of students cannot or should not be expected to be of financial assistance. Nevertheless, it is anticipated that the student will seek and obtain help from the family when it is feasible. With some, assistance can be expected and should be sought from the home church or other interested groups.

---

[1]Depending on degree program; includes Summer Language program tuition of $384.00.

[2]Computed for fall, winter and spring quarters.

[3]Computed at $100.00 per month for 12 months.

[4]Includes student and family.

ɪere are presently three sources for student loans:

ɪited Student Aid Funds and Federally Insured
ɪans. This program of guaranteed student loans
ɪerates through lenders (banks, savings and loan
ɪociations, etc.) in the place of residence of the
ɪdent. There is no payment of interest or principal
ɪtil graduation.

ɪational Defense Student Loans. Government
ɪnds for student loans have been made available
ɪ the Seminary. This loan repayment is also defer-
ɪ until after graduation.

ɪller Seminary Student Loans. Short or long term
ɪans are available. Short term is for financial emer-
ɪncy and carries no interest. Long term is subject
ɪ negotiation based on student need. Included in
ɪese loans are four which have been named as
ɪlows:
    Charles E. Fuller
    Gerrit P. Groen
    Maud Aikens Harper Loan Fund
    Hazlett Memorial Loan Fund

ɪXILIARY SCHOLARSHIPS
ɪe Fuller Seminary auxiliary grants a limited
ɪmber of scholarships to Seminary students each
ɪar. All auxiliary scholarship applications must be
ɪmplete and in the hands of the scholarship com-
ɪttee by March 15.

ɪVARD

ɪnald Anderson McGavran Award in Church
ɪowth. This annual award is granted to the mission-
ɪy associate who in the judgment of the School of
ɪorld Mission faculty has made the most significant
ɪntribution to research in church growth overseas.
ɪis $100 award has been made possible by the
ɪ72-1973 class.

degree requirements

Competence in three of the eight branches of the
discipline of missions is required for the Master of
Arts degree. Competence in five will be required for
the Doctor of Missiology. For the M.A. in missions,
72 quarter hours past the B.A. are required; for the
M.A. in missiology, 36 quarter hours past the M.Div.,
and for the doctorate in missiology, 72 quarter hours
past the M.Div. For experienced mission leaders
with no M.Div., about three years graduate education is required in mission-related subjects. Degree
requirements are: B average in all courses, passing
comprehensive examinations, writing and defending
a thesis which is a contribution to knowledge and
functional knowledge of a foreign language (which
may be that of the land in which the missionary
works).

Graduate work in missions done at other institutions may, under some circumstances, be accepted
toward these requirements.

graduation

The prescribed course of study as outlined in the
curriculum for each degree must be satisfactorily
completed.

In order to qualify for the M.Div. or M.A. degree,
the student must have obtained at least twice as
many grade points as the total number of units he
has undertaken. For the Th.M., Th.D. and Ph.D.
degrees a minimum grade of B is required for each
course taken for credit in the program.

In addition to these academic requirements for
graduation, the student must present a satisfactory
clearance of his financial accounts and must be
approved by the faculty as having conducted himself in accord with standards of wholesome Christian
character.

Statement of intention to graduate must be
made at the time of registration each quarter of
the year of the student's graduation, with formal
application for graduation and payment of graduation fees being made at the registration for the last
quarter of residence.

Students expecting to graduate must notify the
registrar in writing by April 1.

19

CALENDAR

summer session   June 27-September 17, 1974

June 27, 10:00 a.m.-noon; 2:00-4:00 p.m. Registration for Greek 10 (extended) and Hebrew 15 (extended)
June 27, 6:00 p.m. Greek 10 (extended) and Hebrew 15 (extended) begin
July 23, 10:00 a.m.-noon; 2:00-4:00 p.m. Registration for Greek 10 (concentrated) and Hebrew 15 (concentrated)
July 24, 8:00 a.m. Greek 10 (concentrated) and Hebrew 15 (concentrated) begin
September 17 Classes end; Research and clinical training continue
September 19-20 School of Psychology faculty counseling and programming appointments

first quarter   September 23-December 13, 1974

September 23   Foundations for Ministry and orientation to Seminary begins for juniors. Includes Greek examination for entering students who have taken Greek elsewhere than in the summer session, personality testing for all incoming students, and matriculation and registration for new students.
September 23-27, Monday-Friday, 8:30 a.m.-4:00 p.m. Matriculation and registration of students (registration appointment sign-up sheet available on registrar's board after August 23)

> Middlers   Monday and Tuesday
> Seniors   Wednesday
> Juniors   Friday

September 24-26   School of Psychology comprehensive exams
September 30   Classes commence for returning students
November 26-27   School of Psychology faculty counseling and programming appointments
November 28-29   Thanksgiving recess
December 2-6   Registration for second quarter
December 6   Classes end; Research and clinical training continue
December 9-13   Quarterly examinations
December 16-January 3   Christmas recess

second quarter   January 6-March 21, 1975

January 6   Classes commence
January 7-8   School of Psychology comprehensive exams
February 17   Washington's birthday
March 3-5   School of Psychology faculty counseling and programming appointments
March 10-14   Registration for third quarter
March 14   Classes end; Research and clinical training continue
March 17-21   Quarterly examinations
March 24-28   Spring recess

third quarter   March 31-June 13, 1975

March 31   Classes commence
March 28   Good Friday — no classes
April 1-3   School of Psychology comprehensive exams
May 30   Faculty-senior dinner
June 6   Classes end; Research and clinical training continue
June 8   11:00 a.m. Baccalaureate
June 9   Senior and faculty communion service
June 9   7:30 p.m. Commencement
June 10-13   Quarterly examinations

Summer session   June 26-September 16, 1975

ne 26, 10:00 a.m.-noon; 2:00-4:00 p.m. Registration for Greek 10 (extended) and Hebrew 15 (extended)

ne 26, 6:00 p.m. Greek 10 (extended) and Hebrew 15 (extended) begin

ly 22, 10:00 a.m.-noon; 2:00-4:00 p.m. Registration for Greek 10 (concentrated) and Hebrew 15 (concentrated)

ly 23, 8:00 a.m. Greek 10 (concentrated) and Hebrew 15 (concentrated) begin

ptember 16   Classes end; Research and clinical training continue

ptember 16-19   School of Psychology faculty counseling and programming appointments

rst quarter   September 22-December 12, 1975

ptember 22   Foundations for Ministry and orientation to Seminary begins for juniors. Includes Greek examinations for entering students who have taken Greek elsewhere than in the summer session, personality testing for all incoming students, and matriculation and registration for new students.

21

ptember 24   School of Psychology comprehensive exams

ptember 22-26, Monday-Friday, 8:30 a.m.-4:00 p.m. Matriculation and registration of students (registration appointment sign-up sheet is available on registrar's bulletin board after August 22)

    Middlers   Monday and Tuesday

    Seniors   Wednesday

    Juniors   Friday

ptember 29   Classes commence for returning students

ovember 17-21   School of Psychology faculty counseling and programming appointments

ovember 27-28   Thanksgiving recess

cember 1-5   Registration for second quarter

cember 5   Classes end; Research and clinical training continue

cember 8-12   Quarterly examinations

cember 15-January 2   Christmas recess

cond quarter   January 5-March 19, 1976

nuary 5   Classes commence

nuary 7   School of Psychology comprehensive exams

bruary 16   Washington's birthday

rch 2-5   School of Psychology faculty counseling and programming appointments

rch 8-12   Registration for third quarter

rch 12   Classes end; Research and clinical training continue

rch 15-19   Quarterly examinations

rch 22-26   Spring recess

ird quarter   March 29-June 11, 1976

rch 29   Classes commence

rch 31   School of Psychology comprehensive exams

ril 16   Good Friday — no classes

y 28   Faculty-senior dinner

ne 4   Classes end; Research and clinical training continue

ne 6   11:00 a.m. Baccalaureate

ne 7   Senior and faculty communion service

ne 7   7:30 p.m. Commencement

ne 8-11   Quarterly examinations

questions most frequently asked

1. If I have never been a missionary can I enroll?

The SWM grants degrees to those who have had at least three years in cross-cultural Christian ministry. If you have not had this experience, seek to enroll in one of the School of Theology mission concentration programs.

2. What kind of scholarship assistance is provided?

Tuition, fees, books, room and board amount to about $3,100 per year. Some tuition scholarships ($1,600) are available to persons holding responsible positions in their missions or churches. It is expected, however, that the church or mission served will supplement the tuition grant as an expression of its endorsement of this graduate study. The Seminary does not make grants toward transportation expenses.

3. What is the difference between an M.A. in Missions and an M.A. in Missiology?

The M.A. in Missions is built upon the B.A. and requires 72 credits (2 years). The M.A. in Missiology requires 36 credits (1 year) beyond the M. Div. or its equivalent. The professional Doctorate of Missiology requires 72 credits (2 years) beyond the M. Div. or its equivalent. The first year of the doctoral program is devoted to master's level work in Missiology. If performed with "honors," the second year is devoted to meeting doctoral level requirements.

4. How do I qualify for degree candidacy?

See "Admission," page 4.

5. Does the SWM enroll special students, that is, those who don't want a degree?

Yes. See "Admission," page 4.

6. If I can come for only one quarter which would be best?

Fall quarter. See "Admission," page 4.

7. What can I do to prepare beforehand?

Join the Church Growth Book Club ($1.00 per year) and read the Church Growth Bulletin, Dr. McGavran's *Understanding Church Growth*

and Dr. Tippett's *Church Growth and The Word of God.* (The Book Club gives 40% discount.) Begin to gather data on the church or mission you serve. Request *How to Do a Chu Growth Survey.* The more information you assimilate on the Christian movement in your area the more profitable will be your SWM st

8. What languages are required for SWM degree programs?

One must display competence in the language the people he serves. The biblical languages, C and Hebrew, are normally part of the M. Div. are not required in the M.A. in Missions.

9. If English is not my first language, must I mee any English proficiency requirements?

Yes. The Seminary requires the examination s by the English Language Institute, Division o Testing and Certification of the University of Michigan. There is probably a center in your country where these tests are conducted. Writ for details.

10. How can I know if there are other SWM gradu serving the same country I am?

Write to the Dean of the School of World Mission. Occasionally potential SWMers are as to contact graduates relative to their desire to attend the SWM.

11. Are School of World Mission courses available any other graduate institutions?

There is a directory of missionary courses off in North America* which will help one choos school for missionary preparation. The SWM begun to establish relationships with institutic in various parts of the world where, it is hope similar courses and SWM credit will soon be available.

*An American Directory of Schools and Colleges Offering Missionary Courses, Glenn Schwartz, ed., William Carey Library, South Pasadena, California 1973 ($2.95).

2. GENERAL AREAS OF STUDY CONSTITUTING MISSIOLOGY

Missiology is a new academic discipline. The simplest
definition of the term missiology, a term that has been in
use for nearly sixty years, is "the study of man being
brought to God in history." Missiology belongs to the
interdisciplinary realm. It requires a vocabulary of its
own. That vocabulary must relate "to the theory and
research of each of the related disciplines" such as
theology, anthropology, sociology, psychology, history,
linguistics and communications.

23

A. Missiology, a new Discipline 25

B. Theology at the School of World Mission 29

C. Bibliography for the Areas of Study Constituting
    Missiology 32

24

MISSIOLOGY, A NEW DISCIPLINE

The School of World Mission and Institute of Church
Growth has been brought into being to meet several urgent
needs. One of these is to provide in-service training and
graduate education for experienced missionaries and bi-
cultural national church and mission leaders. To achieve
this objective, the School of World Mission has developed
a unique educational program. The program emphasizes
church growth and is devoted to the development of the new
science of missiology. C. Peter Wagner's article, reprinted
in Appendix B from the December 7, 1973 issue of Christianity
Today, is entitled"'Church Growth': More than a Man, a
Magazine, a School, a Book."* He succinctly describes six
distinctives which characterize the SWM educational program.

Another urgent need is the development of mission
research to provide the necessary data base for objective
evaluation. Why do some churches and areas of mission grow
rapidly while others don't? is the major question. Professor
Alan R. Tippett's article (Appendix D), "Research Method
and the Missiological Process at the School of World Mission,"
discusses this important aspect of the new discipline.

A major purpose of the School of World Mission is to
accelerate the rate of church growth and world-wide
evangelization. The means chosen to accomplish this goal
is missiological education. An unusual academic curriculum
centered around this new discipline has been developed.
Several disciplines are involved in this interdisciplinary
search for knowledge. The two major disciplines of theology
and anthropology "integrate and interact continually" in the
science of missiology. The major purpose of this new science
"is to aid in bringing men and God together in what might be
called the divine-human relationship in accordance with the
scriptural mandate." Professor Tippett also affirms:

I believe that by men God communicates to men what he
has done for men. I believe also that the ultimate
goals of theology and anthropology bring us into that
great area of true adventure - discovering under God
the new man in Christ (p. vii).

---

* Copyright 1973 by Christianity Today; reprinted in the
Appendix by permission.

A person "engaged in any kind of cross-cultural communication or service - medical, educational, agricultural,
technological or missionary - should be trained in basic
social anthropology." Professor Tippett (p. vi) further
states:

> I see no hope for the Christian mission of today or
> tomorrow except in terms of a simple biblical theology
> on a soundly anthropological base. God's message to
> men has to be presented to men, by men, in precise
> human contexts.

The above quotations are from an unpublished manuscript
entitled "Adventures in Missiology." The manuscript contains
an explanation and definition of missiology, the discipline
that has been brought into prominence by Professors Tippett
and McGavran and their colleagues at the School of World
Mission and Institute of Church Growth. The rest of this
article, MISSIOLOGY, A NEW DISCIPLINE, is devoted to the
explanation given by Professor Tippett (pp. vii-x).

26

There are also other dimensions of the discipline of
missiology. One of these, for instance, is history. God
is active in history and through history. The action of
God in the midst of human history may be studied, as the
anthropologist would put it, as synchronic (horizontal,
world-wide in its sweep) or as diachronic (vertical through
time). God revealed Himself in history - at a precise place,
in a precise culture, and at a precise point of time. God's
revelation of Himself in "the word made flesh" from the
incarnation to the enthronement is the supreme divine
revelation and is of eternal significance to man, but it is
not by any means God's only revelation to man down through
history. The whole of history - especially Christian
history - is charged with God's self-declaration. This
permits us to study His methods of work with man, such
divine/human encounters as the conversion of men to God -
one of the important themes of missiology, both in its
anthropological and theological dimensions. Only when the
two aspects are studied together in, say, a people-movement
from animism to Christianity, do we experience even a
glimpse of the amazing things God is doing among men in our
day.

The simplest definition of missiology is "the study of man being brought to God in history," but perhaps for the clear understanding of what lies before us in these pages one should attempt a more formal definition showing the component parts of the discipline. Such a working definition is badly needed. When I wrote the introduction to <u>Solomon Islands Christianity</u>. which was a missiological study, I struggled with a paragraph which had to say that this was "historical but not a history," and with another that had to say it was "anthropological but not an anthropology" and I might well have added a third saying it was "theological but not a theology." It was, in point of fact, <u>missiology</u>, belonging to an interdisciplinary realm, with a vocabulary of its own that somehow needs to be related to the theory and research of each of the related disciplines. Here then is an attempt which I have shared for criticism with my colleagues:

27

Missiology is defined as the academic discipline or science which researches, records and applies data relating to the biblical origin, the history (including the use of documentary materials), the anthropological principles and techniques and the theological base of the Christian mission. The theory, methodology and data bank are particularly directed towards:

1. the processes by which the Christian message is communicated,
2. the encounters brought about by its proclamation to non-Christians,
3. the planting of the Church and organization of congregations, the incorporation of converts into those congregations, and the growth and relevance of their structures and fellowship, internally to maturity, externally in outreach as the Body of Christ in local situations and beyond, in a variety of culture patterns.

Immediately it will be apparent that such research requires some familiarity with the tools and techniques of anthropology, theology and history. Yet even this is not all. The missiologist may find himself calling on the resources of, say, linguistics or psychology. Nevertheless,

missiology is a discipline in its own rights.* It is not a
mere borrower from other fields, for these dimensions are
related to each other in a unique manner. They interact,
influence, modify each other. Missiology is dynamic not
static. It is not like a physical mixture but is more like
a field of chemical interaction, combination and recombi-
nation, producing new substances by what I believe is called
"the transmutation of elements," or in biology, the coming
together of germ cells to form some completely new organism.
Missiology is a new thing with its own autonomous entity.

- - - -

A Curriculum Committee on the Training of Missionaries
met at Milligan College, Tennesse,during the William S.
Carter Symposium, April, 1974, to examine guidelines for a
curriculum suitable for the training of missionaries in
cross-cultural understanding. The proposed statement and
suggested three-level missiological curriculum, drafted under
the chairmanship of Professor Tippett is included as Appendix C

28

---

*Some critics have objected to the term missiology because
of its derivation, being half Latin and half Greek. The
English word mission came into common use in a number of
ways in the 16th and 17th centuries - theological,
ecclesiastical and political. The common element was the act
of sending forth with authority. Although the word itself is
not biblical the concept is. Whether we see the Christian
mission as "in the world" (John 17:18) or "to the nations of
the world" (Matt. 28:19) both are sending forth under the
authority of Christ and the modern word mission would seem
appropriate.

The suffix ology from the Greek logia, is regularly used
in modern lexical formations, especially as referring to
"science and departments of science." Since the beginning of
the last century this procedure has been used in English to
define new areas of scientific study, regardless of the
character of the root to which the suffix is affixed: i.e.
in modern usage it makes no real difference that a Latin
root may have a Greek suffix. Many such words came into
English scientific writing in the last century via the
European languages, and the process is still active. Sociology
terminology, numerology, ... are examples.

THEOLOGY AT THE SCHOOL OF WORLD MISSION

Those committed to the Church Growth point of view bear a
solemn responsibility under God to work for the renewal of
the Church's sense of mission and her return to the task of
world-wide evangelism and church-planting as biblically defined and traditionally understood. Our studies in theology
are designed to enable missionary associates to perform
this task better.

A. We offer two primary courses in Biblical Theology:

   1. THEOLOGY OF MISSION I (610) - The mission of the
       people of God in the Old Testament (focus: Israel
       and the Nations)

   2. THEOLOGY OF MISSION II (611) - The mission of the
       people of God in the New Testament (focus: Church   29
       and the Nations)

B. We do not offer any courses in Systematic Theology:

This means that we do not seek to face all the questions
that Reality directs toward man. Of course, we believe in
Systematic Theology! Man is capable (he is free to reason!)
of being constantly challenged to inquire what is in and
beyond the questions by which he is incessantly struck. He
has to account for himself and his environment as a responsible person. Systematic Theology attempts to "learn how
things are related" in the perspective and within the horizon
of God, and with Holy Scripture as the trustworthy record
of His disclosure of Himself to man.

C. We offer two courses in Theology of Mission, a subject
that has had a long past, but only a brief history.

   1. THEOLOGY OF MISSION III (612) - The pre-history of
       mission up to the 19th century and its history--
       Orthodox Protestant, Roman Catholic and Conciliar
       Protestant--up to New Delhi 1961.

   2. THEOLOGY OF MISSIONS TODAY (613) - We review all
       alternative theologies of mission currently being
       advocated and practiced. These shall be traced to
       their sources and evaluated in the light of
       Scripture, the history of the Church, and the

contemporary phenomenon of the receptivity of the
Gospel by large segments of the human family.

D. The Traditional Themes in a Theology of Mission:

Down through the history of the Church, whenever Christians
have reflected on the mandate to disciple the nations, they
have invariably and inevitably become aware of five basic
issues.

  1. The Church's Apostleship.

      Since the central purpose of the Church is to glorify
      God through obedience to the Great Commission, how
      does she bring about this obedience? What is her
      collective responsibility touching the sending forth
      of laborers? What is the individual Christian's
      responsibility? How shall Church and Christian
      "bring about the obedience of faith for the sake of
      Jesus' Name among all the nations" (Romans 1:5)?

  2. Church-Mission Relationship.

      Since the Lord has given gifts to His Church
      (apostles, prophets, evangelists and pastor-teachers)
      to make possible the total and corporate participation
      of His people in the ongoing of the Christian mission,
      what is the relation between the Church's structured
      congregations and those sodalities within her life,
      whether voluntary or authorized, whose objective
      is to extend or support the Christian movement as it
      extends "to the regions beyond"? And more, what is
      the relation between these para-church structures
      (missions, societies, orders, fellowships, etc.) and
      the structured congregations they bring into being?

  3. The Gospel and the Religions.

      Since Scripture clearly teaches that God has spoken
      and acted, finally and decisively in Jesus the Christ,
      His eternal Word made flesh, for the salvation of
      mankind, what is the relation between this Good News
      and all the religious systems of mankind that do not
      acknowledge His Lordship? Do they only represent

30

unrelieved blackness, Godforsakeness and human
rebellion? Or, if some good is found in them, can
they be totally devoid of salvation? Is non-Christian
religious experience completely invalid?

4. The Salvation of the Heathen. Since Jesus Christ
   clearly taught that the Salvation of man was made
   possible by His death, burial and resurrection, and
   by this alone, what is the relation between His
   redemptive work and the eternal destiny of the
   heathen? What of those who have died without ever
   hearing the Gospel? Or those who while ignorant of
   this message have perceived the divine through
   nature and have cried out, "God, be merciful to me
   a sinner!"

5. God in History. Since the God in Scripture is the   31
   God of the nations, we must believe that He has been
   at work down through history. He watches over people
   and makes them ready for the coming of the Gospel.
   What then is the validity of each separate culture?
   Should its elements be "possessed" by the missionary
   and incorporated into the indigenous churches he
   plants in its midst? Or should they be rejected
   as "worldly"?

E. A Contemporary Problem:

In recent decades Christians have been pressed to probe
the relation between Great Commission evangelism and social
action. When the issue of priority is raised, how is it
to be resolved?

BIBLIOGRAPHY OF AREAS OF STUDY CONSTITUTING MISSIOLOGY

A seven-page BIBLIOGRAPHY ON MISSION AND MISSIONS,
which provides an anotated listing of books in four areas
of missiology, has been enlarged. The following bibliographic
listing is by no means exhaustive. It is of a very general
nature and is divided according to six of the general areas
of missiology. The syllabus of specific courses being offered
at the School of World Mission in each area, also includes a
limited bibliography to guide the associate or student in
his research.

A.   THEORY AND THEOLOGY OF MISSION

1. Allen, Roland: Ministry of the Spirit. (Eerdmans,
   1965.) The essence of missions is communicating
   the Holy Spirit. Highly relevant to today's real
   problems.

2. Allen, Roland: Missionary Methods: St. Paul's or Ours?
   (Eerdmans, 1966.) An influential statement of basic
   missionary theory.

3. Anderson, Gerald H.: Bibliography of the Theology of
   Missions in the Twentieth Century. 3rd ed.
   (Missionary Research Library.)

4. Anderson, Gerald H., ed.: Christian Mission in
   Theological Perspective. (Abingdon, 1967.) Several
   authors seek to discover the theological basis and
   aim of missions.

5. Anderson, Gerald H., ed.: The Theology of the Christian
   Mission. (McGraw-Hill, 1961.) Twenty-five great
   theologians set forth their theologies of mission -
   very unequal essays - using 'mission' in many different
   senses, only a few interested in world evangelization.

6. Barrett, David B.: Schism and Renewal in Africa. (Oxford
   1968.) An investigation of the great independent
   church movements in Africa delineating the causes for
   these new churches to break with the traditional
   mission-related churches. A very revealing and
   provocative study.

32

7. Bavinck, J. H.: Introduction to the Science of
   Missions. (Presbyterian and Reformed, 1964.)
   An excellent discussion of theory of missions,
   Christian presuppositions in Comparative Religions,
   and history of missions. Rewarding reading.

8. Beaver, R. Pierce: The Missionary Between the Times.
   (Doubleday, 1968.) An analysis of the missionary
   vocation in the changing world with constructive
   suggestions for modern missionaries.

9. Beaver, R. Pierce: To Advance the Gospel. (Eerdmans,
   1966.) The best of Rufus Anderson, "the most original,
   constructive, and courageous exponent of missionary
   theory and theology America has produced and an
   aggressive creative administrator of missionary work." 33

10. Bennett, Charles: Tinder in Tabasco. (Eerdmans, 1968.)
    A depth study of the rapidly growing church in the
    state of Tabasco, Mexico.

11. Beyerhaus, Peter: Missions Which Way? Humanization or
    Redemption. (Zondervan Publishing House, 1971.)

12. Beyerhaus, Peter: Shaken Foundations. Theological
    Foundations for Mission. (Zondervan Publishing
    House, 1972.)

13. Beyerhaus, Peter and Lefever, Henry: The Responsible
    Church and the Foreign Mission. (Eerdmans, 1964.)
    A study of the relationship of the indigenous Church
    with the foreign mission from an historical and
    theological perspective.

14. Blauw, Johannes: The Missionary Nature of the Church -
    A Survey of the Biblical Theology of Mission.
    (McGraw-Hill, 1962.)

15. Boer, Harry: Pentecost and Missions. (Eerdmans,
    Lutterworth, 1961.) A competent discussion from
    the viewpoint of conservative Dutch theology of
    Christian mission and the work of the Holy Spirit.
    Essential reading.

16. Campbell, Robert Edward, ed.: The Church in Mission.
    (Maryknoll Publications, 1965.)

17. Church Growth Bulletin, 265 Lytton Avenue, Palo Alto,
    California 94301. Bimonthly publication of news
    and opinion concerning the growth of the Church
    around the world.

18. Cook, Harold R.: An Introduction to the Study of
    Christian Missions. (Moody Press, 1954.) The
    clear, biblical basis for the evangelization of
    the world. An excellent book for a beginning.

19. Cullmann, Oscar: Salvation in History. English
    translation from the German, drafted by Sidney G.
    Sowers and afterwards completed by the editorial
    staff of S.C.M.Press. (S.C.M.Press, 1967.)

20. Ferre, Nels Fredrick Solomon: The Finality of Faith
    and Christianity among the World Religions. 1st ed.
    (Harper and Row, 1963.)

21. Freytag, Walter: The Gospel and the Religions; a
    Biblical Enquiry. (S.C.M., 1957.)

22. Gottwald, Norman Karol: The Church Unbound; a Human
    Church in a Human World. 1st ed. (Lippencott,
    1967.)

23. Grassi, Joseph A.: A World To Win. The Mission Methods
    of Paul the Apostle. (Maryknoll Publications, 1965.)

24. Grimley, John P. and Robinson, Gordon E.: Church Growth
    in Central and Southern Nigeria. (Eerdmans, 1966.)
    A detailed analysis of the church growth in Nigeria.

25. Hahn, Ferdinand: Mission in the New Testament.
    (Allenson, 1965.) An exegetical study of the words
    in the New Testament related to the mission of the
    Church.

26. Henry, Carl F. H., ed.: One World One Gospel One Race.
    2 vols. (World-Wide Publications, 1967.) Reports
    and papers of the Berlin World Congress on
    Evangelism.

34

27. Hillman, Eugene: The Church as Mission. (Herder and Herder, 1965.)

28. Hocking, William Ernest: The Coming World Civilization. (Harper, 1956.)

29. Hocking, William Ernest: Living Religions and a World Faith. (The Macmillan Co., 1940.)

30. Hodges, Melvin L.: The Indigenous Church. (Gospel Publishing House, 1953.) A guide to understanding the theory and practice of forming an indigenous Church.

31. Horner, Norman A.: Protestant Cross Currents in Mission. (Abingdon, 1969.) Three liberals, three conservatives 35 discuss what mission essentially is. Shaull, Stowe, Scherer and Glasser, Lindsell, Shepherd.

32. Jeremias, Joachim: Jesus' Promise to the Nations. The Franz Delitzsch lectures for 1953. (Allenson, 1958.)

33. Kessler, J. B. A.: A Study of the Older Protestant Missions and Churches in Peru and Chile. (Oosterbaan, Netherlands.)

34. Kraemer, Hendrik: The Christian Message in a Non-Christian World. (Harper and Brothers, 1938.)

35. Kraemer, Hendrik: Religion and the Christian Faith. (Westminster, 1956.) A difficult but rewarding book: what is the enduring relationship between religions (man's constructs however much or little irradiated by God), and the revelation of God in Jesus Christ.

36. Kraemer, Hendrik: World Cultures and World Religions. (Lutterworth, 1960.) The encounter of great world cultures on the world religions and the meaning of the encounter for the Church's mission.

37. Laurentin, Rene: Liberation, Development and Salvation. Translated by Charles Underhill Quinn. (Maryknoll Orbis Books, 1972.)

38. Lindsell, Harold: A Christian Philosophy of Missions.
    (Van Kampen, 1949.) Classical biblical missions
    ably set forth. Must reading for Christians
    concerned with mission.

39. Lindsell, Harold: The Church's World-Wide Mission.
    (Word Books, 1966.) Study papers and reports from
    the EFMA-IFMA Congress on the Church's world-wide
    mission, at Wheaton, Illinois.

40. Lindsell, Harold: An Evangelical Theology of Missions.
    (Zondervan Publishing House, 1970.)

41. McGavran, Donald A.: Bridges of God. (Friendship
    Press, 1955.) A presentation of the thesis that the
    majority of people become Christian through people
    movements. This book is a foundation study in the
    science of church growth.

42. McGavran, Donald A.: Church Growth and Christian
    Mission. (Harper & Row, 1966.) Nida, Guy, Hodges
    and McGavran (ed.) discuss the propagation of the
    Gospel (church growth) as a chief and irreplaceable
    goal of Christian mission. A basic and readable
    book.

43. McGavran, Donald A. ed.: The Eye of the Storm, The
    Great Debate in Mission. (Word Books, Publishers,
    1972.)

44. McGavran, Donald A.: How Churches Grow. (Friendship
    Press, World Dominion, 1959.) A study of the
    patterns of church growth and setting forth of
    methods that will produce a growing church.

45. McGavran, Donald A.: Understanding Church Growth.
    (Eerdmans, 1969.) Principles and procedures to
    understand and produce church growth.

46. Missiology, An International Review (Continuing
    Practical Anthropology), 135 N. Oakland Avenue,
    Pasadena, California 91101. A quarterly publication,
    and official organ of the American Society of
    Missiology. Yearly subscription rate: $8.00.

36

47. Martin-Achard, Robert: A Light to the Nations.
    A study of the Old Testament conception of Israel's
    mission to the world. Translated by John Penney
    Smith. (Oliver and Boyd, 1962.)

48. Munck, Johannes: Paul and the Salvation of Mankind.
    (John Knox Press, 1959.)

49. Newbigin, Lesslie: The Household of God. (Friendship
    Press, 1954.) Fifth printing 1965. The nature of
    the Church and its place in mission.

50. Orr, J. Edwin: The Light of the Nations. (Eerdmans,
    1965.) A survey of evangelical revivals of the
    nineteenth century.

51. Orr, J. Edwin: The Flaming Tongue. (Moody Press, 1973.)
    This account of the impact of 20th Century revivals
    sheds light on the worldwide spiritual awakenings of
    our day, their significance and implications for
    tomorrow.

52. Peters, George W.: A Biblical Theology of Missions.
    (Moody Press, 1972.) Encompassing all of the issues
    fundamental to missions, the text makes a comprehensive
    evangelical statement.

53. Power, John: Mission Theology Today. (Maryknoll Orbis
    Books, 1971.)

54. Read, Monterroso, and Johnson: Latin American Church
    Growth. (Eerdmans, 1969.) The authoritative statement
    on Protestant mission in Latin America - Mexico to
    Argentina. The facts concerning them. A creative,
    courageous exposition of their meaning. Essential
    reading. Every church should own a copy.

55. Read, William R.: Brazil 1980. (MARC, 1973.)

56. Read, William R.: New Patterns of Church Growth in Brazil.
    (Eerdmans, 1965.) Sets forth the real evangelical
    story in Brazil, including both the amazing growth
    of great Pentecostal denominations and the varied
    growth of other Protestants. Factual and inspirational.

57. Roberts, W. Dayton: Revolution in Evangelism.
     (Moody Press, 1967.) The origin and expansion of
     Evangelism-in-Depth in Latin America.

58. Schlette, Heinz Robert: Towards a Theology of
     Religions. Translated by W.J.O'Hara. (Herder
     and Herder, 1966.)

59. Seamands, J. T.: The Supreme Task of the Church.
     (Eerdmans, 1964.) Should be in every minister's
     library. Constructive, imaginative, heartening
     and useable exposition of great commission missions.

60. Smith, Eugene L.: God's Mission - And Ours.
     (Abingdon, 1961.) The Church's role in foreign
     missions.

61. Smith, Wilfred Cantwell: The Meaning and End of
     Religion; a new approach to the religious traditions
     of mankind. (Macmillan, 1963.)

62. Taylor, Mrs. Howard: Behind the Ranges. (Moody Press,
     1964.) A biography of I. O. Fraser, vividly
     portraying the great response to the Gospel by the
     Lisu tribes-people of Southwest China.

63. Tippett, A. R.,ed.: God, Man and Church Growth.
     (Eerdmans, 1973.) This Festschrift, honoring Donald
     Anderson McGavran, is divided into six sections.
     After the biographical section, the five parts bring
     out the aspects of church growth McGavran recognized
     and incorporated into the missiological institution
     he founded at Fuller Theological Seminary, Pasadena.

64. Tippett, A. R.: Solomon Island Christianity.
     (Lutterworth, 1968.) A beautifully clear, accurate
     picture of what a "younger Church" really looks like.
     Typical of hundreds of Asian and African denominations
     A meaty, rewarding book.

65. Tippett, A. R.: Verdict Theology in Missionary Theory.
     (William Carey Library, 1973.) An examination of
     current issues in missionary theory by a missionary
     scholar.

38

66. Van Leeuwen, Arend Th.: Christianity In World History; the meeting of the faiths of East and West. Translated by H. H. Hoskins. (Edinburgh House Press, 1964.)

67. Vicedom, Georg F.: Church and People in New Guinea. (Lutterworth, 1961.) Vivid portrayal of mission theory around the tremendous turnings to Christian faith of the peoples of New Guinea.

68. Vicedom, Georg F.: The Mission of God. An Introduction to Theology of Mission. (Concordia, 1965.) A scholarly treatment of the principal themes of the theology of mission from a biblical point of view.

69. Warren, Max, ed.: To Apply the Gospel, Selections from the Writings of Henry Venn. (Eerdmans, 1971.)

70. Weld, Wayne C.: Ecuadorian Impasse. Evangelical Covenant Church (Fuller Seminary Bookstore, Pasadena, California, 1968.) A comprehensive study of church growth in Ecuador.

71. Wold, Joseph: God's Impatience in Liberia. (Eerdmans, 1968.) Excellent portrayal of the gut issues in missions today in the Liberian setting.

39

B.   APOLOGETICS OF THE CHRISTIAN MISSION
     vis á vis non-Christian religions
     (Commonly called Comparative Religion by secularists)

1. Ashby, Philip: The Conflict of Religions. (Charles
   Scribner's Sons, 1955.) A professor of History of
   Religions, Princeton University, presents in turn:
   Christianity, Islam, Hinduism, Buddhism. He then
   goes on to describe two basic conflicts in each
   major religion and offer come ideas on reconciliation
   and "a united witness."

2. Dewick, E. C.: The Christian Attitude to Other Religions
   (Cambridge, 1953.) Does not set forth any system of
   religion - Hinduism, Judaism, or Marxism, for example.
   Wide discussion of attitudes Christians should hold
   toward religions. Written from within the biblical
   perspective with kindliness toward the religions.

3. Forman, Charles W.: A Faith for the Nations.
   (Westminister, c. 1955.) Christianity is a faith for
   the nations. Its value can be established from
   within the human situation in a way appealing to
   those who have yet to believe. A valuable small book.

4. Kraemer, Hendrik: Why Christianity of All Religions.
   (Westminister, 1965.) Excellent for Christians
   seeking an irenic, intelligent attitude toward non-
   Christian religions. Kraemer has scholarly knowledge
   of other religions and unshakeable conviction that
   Jesus Christ is judge of all religions.

5. Neill, Stephen: Christian Faith and Other Faiths.
   (Oxford, 1961.) Discusses Judaism, Islam, Hinduism,
   Buddhism, Animism, and Marxism, asking how should the
   Christian regard these, why the Gospel should be
   proclaimed to them, and what place the Christian
   religion should occupy vis a vis 'other' religions.

6. Perry, Edmund: The Gospel in Dispute. (Doubleday, 1958.
   The relation of Christian faith to other missionary
   religions. Lets each be set forth by an ardent
   exponent. Since each has 'a gospel,' the title
   becomes meaningful. What in other religions Christian
   can expect to live and what will die.

40

C.   MISSIONS ACROSS CULTURES

1. Applied Anthropology in Missions

Luzbetak, Louis J.: The Church and Cultures: Applied
Anthropology for Religious Workers. (Divine Word, Techny,
1963.) Roman Catholic. (See especially Bibliography.)

Nida, Eugene: Customs and Cultures: Anthropology for
Christian Missions. (Harper & Row, New York, 1954.)

Smalley, William A.: "Selected and Annotated Bibliography
of Anthropology for Missionaries." Occasional Bulletin
XI. 1. (Missionary Research Library, New York, 1960.)   41

Smalley, William A.,ed.: Readings in Missionary
Anthropology. (Practical Anthropology, Tarrytown, New York,
1967.)

Tippett, Alan R.: Bibliography for Cross-Cultural Workers.
(William Carey Library, South Pasadena, California, 1971.)

Note: The technical journal in this field is
Practical Anthropology (which has now been taken over
by a new editorial staff and renamed Missiology).
Another journal is Anthropological Quarterly (Roman
Catholic).

2. General Social Anthropology, (including Acculturation,
    Directed Change, Diffusion of new ideas, Communication)

Arensberg, Conrad M. and Arthur H. Niehoff: Introducing
Social Change: A Manual for Americans Overseas. (Aldine
Publishing Co., Chicago, 1964.)

Barnett, Homer G.: Innovation: The Basis of Cultural
Change. (McGraw-Hill, New York, 1953.)

Beals, Alan R.: Culture in Process. (Holt, Rinehart and
Winston, New York, 1967.)

Beattie, John: Other Cultures. (The Free Press of Glencoe, New York, 1964.)

Bock, Phillip K.: Modern Cultural Anthropology. Second Edition. (Alfred A. Knopf, New York, 1974.)

Foster, George M.: Traditional Societies and Technological Change. (Harper & Row, New York, 1973.)

Harris, Marvin: The Rise of Anthropological Theory. (Thomas Y. Crowell Co., New York, 1968.)

Keesing, Roger M., and Felix M. Keesing: New Perspectives in Cultural Anthropology. (Holt, Rinehart and Winston, New York, 1971.)

Kroeber, A. L., ed.: Anthropology Today. (University of Chicago Press, 1953.)

Nida, Eugene: Message and Mission: The Communication of the Christian Faith. (Harper & Bros., New York, 1960.)

3.   Encounter with Magico-Religion

Barrett, David B.: Schism & Renewal in Africa, An Analysis of Six Thousand Contemporary Religious Movements. (Oxford University Press, 1968.)

Lessa, William A. and Evon Z. Vogt: Reader in Comparative Religion: An Anthropological Approach. (Harper & Row, Evanston, 1965.)

Lowie, Robert H.: Primitive Religion. (Peter Owen Ltd., London, 1952.)

Malinowski, B.: Magic, Science and Religion. (Doubleday & Co., New York, 1948.)

Middleton, John, ed.: Gods and Rituals. (Natural History Press, New York, 1967.)

Middleton, John, ed.: Magic, Witchcraft and Curing. (Natural History Press, New York, 1967.)

Notes and Queries on Anthropology. (6th edition revised
and rewritten by a committee of the Royal Anthropological
Insitute of Great Britain. Routledge and K. Paul, London,
1951.)

Parrinder, E. G.: African Traditional Religion.
Hutchinson's Home University Library, London, 1954.)

Radin, Paul: Primitive Religion. (Dover Publications,
New York, 1957.)

Sundkler, B. G. M.: Bantu Prophets in South Africa.
(Oxford University Press, London, 1961.)

Taylor, John V.: The Primal Vision. (S.C.M. Press,   43
London, 1963.)

Tempels, R. P. Placide: Bantu Philosophy. (Presence
Africaine, Paris, 1959.)

Warneck, Joh.: The Living Christ and Dying Heathenism.
Baker Book House, Michigan, 1954.)

    4. Culture and Personality

Barnouw, V.: Culture & Personality. (Dorsey Press, 1973.)

Hallowell, A Irving: Culture and Experience. (University
of Pennsylvania Press, 1955.)

Haring, Douglas G., ed.: Personal Character and Cultural
Milieu. (Syracus University Press, 1956.)

Honigman, John J.: Personality in Culture. (Harper & Row,
New York, 1967.)

Kardiner, Abram, et al.: The Psychological Frontiers of
Society. (Columbia University Press, New York, 1945.)

Hunt, Robert, ed.: Personalities and Cultures. (The
Natural History Press, New York, 1967.)

Linton, Ralph: The Cultural Background of Personality.
(Appleton-Century-Crofts, New York, 1945.)

Linton, Ralph: The Study of Man. (Appleton-Century-Crofts,
New York, 1936.)

D. TECHNIQUES, ORGANIZATION AND METHODS IN MISSION

    (See Bibliography for F. CHURCH GROWTH.)

44

E. HISTORY OF MISSIONS AND CHURCH EXPANSION

1. Aberly, John: An Outline of Missions. (Muhlenberg
   Press, Philadelphia, 1945.) Excellent as an outline.

2. Addison, James Thayer: The Medieval Missionary.
   (The International Missionary Council of the World
   Council of Churches, New York, 1936.) Excellent
   on the medieval period; shows the missionary
   influence of the monastic system.

3. Dawson, Christopher: The Making of Europe. (Meridian
   Books, New York, 1956.) Paperback. More balanced
   than most Protestant accounts of the effect of
   Christianity on the various cultures of the early 45
   Middle Ages. Fascinating. Hard back printing 1932.

4. Dawson, Christopher: Religion and the Rise of Western
   Culture. (Image Books, Doubleday, New York, 1958.)

5. Edman, V. Raymond: The Light in Dark Ages. (Van Kampen
   Press, Wheaton, 1949.) A returned missionary's
   scholarly investigation of the course of missions
   before Carey. Rich footnotes and quotations.

6. Elsbree, O. W.: The Rise of the Missionary Spirit in
   America, 1790-1815. (Williamsport Printing and
   Binding Co., Pa., 1928.)

7. Foster, John: After the Apostles: Missionary Preaching
   of the First Three Centuries. (S.C.M. Press, London,
   1951.) Uses original sources in discussing the
   approach of the early missionaries to the different
   cultures of the time.

8. Glover, Robert H., and J. Herbert Kane: The Progress
   of World-wide Missions. (Harper and Row, New York,
   1960.) The title does not fit. Except for brief
   introduction, it is a catalog of the countries of
   the world, mentioning for each in a page or two the
   data of mission interest. Good bibliography.

9. Goodard, Burton L, ed.: The Encyclopedia of Modern
   Christian Missions, Vol. 1. (Thomas Nelson & Sons,
   Camden, New Jersey, 1967.) Excellent, exhaustive.
   This first volume is an encyclopedia of 1437
   Protestant Mission agencies.

10. Harnack, Adolf H. von: The Mission and Expansion of
    Christianity in the First Three Centuries. (Harper
    Torchbooks, New York, 1962.)

11. Harr, Wilber C., ed.: Frontiers of the Christian
    World Mission Since 1938. (Harper and Brothers,
    New York, 1962.)

12. Hoffman, Ronan: Pioneer Theories of Missiology.
    (The Catholic University of America Press,
    Washington, D.C., 1960.) A comparative study of
    the mission theories of Cardinal Brancati de
    Laurea, O.F.M. Conv., with those of three of his
    companions.

13. Kane, J. Herbert: A Global View of Christian Missions.
    (Baker Book House, Grand Rapids, 1971.)

14. Latourette, Kenneth Scott: A History of the Expansion
    of Christianity, Volumes I-VII. (Zondervan
    Publishing House, Grand Rapids, 1970.) The most
    exhaustive ever, this seven volume series is the
    only really authoritative work on the precise
    subject written in the last 75 years.

15. Latourette, Kenneth Scott: Christianity in a
    Revolutionary Age, A History of Christianity in the
    Nineteenth and Twentieth Centuries. (Harper, New
    York, 1958-62.) Five volumes that are unique.
    Quietly shatters geographic and institutional
    limitations of the usual accounts.

16. Latourette, Kenneth Scott: History of Christianity.
    (Harper, New York, 1953.) Unusual in its fairness
    to Christianity as a world movement, not just a
    Western phenomenon. The most balanced, readable
    work of its length.

46

17. McEvedy, Colin: The Penguin Atlas of Medieval History.
(Penguin Books, Baltimore, 1961.) Indispensable.
First book to make graphic sense out of the
thousand years of human flux in medieval Europe.

18. Maury, P., ed.: History's Lessons for Tomorrow's
Mission. (World's Student Christian Federation,
Geneva, 1960.)

19. Neill, Stephen: A History of Christian Missions.
(Penguin Books, Baltimore, 1966.) Best brief
single volume paperback treatment.

20. Robinson, Charles H.: A History of Christian Missions.
(Chas. Scribner's Sons, New York, 1923.) Very good
for the period up to date of publishing.   47

21. Schmidlin, Joseph: Catholic Mission History.
Translated from the German by Matthias Braun.
(Mission Press, S.V.D., Techny, Ill., 1931.) The
classic work of Catholic missions. Contains 862
pages. Has a useful bibliography. Now superseded
by A. Mulders: Missiegeschiedenis.

22. Speer, Robert E.: Missions and Modern History. 2
volumes. (Revell, New York, 1904.) Detailed
descriptions of significant events in the 19th
century by one of the greatest missionary statesmen.

23. Syrdal, Rolf A.: To the End of the Earth. (Augsburg
Publishing House, Minneapolis, 1967.) One-third
devoted to Biblical times, one-third to the theory
of missions, and one-third to history of missions.
Very sketchy.

24. Van Den Berg, Johannes: Constrained by Jesus' Love.
(J. H. Kok, Kampen, 1956.) An inquiry into the
motives of the missionary awakening in Great Britain
in the period between 1698 and 1815.

25. Warneck, Gustav: History of Protestant Missions.
(Fleming H. Revell, New York, 1906.) Classical work.

26. Winter, Ralph D.: The Twenty-Five Unbelievable Years,
1945 to 1969. (William Carey Library, South Pasadena,
1970.)

F. CHURCH GROWTH (TECHNIQUES, ORGANIZATION AND METHODS)

1. Cogswell, James A.: Response: The Church in Mission
   to a World in Crisis. (CLC Press, Richmond, 1971.)

2. Collins, Marjorie A.: Manual for Accepted Missionary
   Candidates. (William Carey Library, South Pasadena,
   1972.), paper.

3. Covell, Ralph R. and C. Peter Wagner: An Extension
   Seminary Primer. (William Carey Library, South
   Pasadena, 1971.), paper.

4. Gerber, Vergil: God's Way to Keep a Church Going and
   Growing. (Regal Books, Glendale, 1974.), paper.

5. Griffiths, Michael C.: Give Up Your Small Ambitions.
   (Moody Press, Chicago, 1971.), paper.

6. Kane, J. Herbert: Winds of Change in Christian Mission.
   (Moody Press, Chicago, 1973.), paper.

7. McGavran, Donald A., ed.: Church Growth and Christian
   Mission. (Harper & Row, New York, 1965.)

8. McGavran, Donald A., ed.: Church Growth Bulletin, Vols.
   1-5. (William Carey Library, South Pasadena, 1969.)

9. McGavran, Donald A., ed.: Crucial Issues in Missions
   Tomorrow. (Moody Press, Chicago, 1972.)

10. McGavran, Donald A.: How Churches Grow. (World
    Dominion Press, London, 1959.)

11. McGavran, Donald A.: Understanding Church Growth.
    (Eerdmans, Grand Rapids, 1970.), cloth and paper.

12. Mathews, Basil: Forward Through the Ages. (Friendship
    Press, New York, 1960.)

13. Neill, Stephen: Call to Mission. (Fortress Press,
    Philadelphia, 1970.)

48

14. Strachan, R. Kenneth: The Inescapable Calling. (Eerdmans, Grand Rapids, 1968.), paper.

15. Tippett, Alan R.: Church Growth and the Word of God. (Eerdmans, Grand Rapids, 1970.), paper.

16. Tippett, Alan R.: People Movements in Southern Polynesia. (Moody Press, Chicago, 1971.)

17. Trueblood, Elton: The Validity of the Christian Mission. (Harper & Row, 1972.)

18. Wagner, C. Peter, ed.: Church/Mission Tensions Today. (Moody Press, Chicago, 1972.)

19. Wagner, C. Peter: Frontiers in Missionary Strategy. 49
    (Moody Press, Chicago, 1971.)

20. Wagner, C. Peter: Look Out! The Pentecostals Are Coming. (Creation House, Carol Stream, 1973.)

21. Wagner, C. Peter: Stop the World, I Want to Get On. (Regal, Glendale, 1974.)

22. Winter, Ralph D., ed.: Theological Education by Extension. (William Carey Library, South Pasadena, 1969.)

23. Winter, Ralph D., and R. Pierce Beaver: The Warp and the Woof. (William Carey Library, South Pasadena, 1970.), paper.

24. Wong, James, Peter Larson, and Edward Pentecost: Missions from the Third World. (Church Growth Study Center, Singapore, 1973.), paper.

25. Yamamori, Tetsunao, and E. LeRoy Lawson: Introducing Church Growth. (Standard Publishing, Cincinnati, 1974.)

G. THE WORLD CHURCH -- ECUMENICS

1. Bea, Augustin Cardinal: The Unity of Christians.
   Edited by Bernard Leeming, S.J. (Herder and
   Herder, New York, 1963.)

2. Beaver, R. Pierce: Ecumenical Beginnings in
   Protestant World Mission, A History of Comity.
   (Nelson, New York, 1962.)

3. Bridston, Keith R., and Walter D. Wagoner, eds.:
   Unity in Mid-Career. An Ecumenical Critique.
   (The Macmillan Company, New York, 1963.)

4. Brown, Robert McAfee: The Ecumenical Revolution.
   An Interpretation of the Catholic-Protestant
   Dialogue. (Doubleday & Co. Inc., Garden City, New
   York, 1967.)

5. Fey, Harold E., ed.: A History of The Ecumenical
   Movement. Volume 2 / 1948-1968--The Ecumenical
   Advance. (The Westminister Press, Philadelphia,
   1967.)

6. Groscurth, Reinhard, ed.: What Unity Implies. Six
   Essays After Uppsala. (World Council of Churches
   Studies No. 7, 1969.)

7. Hillman, Eugene: The Wider Ecumenism. (Herder and
   Herder, New York, 1968.)

8. Hogg, William Richey: Ecumenical Foundations.
   A History of the International Missionary Council
   and Its Nineteenth-Century Background. (Harper &
   Brothers, New York, 1952.) Valuable for a basic
   understanding of developments in this period.
   Extensive footnotes and bibliography.

9. Lambert, Bernard: Ecumenism, Theology and History.
   Translated by Lancelot C. Sheppard. (Herder and
   Herder, New York, 1962.)

50

10. Mackay, John Alexander: Ecumenics; The Science of
    The Church Universal. (Prentice-Hall, Englewood
    Cliffs, N. J., 1964.)

11. Newbigin, Lesslie: The Reunion of The Church,
    A Defence of the South India Scheme. New and
    Revised Edition. (SCM Press Ltd., London, 1960.)

12. Rouse, Ruth and Stephen Charles Neill: A History of
    The Ecumenical Movement, 1517-1948. Second
    Edition with Revised Bibliography. (The Westminster
    Press, Philadelphia, 1967.)

13. Stowe, David M.: Ecumenicity and Evangelism. (Eerdmans,
    Grand Rapids, 1970.)

14. Van den Heuvel, Albert H., ed.: Unity of Mankind.
    Speeches from the Fourth Assembly of the World
    Council of Churches, Uppsala 1968. (World Council
    of Churches, Geneva, 1969.)

15. Vischer, Lukas, ed.: A Documentary History of the
    Faith and Order Movement, 1927-1963. (The Bethany
    Press, St. Louis, 1963.)

16. Weber, Hans-Ruedi: Asia and The Ecumenical Movement
    1895-1961. (SCM Press Ltd., London, 1966.)

51

SUBJECT: COMPREHENSIVE EXAMINATIONS
MEMORANDUM TO: All SWM Degree Candidates
            FROM: Arthur F. Glasser   December 11, 1973

Introduction

The comprehensive examination assumes the data base of several disciplines and is designed to probe into the degree candidate's grasp of their relevant issues. It is a four-hour examination that involves writing comprehensive answers to four questions (which he is generally at liberty to select from six possibilities). Since the examination is particularly designed to test one's ability to organize the data into a coherent whole, the examiner particularly looks for the following:

1. Comprehensiveness in treatment.

2. Orderly sequence of development.

3. Expressed indebtedness to those scholars who have contributed to the development of the subject.

4. An awareness of its inherent problems.

5. A style of presentation that demonstrates his grasp of the subject.

Specific Regulations:

1. **PREREQUISITE**

   No comprehensive examination can be taken without having been first advanced to degree candidacy.

2. **CANDIDACY**

   Degree candidacy will be decided at the last December meeting of the SWM Faculty.

3. MASTERS

Candidates for the degrees of a <u>Master of Arts</u>
<u>in Missions</u> as well as <u>in Missiology</u> shall take
comprehensives in:

a.   Church Growth and Biblical Theology

b.   Anthropology and Animism

c.   History and Case Studies

4. REPEATING

Those who have already taken M.A. comprehensives
will not have to repeat them if they are candidates
for <u>D.Missiology</u>.

53

5. DOCTORAL

All doctoral candidates shall take a fourth
examination covering the field of Missiology, in
order to demonstrate their competence in integrat-
ing its separate components. Its focus will be
the "core" 700 level courses.

6. GRADES

M.A. comprehensives will be marked "pass with
honors," "pass" or "fail." A "pass with honors"
must be attained by all doctoral candidates,
whereas a "pass" will satisfy the M.A. requirements.

7. GRADING PROCESS

When a paper is marginal and its grade is in doubt,
a second faculty member shall be called in to review the paper in the light of the best and poorest
papers turned in.

8. <u>FAILURE</u>

Should any degree candidate fail to qualify in any
specific examination, he will be permitted to repeat the examination the following year.

9. <u>SCHEDULE</u>

Comprehensive examinations are scheduled during
the first week of May. Each four-hour examination
is written from 1-5 p.m. The time and place for
each examination will be posted by the 15th of
April.

54

COMPREHENSIVE EXAMINATION - May 9, 1973
Theory and Theology of Missions and Church Growth

Select two of the following:

1. Discuss the major emphases of the Church Growth
   school of thought.

2. Describe people movements in the sociological-
   anthropological, historical, and theological-
   biblical dimensions.

3. Set forth the major objections to Church Growth
   as a key consideration in mission policy and
   answer them from the biblical and practical points
   of view.

Select two of the following:

1. Blauw says "We must be much more reserved in
   speaking of the missionary message of the Old
   Testament than of its universal message" (p.17).
   Discuss.

2. What is the relation between the Jesus proclamation of the Kingdom of God and His issuance of the
   Great Commission?

3. Discuss the Apostolic Band(s) of the New Testament,
   their nature, function and relation to local
   congregations.

                    McGavran/Glasser

COMPREHENSIVE EXAMINATION - May 12, 1972
Church Growth and Theology

Church Growth - Two Hours

1. Discuss the many ways in which missions and Churches - while holding to the biblical priority of proclaiming the Gospel - work quietly forward winning few to Christ and planting few churches.

2. Set forth five principles of church growth (described in Understanding Church Growth) most germane to and needed by the missions and Churches in your field. Spend about twelve minutes on each principle.

Theology - Two Hours (Use your Bible if you wish.)

1. The unifying theme of the Bible is the theme of REDEMPTION. It is not artificially imposed on either Old or New Testaments but is inherent in the concept of a people called by God to be His--to live under His rule and to hope in His coming Kingdom (Bright 1953:10). We accept this. How then should we relate the Old Testament portrayal of the people of God to His purpose touching the nations? (Don't use extended prose. The more sub-headings the better.)

2. By His crucifixion Jesus Christ removed "the enmity" between Jew and Gentile and "broke down the middle wall of partition" between them. As a result, "whatever divisions exist in society, and whatever may be the right solution of them, within the body of Christ such divisions have no relevancy whatever. In the Church of Christ there is neither Jew nor Greek, slave nor free (I Cor. 12:13): all are, without exception, one" (Bright 1953:264). We accept this. And yet we cherish the thesis that "men like to become Christians without crossing racial, linguistic or class barriers" (McGavran 1970:198). We tend to challenge the wisdom of seeking to plant conglomerate churches in pluralistic societies. But how should we defend this Church Growth principle on Biblical grounds?

COMPREHENSIVE EXAMINATION - May, 1973
Mission Across Culture - Anthropology and Animism

Answer Four Questions Only

1. Discuss the nature and significance of the urban
anthropological theory of Max Weber, Emile Durkheim,
Oscar Lewis and William Mangin.

2. Write an essay on the magical treatment of sickness,
and how it relates to the Christian mission.

3. How does the approach of one of Philip Bock, Homer
Barnett or Louis Luzbetak differ from that of other
anthropologists, and what does his writing signify for
missiology?

4. How does the notion of dynamic equivalence relate to
the concept of indigeneity?

5. Discuss the place of dynamics in religion, using data
from the Reader in Comparative Religion, Solomon Island
Christianity and Schism and Renewal in Africa.

6. Explain the place of the functional substitutes in
cross-cultural church planting, its importance and its
dangers.

7. Write notes on the contribution of any six of the
following to anthropological literature, and how it may
be used in missiology:
    a. John Gillen
    b. Morris Opler
    c. W. E. H. Stanner
    d. S. C. Dube
    e. E. B. Tylor
    f. Kenneth Little
    g. W. H. Goodenough
    h. Walter Goldschmidt
    i. Arnold van Gennep
    j. Laurenson Sharp
    k. Anthony Wallace
    l. M. N. Srinivas
    m. Francis Hsu
    n. Robert Redfield
    o. G. P. Murdock
    p. Lalive d'Epenay
    q. Gilberto Freyre
    r. Robert Lowie
    s. Cornelius Osgood
    t. Stafford Beer
    u. Samuel Ramos

8. Write an essay on one of the following books, relating
it to the science of mission:

    a. The Other Covenant (Theology of Paganism)
    b. Traditional Cultures and the Impact of
        Technological Change
    c. Juan the Chamula
    d. Science, Magic and Religion
    e. Primitive Man as a Philosopher
    f. People Movements in Southern Polynesia
    g. Theory and Practice of Translation
    h. Readings in Missionary Anthropology.

58

COMPREHENSIVE EXAMINATION - May, 1972
Missions Across Cultures - Anthropology and Animism

Answer any four questions. Illustrate from your year's
reading. Plan your answering to spend about an hour on
each question you select.

1. Write an essay on "Cultural Values."

2. Discuss cross-cultural conversion in terms of
advocacy, acceptance and rejection.

3. What did you learn from Solomon Islands Christianity
or The Peoples of Southwest Ethiopia?

4. What lessons do Nativism, Independency or Negritude
have for the Church in mission?

5. How is the biblical message relevant for an animist
world of power encounter?

6. Discuss the contribution of Anthony Wallace or Homer
Barnett to church growth theory.

7. Discuss the nature and dangers of syncretism in New
Testament times and in two present-day regions of the world.

8. What have your learned from anthropology about how to
plant a church in a frontier situation - either rural or
urban?

9. Distinguish between - Witchcraft and Sorcery;
Possession and Shamanism; Religion, Magic and Science.

10. Enumerate some of the conceptual contributions of any
four of these and how they can be used in church growth
theory:

Edward Hall	John Mbiti
Bronislaw Malinowski	Joel Aronoff
Jacob Loewen	David Barrett
Ralph Linton	Oscar Lewis
F. E. Williams	George Foster

COMPREHENSIVE EXAMINATION - May 11, 1973
SUBJECT: History and Case Studies

Instructions: Answer questions with as few words as
possible. Write very clearly please. Select 3 of the
first 4 questions. The 5th question is required.

1. WHAT LIGHT IS SHED ON MISSIONS BY WHAT WE KNOW OF THE
    CREATIVE INTENT OF GOD?
    a. What logical relation is there between creation,
        redemption and the Christian Mission?
    b. What are the various enigmas that still remain in
        the story of mankind, as this may be related to
        question 1.a?
    c. What do we know pretty clearly about the story of
        mankind prior to Christ which provides any kind
        of pattern?
    d. Does this pattern contrast with the A.D. period?
        (Extra credit: How soon, and where, did the
        significance of the A.D. period as a period
        become recognized?)

60

2. WE ATTEMPTED TO DESCRIBE THE "WESTERN" EXPANSION OF
    THE CHRISTIAN MOVEMENT IN 400 YEAR PERIODS.
    a. Describe this scheme very briefly.
    b. What discernable pattern is there?
    c. What is signified (on this broad canvass) by
        Pearl Harbor?
    d. Going strictly by analogy to earlier periods, what
        cataclysmic event may the Western World face in
        the near future?
    e. What significance does this have right now for
        missions?
    f. After it happens?
    g. What might we--going strictly by analogy--best do,
        as Christians in view of these possibilities?
        E.G. What, if these events take place, is the
        logical approach we should have as mission
        leaders today and tomorrow?

3. IN TERMS OF ORGANIZED, INTENTIONAL EXPANSION OF THE
    CHRISTIAN MOVEMENT PRIOR TO 1800.
    a. What did Paul do, or what would he have to
        have done, to qualify as the founder and manager
        of a mission sodality?

b. What two kinds of radically different Christian
    communities were part and parcel of the expansion
    of Christianity, even prior to Constantine?
c. Did one gain strength and the other weakness as
    the result of the Constantian revolution in Roman
    religious history? (Extra credit: How does
    McGavran's view of Constantine's impact differ
    from the more common view?)
d. Sketch briefly the most active structural mechan-
    isms in all of Christian history (in regard to
    expansion, remember). Note the periods, types,
    styles, with their strengths and weaknesses (you
    should be able to point out at least three and
    perhaps six stages).
e. What great event at about 1800 drastically re-
    duced the number of Christian missionaries
    across the world?

61

4. SUMMARIZE BRIEFLY THE STORY OF THE RELATIONSHIP
BETWEEN THE PROTESTANT MOVEMENT AND MISSIONS.
    a. Mark off the major periods.
    b. What Spiritual movements were significantly
        involved?
    c. How did structures for mission vary across the
        decades of Protestant mission activity?
    d. Do your best to draw roughly a growth curve of
        total Protestant missionaries between 1500 and
        1973. At least point out the new bursts of vigor.
    e. Give three examples of the powerful interplay of
        political/military events and mission outreach.
    f. What were some of the heartening early (prior to
        1860) mission breakthroughs on a fairly large
        scale?
    g. What happened for the first time at Edinburgh
        in 1910?
    h. What would have to happen today for something
        fairly to be called Edinburgh II? (Why does
        Bangkok not qualify?)

5. CASE STUDIES

Answer either of the following two questions:

a. Describe the three expansions of the Methodist
    Church in the Gold Coast, emphasizing the
    context and the growth principles involved
    in each.

b. Describe the four main types of churches in
    India and assess the meaning of each for the
    strategy of evangelism and mission.

62

COMPREHENSIVE EXAMINATION - May, 1972
SUBJECT: History

1. a. According to the author of the Twenty-Five
      Unbelievable Years, what is the crucial
      distinction that needs to be drawn between
      ecumenical structures and oikoumenical structures?
      Describe this distinction both with and without
      the use of the two words modality and sodality.

   b. What are the major differences between the IFMA
      and the EFMA and the DWME? In what way are the
      first and last opposites and the middle one like
      both the others? Which of these is more
      oikoumenical than the other two?

   c. Identify the major structures and the major kinds
      of structures of cooperation and coordination   63
      which involve missions today.

   d. What, according to Hogg, are the four streams of
      influence that developed in the past century and
      a half into the Ecumenical movement today?

   e. Following the 1910 conference at Edinburgh, Mott
      went around the world encouraging into existence
      National Christian Councils. What gradual changes
      took place over the years in the nature of the
      field situation and the membership of these bodies
      which eventually, in almost every case, profoundly
      altered their structure and character?

2. Treat the following questions from historical
   perspective (drawing illustrations from major periods):

   a. What, structurally speaking, are most Christian
      mission agencies? Did Paul operate a mission, for
      example? If you don't feel you know enough about
      what Paul did, then tell what he would have had
      to do for his role to be definable, in structural
      terms, as that of operating a mission. What about
      later periods of history, etc.?

b. From the standpoint of purpose, of the nature of
work being accomplished, what are most Christian
mission agencies doing? That is, what are the
end results of their work? What do they often
overlook?

c. From the standpoint of traversing cultural
distances, how might we classify mission agencies?

d. From the standpoint of how missions are supported,
what varieties of relationship do we see?

3. a. Stories of King Arthur have been far more popular
in France than in England. In terms of cultural
factors, what obvious explanation comes to mind?
How did similar cultural factors defer the
evangelization of the Saxons who invaded Britain
in the 5th century?

b. How would you compare the role and task of
Boniface to that of Wesley? What parallels to
each do you see in the world at this moment?

c. Suggest the ways in which the use of the
vernacular affected mission work during the first
millenium.

d. What sharp distinction can be drawn between the
process whereby the invading Goths became
Christian and the Vikings became Christian?

e. How, briefly, do you explain the sudden dual
campaign of Cathedral and Crusade? Do you see
any modern parallels?

64

COMPREHENSIVE EXAMINATION - Doctoral Level, May 12, 1973
SUBJECT: "700" Level Courses

Method: This examination will last 4 hours. Run through
the courses listed below. Check all that you have taken.
You MUST provide answers to questions of these courses.
Obviously, you will not attempt answers to any you have
not taken! This means you must plan your time very carefully to cover these questions within the time allotted.
Return this sheet with your paper.

Course SWM 720 - ANIMISTIC BASES OF THE GREAT RELIGIONS

Discuss the place of Christianity among the religions
of the world: comparing or contrasting it with Hinduism or Buddhism. How would you rate Jean Danielou,
Walt Whitman and Toynbee in your comparison?

Course SWM 732 - CULTURE PERSONALITY AND THE GOSPEL

Discuss the relationship of the concepts dealt with
by e. g. Honigmann, Aronoff, Maslow (treated in the
Culture and Personality course) to Missiology.

Course SWM 733 CONVERSION WITH A MINIMUM OF DISLOCATION

Briefly state the contributions of Barclay, Weins,
Loewen and Tippett to a more adequate understanding
of Christian conversion. Summarize such an understanding (with or without a diagram).

Course SWM 734 ANTHROPOLOGICAL THEORY

Who have been the most useful secular anthropological
theorists you have met in your studies at Fuller, and
how do you apply their theories to missiology? (Do no
more than 3 anthropologists but you can confine yourself to one if you write on him for 60 minutes.)

Course SWM 735 ETHNOLINGUISTICS

Discuss the value of various kinds of linguistic and
ethnolinguistic data to the discovery of the world view
and value system of a people.

Course SWM 736   ANTHROPOLOGICAL BASIS OF LEADERSHIP

What is the value of anthropology in cross-cultural
leadership planning? Illustrate your answer from
three or four different kinds of social structure.
What does this say to denominational Missions?

Course SWM 760   ADVANCED CHURCH GROWTH   (Choose 1 of 2)

1.   The church typology most commonly used today is
     based on doctrine and polity by which we distin-
     guish Greek Orthodox, Roman Catholic, Lutheran,
     Calvinist, Congregational, Baptist or other
     subdivisions of the Church. Often more revealing
     and more important as concerns growth potential is
     a typology based on sociological linguistic and
     ethnic considerations. Discuss the theory of this
     second "typology of churches" and illustrate it
     from Afericasia.

2.   Two essential positions of the School in regard
     to Culture and Christianity are: that men should
     become Christian within their culture, and at the
     same time that biblical requirements should over-
     ride all personal, traditional, western, cultural
     and ethnic norms.
          Why is it necessary to hold to both these
          positions?
          What are the results of understressing each?
          What are the proper limits of each?

Course SWM 766   STRATEGY OF MISSIONS

Describe the syndrome of church development, comment
on its importance in missionary strategy, and give
some examples.

66

COMPREHENSIVE EXAMINATION - Doctoral Level, May, 1972
SUBJECT: "700" Level Courses

Select four questions only, giving one hour to each.
Mention the literature on the subject, and apply your
answers to the general program of Christian mission.

1. What problems in Christian mission are brought to
light in the new book Eye of the Storm?

2. What is historiography? How would you handle personal
documents? What methodology would you use for using and
evaluating cross-cultural materials and statistical records?
Give examples from situations with which you are familiar.

3. Discuss the new ethnolinguistic approach to Scripture
translation and its bearing on church planting.

4. Outline four different culture patterns of authority
and social control, and indicate how they should be
approached by the church planter, who seeks to see a
reasonable leadership pattern in the young church.

5. Discuss the claim that the great religions of Asia are
basically animistic. Where Asian religions have spread to
other lands such data may also be used to illustrate your
points e.g. Islam in Africa.

6. What theoretical issues came into focus with the
meeting of: Linton and Kardiner; White and Bidney;
Boas and Graebner; Linton, Herskovits and Redfield.

7. Distinguish between the notions of "Race" and "Culture"
and the implications of the distinction for Christian
mission.

8. Discuss the dynamics of the process of conversion and
what this means for evangelist and pastor.

9. Have you done any personal research or study on the
relationship of personality, culture and Christian
mission? In what direction do you think this subject
speaks to church growth theory?

I.   Purpose of the Degree

Missions is a highly specialized activity of extra-
ordinary challenge and difficulty firmly rooted in purposes
of God as revealed in the Bible. Leaders of the missionary
enterprise require much advanced professional education.
Explosion of knowledge, new insights available through the
sciences of man such as anthropology, sociology, communication
science and history, the widespread use of new forms of
communication, revolutionary changes on every hand, and the
remarkable receptivity of many populations toward the Gospel,
all make it necessary for career missionaries and leaders of
younger Churches to seek advanced education in the science
of missions--missiology.

The program leading toward the degree has been designed
to meet this need. The Doctor of Missiology is a professional
degree (similar to an M.D. or Ed.D.) rather than a research
or academic degree (like a Ph.D.). This program requires a
great deal of research but does not (like many Ph.D. programs)
focus on research merely for the sake of the research itself.
The program requires research for the purpose of application
to the multitude of missionary problems. It fits men to
administer missionary societies, train leaders of the younger
Churches, solve the crucial problems of modern missions, plan
advances, think strategically and biblically about missions,
and in short, to be more effective missionaries in the era of
great change and Christian advance now in progress.

II.   Entering the Program

A.   The program involves a minimum of five years study
     beyond the B.A. Of these, three are normally spent
     in biblical and theological studies leading to a
     B.D., M.Div. or equivalent, one is spent in graduate
     missions studies leading to an M.A. in Missiology,

*As of Nov. 29, 1973: request latest revision if exploring
the possibility of entering this program.

and one is spent in advanced missions studies in special interest courses and in writing a doctoral dissertation.

B. The Steps Involved in Entering the Program:

1. Completion of B.D., M.Div. or equivalent. When this step has been satisfactorily completed the student is eligible for consideration as an Applicant for the Degree M.A. in Missiology.

2. Upon application for entrance into the program the applicant may be admitted at this point to the status of Prospective Candidate for the Degree M.A. in Missiology.   69

3. If by faculty action the Applicant is approved for entrance into the M.A. program, he becomes a Candidate for the Degree M.A. in Missiology. Such faculty action is normally taken at the end of the Prospective Candidate's first term in residence at SWM/ICG.

4. Upon completion of the M.A. requirements (including the Comprehensive Examinations and, normally, an M.A. thesis) the M.A. Candidate may apply for admission to the Doctorate in Missiology program. Such application may be made at any time prior to the taking of the Comprehensive Examinations but will not be evaluated by the faculty until the results of those examinations are known. No Prospective Candidate for the D.Miss. may consider himself a part of the D.Miss. program until such faculty action has elevated him to the status of Candidate for the D.Miss.

5. If by faculty action the Prospective Candidate is approved for entrance into the D.Miss. program, he becomes a Candidate for the Degree Doctorate of Missiology.

C. The Timing of These Steps:

1. Step 1 (the B.D., M.Div. or equivalent) is normally completed before the Applicant arrives at SWM/ICG. If this step has not been completed, the Applicant is normally encouraged to complete it by means of study in the School of Theology of Fuller Theological Seminary.

2. Steps 2-5 may be completed at any time after the Applicant has completed step 1, his cross-cultural field experience and the remaining requirements listed under VI below.

3. The M.A. and the D.Miss. work may be done either in two consecutive years or with an intervening period of field experience between the M.A. residence and the D.Miss. residence.

D. Other Procedures:

1. Those who take a two-year M.A. in Missions (built on a B.A. rather than a B.D. or M.Div.), will normally be required to complete a B.D., M.Div. or equivalent before applying for admission to the D.Miss. program. Upon success-ful completion of the B.D. or M.Div., such applicants become Prospective Candidates for the D.Miss. (step 5 above).

2. Those bringing a B.D., M.Div., M.A. in Missions, Th.M. and/or other degrees from other institution may, by special faculty action, be admitted to the doctoral program at a place fixed by evalua-tion of the missions content of their previous work.

3. The Candidate must normally complete the doctoral degree within five years after being advanced to candidacy. If for some reason this proves impossible, the Candidate may petition the faculty for an extension of the time limit.

4. In the case of properly qualified international
   students, the faculty will apply these procedures to each person individually after a
   period of residence at SWM/ICG during which
   time the Applicant is regarded as studying with
   probationary status.

III. <u>Language Requirement</u>

A. Fluency in the language of the country in which the
   candidate works is the normal language requirement.
   Fluency is attested by his writings in that language,
   by rating as to proficiency in speech, understanding,
   and reading by nationals or other fellow missionaries,
   or by other approved examiner.

                                                     71

B. Other language competence may, upon petition to the
   faculty, be considered in fulfillment of this requirement. Justification of such an alternative on the
   basis of the Prospective Candidate's thesis research
   is the only basis envisaged for an alternative
   language.

IV. <u>Residence Requirement</u>

A minimum of three quarters in continuous residence
after being advanced to doctoral candidacy is normally
required. "Residence" is defined as presence at Fuller,
carrying twelve hours per quarter, under supervision of
the Candidate's dissertation committee.

V. <u>Course Requirements</u>

Doctoral candidates must choose eight of the following
core courses, <u>at least one under each faculty member</u>:
(all are three hour courses)

713. MODERN THEOLOGIES OF MISSION, Glasser
770. HERMENEUTICS-ECCLESIOLOGY-ECUMENICS AND MISSION,
     Glasser
730. CHRISTIANITY AND CULTURE I, Kraft
737. INDIGENEITY, Kraft
731. CHRISTIANITY AND CULTURE II, McGavran
760. ADVANCED CHURCH GROWTH, McGavran

734. ANTHROPOLOGICAL THEORY, Tippett
736. ANTHROPOLOGICAL BASIS OF LEADERSHIP, Tippett
738. MISSIONS AND SOCIAL CHANGE, Wagner
(766.) STRATEGY OF MISSIONS, Wagner
756. THE CHURCH GROWTH MOVEMENT IN HISTORICAL
     PERSPECTIVE, Winter
767. CURRENT CHURCH HISTORY, Winter

VI. Admission to Doctoral Program Requires:

A. A 3.0 GPA in all B.D. or M. Div. work, and 3.3 in
   all work at SWM/ICG (on a scale where B is 3.00);

B. The attainment of a certain minimal score on the
   Graduate Record Examination;

C. Passing examinations as specified (qualifying,
   post-M.A., deficiency examinations, written and
   oral, etc.);

D. Ability to do acceptable research and writing,
   demonstrated through submitting a thesis,
   independent research papers, or published mss.;

E. At least three years of successful cross-cultural
   experience, or the equivalent.

VII. Advancement to Candidacy

A. Advancement to D.Miss. candidacy normally occurs
   in late May on the basis of the candidate's record
   during the M.A. year, and the fulfillment of "C"
   below.

B. For those with an M.A. Missiology from Fuller, not
   presently in residence, advancement to candidacy
   may occur at any time the faculty, (acting on the
   candidate's record and fulfillment of "C" below)
   deem appropriate.

C. The three steps toward advancement to candidacy to
   be taken by the candidate are:

72

1. File an application for advancement to D.Miss. candidacy at some time prior to the taking of the M.A. Comprehensive Examinations.
2. Secure prospective agreement by one resident faculty member of SWM/ICG to serve as sponsor and chairman of the dissertation committee, and of at least two additional faculty members who will ordinarily become the other two members of the doctoral committee.
3. Pass such written and/or oral qualifying examinations as are determined by the faculty. These are normally the same as the M.A. Comprehensive Examinations which are, in the case of a Prospective Candidate for the D.Miss., graded according to higher standards than for the other M.A. Candidates.

73

D. Agree to enroll thereafter each quarter in Research Seminar 790, or Reading and Conference 791 (at the discretion of the chairman) until dissertation is completed.

VIII. Comprehensive Examinations

After two terms in the doctoral program, the candidate takes comprehensive examinations in four branches of the discipline of missions. At the discretion of the faculty, research papers may be substituted for one or more of these.

IX. Dissertation

A. The candidate must have completed at least three terms, i.e. 36 hours (or the equivalent) of graduate missions study before being allowed to start the dissertation. These hours normally constitute his M.A. residence study.

B. The dissertation embodies the results of the candidate's independent work.

C. The dissertation topic selected must fall within the linguistic competence of the candidate, for documentation and/or interviewing.

D. The dissertation must constitute a professional contribution to missiology.

E. In preparing the dissertation, the candidate is guided by his committee.

F. Approval of the dissertation by the committee after an oral defense is required before the candidate may be recommended for the degree.

X. Doctoral Candidates and Thesis Supervision

All doctoral candidates will be required to participate in helping M.A. men as adjunct mentors. They will work under the faculty members serving as mentors; this will greatly diminish the present heavy burden that all faculty members carry.

CHECKLIST FOR THE D.MISS DEGREE CANDIDATE

NAME[1] (Last) _____ (First) _____ (Middle) _____

Degree _____ Plan _____ Graduation-Expected Date _____

..D. Completed (date) _____ (place) _____

..A. (Missiology) Completed (date) _____ (place) _____ G.P.A. _____

..R.E. Taken (date & place) _____ Recorded in file _____

esearch & Writing Ability Demonstrated (date) _____ (M signature) _____

..dvanced to D.Miss Candidacy (date) _____ (D signature) _____

..ADLINE	DATE	APPROVAL[2]	
_____	(M) _____	_____	1. Committee Mentor _____ 2. _____ 3. _____
_____	(M) _____	_____	2. Language (name) _____ (requirement met) _____
_____	(M) _____	_____	3. Examination(s) (req.) _____ (met) _____
			(req.) _____ (met) _____
_____	(M) _____	_____	4. Thesis Subject: Outline,Method,Prelim. Bibliog. Acptd.
_____	(R) _____	_____	5. Course work: First Term (hours) _____ (GPA) _____
_____	(R) _____	_____	Second Term (hours)_____ (GPA) _____
_____	(R) _____	_____	Third Term (hours) _____
_____	(R) _____	_____	6. Residence Req. met (3 qtrs. continuous residence)
_____	(M) _____	_____	7. Thesis: Defended (rough draft)
_____	(M) _____	_____	Final Draft Approved (Front page signed, paging, index, 200 word abstract, Vita checked)
_____	(L) _____	_____	Deposited: Library (2 copies)
_____	(D) _____	_____	Dean (1 copy) + (the original)
_____	(D) _____	_____	8. Permission to graduate
_____	(D) _____	_____	9. One copy of this form to Dean[3]
_____	(R) _____	_____	10. One copy to Registrar[3]
_____	(M) _____	_____	11. One copy to Mentor[3]

PRINT name as you want it to appear on your diploma _____
Authorized approval (indicated by initials & date) to be obtained from
  Dean (D), Mentor (M), Registrar (R), or Librarian (L) as indicated.
Keep original yourself, photocopy for Dean, Mentor & Registrar.

SCHOOL OF WORLD MISSION
CHECKLIST FOR M.A. DEGREE CANDIDATE

NAME[1]   (Last) _____ (First) _____ (Middle) _____

ᴅegree anticipated _____ Date of Anticipated Graduation _____

G.P.A. _____ G.R.E. taken (date and place)_____

DATE   APPROVAL[2] & INITIALS

(M) _____ _____ 1. a. Language _____
                                   b. Country _____
                                   c. Years of field experience _____
                                   d. Denomination _____
                                   e. Mission board _____

(D) _____ _____ 2. Thesis Committee 1.(M) _____ 2. _____ 3. ___

(M) _____ _____ 3. Thesis/Project: a. Subject _____
                                   _____

(M) _____ _____   b. Outline, Methodology & Preliminary
                                      Bibliography approved.

(D) _____ _____ 4. Advancement to candidacy

(R) _____ _____ 5. Position at end of First Term (hours) _____
                                   GPA _____

(M) _____ _____ 6. Thesis successfully defended (rough draft)

(R) _____ _____ 7. Course work completed and in process (end of
                                   Second Term). Fill out curriculum chart
                                   on back of this form

(M) _____ _____ 8. Final draft of thesis approved (front page
                                   signed, paging checked)

(D) _____ _____ 9. Comprehensive examinations approved

(L) _____ _____ 10. Thesis deposited: Library (2 copies)

(D) _____ _____   Dean   (1 copy) + (the origi̇

(D) _____ _____ 11. Permission to graduate

(D) _____ _____ 12. One copy of this form to Dean[3]

(M) _____ _____   One copy to Mentor[3]

(R) _____ _____   One copy to Registrar[3]

1. PRINT name as you want it to appear on your diploma _____

2. Authorized approval (indicated by initials & date) to be obtained from
   Dean (D), Mentor (M), Registrar (R), or Librarian (L) as indicated.

3. Keep original yourself, photocopy for Dean, Mentor & Registrar.

GENERAL MISSIOLOGICAL TEXTBOOK REQUIREMENTS
School of World Mission of Fuller Theological Seminary

General Textbooks

In addition to the textbooks required for specific
SWM courses, the following missiological textbooks are
required for the various fields of study offered at the
School of World Mission.

Each research associate should add these volumes to
his personal library. Nearly all of these required books
may be purchased at a discount from the William Carey
Library through the Church Growth Book Club, 305 1/2
Pasadena Avenue, South Pasadena, California 91030.

BARRETT, David B. (et al.)
1973 Kenya Churches Handbook. The development of
      Kenya Christianity, 1498 - 1973. Kisumu, Kenya
      Evangel Publishing House.

EVANGELICAL MISSIONS QUARTERLY
      Three bound volumes -- First nine years. South
      Pasadena, William Carey Library.

GLASSER, Arthur F. (ed.)
1971 Crossroads in Missions. (Five books in one, by
      BLAUW, Johannes, SCHERER, James A., BEYERHAUS,
      Peter and Henry LE FEVER, STREET, Watson, and
      BEAVER, R. Pierce.) South Pasadena, William
      Carey Library.

MC GAVRAN, Donald A.
1955 Bridges of God. New York, Friendship Press, and
      London, World Dominion.

1959 How Churches Grow. New York, Friendship Press,
      and London, World Dominion.

MC GAVRAN, Donald A. (ed.)
1969 Church Growth Bulletin Volumes I-V. (One volume,
1964-1968.) South Pasadena, William Carey Library.

1972 Crucial Issues in Missions Tomorrow. Chicago,
Moody Press.

MARC (DAYTON, Edward R. ed.)
1973 Mission Handbook: North American Protestant
Ministries Overseas. 10th edition, 1973. Monrovia,
Missions Advanced Research and Communication Center.

TIPPETT, Alan R. (ed.)
1971 Bibliography for Cross-Cultural Workers. South
Pasadena, William Carey Library.

1973 God, Man and Church Growth. A Festschrift in
Honor of Donald Anderson McGavran. Grand Rapids,
Eerdmans.

TIPPETT, Alan R.
1970 Church Growth and the Word of God. The Biblical
Basis of the Church Growth Viewpoint. Grand
Rapids, Eerdmans.

1973 Verdict Theology in Missionary Theory. (2nd
edition.) South Pasadena, William Carey Library.

WAGNER, C. Peter (ed.)
1972 Church / Mission Tensions Today. Chicago, Moody
Press.

MISSIOLOGY, An International Review (Continuing
Practical Anthropology). South Pasadena,
American Society of Missiology.

TIPPETT, A. R., (ed.)
1971 Bibliography for Cross-cultural Workers. South
      Pasadena, William Carey Library.

The sections in this bibliography are classified
according to the courses offered at the School of World
Mission, Fuller Theological Seminary, in cross-cultural
subjects. Cross reference notes are found at the head of
several sections. Entries within the sections are by
author in alphabetical arrangement

General Material   Pages

    Technical Journals   15-20
    Symposia   21-24
    Abbreviations   25
    Cyclopedias & Bibliographies   29-34
    Cultural Anthropology   35-38   79
        Single Country Case Studies   38-47
        Comparative Case Studies   47-49

Course No.   Title

622 Animism I (General Works on Primitive
         Religion, Philosophy of Animism) 171-188
623 Animism II (Systems & Practitioners) 189-216, 228-232
630 Anthropology I (Social Structure,
         Values, Missionary Anthropology)   63-98, 159-170
631 Anthropology II (Culture Change)   107-121, 136-143
634 Urban Anthropology   144-152
640 Research Methods   233-252
667 African Movements   207-216
720 Animistic Bases of The Great Religions 217-227
732 Culture and Personality   122-135
733 Conversion with a Minimum of
         Dislocation   159-170
734 Anthropological Theory   53-62
735 Ethnolinguistics   153-158
736 Anthropological Basis of Leadership
         (Authority Patterns)   99-106

[Bring your bibliography to class. It will be used as a
reference tool.]

3. COURSES OF STUDY

Specific Course Syllabi and Required Textbooks

THE CURRICULUM

In a wider sense, the curriculum consists of a combination of course work, reading and directed research tailored to fit the individual missionary's problems and opportunities. In a narrower sense, the curriculum consists of courses of study which develop a part of one of the following eight major branches of learning and together make up the discipline of missiology. 700 courses are in the corresponding areas but are considered doctoral level.

81

In any given quarter, courses will be selected from among the following, depending upon the availability of faculty and composition of the anticipated student body.

I. Theory and Theology of Missions 86

    610 THEOLOGY OF MISSION I. 87

    611 THEOLOGY OF MISSION II. 90

    612 THEOLOGY OF MISSION III. 94

    613 THEOLOGY OF MISSIONS TODAY. 96

    614 (714) THEOLOGY OF RELIGIOUS ENCOUNTER. 104

700 courses are considered doctoral level.

85

I. Theory and Theology of Missions

    610 THEOLOGY OF MISSION I.

    611 THEOLOGY OF MISSION II.

    612 THEOLOGY OF MISSION III.

    613 THEOLOGY OF MISSIONS TODAY.

    614 (714) THEOLOGY OF RELIGIOUS ENCOUNTER.

THEOLOGY OF MISSION I, SWM 610   First Quarter
Professor A. F. Glasser   2 hours credit

Description of Course

A comprehensive study of the Old Testament as preparation for the Christian mission, focusing particular
attention on the cultural imperative, Israel and the
nations, the Kingdom of God, religious encounter and the
missionary awakenings of Judaism during the intertesta-
mental period.

Reading Requirements

BLAUW, Johannes
   1962   The Missionary Nature of the Church. Vol. 1 of
          Crossroads in Missions, South Pasadena, William
          Carey Library, 1971, chapters 1-4 (55 pages).

BRIGHT, John
   1953   The Kingdom of God. Nashville, Abingdon Press,
          chapters 1-6, (179 pages).

WRIGHT, G. Ernest
   1950   The Old Testament Against its Environment.
          London, SCM Press Ltd., chapters 1-3 (103 pages).

   1952   God Who Acts, Biblical Theology as Recital.
          London, SCM Press Ltd., chapters 1-5 (117 pages).

Reading Schedule:

Week	Blauw	"God Who Acts"	"O.T. Against"	Bright
1.	ch 1	ch 1 (22 pp)		
2.	-	ch 2 (26 pp)		
3.	-	ch 3 (28 pp)		

Week	Blauw	"God Who Acts"	"O.T. Against"	Bright
4.	-	-	ch 1 (32pp)	ch 1 (28pp)
5.	-	-	ch 2 (34pp)	ch 2 (26pp)
6.	ch 2	-	ch 3 (37pp)	ch 3 (27pp)
7.	-	-	-	ch 4 (29pp)
8.	ch 3	ch 4 (20 pp)	-	ch 5 (29pp)
9.	ch 4	ch 5 (22 pp)	-	ch 6 (31pp)
10.	-	-	-	-

Other Books: get acquainted!

BRIGHT, John
  1972 A History of Israel. 2nd edition, Philadelphia,
        Westminister Press.

BRUCE, Frederick Fyvie
  1963 Israel and the Nations: from the Exodus to the
        Fall of the Second Temple. Grand Rapids, Eerdmans.

88

  1969 New Testament Development of Old Testament Themes.
        Grand Rapids, Eerdmans (c1968).

HARRISON, Roland Kenneth
  1971 Introduction to the Old Testament with a Compre-
        hensive Review of Old Testament Studies and a
        Special Supplement on the Apocrypha. Grand Rapids,
        Eerdmans (c1969).

HASEL, Gerhard F.
  1972 Old Testament Theology: Basic Issues in the
        Current Debate. Grand Rapids, Eerdmans.

KAUFMANN, Yehezkel
  1960 The Religion of Israel, from its Beginnings to the
        Babylonian Exile. Translated and abridged by
        Moshe Greenberg. Chicago, University of Chicago
        Press.

VAN RULER, Arnold Albert
  1971 The Christian Church and the Old Testament.
        Translated by Geoffrey W. Bromiley. Grand Rapids,
        Eerdmans.

Writing Projects:

1. Single Page Reflections

   Week by week you will encounter ideas in the Old
   Testament that bear on the mission of the people of
   God today. Select two per week that appear most
   relevant to you in your work. Comment briefly on
   them in such a way that your "single page
   reflections" could be published in your Church or
   Mission periodical. Don't present bland homilies
   or "Preachments" on ideas that are probably already
   familiar to your readers. Introduce them to new
   thoughts that will send their minds soaring!

       NUMBER THEM IN SEQUENCE. THEY ARE DUE EVERY
       TUESDAY. ONLY THOSE TURNED IN ON TIME WILL
       BE RECORDED.

2. Longer Reflections

   89

   Select any Old Testament subject that has intrigued
   you and develop it for at least five pages.
   Suggested themes:
       The Cultural Mandate;
       The Use of Violence to Attain Social Justice;
       Jehovah (JHWH) versus Baal;
       Nationalism; Election; Ghettoism; Election;
       Israel and the Nations;
       The People of God and Totalitarianism;
       Syncretism; Conversion;
       Sodalities in the Old Testament;
       Evangelism in the Old Testament;
       Humanization; etc.

       DO NOT BEGIN THIS ASSIGNMENT UNTIL THE EIGHTH
       WEEK. IT IS DUE ON THE LAST DAY OF THE
       EXAMINATION PERIOD.

Examination:

   Note: There is no final examination in this course.

THEOLOGY OF MISSION II, SWM 611   Second Quarter
Professor A. F. Glasser   2 hours credit

Description of Course

A comprehensive study of the New Testament as revelation of the Christian mission, focusing particular
attention on the evangelistic mandate, Jesus and the
nations, the Kingdom of God, apostolic understanding of
mission and the missionary obedience of the Church in
the apostolic age.

Purpose of the Course

To develop a theology for the Christian Mission based
on the Old Testament foundation and consummated in the
life, ministry, redemption, and instruction of Jesus
Christ and His Apostles, relating this to the Kingdom of
God and the growth expansion of the Apostolic Church
from Pentecost onward. Collateral themes such as conversion, communication, satanic opposition, religious
encounter, social service, Christian "presence," the
State, prayer, the gifts of the Spirit, and the tension
between charismatic and hierarchical orders of Church
structure will be explored since all are related to
Mission as traditionally understood by the Christian community down through the centuries.

Reading Requirements: (to be finished at end of term)

BLAUW, Johannes
    1962 The Missionary Nature of the Church. Vol. 1 of
          Crossroads in Missions, South Pasadena, William
          Carey Library, 1971, pp. 65-172.

BRIGHT, John
    1953 The Kingdom of God. Nashville, Abingdon Press,
          pp. 187-274.

Reading Requirements continued: (400 pages in the following:)

FILSON, Floyd V.
  1950 The New Testament Against its Environment. London,
        SCM.

HAHN, Ferdinand
  1965 Mission in the New Testament. Naperville, Ill.,
        A. R. Allenson. (Translated by Frank Clarke from
        the German.)

JEREMIAS, Joachim
  1958 Jesus' Promise to the Nations. The Franz Delitzsch
        lectures for 1953. Naperville, Ill., A. R. Allenson.

LADD,George Eldon
  1964 Jesus and the Kingdom; The Eschatology of Biblical
        Realism. New York, Harper and Row.

Book Studies: (5 pages, due: February 15)   91

    You will be given a New Testament book. Summarize in
    a comprehensive fashion what it says about the mission
    of the Church.

Topical Studies: (5 pages, due: March 15)

    Develop one of the following themes (or one of your
    choice) and expound it in terms of the New Testament.
    List relevant passages, give their meaning in a
    comprehensive sense, summarize your conclusions, and
    detail any unresolved problems.

    1. The lostness of man and mission

    2. The sovereignty of God and mission

    3. Evangelism: Power Encounter

    4. Proclamation: "By Word and Deed"

    5. Conversion

    6. Church renewal and mission

7. Mission and the Synagogue

8. Principalities and powers

9. The State and Mission

10. History and mission

11. The Church and her ministry

12. Recaptivity and mission

Note: No final examination. Reading report due on March 15.

Sequence of Presentation

Objective:

To identify the components of a biblical theology of mission based on the Old Testament foundation and consummated in the life, service, instruction, redemption and mandate of Jesus Christ.

To relate these components to the Kingdom of God and the growth of the Apostolic Church from Pentecost onward.

WEEK 1-2   "The Time is at Hand"
        a. Linkage with the Old Testament - Inter-
           testamental Period
        b. The First Century World - context
        c. The Advent of Jesus of Nazareth

WEEK 3   The Words of Jesus of Nazareth
        a. Concerning the Kingdom
        b. Concerning the Nations

WEEK 4   The Mandate of Christ the Lord
        a. Five Utterances of one Great Commission
        b. The Promise of the Father - Baptism of
           the Spirit
        c. The Ascension

WEEK 5   The Coming of the Spirit of God
        a. The People of God
        b. The Body of Christ
        c. The Gifts of the Spirit

92

WEEK 6   The Universalization of the Christian Movement
          a. Aramaic Speaking Jewish Church
          b. Greek Speaking Jewish Church
          c. Greek Speaking Gentile Church

WEEK 7-8 Paul and the Salvation of Mankind
          a. The Evangelistic Task: Conversion and
              Incorporation
          b. The Inevitable Encounter: Confrontation
              with Religion
          c. The Arena of Conflict: Principalities
              and Powers
          d. The Essence of Service: Suffering and
              Fruitbearing
          e. The Lostness of Man: Sovereign Election
              and Human Responsibility
          f. The Unexpected Insight: Israel and
              the Church
          g. The Missionary Objective: The Nations
              and Christ's Return
          h. The Apostolic Pattern for Outreach: 93
              By Congregations and Sodalities
          i. The Model for Church-Mission Relationships:
              The Church at Rome and the Mission to Spain

WEEK 9   Pastoral Epistles and the First Century Church

WEEK 10   Mission in Time and in Consummation
          a. For the 2nd Generation: test of nominality
          b. For the Last Generation: test of endurance

THEOLOGY OF MISSION III, SWM 612   Third Quarter
Professor A. F. Glasser   2 hours credit

Description of Course

An evaluation of the development of missiological
thought down through the history of the Church until the
International Missionary Council-World Council of Churches
merger at New Delhi in 1961, with particular attention
given to the writings of Orthodox, Roman Catholic and
Continental Protestant missiologists.

Reading Requirements

94

By April 26

BEYERHAUS, Peter, and LEFEVER, Henry
  1964 The Responsible Church and the Foreign Mission.
        Vol. 3 of Crossroads in Missions. South
        Pasadena, William Carey Library, 1971.

By May 31

ABBOTT, Walter M., gen. ed., and GALLAGHER, J.,trans. ed.
  1966 The Documents of Vatican II, All Sixteen
        Official Texts Promulgated by the Ecumenical
        Council, 1963-1965. (Translated from the Latin)
        New York, Guild Press.

        Read: Lumen Gentium, pp. 9 - 106.
               Ad Gentes, pp. 580 - 633.

Writing Assignments: (Due by May 24.)

1. Missiologist: Select a man related to your area of
    interest and
    a. Secure as complete a bibliography as possible
        of his work, marking with an asterisk FTS
        holdings, or

b. Review one of his books.

2. Bible:

Explore a theme of your choice, but first clear it
with your professor who may have counsel and sources
to share. We are particularly concerned at the
range of sources you explore. Do not feel you must
answer the questions you raise.

Examination: There will be no final exam.

Sequence of Presentation

Introductory Remarks

A. Missiology - Its Pre-History
    1. During the Roman Period
    2. The Crusades - Raymond Lull (Liull)
    3. 1st Catholic Missionary Revival (13/14th C.)   95
    4. 2nd Catholic Missionary Revival (16/17th C.)
    5. 16th Century Reformers
    6. Post-Reformation Era and Early Pietism
    7. Puritanism (17th C.) and the Salvation of Mankind
    8. Evangelical Awakening (18th C.) and later Pietism

B. Missiology - Its Formal Quest
    1. Henry Venn and the Anglo-Americans
    2. Gustav Warneck and the Germans

C. Missiology - Its Roman Catholic Contribution
    1. General Orientation
    2. Schools of Louvain and Munster
    3. Missionary Popes of the 20th Century
    4. Vatican II
    5. Post-Vatican II Era

D. Missiology - Its Conciliar Contribution (prior to
                  New Delhi 1961)
    1. Conservative Evangelicals and the WCC
    2. The Religions - Fulfilment vs Discontinuity
    3. The Godhead - Finality vs Particularity (Newbigin)
    4. The Church - Mission as Church (Hoekendijk)
    5. The Church - Event vs Structure.

THEOLOGY OF MISSIONS TODAY, SWM 613   Third Quarter
Professor Donald A. McGavran   2 hours credit

Description of Course

A study of the mission of the Church interpreted in
terms of the Great Commission, in the light of the contemporary world-wide struggle for brotherhood, justice
and equality, the revolution of rising expectations, and
the growing pluralism of most societies with particular
attention given to British and American missiologists,
the World Council of Churches since 1961, the Wheaton and
Frankfurt Declarations.

Textbooks

Buy and read carefully, in the order listed in the
Synopsis or Sequence of Lectures, the following books.
(They will be on reserve, but they are mostly small books,
and you will want them in your library.)

BEYERHAUS, Peter
    1972 Shaken Foundations, Theological Foundations for
          Mission. Grand Rapids, Zondervan Publishing House.

    1971 Missions Which Way? Humanization or Redemption.
          Grand Rapids, Zondervan Publishing House.

LINDSELL, Harold, edited by
    1966 The Church's World Wide Mission, Waco, Texas,
          Word Books.

McGAVRAN, Donald, editor
    1972 The Eye of the Storm, The Great Debate in Mission.
          Waco, Texas, Word Books, Publisher.

NEWBIGIN, James Edward Lesslie
  1969 The Finality of Christ. Richmond, Virginia,
        John Knox Press.

SPEER, Robert Elliott
  1933 The Finality of Jesus Christ. New York,
        Fleming H. Revell Company.

TIPPETT, Alan R.
  1969 Verdict Theology in Missionary Theory. Lincoln,
        Illinois, Lincoln Christian College Press.

VISSER'T HOOFT, Willem Adolph
  1963 No Other Name; the Choice between Syncretism and
        and Christian Universalism. Philadelphia,
        Westminster Press.

WAGNER, C. Peter
  1970 Latin American Theology; Radical or Evangelical?
        Grand Rapids, Eerdmans.

WINTER, Ralph D., edited by
  1973 The Evangelical Response to Bangkok. South
        Pasadena, William Carey Library.

97

Term Papers

1. Critique of Two Contrasting Essays in The Theology
   of the Christian Mission. About 4 pages, due April 1]

2. Four Doctrines Revised Toward Missionary Adequacy and
   Biblical Exactness. Use any out of LEITH, J. H.
   Creeds of the Churches, 39 Articles
                         Canons of Dort
                         Augsburg Confession
   Or, if you prefer, that of your own communion.

3. The Theological Issues in: (About 6 pages)
        Christianity and Cultures;
        Salvation Today;
        The Pluralistic Hermeneutic;
        Christianity and Other Religions.

Synopsis or Sequence of Lectures

PART I. CAN THERE BE A THEOLOGY OF MISSION?

Required Reading-No. of Pages

Mar. 28 What Is Mission? The Eye of The Storm   200
      30 Can There Be a Theology of Mission?

Apr. 4 The Books Developing
         Theology of Mission   Verdict Theology   100
       6 A Theology of Mission
         Conceived as Church Growth

PART II. THEOLOGY THAT IS BIBLICAL & MISSIONARILY ADEQUATE

Apr. 11 Making Each Doctrine True to the Bible
         at the Point of Mission   Missions Which Way?
      13   ditto
      18   ditto
      20   ditto   Finality of Christ
                              (both books...) 300

98

PART III. CURRENT DEVIATIONS

Apr. 25 The Clash Between Christianity and Cultures
      27   ditto
May   2   ditto   The Evangelical Response
      4   ditto   to Bangkok....   100
      9 Presence as Method and as End
     11 This Worldly Improvement as
         Salvation   Latin American Theology 100
     16 The Pluralistic Hermeneutic
         and Salvation   Shaken Foundations   100

PART IV. A MORE BIBLICAL THEOLOGY OF MISSION: CURRENT
          OPPORTUNITIES

May 18 The Church: One and Many   The Church's
                              World Wide Mission   100
     23 Theological Implications of "Statistical
         Compassion" BARRETT: God, Man and Church Growth
     25 Eight Crucial Issues:
         Frankfurt Declaration. No Other Name   100
     30 Ten Crucial Issues: Wheaton Declaration.

Bibliography on Theology of Mission

Many books touch on the theology of missions, developing
some one or more of its many facets. A partial list of
these books follows. Many set forth theological considerations which have been held in the days past, and hence are.
more strictly in the field of Dean Glasser's Theology of
Mission III. They are nevertheless listed because current
ideas (which is what I deal with in Theology of Missions
Today) have deep roots in yesterday.

Books marked by a single asterisk are especially
important. But, as you build up a library of books on the
theology of missions, all these will help you get a 'feel'
of the trends and currents.

ADENEY, David Howard
  1955 The Unchanging Commission. Chicago, Inter-Varsity

*ALLEN, Roland
  1960 The Ministry of the Spirit; selected writings.   99
         London, World Dominion Press.

*ANDERSON, Gerald H., ed.
  1961 The Theology of the Christian Mission. New York,
         McGraw Hill.

*ANDERSON, W.
  1956 Towards A Theology of Mission. (end ed.) London,
         S. C. M. Press.
BARTH, Karl
  1936 Church Dogmatics IV, Part 2, The doctrine of
         reconciliation. Tr. IV Parker, Thomas Henry Lewis.
         Edinburgh, T. & T. Clark.

BAVINCK, J. H.
  1960 An Introduction to the Science of Missions.
         Translated by David Hugh Freeman. Grand Rapids,
         Baker Book House.

BEAVER, Robert Pierce, ed.
  1966 Pioneers in Mission; the early missionary ordina-
         tion sermons, charges and instructions. Grand
         Rapids, W. B. Eerdmans.

*BEAVER, Robert Pierce, ed.
1967 To Advance the Gospel, Selections from the Writings of Rufus Anderson. Grand Rapids, W. B. Eerdmans.

ANDERSON, Gerald H.
1958 Bibliography of the Theology of Missions in the 20th Century. New York, Missionary Research Library.

BLAUW, Johannes
1962 The Missionary Nature of the Church. Volume 1 of Crossroads in Missions, South Pasadena, William Carey Library.

BOER, Harry R.
1961 Pentecost and Missions. Grand Rapids, Eerdmans.

*CRAGG, Kenneth
1968 Christianity in World Perspectives. New York, Oxford University Press.

DAVIES, John Gordon
1967 Dialogue With the World. London, S.C.M. Press.

*GENSICHEN, Hans Werner
1966 Living Mission: The Test of Faith. Philadelphia, Fortress Press.

*HAHN, Ferdinand
1965 Mission in the New Testament. Translated by Frank Clarke. Naperville, Illinois, A. R. Allenson.

HARKNESS, George
1939 "The Theological Basis of the Missionary Message," in October issue, International Review of Missions New York, Published by the Commission on World Mission and Evangelism of the World Council of Churches.

HAYWARD
1964 "Hayward-Strachan Debate," in April issue, International Review of Missions.

100

HENRY, Carl F. H., and W. Stanley MOONEYHAM, editors
  1967 World Congress On Evangelism (Berlin 1966).
        Minneapolis, World Wide Publications.

*HILLIS, Don W., ed.
  1965 The Scriptural Basis of World Evangelization.
        Grand Rapids, Michigan.

HILLMAN, Eugene
  1965 The Church As Mission. New York, Herder and Herder

HOFFMAN and SCHERER
        The Theology of the World Apostolate. Chicago,
        Association of Professors of Missions Proceedings.

*HORNER, Norman
  1968 Protestant Cross Currents in Mission; the ecumen-
        ical-conservative encounter. Nashville,
        Abingdon Press.

*INGRAM, William Thomas   101
  1956 The Missionary Content of Contemporary American
        Theology. Microfilmed Ph.D., Pub. No. 16,578,
        Ann Arbor, University Microfilms.

JERUSALEM SERIES, Volume IV

LATULHALLO, P. D.
        Church and World (in H. Kraemer's writings)
        Microfilmed Ph.D.

LEITH, John H., ed.
  1963 Creeds of The Churches; a Reader in Christian
        Doctrine from the Bible to the Present. Garden
        City, N. Y., Anchor Books.

*LINDSELL, Harold
  1970 An Evangelical Theology of Missions. (Rev. ed.)
        Grand Rapids, Zondervan.

*NEWBIGIN, James Edward Lesslie
  1964 Trinitarian Faith and Today's Mission. Richmond,
        John Knox Press.

RÉTIF, Louis and André RÉTIF
1962 The Church's Mission in the World. New York,
      Hawthorn Books.

*ROOY, Sidney H.
1965 The Theology of Missions in the Puritan Tradition.
      Grand Rapids, Eerdmans.

*ROSSEL, Jacques
1968 Mission in a Dynamic Society. London, S.C.M. Press

SCHERER, James A.
1971 "Salvation Today" (Occasional Bulletin, August).

SCHULTZ, Hans Jürgen
1967 Conversion To The World. New York, Scribner.

- - - "Salvation Today'.' International Review of Missions
       October 1971, and January 1972.

SPEER, Robert Elliott
1919 The Gospel and the New World. New York, Fleming
      H. Revell Co.

- - - Student World. Articles on Presence in July, 1964,
       Number 3, 1965 and Number 4, 1966 issues.

SUNDKLER, Bengt Gustaf Malcolm
1966 The World of Mission. English translation by Eric
      J. Sharpe, Grand Rapids, Eerdmans.

TAYLOR, John Vernon
1966 For All The World; the Christian Mission in the
      Modern Age. Philadelphia, Westminister Press.

- - - "Tenth Biennial Meeting of the Association of
       Professors of Missions," Salvation and Mission.

GOODALL, Norman, ed. by
1968 The Uppsala Report '68 - Drafts For Sections
      World Council of Churches, Fourth Assembly,
      Uppsala, Geneva, Official Report of WCC.

102

- - - Uppsala Speaks

VICEDOM, Georg F.
  1965 The Mission of God; an Introduction to a Theology
        of Mission. Translated by Gilbert Thiele and
        Dennis Hilgendorf. St. Louis, Concordia Publishing
        House.

WHITE, Hugh Vernon
  1937 A Theology of Christian Missions. New York,
        Willett, Clark and Company.

WORLD COUNCIL OF CHURCHES
        The Missionary Task of the Church
        A Theological Reflection on the Work of Evangelism

ZWEMER, Samuel Marinus
  1920 Christianity the Final Religion; addresses on the
        missionary message for the world today, showing
        that the old gospel is the only gospel. Grand
        Rapids, Eerdmans-Sevensma Company.

  1943 'Into All the World,' the Great Commission; a
        Vindication and an Interpretation. Grand Rapids,
        Zondervan Publishing House.

ISHIDA, Y.
  1971 Salvation, Mission and Humanization in Lutheran
        World, pp 370ff.

BRAUN, Charles McAfee
        "Uppsala, An Informal Report." Journal of
        Ecumenical Studies, 5:633-660. pp 653-654 have a
        top quote - states clearly that Uppsala favored
        secular ecumenism and turned from conversion and
        church planting.

103

THEOLOGY OF RELIGIOUS ENCOUNTER, SWM 614   Second Quarter
Professor Arthur F. Glasser   2 hours credit

Description of Course

An investigation of the relation between Revelation
and Christianity in the context of elenctic missionary
encounter with men of other faiths, or no religious
allegiance. Particular attention will be given to Roman
Catholic and Protestant theologians throughout the 20th
century.

Sequence of Presentation

104

Week 1-4 Part I Revelation and Religion
          a. The Old Testament and Religion
             Is this normative for us today?
          b. The New Testament and Religion
             Did Jesus differ with the Old Testament?
          c. The Finality of Jesus Christ
             How did Paul affirm this before
             Non-Christians?

Week 5-7 Part II Theologians and Religion
          a. A Lutheran Model: Walter Freytag
          b. The Vatican II Document: Non-Christian
             Religions
          c. The IMC Debates
          d. Contemporary Evangelical Approach

Week 8   Part III Devotees of Non-Christian Religions
          The Maurier Model

Week 9-10 Part IV Mission and Religion
          a. The Role of Conscience
          b. The Kerygmatic Approach
          c. The Elenctic Approach

Sequence of Assignments

Week 1   Paper (1 page) on "paroxuno" in Acts 17:16
          expounding on the significance of this word
          (its Hebrew equivalent) in the Old Testament.
                          DUE: End of 1st week
Week 2   Read Yehezkel Kaufmann: The Religion of Israel
          (Chicago University), pp. 7-59 and write a one-
          page paper on its most illuminating insights.
                          DUE: End of 2nd week
Week 3   Read the Apocryphal Wisdom of Solomon, 12-14
          alongside Paul's argument in Romans 1:18-32
          and write a one-page paper describing their
          interrelation.
                          DUE: End of 3rd week
Week 4   Read two good commentaries on I Cor. 8:5,6 and
          II Cor. 6:16,17 and describe your findings (1p.).
                          DUE: End of 4th week
Week 5   Read Vatican II on Non-Christian Religions.
                          DUE: End of 5th week
Week 6-7 Read J. H. Bavinck, Introduction to the Science   105
          of Missions: The Kerygmatic (pp. 79-141) and
          Elenctic (pp. 221-266) approaches.
                          DUE: End of 7th week
Week 7-10 Read Henri Maurier, The Other Covenant: A
           Theology of Paganism.   DUE: End of Quarter

Term Paper: You have been asked to speak on Evangelism
           at a conference of Church and Mission workers in
           your area with Acts 26:18 as your assigned text.
           What will you say, keeping in mind that "power
           encounter" and "elecntic presentation" are your
           objectives. Five pages. DUE: End of Quarter

Note: No final examination.

A Working Bibliography

ALLPORT, Gordon W.
   1950   The Individual and His Religion.   New York,
          MacMillan.

ANDERSON, J. N. D.
   1970   Christianity and Comparative Religion.
          Downer's Grove, Inter-Varsity Press.

BAVINCK, J. H.
   1960   An Introduction to the Science of Missions.
          Translated by David Hugh Freemen.   Grand Rapids,
          Baker Book House.

   1966   The Church Between Temple and Mosque.
          Grand Rapids, Eerdmans.

BOUQUET, A. C.
   1962   Comparative Religion.   Baltimore, Penguin Books.

BROW, Robert
   1966   Religion: Origins and Ideas.   Chicago,
          Inter-Varsity Press.

CHALMERS, R. C. and J. A. IRVING, Eds.
   1965   The Meaning of Life in Five Great Religions.
          Philadelphia, Westminster Press.

DANIELOU, Jean
   1964   Great Religions.   Notre Dame, Fides Publishers.

DEWICK, E. C.
   1948   The Gospel and Other Faiths.   London,
          Canterbury Press.

   1963   The Christian Attitude to Other Religions.
          Cambridge, University Press.

FREYTAG, W.
   1957   The Gospel and The Religions.   London, SCM Press.

106

KAUFMANN, Yehezkel
1960 History of the Religion of Israel, from its
      beginnings to the Babylonian exile. Vols. 1-3,
      Chicago, University of Chicago Press.

KELLOGG, S. H.
1957 Handbook on Comparative Religion. Grand Rapids,
      W. B. Eerdmans.

KERKHOFS, Jan, Ed.
1968 Modern Mission Dialogue. Shannon, Ecclesia Press.

KOESTLER, Arthur
1961 The Lotus and The Robot. New York, The
      MacMillan Company.

KRAEMER, Hendrik
1938 The Christian Message in a Non-Christian World.
      Grand Rapids, Kregel Publications.

1956 Religion and The Christian Faith. London,   107
      Lutterworth Press.

1960 World Cultures and World Religions. Philadelphia,
      Westminister Press.

MOSES, D. G.
1950 Religious Truth and the Relation Between Religions.
      Madras, Christian Literature Society for India.

NEILL, Stephen
1961 Christian Faith and Other Faiths. London,
      Oxford University Press.

NEWBIGIN, Lesslie
1968 The Finality of Christ. Richmond, John Knox Press.

OHM Thomas
1959 Asia Looks at Western Christianity. New York,
      Herder and Herder.

SCHOEPS, Hans-Joachim
1968 The Religions of Mankind. Garden City, Doubleday-
      Anchor Book.

SMITH, Huston
  1958 The Religions of Man. New York, Perennial
        Library, Harper and Row.

SOPER, E. D.
  1957 The Inevitable Choice: Vedanta Philosophy or
        The Christian Gospel. Nashville, Abingdon Press.

SPEER, R. E.
  1933 The Finality of Jesus Christ. Westwood, F.H.Revell.

TILLICH, Paul
  1964 Christianity and The Encounter of the World
        Religions. New York, Columbia University Press.

TOYNBEE, Arnold
  1956 An Historian's Approach to Religion. London,
        Oxford University Press.

  1957 Christianity Among the Religions of the World.
        New York, Scribner.

TRUEBLOOD, D. E.
  1957 The Philosophy of Religion. New York, Harper and
        Row.

TH. VAN LEEUWEN, Arend
  1964 Christianity in World History. London,
        Edinburgh House Press.

VICEDO, George F.
  1963 The Challenge of the World Religions.
        Philadelphia, Fortress Press.

VISSER 'T HOOFT, W. A.
  1963 No Other Name. London, SCM Press.

WARREN, Max
  1964 Perspective in Mission. New York, Seabury Press.

YOUNG, Robert D.
  1970 Encounter with World Religions. Philadelphia,
        Westminister Press.

108

II. Apologetics of the Christian Mission
vis á vis non-Christian religions

622 ANIMISM AND CHURCH GROWTH I.

623 ANIMISM AND CHURCH GROWTH II.

624 HINDUISM AND APPROACH TO HINDUS.

ANIMISM AND CHURCH GROWTH I, SWM 622   First Quarter
Professor A. R. Tippett   2 hours credit

Description of Course

The basic features of the animistic view of life common
to the masses in Asia, Africa, Oceania and Latin America,
and its bearing on the acceptance of the gospel and the
spread of the indigenous church.

This course (SWM 622) deals with the philosophical and
experiential encounter of Christianity with Animism, Course
SWM 623 deals with the practical face to face encounter with
practitioners and structures of Animism. Course 622 is a
pre-requisite for 623. The two courses should be regarded
as a whole.

Bibliography: The Phenomenology of Animism

TIPPETT, A. R., (ed.)
  1971 Bibliography For Cross-Cultural Workers. South
        Pasadena, William Carey Library.

Participants in this course should familiarize themselves
with the following: pp. 173-178 (overall), pp. 179-188
(Course SWM 622) and pp. 189-216 (Course SWM 623).

Reading Requirement:

1) Assigned readings from a Reader.

LESSA, Wm. A., and Evon Z. VOGT, (eds.)
  1965 Reader in Comparative Religions: An Anthropolog-
        ical Approach. 2nd edition. New York, Harper
        and Row.

MIDDLETON, John (ed.)
  1967 Myth and Cosmos: Readings in Mythology and
        Symbolism. New York, The Natural History Press.

110

2) Read one of the following books:

DE WAAL MALEFIJT, Annemarie
   1968 Religion and Culture, An Introduction to Anthro-
         pology of Religion. New York, Macmillan Co.

LOWIE, Robert H.
   1952 Primitive Religion. London, Peter Owen Ltd.

MALINOWSKI, Bronislaw
   1948 Magic, Science and Religion. New York, Doubleday
         and Co. Paperback Anchor 23.

MAURIER, Henri
   1968 The Other Covenant, A Theology of Paganism.
         New York, Newman Press.

RADIN, Paul
   1957a Primitive Man as a Philosopher. New York, Dover
         Publications. Paperback T392.

   1957b Primitive Religion. New York, Dover Publications.
         Paperback T393.

111

TIPPETT, A. R.
   1970 Peoples of Southwest Ethiopia. South Pasadena,
         William Carey Library.

WALLACE, A. F. C.
   1966 Religion: An Anthropological View. New York,
         Random House.

Examination: There will be an EXAM.

Sequence of Presentation

1. The relevance of the study of animism for church planting.
2. Survey of the literature.
3. The nature and psychology of group behavior in animist
   society. Dynamism and the concept of Power encounter
   within the biblical world view. The power of the Name.
4. The concept of Mana. Should it be captured for Christ
   or discarded as pagan? An ethnolinguistic study.

5. Taboo. The concept of the Holy, an ethnolinguistic study. Soul stuff, skull cults, toh, magic and other allied concepts.
6. The animistic World Views, and the High God concept, Hierarchy of Gods; Gods, Spirits and Ghosts.
7. Man's Psychic Nature in animistic thought. An example of animist conceptualization.
8. Conflicting concepts of the Soul or Souls: their nature, activity and destiny.
9. Animistic notions of Pre-existence and Survival Conceptualizing the role of the Ancestor (a) Oriental (b) Afro-Oceanic.
10. The thought patterns of Magic, Science and Religion.
11. The philosophy and logic of Myth. Its significance to the missionary.
12. The logic of Symbolism. Symbolism in communication. Symbolic patterns in ritual.
13. The animistic concept of sin and salvation.
14. The concepts of Sacrifice, Sacrificial Place and Paraphernalia and Persons.
15. The animist's notion of Prayer. Examination of specific cases.
16. 'Primitive' man's capacity for a gospel of salvation. Specific cases to be examined.
17. The process of Conversion from animism to Christianity.

112

ANIMISM AND CHURCH GROWTH II, SWM 623   Second Quarter
Professor A. R. Tippett   2 hours credit

Description of Course

Christian mission in confrontation with persons and
institutions of animistic society -- witchcraft, sorcery,
possession, shamanism, priesthoods, prophetic movements.

Prerequisite: Course SWM 622 ANIMISM AND CHURCH GROWTH I.

Bibliography: Animistic Practitioners and Systems

MIDDLETON, John (ed.)
  1967 Gods and Rituals, Readings in Religious Beliefs and 113
        Practices. New York, Natural History Press.

  1967 Magic, Witchcraft and Curing. New York, Natural
        History Press.

TIPPETT, A. R., (ed.)
  1971 Bibliography For Cross-Cultural Workers. South
        Pasadena, William Carey Library. [pp. 189-216].

Examination: There will be an EXAM.

Sequence of Presentation

1. General introduction to 'primitive' religious systems
    and their organization.
2. Fetishism, nature of the fetish, various types, competent
    authority for using them, significance for the Christian
    evangelist. Comments on Totemism and Idolatry.
3. Divination, the place of diagnosis in determining the
    nature and treatment of sickness and misfortune,
    relationship between diviner and medicine-man, equipment
    used, other uses of divination.
4. Vision Quest among American Indians, specific cases to
    be dealt with, how the medicine-man is prepared, trained
    and accredited, his role in the life of the tribe.

5. Shamanism, attempt to reach a precise definition of Shamanism and the role of the Shaman - an Asian study. Further development in relation to sickness, transvestites.

6. Afro-Oceanic Ancestor Worship, how it differs from the Orient, problems for the missionary. Individual village priests, Fijian Vu-worship.

7. The Organized Priesthood, West African Case Study of an historic encounter of Christianity and organized Paganism in old Gold Coast.

8. Polynesian religious practitioners - Divine Chief, Temple Priest and Craft Priest; some specialized treatment of the craft priest (Study of the Prophet will come later).

9. Analysis of a religious system (Navaho Case Study), discussion on why this still functions after so many years of Christian mission, Navaho Witchcraft.

10. General analysis of Wizardry. Witchcraft in Africa - several treatments - the role of the Witchfinders and their organization.

11. Sorcery - general survey and a special look at the Solomon Islands.

12. Demon Possession, an attempt to classify the forms in which a missionary may meet it, and a discussion on dealing with it.

13. The place of Glossolalia in non-Christian religion, classification of types and an examination of the reported data.

14. Brazilian Spiritism, its historic antecedents and current ingredients, and the approaches of the various Christian missions to it.

15. The Prophet in Polynesia, his revelationary experience and what this means for the Church. Some African and American Indian comparisons.

16. Neo-paganism, Nativistic Movements, Negritude; attempt to classify some of the common features, discussion on why these elements reappear, investigation of how they should be dealt with when they disrupt a Christian cause.

17. The emergence of Folk Churches, comparison of several cases - Ringatu, Peyote, Eto, and one African case. What this signifies to Missions and its warnings.

18. General concluding summary relating courses 622 and 623 to church planting and to church growth.

HINDUISM AND APPROACH TO HINDUS, SWM 624   Quarter
Professor, Donald A. McGavran   2 hours credit

Description of Course

A systematic presentation of both philosophic and popular Hinduism, its doctrinal base and social structure. Approaches to Hindus which have multiplied churches among them. Secularism as an outcome of Christian mission.

III. Mission Across Cultures--anthropology, sociology, world revolution, secularism, urbanization

630 ANTHROPOLOGY AND MISSION I.

631 ANTHROPOLOGY AND MISSION II.

634 URBAN ANTHROPOLOGY.

636 FUNDAMENTALS OF LANGUAGE LEARNING.

637 LINGUISTICS AND MISSION.

ANTHROPOLOGY AND MISSION I, SWM 630   First Quarter
Professor Charles H. Kraft   2 hours credit

Description of Course

What anthropology offers the missionary in his task
of discipling the nations and avoiding cultural barriers
to the redemptive work of the Holy Spirit, and patterns
of culture within which the Christian operates.

Bibliography: Textbooks

1. Prerequisite
   NIDA, Eugene A.   --(N)
   1954   Customs and Cultures. New York, Harper.   117

   We expect that you will have read Customs and
   Cultures before you take this course. If you
   have, you will find it worthwhile to refer to it
   as we proceed. If you have not previously read
   Nida, by all means get the book and get through
   it as soon as possible.

2. Required for Course
   BOCK, Philip K.   --(B)
   1969   Modern Cultural Anthropology. New York,
          Alfred A. Knopf.
   SMALLEY, William A., Editor   --(S)
   1967   Readings In Missionary Anthropology.
          Tarrytown, N. Y., Practical Anthropology.

3. Corequisite: Read one additional Anthropology
   textbook, selected from the following list:
   BEALS, Ralph L., and HOIJER, Harry
   1965   An Introduction to Anthropology. (Third
          edition) N. Y., The Macmillan Co.
   HERSKOVITS, Melville J.
   1951   Man His Works: The Science of Cultural
          Anthropology. N. Y., Alfred A. Knopf.

HONIGMANN, John J.
    1963 Understanding Culture. N. Y., Harper
          and Row.
KEESING, Roger M., and KEESING, Felix M.
    1971 New Perspectives in Cultural Anthropology.
          N. Y., Holt, Rinehart and Winston, Inc.
KEESING, Felix M.
    1963 Cultural Anthropology: The Science of
          Custom. N. Y., Holt, Rinehart and
          Winston, Inc.
KROEBER, A. L.
    1948 Anthropology. N. Y., Harcourt, Brace
          and Co.
TAYLOR
        Cultural Ways.

4. PRACTICAL ANTHROPOLOGY, vols., 1, 2, 6, 7, 10, 13,
        14. Tarrytown, N. Y., Practical Anthro-
        pology. (on Reserve in Library) --(PA)

118 Class Schedule:

Date	Discussion Topic	Assigned Readings
Sept 26	Perspective - Anthropology and Mission	S307-13; (N1; N10)
28	- Ethnotheology	B1; (N2)
Oct 3	- God and Culture	PA1:120-21; 2:58-71; (N48-52)
10	- The Cultural & the Supracultural	Handout; PA10:179-86
12	Anthropological Method	B10; Other Text
17	Learning Culture - Language	B2; Other Text; S341-58
19	- Enculturation	B3; Other Text; PA6:29-42:7:36-42
24	Social Systems - Kinds of Persons	B4; Other Text; S31-51
26	- Kinds of Groups	B5: Other Text: S65-97
31	- Social Time and Space	B6; Other Text
Nov 2	- Cultural Processes and Change	S124-31 B7; Other Text;

Nov	7	Technology - Tools and the Physical World	B8; Other Text; [Tippett, Solomon Islands, ch. 12]
	9	- Techniques and Skills	B9; Other Text
	14	Ideology - Belief Systems	B11; Other Text; S52-61, 103-6
	16	- Value Systems	B12; Other Text; PA13:34-46
	21	Application - Christianity in Culture I	S147-203
	28	- Christianity in Culture II	S204-54
	30	- The Missionary-- Roles & Statuses	S255-306; PA14:145-60,193-208

Readings:
1. To be read <u>by the date listed above</u> so they can be discussed in class on that date.
2. Read the assigned chapter or pages plus the corresponding section in the supplementary textbook of your choice. In some cases there will not be a whole chapter in that text corresponding to the listed topic. If so, find the relevant portions of that text by going through the index.

Writing Assignments: (Due <u>by the end of the term.</u>)
1. A comparison and contrast between Bock and the supplementary text that you choose (about 5 pages-- outline plus comment format preferred).
2. Choose 50 important insights that you feel you have gained from this course (from reading, lectures + class discussion). List these and comment briefly on why each insight is valuable to you in your work. ("Comment briefly" means no more than a paragraph or two per item).

Suggestion (to minimize the effort involved in producing paper #2 and to maximize the value of the course to your specific situation)
Keep a running notebook of insights gained as you go along, noting their actual or potential application to your work. Then simply select from this list for your paper. You may find it helpful to do this also for paper #1.

119

ANTHROPOLOGY AND MISSION II, SWM 631   Second Quarter
Professor Charles H. Kraft   2 hours credit

Description of Course

The cross-cultural communication of the Gospel and directed culture change, with particular attention to the diffusion, acceptance or rejection of the supra-cultural message of the Scriptures.

Bibliography: Textbooks

FOSTER, George M.
  1962 Traditional Cultures: and the Impact of
        Technological Change. N. Y., Harper and Row.
LUZBETAK, Louis J.
  1963 The Church and Cultures. Techny, Ill.,
        Divine Word Pub.
NIDA, Eugene A.
  1960 Message and Mission: The Communication of the
        Christian Faith. South Pasadena, William
        Carey Library.
NIDA, Eugene A., and TABER, Charles R.
  1969 The Theory and Practice of Translation. Leiden,
        E. J. Brill for The United Bible Societies.
WALLACE, Anthony, F. C.
  1956 "Revitalization Movements," American
        Anthropologist, 58:264-281. (Also available in
        The Bobbs-Merrill Reprint Series in The Social
        Sciences, A-230, Indianapolis, Indiana.)

Required Reading for Special Papers:

Paper II
  BARNETT, Homer G.
  1953 Innovation: The Basis of Cultural Change.
        N. Y., McGraw - Hill Book Co.

Paper III
  NIDA, Eugene A.
        "Christo-Paganism," Practical Anthropology,
        8:1-14, (1961)-
  SHARP, Lauriston
  1952 "Steel-Axes for Stone-Age Australians,"
        Practical Anthropology, 7:62-73, (1960).
        (Also available in The Bobbs-Merrill Reprint
        Series in The Social Sciences, A-208,
        Indianapolis, Indiana.)
  TIPPETT, Alan R.
    n.d. "Ethnic Cohesion...Indonesia." From: Accept-
          ance and Rejection of Christianity, (unpub-
          lished manuscript).   121
    n.d. "Patterns of Religious Change." Draft of
          chapter in forthcoming introduction to
          Missiology.

Required Papers:

Paper I, Due Jan. 23. Discuss 15 Important Insights into
    your work that have come up so far. Also, go to the
    movie, "Fiddler on the Roof" and write up a 2-3 page
    analysis of the culture change process and the
    response to it as portrayed in the movie.

Paper II, Due Feb. 8. --15 more Insights or [for EXTRA
    CREDIT] skim-read and report on 15 Important Insights
    from Barnett.

Paper III, Due Feb. 27.--15 more Insights or [for EXTRA
    CREDIT] read and report on at least 15 Insights from
    the four papers listed above (Nida, Sharp and Tippett).

Class Schedule

Jan. 4 Introduction: Luzbetak, chapters 1-5, 13.
                  Culture Change
    9 Cultural Integration: Luzbetak, chs. 6, 7, 8.
  11 Cultural Dynamics; General Notions:
      Luzbetak, ch. 9; Foster, ch. 1.
  16 Processes of Culture Change I: Luzbetak, ch. 10.
 *18 Processes of Culture Change II: Foster,
      chs. 2, 3, 4. Hand in Discussion Topics.
 *23 Feedback Session I -- Paper I Due.
  25 Barriers to Change: Foster, chs. 5, 6, 7.
  30 Conditions Favoring Change: Luzbetak, ch. 11;
      Foster, ch. 8.
Feb. 1 Advocates of Change: Foster, chs. 9, 10, 13.
  *6 Key Concepts from Barnett: Read PA 1:98-104.
      Hand in Discussion Topics.
  *8 Feedback Session II -- Paper II Due.

122

      Advocating Change: Cross-Cultural Communication
  13 Theological and Religious Aspects: Nida 10, 1, 2.
  20 Models, Symbols & Social Structure: Nida 3, 4, 5.
 *22 Christian Movements, Psychology and Culture:
      Nida 6, 7, 8; Wallace. Hand in Discussion Topics.
 *27 Feedback Session III -- Paper III Due.

      Ethnolinguistics: Bible Translation as a Case Study
Mar.*1 Nature and Value of Ethnolinguistics: Nida 9;
      Nida & Taber 1, 2. Write Problems 1-7.
  *6 A New Concept of Translating I; Skim-read Nida &
      Taber 3, 4, 5. Write Problems in chs. 3-5;
      choose any 8 of them.
  *8 A New Concept II: Skim-read Nida & Taber 6, 7, 8.
      Write any 8 problems in chs. 6-8. Hand in
      Discussion Topics.
  13 Feedback Session IV.

*Written Assignment Due

Discussion Topics: On the session before each Feedback Session, please hand in any questions that you
would like to have discussed in the Feedback Sessions.

URBAN ANTHROPOLOGY, SWM 634 (734)   Second Quarter
Professor A. R. Tippett   2/3 hours credit

Description of Course

A seminar for interaction, with a limited amount of
lecturing on the following topics:

Theoretical
    Basic Concepts and Theories, The Culture of Poverty,
Primary Homogeneous Units and Secondary Associations,
Urbanization, Industrialization, Modernization,
Suburbanization, Population Mobility, Anomie, Ethnic
Minorities in Urban Situations, the Second Generation
Urban-born, Current Problems.   123

Practical
    Cross-cultural Urban and Industrial Studies of Places
open for Innovation Today, the Character of Religious
Encounter, Sociological and Economic Factors, Methodo-
logical Procedures for Investigating Potential for
Church Planting, Structures for Urban Christianity, the
Significance of Mobility etc.

Seminar Discussions

The seminar will be based on the reading of published
modules on Urban Anthropology and Sociology. These are
available at the bookstore as the "Urban Anthropology
Packet."

Book Report

Each participant will read one book of his own
selection from a list prepared by the professor (or in
consultation with the professor), and provide a brief
summary and critique for presentation to the class (10 to
20 minutes, according to the size of the class). These
books will cover urban case studies. The scripts will be

distributed, so that each participant acquires as many
book outlines as there are members in the class.

Grading

Grading will be based on (1) Book report and presentation, (2) Class participation (3) Test at the end.

1. Bibliography:

See A. R. Tippett: Bibliography for Cross-cultural
Workers, 1971, South Pasadena, William Carey Library.
pp. 144-152.

2. Collection of Essays on Urban Anthropology:

ANDERSON, Nels
    1964 Urbaniam & Urbanization. Leiden, E. J. Brill.

EDDY, Elizabeth M.
    1968 Urban Anthropology: Research Perspectives and
          Strategies. Southern Anthropological Society
          Proceedings #2, Athens, University of Georgia
          Press.

LUZBETAK, Louis J. (Ed.)
    1966 The Church in the Changing City, Techny,
          Divine Word Publications.

WEAVER, Thomas and Douglas WHITE (Eds.)
    1972 The Anthropology of Urban Environments.
          Society of Applied Anthropology, Monograph #11,
          Boulder, University of Colorado.

3. Participants are also recommended to make use of the
   international urbanization surveys, from the Ford
   Foundation Office of Reports. (ERIC,LIPCO, Bethesda).

4. The Urban Anthropology Packet, which each participant
   will need, contains the following papers:

DAVIS, K.
    1955 "The Origin and Growth of Urbanization in the
          World." American Journal of Sociology. Vol.
          LX, March 1955, pp. 429-437.

124

DAVIS K.
1965 "The Urbanization of the Human Population"
      Scientific American. Vol. 213, No. 3, pp. 40-
      53, Sept. 1965.

GLAZER, Nathan
1965 "The Renewal of Cities" Scientific American.
      Vol. 213, No. 3, pp. 194-204, Sept. 1965.

GOODE, W. J.
1957 "Community Within a Community: the Professions"
      American Sociological Review. Vol. 22, pp.
      195-200.

KOMAROVSKY, M.
1946 "The Voluntary Association of Urban Dwellers"
      American Sociological Review. Vol. XI, pp.
      686-698, Dec. 1946.

LEWIS, Oscar
1966 "The Culture of Poverty" Scientific American. 125
      Vol. 215, No. 4, pp. 19-25, Oct. 1966.

1969 "The Possessions of the Poor" Scientific
      American. Vol. 221, No. 4, pp. 114-124.

LITTLE, K.
1971 "Some Aspects of African Urbanization South of
      the Sahara" McCaleb Module in Anthropology,
      Reading, Mass., Addison Wesley Publishing Co.,
      Inc.

MANGIN, W.
1967 "Squatter Settlements" Scientific American.
      Vol. 213, No. 4, pp. 21-29, Oct. 1967.

MINER, H.
1952 "The Folk-Urban Continuum" American Sociologi-
      cal Review. Vol. XVII, pp. 529-537, 1952.

MINTZ, S. W.
1960 "Peasant Markets" Scientific American. Vol.
      203, No. 2, pp. 112-122, August, 1960.

REDFIELD, R. and M. B. SINGER
    1954 "The Culture Role of Cities" Economic
          Development and Cultural Change. Vol. III,
          No. 1, pp. 53-73.

SCHWERDTFEGER, F. W.
    1972 "Urban Settlement Patterns in Northern Nigeria"
          Man, Settlement and Urbanism, by Peter J. Ucko,
          Ruth Tringham and G. W. Dimbleby. Cambridge,
          Mass., Schenkman Pub. Co.

SMITH, M. G.
    1972 "Complexity, Size and Urbanization" Man,
          Settlement and Urbanism, by Peter J. Ucko,
          Ruth Tringham and G. W. Dimbleby. Cambridge,
          Mass., Schenkman Pub. Co.

WHEATLEY, P.
    1972 "The Concept of Urbanism" Man, Settlement
          and Urbanism, by Peter J. Ucko, Ruth Tringham
          and G. W. Dimbleby. Cambridge, Mass.,
          Schenkman Pub. Co. Oct. 1972, pp. 1-37.

WHYTE, W. F.
    1941 "Corner Boys: A Study of Clique Behavior"
          The American Journal of Sociology. Vol. XLVI,
          pp. 647-664.

    1943 "A Slum Sex Code" American Journal of
          Sociology. Vol. XLIX, pp. 24-31.

WIRTH, Louis
    1938 "Urbanism as a Way of Life" The American
          Journal of Sociology. Vol. XLIV, pp. 1-24,
          July, 1938.

FUNDAMENTALS OF LANGUAGE LEARNING, SWM 636   Third Quarter
Professor Charles H. Kraft /MGK   2 hours credit

Description of Course

The study and practice of techniques of language learning. Insights of modern linguistics are employed to
assist the learner in developing his understanding of and
ability to go about language learning and/or improving
competence in a language he already knows.

Textbooks

NIDA, Eugene A.
  1950   Learning A Foreign Language. New York, National   **127**
         Council of Churches of Christ in the U. S. A.

LARSON, Donald N. and William A. SMALLEY
  1972   Becoming Bilingual, A Guide to Language Learning.
         New Canaan, Conn., Practical Anthropology.
         (Order from Practical Anthropology, Box 1041,
         New Canaan, CT 06840 - $6.00 paper, postpaid.)

Reading Assignments

March 27
        NIDA, Chapter 1 "Languages Must and Can be Learned"
        LARSON-SMALLEY, Chapter 7 "A Language Can be
            Learned"

April 3
        NIDA, Chapter 2 "Principles of Language Learning"
        LARSON-SMALLEY, Chapters 1 and 2 "When One
            Language is Not Enough" and "Learning the
            Next One"

April 10
> NIDA, Chapter 3 "Learning by Listening"
> LARSON-SMALLEY, Chapters 3-5 "Learning in a New
>   Community," "Learning Through Cultural
>   Perspectives," and "Learning Under Anxiety"

April 17
> NIDA, Chapter 4 "Learning a Foreign Language
>   From a Teacher"
> LARSON-SMALLEY, Chapters 8 & 9 "Learning in Ideal
>   Programs" and "Learning in Typical Programs"

April 24
> LARSON-SMALLEY, Chapters 6-10 "Learning From a
>   New Family" and "Resources For Learning"

May 1
> NIDA, Chapter 5 "Learning a Foreign Language From
>   an Informant"
> LARSON-SMALLEY, Chapter 13 "Organizing Practice"
> NIDA, Chapter 6 "Mastering the Sounds"

May 8
> LARSON-SMALLEY, Chapters 16-18 "Practicing For
>   Pronunciation," "Practicing For Grammar,"
>   and "Practicing For Vocabulary"

May 15
> LARSON-SMALLEY, Chapters 12, 14 & 15 "Learning
>   From Mistakes," "Planning Learning Cycles:
>   Preparing the Text," "Planning Learning
>   Cycles: Filling Out the Cycle"

May 22 REYBURN, William D., from Practical Anthropology
>   Volume 5, Number 4 (1958), pages 151-178,
>   "Don't Learn That Language"
> LARSON-SMALLEY, Chapter 19 "Learning to Make
>   Sense" or SMALLEY, William A., Editor,
>   Readings in Missionary Anthropology, pp 341-
>   358.

May 29
> A session with a language informant.

LINGUISTICS AND MISSION, SWM 637   Third Quarter
Professor F. Peter Cotterell   2 hours credit

Description of Course

An introduction to the study of language ranging from
its form and function to the field of applied linguistics
and with particular reference to illiteracy, Bible translation and exegesis, and church growth.

Texts:

BOLINGER, Dwight
1968 Aspects of Language. New York, Harcourt,
Brace and World.   129

NIDA, Eugene A.
1961[2] Bible Translating. New York, United Bible
Societies.

A Selected Bibliography

BLOOMFIELD, L.
1933 Language. New York, Henry Holt and Company.

BRUCE, F. F.
1963[3] The Books and the Parchments: Some Chapters
on the Transmission of the Bible. Westwood,
N. J., Fleming H. Revell.

CARROLL, J. B.
1953 The Study of Language. Cambridge, Harvard
University Press.
1964 Language and Thought. New Jersey, Prentice-
Hall.
COTTERELL, F. Peter
1972 "Control in Amharic," Journal of Ethiopian
Studies, Addis Ababa.

DIACK, H.
1965 In Spite of the Alphabet. London, Chatto and
      Windus.

LANGACKER, R. W.
1967 Language and its Structure. New York,
      Harcourt, Brace and World.

LYONS, J., (ed.)
1970 New Horizons in Linguistics. London, Pelican.

METZGER, B. M.
1971 Lexical Aids for Students of New Testament
      Greek. Princeton, published by the author.

MILLER, G. A.
1956 "The magical number seven, plus or minus two;
      some limits on our capacity for processing
      information," Psychological Review, 63.

NIDA, Eugene A.
1972[2] Message and Mission. South Pasadena, William
      Carey Library.

PEI, M. A., and GAYNOR, F.
1954 Dictionary of Linguistics. London

PIKE, K. L.
1946 Phonetics. Ann Arbor, University of Michigan
      Press.

1947 Phonemics. Ann Arbor, University of Michigan
      Press.

POSTMAN, L., and KEPPEL, G.
1969 Verbal Learning and Memory. London, Pelican.

ROBINS, R. H.
1964 General Linguistics, an Introductory Survey.
      Bloomington, Indiana University Press.

SWADESH, M.
1955 "Towards greater accuracy in lexicostatistic
      dating," Int'l. Journal of Am. Linguistics,21.

130

TOWNSEND, W. C.
   1972 They Found a Common Language. New York,
         Wycliffe Bible Translators.

Required Paper and Tests

   A term paper of 5,000 words on any topic covered in
   the syllabus as applied to a specific area of the
   student's interest. Due June 1st.

   A test paper on the first two areas of study as
   listed. Scheduled for April 12th.

   A test paper on the 4th and 5th areas of study as
   listed. Scheduled for May 17th.

Sequence of Presentation

1. INTRODUCTION. The function of language: inter and
   intra personal communication; descriptive, historical
   and comparative linguistics.   2 lectures   131

2. APPLIED LINGUISTICS. Phonetics and phonology:
   acoustic, auditory and articulatory phonetics, vowels
   and consonants; morphonology, the morpheme, allomorphs;
   syntax: word classes, immediate constituents,
   sentence classification; transformational grammar;
   semantics.   3 lectures

3. LANGUAGE LEARNING. Goals, myths and methods: learning in children, in adults, classical and immersion
   learning; structured learning; physiology of language
   learning, learned patterns; language and
   acculturation.   2 lectures

4. LINGUISTICS AND LITERACY. Literacy and poverty;
   problems of the illiterate, illiteracy and the second
   language; structure in literacy programs: letter,
   word, phrase, sentence, the primer, readers; psychological factors; simplified texts, measuring
   techniques.   3 lectures

5. LINGUISTICS AND TRANSLATION. Translation and interpretation: using an interpreter; written translations, some problems and some answers. Bible translation: problems from Greek and Hebrew; types of
   translation.   2 lectures

6. LINGUISTICS AND BIBLICAL EXEGESIS. Bible languages,
   role of language, role of culture; Babel and Pentecost, the Rabshakeh, the logos; Barr's criticisms;
   rightly dividing or wresting.   2 lectures

7. LINGUISTICS AND CHURCH PLANTING. Homogeneous groups:
   ethic and linguistic factors; historical linguistics
   and cultural acceptability; socio-economics; Ethiopia,
   a case study: language families and the pattern of
   growth, a power to predict.   4 lectures

132

IV. Techniques, Organization and Methods in Mission

640 RESEARCH METHODS.

642 TRAINING THE MINISTRY-LAY AND ORDAINED.

643 THEOLOGICAL EDUCATION BY EXTENSION WORKSHOP

644 PROGRAMMED INSTRUCTION

133

RESEARCH METHODS SWM 640   Third Quarter
Professor Alan R. Tippett   2 hours credit

Description of Course

An introductory study designed to equip the missionary
working in alien cultures to discern truly and describe
exactly the structures of society and Church, personality
conflicts and human environment, customs, and beliefs.
Techniques of interviewing, observing, and documenting.

Class meets on Wednesdays and Fridays at 11:40 a.m.

Bibliography: Recommended

134

BEATTIE, John
    1964   Other Cultures: Aims, Methods and Achievements
           in Social Anthropology. New York, Free Press of
           Glencoe.

    1965   Understanding An African Kingdom. New York,
           Holt, Rinehart & Winston, Inc.

BEVERIDGE, W. I. B.
    1957   The Art of Scientific Investigation. New York,
           Alfred A. Knopf Inc.

COLLIER, John, Jr.
    1967   Visual Anthropology: Photography as a Research
           Method. New York, Holt, Rinehart & Winston, Inc.

COMMITTEE of ROYAL ANTHROPOLOGICAL INSTITUTION
    1971   Notes and Queries on Anthropology. London,
           Routledge & Kegan Paul Ltd.

MADGE, John
    1965   The Tools of Social Science. New York,
           Doubleday, Doran.

MURDOCK, G. P. et al.
1971 Outline of Cultural Materials. New Haven,
   Human Relations Area Files Inc.

NAROLL, Raoul and Ronald COHEN
1970 A Handbook of Method in Cultural Anthropology.
   New York, Natural History Press. [Professor's
   Reference Book.]

SCHUSKY, Ernest L.
1972 Manual for Kinship Analysis. New York, Holt,
   Rinehart & Winston.

TIPPETT, A. R., Compiled by
1971 Bibliography for Cross-Cultural Workers. South
   Pasadena, William Carey Library.
   [Anthropology, Ethnohistory and Missiology,
   pp. 234-249. Teaching Anthropology, pp. 246-252.]

WILLIAMS, Thomas Rhys
1967 Field Methods in the Study of Culture. New York, 135
   Holt, Rinehart & Winston, Inc.

Requirements for the Course: RESEARCH METHOD NOTEBOOK

Produce a notebook to cover Research Method.

This should include:

(1) Notes on the Lectures prepared week by week.
(2) Notes on any Reading done.
(3) Bibliography of useful material.
(4) Sample interview.
  (a) Preliminary Plan
  (b) Key Questions
  (c) Report of Interview
  (d) Two-page write-ups as an Article.
(5) Any other items you consider worth preserving.

The notebook should be arranged on a basis of subject
matter classifiers, like your course outline. Use a loose
leaf system so you can build it up during the term.

Notebooks will be handed in for inspection before Friday
June 1st, and will be returned to you on Monday, June 4th.

Sequence of Presentation

March 28 Reasons for the course. Basic terminology and
approach. Literature available.
30 Comparative research in Socio-missiology.
Various types of Missiological Research.
April 4 Ethnohistorical Method and Reconstruction
6 The Pilot Project
11 The Use of Schedules
13 The Use and Abuse of Questionnaires
18 Sampling
20 The Field Situation: Personal preparation,
equipment, etc.
25 Systems for Recording and Classifying Data on
the Field
27 Detached Observation
May   2 Participant Observation
4 Interviewing: (1) Choice of Informants
9   (2) Methods and Rules for
Questioning
11   (3) Problems of Interviewing
16   (4) Informant Reliability
18 Use of Documents
23 Demographic material and Statistical Tables
25 Indirect ways of collecting information
30 Processing Data
June   1 Examination or practical assignment.

TRAINING THE MINISTRY SWM 642
Professor James H. Emery

Second Quarter
2 hours credit

Description of Course

Training lay and ordained ministers to obtain development of the Church and extension of the faith. Theological,
historical, cultural and practical factors in designing
right kinds of training for radically different contexts,
particularly extension programs.

Purpose of the Course

The purpose is to think through the problems of the   137
Christian ministry as it is carried out in different cultures,
and to attain an historical perspective of the possible ways
the ministers have been prepared. It is desired that the
general concepts and factors that influence the training of
the ministry be related to the specific culture in which one
works, so that the relationships between the concepts and
practice become clear.

Reading Requirements

WINTER, Ralph D.
  1969 Theological Education by Extension. South
        Pasadena, William Carey Library.

COVELL, Ralph R. and WAGNER, C. Peter
  1971 An Extension Seminary Primer. South Pasadena,
        William Carey Library.

NIEBUHR, Helmut R., and WILLIAMS, D. D.
  1956 The Ministry in Historical Perspective.
        New York, Harper.

(Further readings as assigned.)

Term Paper

Each person will write a term paper of from 15-20
pages, double spaced analyzing the situation of
theological education in the country and the church
in which he works, discussing the relevant social
and cultural factors that influence the ministry,
and the preparation of those who minister. Include
in this a brief proposal for a design of a training
program to fit the situation, showing how it takes
into consideration the social and cultural factors
involved.

Attach a copy of the detailed outline from which
the paper is written.

Examinations

There will be a midterm and final, each covering
the reading and lecture material for that period.

138

Sequence of Presentation

Jan. 3 Introduction
Problem of theological education in the present.
Discontinuity between preparation and ministry. Dis-
illusionment of people with education in general and
the possible ways to attack the problem.

PART I, Factors Affecting the Ministry and
Theological Education

Jan. 5, 10 A. Historical perspective
1. Resume of historical antecedents of theological
education and preparation for ministry in western
culture from the New Testament until the present time.
The relationship between the varying concepts of the
ministry, and the preparation and selection of those
who exercise it. (2 sessions)

Jan. 12
2. Resume of how leaders have been prepared in the
third world from the beginning of the modern missionary movement to date. The conflicts that have arisen

with respect to the concepts and practices, e.g.
Roland Allen, Nevius, etc.

      B.   The ministry

Jan. 17
    1.   The ministry in relation to culture
    Discussion of the interrelations between cul-
tures, and the concept of the ministry, the biblical
cultures, modern cultures in various parts of the
world. Conflicts between various subcultures within
a given church, and the resolution of these conflicts.
The church as a subsystem within the culture.

Jan. 19
    2.   The ministry and leadership patterns
    How various societies select and validate leader-
ship, and prestige patterns, and the value systems
that relate to leadership. The influence of indigenous patterns on the concepts of ministry and the
practice of theological education.

139

Jan. 24
    3.   The ministry and the church
    The church and the place of the ministry, or
ministries in it. The exercise of the ministry compared with the role perception of the church and the
ministers who exercise it. Biblical concepts of roles
and functions of the ministry.

      C.   Training of the ministry

Jan. 26
    1.   Entering the ministry
    The concept of the call. The selection of candi-
dates for the ministry and its effect upon the exercise and the role of the minister.

Jan. 31
    2.   Preparation for ministry
    How different modes of preparation relate to
different role perceptions and ways of ministering.
The effect this has on the church, its expectations
and practices.

Feb. 2
    3. Teaching modes
    Conflicts between culturally patterned modes of
learning and the material and tasks to be learned.
How people learn in different cultures and how they
learn at different stages of life.

Feb. 7 Mid-term examination

PART II, The Design of Training Programs

Feb. 9   A. Objectives of training
    A consideration of the specific objectives to be
attained in a training program. Definition of these
objectives in terms of the culture and society in
which it is to function. The factors that influence
this design as seen by the church, and in light of
the Bible.

Feb. 14   B. Organizing the system
    How to create a system to fulfill the objectives
of the training course. The possible components and
how they may be created and arranged. The influence
of factors inherent in the church and culture that
modify the educational system.

Feb. 16   C. The curriculum
    Dividing the material and tasks to be learned
into segments capable of being taught. Use of mod-
ular designs, of integrated systems with different
levels, and the projection of the initial teaching
into a program of continuing education.

Feb. 21   D. Teaching methods
    What delivery systems are available to communi-
cate, how efficient they are with respect to cost,
novelty, and long term utilization. The influence of
teaching methods on the perception of the role of the
ministry. Peer learning. Programmed instruction.

Feb. 23   E. Creating study materials
    Provision of the materials necessary to supply
the system, the planning, preparation and distribution
of them. The problems presented by cultures with
little or no written materials. The care and feeding
of indigenous authors.

Feb. 28   F. The faculty
    Problems relating to the building of faculties
and theologians in different cultures. Conflicts between prestige orientation vs. autochotonous communication. Creative thinking and indigenous leadership.

Mar. 2, 7 & 9 The final sessions will be dedicated to
a discussion of the projects presented in the term
papers.

THEOLOGICAL EDUCATION BY EXTENSION WORKSHOP, SWM 643
Professor Ralph D. Winter   Second Quarter - 2 hours credit

Description of Course

    Seminar designed for researchers to present case
studies of their field situations. Usually involves
determining the validity or effectiveness of a residential
or TEE program. Researcher presents a paper about
Theological Education by Extension which is discussed in
class. Designed to be of practical use in problem
solving.

MULTI-LINGUAL CHURCH LEADERS   Taken from the M.A. project of Les Hill

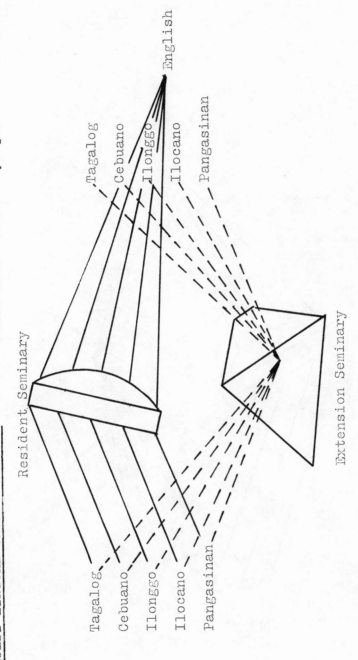

(figure 2)

MULTI-CULTURAL CHURCH LEADERS   Taken from the M.A. project of Les Hill

Resident Seminary

Extension Seminary

Middle socio-econ. pastors
Tribal pastors
Lower socio-econ. pastors
Rural pastors
Urban middleclass Pastors

S O C I E T Y

Middle socio-econ.
Tribal
Lower socio-econ.
Rural
Urban

(figure 1)

PROGRAMMED INSTRUCTION, SWM 644   Second Quarter
Professor Ralph D. Winter (Fred Holland)   2 hours credit

Description of Course

Fundamentals of programming demonstrate use of P I
materials in a TEE program. A production workshop where
P I frames can be written, rewritten and tested.

Classes will include:

1. Working through the Designing Effective Instruction
   Multi-media/workbook exercises.

2. Lectures on programming, writing for new literates 145
   and S-R concepts.

3. Programming under supervision.

Required Textbooks:

HOLLAND, Fred and Grace
  1973 Talking With God. An AEAM Theological Commission
        Text (Revised). Kisumu, Kenya, Evangel
        Publishing House (c.1972).

HOLLAND, Grace and Jonah MOYO

  1973 Bringing People to Jesus. An AEBICAM Programmed
        Text (Two). Kisumu, Kenya, Evangel Publishing
        House.

MAGER, Robert F.
  1962 Preparing Instructional Objectives. Belmont,
        California, Fearon Publishers.

PIPE, Peter
  1966 Practical Programming. New York, Holt, Rinehart
        and Winston, Inc.

WORKBOOK
  n.d. Designing Effective Instruction, Monitors' Manual.
        Palo Alto, General Programmed Teaching.

Required Papers:

    Identify target group--ability, education, interests,
    world view, etc. List concerns--content of subject,
    spiritual needs, cultural, job relatedness.

    Write, test and revise two daily segments of a
    subject of your choice from a subject of students'
    choice and need after given the broad general content
    outline.

Other Readings: (to be referred to individuals as needed)

HARLESS, Joe H.
  1970 (1) An Ounce of Analysis (Is Worth a Pound of
             Objectives), A Self-Instructional Lesson. Falls
             Church, Virginia, Harless Educational Technologists.

  1969 (2) Analysis of Learning Problems. Falls Church,
             Virginia, Harless Educational Technologists, Inc.

  1968 (3) Behavior Analysis and Management. Falls
             Church, Virginia, Harless Educational Technologists.

  n.d. (4) Design of Teaching Strategies. Falls Church,
             Virginia, Harless Educational Technologists, Inc.

  1969 (5) Construction of Teaching Exercises. Falls
             Church, Virginia, Harless Educational Technologists.

MAGER, Robert F.
  1968 (1) Developing Attitude Toward Learning. Belmont,
             California, Fearon Publishers.

MAGER, Robert F., (co-authored by Peter PIPE)
  1970 (2) Analyzing Performance Problems, or 'You Really
             Oughta Wanna.' Belmont, California, Fearon Pub.

146

MARKLE, Susan Meyer
  1969 Good Frames and Bad, A Grammar of Frame Writing.
        New York, John Wiley & Sons, Inc. (Second Edition,
        c. 1964).

POPHAM, W. James and Eva L. BAKER
  1970 (1) Systematic Instruction. Englewood Cliffs,
        Prentice-Hall, Inc.

  1970 (2) Establishing Instructional Goals. Englewood
        Cliffs, Prentice-Hall, Inc.

  1970 (3) Planning an Instructional Sequence.
        Englewood Cliffs, Prentice-Hall, Inc.

V. History of Missions and Church Expansion

651 THE HISTORICAL DEVELOPMENT OF THE
CHRISTIAN MOVEMENT.

652 THE EMERGENCE OF THE WESTERN CHRISTIAN
TRADITION.

653 PROJECT SEMINAR IN THE CHRISTIAN
MOVEMENT.

654 HISTORY OF EVANGELICAL AWAKENINGS.

THE HISTORICAL DEVELOPMENT OF THE CHRISTIAN MOVEMENT, 651
Professor Ralph D. Winter   First Quarter, 2 hours credit

Description of Course

An analysis of the growth dynamics of the Christian
movement, from its roots in the Abrahamic covenant to its
fruits in the age of Billy Graham and its prospects by
the year 2000. Emphasis on the period beginning with
World War I, the indigenization of world Christianity,
the new mission agencies and new rules for old ones, the
structure and function of missions today.

Objective of Course

One objective of The Historical Development of the
Christian Movement, SWM 651, is to give an overall perspective of the entire story of the expansion of the
Christian faith. Actually, rather than to try "to give
all one needs to know" it will be chiefly concerned with
engendering an undying interest in the subject.

Another objective is to allow for a considerable portion of all time spent out of class to be given to the
period following 1910 and, in particular, to those areas
of the world where the individual is personally involved
or interested. Thus three of the four texts zero in on
the recent period, while the fourth, Latourette's one
volume History of Christianity, treats not only the modern
period but will provide a permanent, standard reference
for the entire story. (This book will be used extensively
next quarter as well.)

Textbooks

CLARK, Stephen B.
    1972 Building Christian Communities, Strategy for

Renewing the Church. Notre Dame, Ave Maria
Press.

LATOURETTE, Kenneth Scott
  1953 A History of Christianity. New York, Harper
        and Row, Publishers.

WINTER, Ralph D.
  1970 The Twenty-Five Unbelievable Years, 1945 to
        1969. South Pasadena, William Carey Library.

  1970 The Warp and the Woof, Organizing for Mission.
        South Pasadena, William Carey Library.

Selected Bibliography: (Recommended Books)

  *DAWSON, Christopher
    1958 Religion and the Rise of Western Culture.
          Garden City, N. Y., Image Books, A Division
          of Doubleday & Company, Inc.

  LATOURETTE, Kenneth Scott
    1970 A History of The Expansion of Christianity.
          Volumes I - VII. Grand Rapids, Zondervan
          Publishing House.

    1962 Christianity in a Revolutionary Age. Volumes
          I - V. New York, Harper and Row, Publishers.

  *MCEVEDY, Colin
    1961 The Penguin Atlas of Medieval History.
          Baltimore, Penguin Books.

  *NEILL, Stephen
    1964 A History of Christian Missions.
          Baltimore, Penguin Books.

  *(All of these books will be required in the second
    quarter for History Course SWM 652.)

Reading Suggestions and "Response Papers"

During the first half of the quarter, your outside
reading should relate to the recent, historical dimension
of the area of the world you are concerned about. This
should include all pertinent material in Latourette's
(one-volume) History of Christianity, his (seven-volume)
History of the Expansion of Christianity, and his (five-
volume) Christianity in a Revolutionary Age. The latter
two sets are on reserve. (The seven-volume set, available
for a very low price through the Church Growth Book Club,
will be required next quarter in case you have been want-
ing a good excuse to invest in it.)

On Wednesday of each week, beginning Oct. 4th, a
"response paper" plus a work report will be due. Your
response papers over the quarter (nine total) should
simply record the growth of your knowledge and awareness
in this area of study. Jot down whatever surprises,
puzzles, pleases, concerns you, (a half-page is sufficient) representing your honest reaction to class topics
or outside reading, study, and reflection. Your work
reports each week should simply describe the nature of
the work you have done for this course during the previous
week. These two items can be on the same page.

151

Term Papers or Projects

Note: the second work report Oct. 11 must include two
or three possible term paper/projects subjects. The
fourth work report Oct. 25 must include a final topic
plus a tentative outline and bibliography.

The term papers or term projects will be due no later
than 10 P.M. on Friday of the eighth week. They are to
be placed under the index tab for your name in the three-
ring binder in the library.

During the ninth week you are to read (and write a
one-half page response) for two term papers of other
members of the class. During the tenth week you will re-
ply in a half page to the responses to your own paper.

Examinations

The mid-term and final exams will cover classroom
topics plus assigned related readings (which will occur
mainly in the latter part of the quarter).

Emphasis in work and in grading should be considered
roughly as follows:

Response papers   15%   Mid-term exam   15%
Work reported   15%   Final exam   15%
           Term paper/project   40%

Course Introduction

One way to understand what we expect of you in regard
to your term paper/project in this course is to understand what we think you are!

152

First of all, you are graduate students. One of the
nice things about graduate school is that there it is
assumed students can learn from each other, and even the
professors can learn from the students. That is,
graduate students differ from undergraduates chiefly in
that they rise above a self-educating activity to endeav-
ors that propose seriously to add to the common fund of
knowledge. Graduate students may not quite be professors,
although they are often used as such in first-rate universities, but they are no longer mere students whose only
purpose is self-education: they are expected to make
some contribution of general value.

In the second place, you have enrolled in an academic
institution and are presumably prepared to work academically, that is, in reference to others who are working
on the same subjects. One of the main functions of the
use of the so-called academic apparatus--footnotes, references, library research, etc.--is to allow one to participate effectively at the scholarly roundtable of discussion.
To do so requires you to courteously and respectfully
listen to what others are saying (and have said). To
speak up without first listening would be rash and fool-
hardy, and would not make you welcome. On the other hand,

never to speak up, never to propose anything worthy of
the others to hear, is to cease to listen, and to yield
your place at the table to someone who will properly join
in.

In the third place, those who enroll in the SWM, unlike
the vast majority of graduate students, are pursuing mid-
career or mid-service rather than pre-service studies.
They are not students in the ordinary sense--preparing
for a career, learning on the basis of no actual experience. This is why we refer to our enrollees as Research
Associates rather than students: you are able to teach
not just learn, write to be read not just as an exercise,
and to do research on the basis of previous experience.
This assures higher motivation and usually greater will-
ingness to look at what needs to be done rather than
merely what one would like best to do.

Since this is the quarter when the most recent period
of history is stressed, there are two special challenges
to which it is hoped the majority will respond in select-   153
ing term paper topics.

1. Our school has been requested to assist in a survey
of Asian countries to be published under the title, "Let
Asia Hear." This book, edited by Donald Hoke, has a chapter on each Asian country, and it is desired that the
graphical material from chapter to chapter be comparable
in style. Most of this work was done by the Research
Associates in the spring quarter earlier this year. Two
or three people who are interested in techniques of
graphical presentation of data may volunteer to finish
this project up.

2. A similar, but much more extensive challenge comes
to us as our school has joined forces with MARC to provide
a people-by-people survey of all the people of the world,
defining the percentage and the characteristics of the
non-Christian elements in the population. This year no
one should allow any of the subpopulations in the country
where he is involved to be overlooked in this campaign to
chart the unreached peoples of the world.

What this means is that we must this year pay special attention to those who are yet to be won. This does not in any sense dull our interest in the historic growth and development of the churches, that is, our desire to know how many and what kind of people are Christian, but it does mean that more than ever we want to know how many are not Christian, and what kind of people they are so that serious efforts to reach them can be launched. We will try to get together in teams covering the various regions of the world. Only this way can we be sure we cover every area.

Sequence of Presentation

UNIT I. MISSION AND THE CREATIVE INTENT OF GOD

Sept. 27 Class Topic: The Missio Dei in Space and Time. Can what God has done in space and time tip us off as to the purposes of redemption and there- fore of mission?

154

29 Class Topic: The Missio Dei and the Enigmas of the Human Story.
The mystery of the decline of civilizations, the diversity of race, language, and culture-- clues to redemptive purpose.

UNIT II. REDEMPTION IN THE RECENT PAST

Oct.   4 Class Topic: Cycles of Reduction and Expansion
The four reductions and the four expansions.

6 Class Topic: The First Expansion: The Roman World (0 - 400 A.D.).
The first curtain rises: 312 - 410.

11 Class Topic: The Second Expansion: The Barbarian World (400 - 800 A.D.).
The second curtain rises.

13 Class Topic: The Third Expansion: The Viking World (800 - 1200 A.D.).
Alfred the Great, the first vernacular anchor.

Oct. 18 Class Topic: Expansion Aborted (1200-1600 A.D.)
          Crusades, cathedrals, and friars--the political
          perversion of the Reformation.

      20 Class Topic: The Breakdown of Christendom.
          The Reformation; Lutheranism as a national
          church.

      25 Class Topic: The Fourth Expansion: The Non-
                        Western World (1600 - 2000 A.D.).

      27 Class Procedure: Mid Term Exam.

UNIT III. THE EMERGENCE OF A WORLDWIDE CHRISTIAN MOVEMENT
           (The Fourth Expansion in Detail)

Nov.   1 Class Topic: Roman Catholic Missions During
                        the Fourth Expansion.
          Latin America, China, India, Africa.

       3 Class Topic: The Delayed Renewal of Protes-   155
                        tantism.
          The Evangelical Awakening.

       8 Class Topic: The Emergence of Protestant Orders
                        The Methodists, William Carey,
                        CMS, LMS, ABCFM.

      10 Class Topic: The Rise of an American Pattern
                        The 1837 Decision and subsequent
                        events.

      15 Class Topic: The New Burst of Protestant Orders
                        Hudson Taylor and "Faith Missions."

      17 Class Topic: Edinburgh I
                        Antecedents, subsequent meetings,
                        ICOWE.

NOTE: TERM PAPER IS DUE IN THE BINDERS IN THE LIBRARY

       by 10 P.M., November 17.

UNIT IV: THE TWENTY-FIVE UNBELIEVABLE YEARS

Nov. 22   Class Topic: The Retreat of the West.
           The colonial collapse and the rise of the
           new nations.

      24   Class Topic: The Final Breakdown of the
                          Uniformitarian Hypothesis.
           The third and fourth world <u>churches</u>.

      29   Class Topic: Missions New and Old
           The third burst of Protestant orders; the
           planting of younger missions.

Dec.   1   Class Topic: The Phenomenon of Third and
                          Fourth World <u>Missions</u>.

THE EMERGENCE OF THE WESTERN CHRISTIAN TRADITION, SWM 652
Professor Ralph D. Winter--Second Quarter, 2 hours credit

Description of Course

A more detailed geographical, cultural and structural
analysis of the expansion of Christianity prior to 1914,
emphasizing the Western, Roman tradition and the peoples
involved: the Jews, the Greeks, the Romans, the Celts, the
Goths, the Vikings, the Muslims, the rebel Christians.

Textbooks

DAWSON, Christopher
    1958 Religion and the Rise of Western Culture. Garden 157
          City, N.Y., Image Books, A Division of Doubleday.

LATOURETTE, Kenneth Scott
    1953 A History of Christianity. N.Y., Harper & Row.

    1970 A History of The Expansion of Christianity.
          Volumes I-VII. Grand Rapids, Zondervan Publishing.

MCEVEDY, Colin
    1961 The Penguin Atlas of Medieval History.
          Baltimore, Penguin Books.

NEILL, Stephen
    1964 A History of Christian Missions.
          Baltimore, Penguin Books.

Suggested Reading Assignments

Assignment for January 9, 10, and 11, 1973:

1. Read and notice outline: Introduction, Vol. I HEC.

2. Transfer outline from Bibliographic section to chapters, for Chapters I-IV.(Note A,B,C, in margin for each paragraph beginning on page 370, e. g. A to F for Chapter I, A to B for Chapter II, A to L for Chapter III, etc. THEN find the beginning of the same subject matter within the chapters and mark that spot with A,B,C etc. plus the page on which the original A,B,C, occurs in the Bibliographic section. That is, on page 372 you will have put a D by THE MYSTERY CULTS; then you will accordingly put a D, p. 372 at the beginning of the last paragraph on page 22, where the discussion of that subject comes up in the chapter.)

3. Read Chapter I with some care, skim Chapter II. See how far you can get into Chapters III and IV. Do not hasten through IV.

The 652 course is basically an extension of 651, in that the introduction for that course (page 3 of the handed-out materials) still applies. The area no longer applicable is the omission this quarter of the response papers and work report. Consequently, the emphasis this course is shifted a bit more to the exams and term project, being 30 and 40 respectively out of a possible 70 points.

On page two of the 651 handouts are three books required this quarter. Additionally this quarter are the 1st and 3rd volumes of Latourette's H. E. C.

The following are pages which, I would think, would be of special interest:

DAWSON,   11-100, 199-224
NEILL,   61-82, 177-209
LATOURETTE, H. of C. 221-233, 416-445, 447-457
          (459-491, skim), 523-544, 552-553, 640-678,
          840-882, 970-971, 1018-1048.
LATOURETTE, H. E. C. 300 pp: Vol I, Almost all
          258 pp: Vol II, Chapters I, II, 144-149,
                                        338-342
                   Chapter VIII, IX
          219 pp: Vol III, 1-54, 83-118, 134, 154-156,
                            156-159, 186-239, 276-284,
                            307-321, 339-342, 349-358,
                            372-426, 427-457.

PROJECT SEMINAR IN THE CHRISTIAN MOVEMENT, SWM 653
Professor Ralph D. Winter   Third Quarter, 2 hours credit

Description of Course

Any element of special interest in courses SWM 651 and
SWM652 may be followed out by individuals in a seminar
context whether by presentation of a paper or some other
type of research project.

Select Bibliography

BEAVER, R. Pierce, (Edited by)
1967 To Advance The Gospel, Selections from the
Writings of Rufus Anderson. Grand Rapids,
William B. Eerdmans Publishing Co.

159

WARREN, Max, (Edited by)
1971 To Apply The Gospel, Selections from the
Writings of Henry Venn. Grand Rapids,
William B. Eerdmans Publishing Co.

Research Projects (Describe the sources examined.)

1. An analysis of a missionary society. Select a
missionary society and show its contribution to foreign
missions by displaying on a graph the total number of
missionaries supported by or serving under that society
year by year since its beginning.

2. An analysis of an empire. Plot the expansion of a
colonial empire such as the Spanish, British, German, etc.
by showing the total area in square miles and the number
of people under its control at any given period and at
each period of expansion or decline.

3. Submit significant observations from your reading.

HISTORY OF EVANGELICAL AWAKENINGS, SWM 654   Second Quarter
Professor J. Edwin Orr   2 hours credit

Description of Course

Detailed study of the revivals and awakenings of the
19th and 20th centuries, with emphasis upon their
influence upon missionary expansion and upon national
church growth in all the continents.

Bibliography

ORR, J. Edwin
    1965 The Light of the Nations.
          Grand Rapids, Eerdmans.

    1975 The Eager Feet. 1792-
          Chicago, Moody Press.

    1974 The Fervent Prayer. 1858-
          Chicago, Moody Press.

    1973 The Flaming Tongue. 1905-
          Chicago, Moody Press.

VI. Church Growth

660 PRINCIPLES AND PROCEDURES IN CHURCH
GROWTH I.

661 PRINCIPLES AND PROCEDURES IN CHURCH
GROWTH II.

666 STRATEGY OF MISSIONS.

667 CASE STUDIES IN CURRENT CHURCH
HISTORY:

667a INDIGENEITY AND AFRICAN INDEPENDENCY

667b DISCIPLING CHINA

667c CASE STUDY IN CHURCH GROWTH ILLUSTRATED
FROM WEST AFRICA

667d CHRISTIANITY IN LATIN AMERICA

161

667f THE CHURCH IN INDIA

PRINCIPLES AND PROCEDURES IN CHURCH GROWTH I, SWM 660
Professor Donald McGavran - First Quarter, 2 hours credit

Description of Course

A brief survey of the theological, psychological, and
statistical obstructions to church growth arising from
within the missionary movement; sociological structures
of the societies which are the ground of church multiplication, and procedures which cause stagnation, acceleration, introversion and expansion.

Textbooks

McGAVRAN, Donald A.
1970 Understanding Church Growth. Grand Rapids,
William B. Eerdmans Publishing Co.

HASTINGS, Adrian
1967 Church and Mission in Modern Africa. London,
Burns and Oates.

OLSEN, Gilbert
1966 Church Growth in Sierra Leone. Grand Rapids,
William B. Eerdmans Publishing Co.

PICKETT, J. Waskom
1963 The Dynamics of Church Growth. New York,
Abingdon Press.

READ, Wm. R., MONTERROSO, Victor, and JOHNSON, Harmon A.
1969 Latin American Church Growth. Grand Rapids,
William B. Eerdmans Publishing Co.

SHEARER, Roy E.
1968 Wildfire: The Growth of the Church in Korea.
Grand Rapids, William B. Eerdmans Publishing Co.

TIPPETT, A. R.
   1970 Church Growth and the Word of God, The Biblical
         Basis of the Church Growth Viewpoint.
         Grand Rapids, William B. Eerdmans Publishing Co.

Selected Bibliography: (Select two of the following.)

BRAUN, Neil Henry
   1971 Laity Mobilized, Reflections on Church Growth
         in Japan and Other Lands. Grand Rapids,
         William B. Eerdmans Publishing Co.

ENNS, Arno
   1967 Man Milieu and Mission Argentina. Grand Rapids,
         William B. Eerdmans Publishing Co.

KWAST, Lloyd E.
   1968 The Discipling of West Cameroun: A Study of
         Baptist Growth. Grand Rapids, William B.
         Eerdmans Publishing Co.

163

TUGGY, A. L. and TOLIVER, R.
         Seeing the Church in the Philippines.
         Overseas Missionary Fellowship, Publisher.

WAGNER, C. Peter
   1968 The Protestant Movement in Bolivia. South
         Pasadena, William Carey Library.

                     (Also select TWO THESES to read.)

Reading Assignments

   The Text: Understanding Church Growth. Buy it! Under-
              line and annotate it.

              For each of the 20 days, an assignment is to
              be prepared with a Study Guide for that day.
              (See the sixteen-page Study Guide For
              Principles and Procedures in Church Growth.)

Take notes on class discussions, so your understanding
is increased by comments and answers given by the

career missionaries and national leaders in this class.
You will need them for examinations.

Many in this class will be teaching Understanding Church
Growth and should observe what ways of teaching, what
approaches, what questions, are most helpful in promot-
ing understanding of the subject.

Complementary reading: Purchase books.

A. About a book a week should be read and underlined.

The first five books are listed as textbooks. The
last two you choose from the Selected Bibliography
book list given, plus two SWM THESES representing
the field of your choice.

B. In November read and master two of the researches
(theses or dissertations) done here at SWM-ICG.
There are over 100 of these: titles and author
appear on the mimeographed sheet. By November then
you, who are doing a thesis or dissertation, will
have identified your problem and constructed an
outline. You should fit your reading to your
research need, or your special interest.

C. Do a great deal of background reading beyond the
formal assignments. Read as extensively as
possible in the social organization, the culture,
the religions, and the ethnology of your lands.
All this is essential for adequate understanding
of church growth and will form part of the wide
reading done for your research. See the Study
Guide for a limited selection of books on Africa,
Asia, and Latin America.

Submit a statement at final examination time, giving
titles read and number of pages read in each book.

Examinations: (One question will likely be on the reading)

Mid-term examination on October 27.

Final examination on December 4.

164

Sequence of Presentation

See the sixteen-page Study Guide For Principles and Procedures in Church Growth I for the sequence of lectures and discussion and the daily research and reading assignments.

Most class sessions will have discussions based on the sixteen-page Study Guide.

Most class sessions will have five or ten minutes for free discussion, i.e. you take up what matters you wish.

PRINCIPLES AND PROCEDURES IN CHURCH GROWTH II SWM 661
Professor Donald A. McGavran   Second Quarter
                                                Two hours credit

Description of the Course

Many have contributed to the development of the Church
Growth School of Thought. This course presents twenty-
seven of these. They discuss God's Purpose and Man's
Responsibility, God's Work in Human Structures, God in
Human History, God and Man in Field Situations, and
Research Techniques for the Work of God. The theory
(or philosophy) of missions involved is seen to touch
almost every aspect of modern mission; but always from
the point of view of the propagation of the Gospel.

Purpose of the Course

The Church Growth Movement levies tribute on many
branches of knowledge and experience. This course purposes
to harness theology, ethnology, linguistics, history,
quantitative analysis, research, missionary experience,
goal setting, and disciplined planning to the task of
discipling ta ethne. It is placed in the second quarter
so that, as associates work forward on many different
facets of the task of mission, they may be reminded that
all effective thinking about missions must be done against
the graph of growth, i.e. in consciousness of the degree
to which men are becoming followers of Jesus Christ and
members of His Church.

Reading Required

Texts:

TIPPETT, Alan R., Editor
   1973 God, Man and Church Growth. Grand Rapids,
         Eerdmans.

McQUILKIN, J. Robertson
1973   How Biblical is the Church Growth Movement?
       Chicago, Moody Press.

Supplementary Reading:

McGAVRAN, Donald A., Editor
1972   Crucial Issues in Missions Tomorrow.   Chicago,
       Moody Press.

McGAVRAN, Donald A.
1959   How Churches Grow. London, World Dominion;
       New York, Friendship.

READ, William R., Victor MONTERROSO, Harmon A. JOHNSON
1969   Latin American Church Growth. Grand Rapids,
       Eerdmans.

GREENWAY, Roger S.
1973   An Urban Strategy for Latin America. Grand Rapids,
       Baker Book House.   **167**

Various Authors

       Two theses or dissertations on the continent
       of the candidate.

Term Papers, or Projects, and Examination

1. An accurate Description of My Denomination in Zam Zam.
       Each essay will be proportioned somewhat as follows:
           Country and People   1/2 page
           Graph of Growth   1/2 page
           Major Ethnic or Linguistic Units in which the
       Church is growing with (if possible) growth facts
       for each unit   2 pages
           Reasons for Growth or Stagnation in each major
       movement of the graph   2 pages
           Suggestions for Growth 1975-2000 2 pages.

2. Seven Lectures on Church Growth in Outline Form.
About one page per lecture. To be delivered to colleagues
in the land where you work.

3. The papers will take the place of the examination.

Sequence of Lectures

Theology and Church Growth

> Biblical Imperatives (Glasser)
> What is Mission (Shepherd)
> The Role of the Holy Spirit (Seamands)
> Christian Ethno-Theology (Kraft)
> Perfection Growth (Gates)

God's Word in Human Structures

> Pragmatic Strategy (Wagner)
> Receptiveness (Shearer)
> Modernization (Read)
> Cultural Compulsives (Tippett)
> Administrators and Fields (Guy)
> Cross Cultural Perspectives (Winter)
> New Approaches (Shewmaker)
> Ethno-Linguistics (Kraft)

God in Human History

> Dynamics and Social Action (Orr)
> Historical Method, Digging for Facts (Kessler)
> Ethno-Historical Research (Kwast)

God and Man in the Field

> Psychological Dimensions (Sauder)
> Key Persons in People Movements (Murphy)
> Ethnic Units in New Guinea (Spruth)
> Illiterate Nomads (Kjaerland)
> Symbolism and Syncretism (Romero)

Research Techniques in God's Work

> Comparative Method (Yamamori)
> Discipling Africans in This Generation (Barrett)
> Disciplined Planning (Dayton)
> Aviation and Mission (Bennett)

168

Accurate Descriptions of Notable Overseas Denominations

Five of the best of the term papers will be presented and discussed.

Lectures on Church Growth

Several lectures which associates have prepared for colleagues in lands where they work will be delivered to the class.

STRATEGY OF MISSIONS, SWM 666 (766)   Winter Quarter
Professor C. Peter Wagner

Description of Course

Investigates ways in which a sound theory and theology
of mission is being put into effect by missions and
churches. What missionary structures, ministerial training, patterns of church growth and advanced education for
missionaries best serve the unchanging mandate.

Textbook:

WAGNER, C. Peter
  1971 Frontiers in Missionary Strategy. Chicago,
        Moody Press.

Reading Assignment and Bibliography

Each student will read four books other than the text
during the quarter. Choose the books you read from the
list below, according to the self-explanatory classifications.

I. For M. Div. students only (choose up to two):

1.1 MCGAVRAN, Donald A.
       1955 The Bridges of God, A Study in the Strategy
             of Missions. New York, Friendship Press.

1.2 HODGES, Melvin
       1971 Growing Young Churches. Chicago, Moody
             Press.

1.3 TIPPETT, Alan R.
       1970 Church Growth and the Word of God, The
             Biblical Basis of the Church Growth
             Viewpoint. Grand Rapids, Eerdmans.

170

1.4 KELLEY, Dean M.
     1972 Why Conservative Churches Are Growing,
          A Study in Sociology of Religion. New York,
          Harper & Row, Publishers.

2. Mission Theory (choose up to three):

   2.1 MCGAVRAN, Donald A. and others
       1965 Church Growth and Christian Mission.
           New York, Harper and Row, Publishers.

   2.2 PETERS, George W.
       1970 Saturation Evangelism. Grand Rapids,
           Zondervan Publishing House.

   2.3 BRADSHAW, Malcolm R.
       1969 Church Growth through Evangelism in Depth.
           South Pasadena, William Carey Library.

   2.4 TAYLOR, Clyde W. and Wade T. COGGINS
       n.d. Mobilizing for Saturation Evangelism.
           Wheaton, Evangelical Missions Information
                                  Service.

171

   2.5 WAGNER, C. Peter, editor
       1972 Church / Mission Tensions Today. Chicago,
           Moody Press.

   2.6 MCGAVRAN, Donald A., editor
       1972 Crucial Issues in Missions Tomorrow.
           Chicago, Moody Press.

   2.7 STOTT, John R. W. and others
       1971 Christ the Liberator. Downers Grove,
           Inter-Varsity Press.

   2.8 BEYERHAUS, Peter and Henry LEFEVER
       1964 The Responsible Church and the Foreign
           Missions. Grand Rapids, Eerdmans.

3. Mission Theology (choose up to two):

3.1 BEYERHAUS, Peter
     1971 Missions: Which Way? Humanization or
           Redemption. Grand Rapids, Zondervan.

3.2 BEYERHAUS, Peter
     1972 Shaken Foundations, Theological Foundation
           for Mission. Grand Rapids, Zondervan.

3.3 HORNER, Norman, editor
     1968 Protestant Crosscurrent in Mission: the
           Ecumenical-conservative Encounter.
           Nashville, Abingdon Press.

3.4 PETERS, George
     1972 A Biblical Theology of Missions. Chicago,
           Moody Press.

3.5 WAGNER, C. Peter
     1970 Latin American Theology: Radical or
           Evangelical? Grand Rapids, Wm. B. Eerdmans.

172

3.6 MCGAVRAN, Donald A. editor
     1972 Eye of the Storm, the Great Debate in
           Mission. Waco, Word Books, Publisher.

Method of Reporting

A report on each book should be handed in as the books
are read. Please follow class instructions carefully:
1. Select the chapter from the book you have read
   which you consider the most significant one.
2. Reproduce from that chapter two or three pithy
   quotations from the author which you feel have
   made contribution to your thinking.
3. Write your own reaction in 100-300 words to the
   chapter and particularly to the quotes.

Writing Assignment

Write an article on some aspect of the strategy of
missions for a periodical of your choice. You may
choose a denominational or mission organ, an interdenominational magazine, a scholarly journal, Church Growth

Bulletin, etc. This is not just a trial run -- expect to get your article published. It will help your grade if you do.

As a general rule, the article should be 1500-2000 words (unless your publication has other requirements) on a standard manuscript format. The title must be approved before the article is written.

If you would like me to read your rough draft I will do so, although I can not promise a thorough editorial job. If you prefer, go ahead and write the article, send the original to an editor and hand in to me the carbon copy along with the carbon copy of the letter you wrote to the editor. Whether I see the rough draft or not, no grade on the article will be given until I have evidence that it has been mailed to an editor.

Course Outline -- Sequence of Presentation

173

1. Tues., Feb. 6   THE BIBLICAL IMPERATIVE FOR STRATEGY

2. Thurs.,Feb. 8   NEW TESTAMENT PRINCIPLES OF STRATEGY

3. Tues., Feb. 13   TESTING THE SOIL FOR EFFECTIVE SOWING

4. Thurs.,Feb. 15   SPIRITUAL GIFTS AND WHERE THEY FIT

5. Tues., Feb. 20   THE CULTURAL DIMENSION OF STRATEGY

6. Thurs.,Feb. 22   SATURATION EVANGELISM: THE THEORY

7. Tues., Feb. 27   EVANGELISM IN DEPTH AS A CASE STUDY

8. Thurs.,Mar. 1   RELATING STRATEGY TO THE EMERGING CHURCH

9. Tues., Mar. 6   EVANGELISTIC EFFECTIVENESS IN THE CITIES

10.Thurs.,Mar. 8   ADAPTING STRATEGY TO REVOLUTIONARY
                   CONTEXTS

CASE STUDIES IN CURRENT CHURCH HISTORY, SWM 667
INDIGENEITY AND AFRICAN INDEPENDENCY, SWM 667a
Professor Charles H. Kraft   2 hours credit

Description of Course

Systematic study of denominations in Asia, Africa
and Latin America from their beginning to the present,
with special attention to the spiritual and environmental
factors contributing (1) to healthy expansion, and
(2) to slow growth or arrested development. In various
terms attention will be paid to China, Polynesia, Korea,
New Guinea, Ethiopia, Batakland, the Philippines,
West Africa, Brazil, Orissa, Mexico and Latin America.

174   Textbooks:

BARRETT, D. B.
  1968 Schism and Renewal in Africa, an Analysis of Six
        Thousand Contemporary Religious Movements.
        London, Nairobi (etc.) Oxford University Press.

WELBOURN, Frederick Burkewood and B. A. OGOT
  1966 A Place to Feel at Home: a Study of Two
        Independent Churches in Western Kenya.
        London, Nairobi (etc.) Oxford University Press.

Term Projects: (Ten-fifteen page report)

  1. Study of another Independent Church
  2. Read and evaluate OOSTHUIZEN, G. C., Post-
      Christianity in Africa
  3. Apply the Scale of Measuring Indigeneity to a
      specific Independent or Mission Church
      (preferably one which you know well)
  4. Other

Course Outline:

Sept. 26 Introduction
      28 Barrett - chs 1-6 (pp 3-82); Review in
          PRACTICAL ANTHROPOLOGY 17:137-44 (1970)
Oct.   3 Barrett - chs 7-12 (pp83-160)
      10   - chs 13-15 (pp 161-237)
      12   - chs 16-18 (pp 238-278)
      17 Key concepts from Barrett (about a five-page
          paper) - To be discussed in class
      19 Indigeneity Discussion; Term Project Proposal
          Due
      24 Welbourn and Ogot - chs 1-3, 14, 15
          (pp 1-20, 115-148)
      26 Welbourn and Ogot - chs 4-10 (pp21-72)
      31   - chs 11-13 (pp 73-114)
Nov.   2 Key Concepts from Welbourn and Ogot (about a
          five-page paper) - To be discussed in class
       7 Polygamy Discussion
       9 Ancestor Reverence
      14]   175
      16 [
      21 [Other Specific Issues
      28 [and Term Project Reports
      30]

CASE STUDIES IN CURRENT CHURCH HISTORY, SWM 667
DISCIPLING OF CHINA, SWM 667b   Winter Quarter
Professor Arthur F. Glasser   2 hours credit

Description of Course

Systematic study of denominations in Asia, Africa
and Latin America from their beginning to the present,
with special attention to the spiritual and environmental
factors contributing (1) to healthy expansion, and
(2) to slow growth or arrested development. In various
terms attention will be paid to China, Polynesia, Korea,
New Guinea, Ethiopia, Batakland, the Philippines,
West Africa, Brazil, Orissa, Mexico and Latin America.

176   Textbooks:

LATOURETTE, K. S.
   1929   A History of Christian Missions in China.
          New York, The Macmillan Company.

LUTZ, Jessie Gregor-, edited with an introduction by:
   1965   Christian Missions in China, Evangelists of What?
          Boston, Heath.

Assignments and Sequence of Presentation

Jan. 7   KSL to p. 60 (ch. 1-4)
         Class Discussion: General Introduction

     14 KSL to p. 200 (ch. 5-11)
         LUTZ p. 1-15 (Varg, John, Ohlinger)
         Class Discussion: SYRIAN (NESTORIAN)
         CHRISTIANITY - 7th to 10th centuries

     21 KSL to p. 302 (ch. 12-16)
         LUTZ p. 16-33 (Kepler, Costantini, Rutten)
         Class Discussion: CATHOLIC (FRANCISCAN)
         CHRISTIANITY - 13th and 14th centuries

Jan. 28   KSL to p. 415 (ch. 17-18)
LUTZ p. 34-46 (Dohen, Taiping, Boxer)
Class Discussion: CATHOLIC (JESUIT)
CHRISTIANITY - 16th and 17th centuries

Feb. 4   KSL to p. 526 (ch. 19-22)
LUTZ p. 47-59 (Ch'en, T'ang)
Class Discussion: The Nineteenth Century

      11   KSL to p. 685 (ch. 23-27)
LUTZ p. 60-77 (Hsu, Wu, Chao)
Class Discussion: The Twentieth Century, 1900-49
A. F. Glasser: pp. 1-24 PROTESTANT MISSIONARY
ACTIVITY

      18   KSL to p. 843 (ch. 28-31)
LUTZ p. 78-90 (Ch'ih, Latourette)
Class Discussion: Lessons of Protestant
Missions in China
A. F. Glasser: pp. 25-34 PROTESTANT MISSIONARY
ACTIVITY
R. C. Larson: CHINA TODAY (also article by   **177**
Chang Lit-seng)

      25   LUTZ p. 90-104 (Levenson, Fitzgerald)
Class Discussion: The Communist Takeover
(Christian Encounter)
Paul Szto: The Chinese Communist Mind.
Timothy Yu: What We Know About the Church in
China.

Mar. 4   Class Discussion: The Church Under Communism
(1950-1970) And Its Future
R. C. Larson: POSSIBLE STRATEGY SCENARIOS

      11   Class Discussion: The Church Among Diasporal
Chinese And Its Future
Articles by Moses Chow, Chua Wee Hian, and
David Liao.

CASE STUDIES IN CURRENT CHURCH HISTORY, SWM 667c
CASE STUDY IN CHURCH GROWTH ILLUSTRATED FROM WEST AFRICA
Professor Donald A. McGavran   2 hours credit
                                                First Quarter

Description of the Course

Two denominations - Methodist in Ghana and Lutheran in
Liberia - present a sharp contrast in growth achievements
and patterns. Both are traced in outline throughout a
century. Attention is focussed on the Church, not the
mission.

178

Purpose of the Course

This course is designed for those of all countries who
work at great commission missions. The concrete material,
from West Africa, illustrates a way of conceiving the
task. Factors are shown across ten decades as they
caused or prevented communication of the Gospel.

The four chief purposes of the course are:
a) to develop ways of thinking required by men who intend
   to propagate the Gospel;
b) to help men discern essential action in the welter and
   confusion of contextual data, church work, and mission
   programs, i.e. to discern the long range goals hidden
   on all sides by short range goals;
c) to cultivate ability to see growth patterns and
   describe them honestly;
d) to arouse curiosity as to why some missionary labor is
   blessed of God to great discipling and other labors
   fail of that objective.

The Method of the Course

The method is lecture and reading. There will be a final examination. Students are expected to demonstrate the abilities described above and to know enough of the facts so that their new-found skills are anchored in history.

Reading Requirements

DEBRUNNER, Hans W.
1967   A History of Christianity in Ghana. Accra, Waterville Publishing House.

HALIBURTON, Gordon M
1973   The Prophet Harris. London, Oxford University Press.

METCALFE, George Edgar
1962   Maclean of the Gold Coast--the Life and Times of George Maclean, 1801-1847. London, Oxford University Press.

179

SOUTHON, Arthur Eustace
1935   Gold Coast Methodism. London, Methodist Book Depot and The Cargate Press.

WOLD,Joseph Conrad
1968   God's Impatience in Liberia. Grand Rapids, W. B. Eerdmans Publishing Company.

Reading Suggestions

Books on the Churches and Missions in Ghana are abundant. Over thirty titles are in McAlister Library alone. Browse through the Subjects Catalog under Ghana, West Africa, Liberia. Look up and handle the following books. Inspect the Table of Contents. Savor sections which interest you. If you get hooked, read an entire book!

BARTELS, Francis Lodowic
1965   Roots of Ghana Methodism. London, Cambridge University Press.

DICKSON, Kwamina B.
  1969 Historical Geography of Ghana. London,
      Cambridge University Press.

HILL, Polly
  1963 Migrant Cocoa Farmers of Southern Ghana;
      a Study in Rural Capitalism. London, Cambridge
      University Press.

MANOUKIAN, Madeline
  1950 Akan and Ga-Adangme Peoples of the Gold Coast.
      London, International African Institute.

PRIESTLY, Margaret
  1969 West African Trade and Coast Societies;
      a Family Study. London, Oxford University Press.

WARD, William Ernest Frank
  1963 A History of Ghana. New York, Praeger.

WILLIAMSON, Sydney George
  1965 Akan Religion and the Christian Faith;
      a Comparative Study of the Impact of two Religions.
      Accra, Ghana Universities Press.

180

Writing Assignment

(Due end of Term) (Three pages, all well documented)

"A factor (not emphasized in the lectures) which
according to my reading played a significant part in
growth and stagnancy."

Sequence of Presentation

The Methodist Church of Gold Coast 1834-1954

God Builds a Bridge - Historical Antecedents
The Marvellous Beginning 1834-1839
Why the Slowdown 1840-1906?
The Statistical Picture
Expansion I   - The Cocoa Boom 1907-1914
Expansion II   - The Apolonian People Movement 1914
Expansion III   - Sampson Opon and Highly Intelligent
                    Mission 1920-1922

Ingathering Through Christian Education 1924-1954
The Supra-Tribal Church and Tribal Society

The Lutheran Mission in Liberia in Light of the Great Commission

The Facts of Its History
    The Master Plan
    The Mission Programs
    The Churches Established. The Stopped Church
A Common Interpretation of the Facts
A Church Growth Interpretation
Seven Steps Essential to a Break Out
Other Missions and Churches and Liberian Tribal
Movements
How Break-Out Has Occurred

CASE STUDIES IN CURRENT CHURCH HISTORY, SWM 667
CHRISTIANITY IN LATIN AMERICA, SWM 667d   Spring Quarter
Professor C. Peter Wagner   2 hours credit

Description of Course

Systematic study of denominations in Asia, Africa and
Latin America from their beginning to the present, with
special attention to the spiritual and environmental
factors contributing (1) to healthy expansion, and (2) to
slow growth or arrested development. In various terms
attention will be paid to China, Polynesia, Korea,
Ethiopia, Batakland, the Philippines, West Africa, Brazil,
Orissa, Mexico and Latin America.

182

Course Outline or Sequence of Presentation

(Note: daily topics subject to change at the professor's
discretion.)

Mar. 28 No classes. Professor participating in Evangelism
     30 in Depth pastors' conference in Southern Chile.

Alternate assignment for the several days when classes
are cancelled: Read one of the following church growth
studies and write a 600 to 800 word analytical report on
it. Report due April 11.

BENNETT, Charles
    1968 Tinder in Tabasco; a Study of Church Growth in
         Tropical Mexico. Grand Rapids, Eerdmans.

    1971 Man,Milieu, and Mission in Argentina; a Close
         Look at Church Growth. Grand Rapids, Eerdmans.

ENYART, Paul
         Friends in Central America. South Pasadena,
         William Carey Library.

NORDYKE, Quentin Homer
  1972 Animistic Aymaras and Church Growth. Newberg,
        Oregon, The Barclay Press.

READ, William Richard
  1965 New Patterns of Church Growth in Brazil. Grand
        Rapids, Eerdmans.

WAGNER, Peter
  1970 The Protestant Movement in Bolivia. South
        Pasadena, William Carey Library.

Apr. 4 The Origin and Development of the Latin American
        Theological Fraternity. Guest lecturer: Prof.
        Pablo Perez, Mexico.
    6   Theological Education by Extension in Latin
        America. Guest lecturer: Prof. Peter Savage,
        Bolivia.
    11 Latin America and Latin Americans.
    13 No class -- Biola Church Growth Seminar.   183
    18 The Latin American Social Revolution.
    20 No class -- Good Friday.
    25) No classes. Eastern Church Growth Seminar, Nyack.
    27) All reading reports should be completed this week.
May 2   Religious Roots in the Old World and the New.
    4   The Catholic Evangelization of Latin America.
    9   Contemporary Latin American Catholicism.
    11 Protestant Missions in Latin America.
    16 The Ecumenical Movement in Latin America.
    18 Class panel discussion on Evangelism in Latin
        America.
        Kenneth Strachan - Chinkyung Chung
        Mass evangelism - Curt Gedney
        The Evangelism in Depth Debate - John Mulkey
    23 Pentecostalism in Latin America.
    25 Class panel discussion on contemporary Latin
        American theology.
        Geneva 1966 and Medellín 1968 - Victor Monterroso
        Helder Cámara - Otto Kaiser
        Camilo Torres - Daniel Moncivaiz
    30 A proposal for Christian participation in the
        struggle for social justic.
June 1 Class panel discussion on contemporary Latin
        American theology.

Gustavo Gutiérrez - Wayne Weld.
Rubém Alves - George Fraser
Paulo Freire - Kenneth Rideout

Course Requirements

1. Reading
   1.1 Church growth study (see note under March 30
       above) Due April 11.
   1.2 Read 1000 pages of material not previously read
       from these lists:

READ, William, Victor MONTERROSO, and Harmon JOHNSON
1969 Latin American Church Growth. Grand Rapids,
      Eerdmans (400 pp.)
      [Required for all who have not read it.]

CLEARY, Edward L., edited by
1972 Shaping a New World, An Orientation to Latin
      America. Maryknoll, Orbis Books (300 pp.)
      [Required for all who have not lived in Latin
      America and recommended for the others.]

WAGNER,C. Peter
1970 Latin American Theology. Grand Rapids, Eerdmans
      (100 pp.)
      [Required for all who have not read it.]

COLONNESE, Louis M., edited by
1971 Concientization for Liberation. Washington,
      Division for Latin America United States Catholic
      Conference (300 pp.) [Required.]

The above books are basic for this course. After you
have adequately dealt with them, choose the balance of
your reading from the following:

LALIVE, Christian d'Epinay
       Haven of the Masses or
       El refugio de las masas.

184

SAVAGE, Peter, edited by
     El debate contemporáneo sobre la Biblia.

WILLEMS, Emilio
     Followers of the New Faith.

KESSLER, J. B. A.
     A Study of the Older Protestant Missions and
     Churches in Peru and Chile.

COSTAS, Orlando E.
     La iglesia y su misión evangelizadora.
"Christianismo y Sociedad"-- artículos escogidos.
          Or others, with professor's approval.

     1.3 Report on each book read on one page, single
          spaced, in this manner:
          1.31 Title, author, publisher, date.
          1.32 Your self-grade for your reading
                A = thoroughly read and underlined
                B = read, but somewhat rapidly
                C = speed read
          1.33 The number and title of the chapter you
                found most helpful.
          1.34 Two brief quotations from the chapter
                with your own response after each one.
          1.35 Hand in a summary page of all your
                reading showing a total of 1000 pages
                or more.
          1.36 All reports are to be handed in on May 2.

185

2.   Research project. As you will have seen from the
     course outline above, you have been assigned a topic
     for independent research. Build a bibliography on
     the subject, read all you can, write a report up to
     (but not exceeding) 6 pages (SWM standard format)
     summarizing your findings, and participate in the
     panel discussion on the date assigned. Your final
     paper is due on the same date.

Grading

     Church growth study report 20%, Reading reports 30%
     Research projects 40% and Class participation 10%=100%

CASE STUDIES IN CURRENT CHURCH HISTORY:
THE CHURCH IN INDIA, SWM 667f (767f)   Second Quarter
Professor Donald A. McGavran   Two (three) hours credit

Description of the Course

This course describes the socio-ecclesiastical realities which compose the Church in India. It distinguishes
four main types of church - Syrian, Conglomerate, People
Movement from Caste, and People Movement from Tribe. It
shows the varied forms of each which develop in different
environments and suggests how ministers, missionaries,
and other leaders of the Church should understand and use
these forms in nurturing existing congregations and extending the Christian movement.

Purpose of the Course

To help leaders of the Churches - in India and throughout the world -
a) to supplement theological understandings of the Church
with appreciation of the actual forms which empirical
(embodied) Churches take; and
b) to transcend vague sentimental formulations of methods
and goals by recognizing the forms of Church which God
has caused to emerge out of the social structures of India,
is blessing to the growth of His Church; and wills His
servants to develop.

Text Books and Bibliography

The following brief list, suggestive not exhaustive,
contains books on church and mission history, church
growth studies, Indian anthropology, and missiology.
Asterisked books are required reading - a fair amount from
each books so that the total done adds up to 1200 pages.
Doctoral candidates will complete 2000 pages. Double
asterisked books are required of them only.

ALTER and SINGH
    1961 The Church in Delhi, Nagpur, National Christian
          Council of India.

**ANDERSON and CAMPBELL
    1942 In the Shadow of the Himalayas (United Presby-
          terian - 85 years). Philadelphia, Judson Press,
          U. P. Board of Foreign Missions.

BECK, B. E. F.
    1972 Peasant Society in Konku: a study of right and
          left hand subcastes in South India. Vancouver,
          University of British Columbia.

BOALS, Barbara
    1963 The Church in the Kond Hills, Nagpur, National
          Christian Council of India.

CAMPBELL, E.
    1961 The Church in the Punjab, Nagpur, National
          Christian Council of India.

*CORNELIUS, Gollapalli
    1971 Urban Church Growth Among Telegu Baptists in
          South India. An unpublished M.A. thesis, Pasadena,
          Fuller Theological Seminary, School of World
          Mission.

*DYCK, Paul Irvin
    1970 Emergence of New Castes in India. An unpublished
          thesis, Winnipeg, University of Manitoba.

ESTBORN, Sigfrid
    1961 The Church Among the Tamils and the Telegus,
          Nagpur, National Christian Council of India.

**HUTTON, John Henry
    1961 Caste in India, its nature, function and origins.
          Bombay, New York, India Branch, Oxford Univeristy
          Press, Third Edition.

187

*LATOURETTE, Kenneth Scott
   1970 A History of The Expansion of Christianity,
         Volume 6, The Great Century: North Africa and
         Asia, 1800 A.D. to 1914 A.D.   Grand Rapids,
         Zondervan Publishing House.

**MANDELBAUM, David
   1972 Society in India (Volumes I and II), Los Angeles,
         University of California Press.

NEILL, Stephen
   1970 The Story of the Christian Church in India and
         Pakistan, Grand Rapids, Eerdmans.

**PAUL, Rajaiah
   1958 The First Decade (Church South India), Madras,
         Christian Literature Society.

**PICKET, J. Waskom
   1933 Christian Mass Movements in India, New York,
         Abingdon Press.
   * 1973 Church Growth and Group Conversion, South Pasadena,
            William Carey Library, Fifth Edition.

*RICHTER, Julius
   1908 The History of Missions in India, Edinburgh and
         London, Oliphant, Anderson and Ferrier.

*SCHMITTHENNER, S. W.
   1968 The Structure and Outreach of the Andhra Evangel-
         ical Lutheran Church. An unpublished manuscript,
         Pasadena, Fuller Theological Seminary, School of
         World Mission.

SEAMANDS, John Thompson
   1969 A Church Growth Study of the Methodist Church in
         the South India and Hyderabad Conferences. A
         Th.D. dissertation presented to the Faculty of
         Theology Senate of Serampore College. [Copy at
         Pasadena, Fuller Theological Seminary, School of
         World Mission.]

*STOCK, Frederick E.
  1968 Church Growth in West Pakistan, with special
        emphasis upon the United Presbyterian Church.
        An unpublished manuscript, Pasadena, Fuller
        Theological Seminary, School of World Mission.

*SUBBAMMA, Bathineni Venkata
  1970 New Patterns of Discipling Hindus; the next step
        in Andhra Pradesh, India. South Pasadena,
        William Carey Library.

Term Papers, Term Projects, and Examination

    Choose one of the four types of Church, which you do
not know from first-hand experience, and prepare a ten-
page account of an actual case. Give background, matrix,
graph of growth, causes of growth, stagnation and prescrip-
tion for future growth.

    Alternatives by way of projects are sometimes authorized
by the teacher.

    A final examination is given.

189

Sequence of Lectures

    Introductory Lecture
    The Madhya Pradesh Picture Typical of Much of India
    The Four Basic Types of Church
    The United Churches
    The Pure Conglomerate Church
    The One Dominant Caste Conglomerates
    The People Movement from Caste
    The People Movement from Tribe
    Potential People Movements
    The Andhra Situation
    Receptive Islands in Pakistan
    Samuel's Eight Types in Bombay
    Urban Church Growth - Madras
    Caste and Church Growth
    Seminaries in India and Viable Forms of the Church

VII. The World Church--Ecumenics

   670 ECUMENICS.

ECUMENICS, SWM 670   Quarter
Professor Arthur F. Glasser   2 hours credit

Description of Course

   The rise of a world Christian community and a
cooperative spirit among churches and missions as they
disciple the nations. Ecumenism as spirit of unity and
as relationship to a council. Afericasian churches and
Christian unity. Cooperative "disciplined planning" for
mission. Dangers and opportunities in the ecumenical
movement.

190

VIII. Biblical Studies and Theology

   (680-689)

   [Consult section I. Theory and Theology of Missions, page
86 for courses in Theology.]

IX. Research

    690 (790) RESEARCH.

    691 (791) READING AND CONFERENCE.

    692a,b. CHURCH GROWTH RESEARCH AND WRITING.

    693 (793) SPECIAL PROJECTS.

    695 (795) FIELD RESEARCH IN PROPAGATING THE GOSPEL.

RESEARCH, SWM 690 (790)
Faculty   Hours as arranged

191

Description of Course

    Guidance provided to individual missionaries or small groups pressing forward with research on their own problems in mission. Special attention paid to problems assigned to a missionary by his church or mission.

    SWM 690 may be used for credit in any section of the curriculum I to VIII for special work or for thesis.

READING AND CONFERENCE, SWM 691 (791)
Faculty   Hours as arranged

Description of Course

Reading, report and discussion designed to cover areas of special interest or those in which the student is weak.

The course is a flexible listing aimed at making the offerings more relevant for a wide range of candidates. It provides for any directed reading and discussion in special areas not covered in other courses on any given year, where coverage is required for projects, theses or dissertations, either library research to increase theoretical depth, or methodological direction for the collection and handling of data.

These are individual encounters with a professor; and the following are examples of reading and conference courses offered in recent years:

    Recent Anthropological Writing on New Guinea
    Historiography
    Sociology of Religion
    Spacial Diffusion for Computer Study
    Reconstruction of Cross-cultural World Views--Data
        Collecting
    The Theory of Latin American Anthropologists
    Writing in French on Brazilian Spiritism

[A number of the now regular courses were first introduced in this way--e.g., 634, 636, 730, 732, 734, 735, 736, etc. Sometimes when a case study (667) of some region is badly needed by only one man, it may be dealt with as a Reading and Conference course.]

CHURCH GROWTH RESEARCH AND WRITING, SWM 692a,b. 1st & 2nd
Professor Arthur F. Glasser and faculty   1 hour credit

Description of Course

   An analysis of research methodology for the planning
and construction of the thesis or dissertation, resources
in the Los Angeles area, appraising source materials, note
taking and documentation organization of materials with
particular attention given to graphs of growth during the
winter quarter. SWM 692a is offered in the fall quarter,
and SWM 692b is offered in the winter quarter. Both are
required for degree candidates.

   [For detailed syllabus, including a Thesis Flow Chart, 193
see Chapter Five, Guidelines for Research.]

SPECIAL PROJECTS, SWM 693 (793)
Faculty   Hours as arranged

Description of Course

In connection with one of the eight branches of the
discipline, graduate students under faculty guidance
pursue an investigation of substance.

FIELD RESEARCH IN PROPAGATING THE GOSPEL, SWM 695 (795)
Faculty   Hours as arranged

194

Description of Course

Directed research abroad, in accordance with plans and
programs worked out and approved during residence at SWM-
ICG, probing some aspect of mission which cannot be known
from lectures and books. Prerequisites required.

700 courses are considered doctoral level.

I. Theory and Theology of Missions

   713 MODERN THEOLOGIES OF MISSION.

   (714) THEOLOGY OF RELIGIOUS ENCOUNTER

MODERN THEOLOGIES OF MISSION, SWM 713   Quarter
Professor Arthur F. Glasser and/or   3 hours credit
Professor Donald A. McGavran

Description of Course

   Survey of the recent Evangelical, Ecumenical and
Roman Catholic theologies of mission.

195

THEOLOGY OF RELIGIOUS ENCOUNTER, SWM (714) Second Quarter
Professor Arthur F. Glasser   3 hours credit

Description of Course

   An investigation of the relation between Revelation and
Christianity in the context of elenctic missionary
encounter with men of other faiths, or no religious
allegiance. Particular attention will be given to
Roman Catholic and Protestant theologians throughout the
20th century.

   [See detailed syllabus for this course under SWM 614 (714).]

700 courses are considered doctoral level.

II. Apologetics of the Christian Mission
vis á vis non-Christian religions

720 ANIMISTIC BASES OF THE GREAT RELIGIONS.

ANIMISTIC BASES OF THE GREAT RELIGIONS, SWM 720
Professor Alan R. Tippett -- Third Quarter, 3 hours credit

Description of Course

Study of the animistic substructures of the religion of
the common people of Buddhist, Hindu, Islamic, Confucian
and Shinto lands, with special bearing on the relevance of
evangelistic methods and on conversion to Christianity.

Select Bibliography

DANIELOU, Jean
   1964 Introduction to the Great Religions.
       Notre Dame, Fides Publishers.

197

KITAGAWA, Joseph M.
   1968 Religions of the East. Philadelphia, Westminster.

VOS, Howard, ed.
   1959 Religions in a Changing World.
       Chicago, Moody Press.

TIPPETT, Alan R., Compiled by
   1971 Bibliography For Cross-Cultural Workers.
       South Pasadena, William Carey Library.

       A general bibliography for this course is
       found on pages 217-227 of the above volume.

Class Schedule: Class meets on Wed. and Fri. at 8:55 A.M.

Sequence of Presentation

Mar. 28, 30. General Introduction: The Nature of Religion.
       Animism? Its basic concepts, Christianity and
       Judaism among the Religions. Theological

Encounters. Problem of Syncretism. Distinction between Popular Religion and the Philosophical Super-structures. Place of Sacred
Literature and Faith. Enumeration of the type
of investigations to follow.

April 4,6,11,14. Popular Hinduism. Basic Concepts.
Historical Developments. How Hinduism claims
to be all-inclusive. Popular practice.
Animism in the Koran. Attitudes to Christianity.

April 18,20,25. Popular Buddhism. Basic concepts. Two
forms. Popular beliefs, manifestations and
confrontations.

April 27, May 2,4. Popular Islam. Basic concepts. Con-
trasts of orthodox teaching and popular practice.
Animism in the Koran. Attitudes to Christianity.

May 9,11.   Confucianism, Taoism, Shinto.

May 16.   Bahai, Universalism.

May 18,23.   Judaism, Christopaganism: (Latin American,
Asian, African and Western forms).

May 25   General discussion of Religious Super-structure
as against Popular Religion.

May 30   Nature of Current Non-Christian Religious
Reform Movements and their invasion of the
West.

June 1   Evaluation of the place of Christian Mission in
today's world: (1) Divine/Human Encounter,
(2) Man/World Encounter.

Requirement for the Course: Term paper required.

700 courses are considered doctoral level.

III. Mission Across Cultures--anthropology,
sociology, world revolution, secularism,
urbanization

730 CHRISTIANITY AND CULTURE I.

731 CHRISTIANITY AND CULTURE II.

732 CULTURE PERSONALITY AND THE GOSPEL.

733 CONVERSION WITH A MINIMUM OF DISLOCATION.

(734) URBAN ANTHROPOLOGY.

734 ANTHROPOLOGICAL THEORY.

735 ETHNOLINGUISTICS.

736 ANTHROPOLOGICAL BASIS OF LEADERSHIP.

737 INDIGENEITY.

738 MISSIONS AND SOCIAL CHANGE.

199

CHRISTIANITY AND CULTURE I, SWM 730   First Quarter
Professor Charles H. Kraft   3 hours credit

Description of Course

Explores the cultural concomitants of divine-human
interaction. Topics dealt with include man and culture,
God and culture, revelation and culture, the witness and
culture and the people of God and culture. Attention is
given to the development of a perspective of Christian
truth that combines the insights of theology with those
of anthropology.

200 Textbook

KRAFT, Charles H.
  1973 Christianity and Culture - I (Bound Manuscript)
        Pasadena, California, Fuller Theological Seminary.

  (Note: Chapters 1 and 2 are separate from the bound
  manuscript. These two chapters do away with Chapter
  3 in the bound manuscript, i.e. pages 33-46.

        Chapter 4 in the bound manuscript begins on
  page 47; Chapter 2 of the separate notes ends on
  page 46d.

        The Introduction and Bibliography are also
  to be purchased separately together with Chapter 19
  which does away with Chapter 20 in the bound manuscript.)

  (Additional Note: All chapters in the bound manuscript are to be renumbered one number less, i. e.
  Chapter 4 becomes Chapter 3, 5 becomes 4, etc.)

Course Requirements

1. Reading: Read the chapter before the class period
    during which we will be discussing the material in it.
    The manuscript is in rough shape--any comments with
    regard to either content or style will be appreciated.

2. Writing:
    a. A one-page interaction with each chapter is to be
        handed in each class period.
    b. A 10-15 page term paper examining in detail some
        topic dealt with in the manuscript will be re-
        quired before the end of the term. Follow both
        the leads given in the manuscript and your own
        inclinations in developing both the bibliography
        and the treatment of the topic. What I would
        like you to do is to wrestle a bit with the at-
        tempt to deal with the topic you choose in such
        a way that it is both biblically sound and readily
        perceived as relevant by the audience to which you
        wish to speak.

201

Course Outline or Sequence of Presentation

Oct. 3 Fearlessly into the Present - Chapter 1
    5   Culture, Conceptualization and Perception -Chap. 2
    10 Toward A Christian Ethnotheology - Chapter 3
                            (formerly Chapter 4)
    12 Theories of God and Culture - Chapter 4
    17 The Cultural and the Supracultural - Chapter 5
    19 The Bible and Relativity - Chapter 6
    24 Beyond Relativity - Chapter 7
    26 Molded by Culture - Chapter 8
    31 A Model of Culture - Chapter 9
Nov. 2 Revelation and Perception - Chapter 10
    7   The Personalness of Revelation - Chapter 11
    9   The Inspired Casebook - Chapter 12
    14 The Incarnation Our Model - Chapter 13
    16 Translating the Casebook - Chapter 14
    21 Transculturating the Message - Chapter 15
    23 Theologizing as a Dynamic Process - Chapter 16
    28 Dynamic Equivalence Churchness - Chapter 17
    30 Christian Conversion as a Dynamic Process -Chap.18

Dec. 5 Transforming Culture with God - Chapter 19
     7 Movements and Cultural Transformation - Chapter 20

Prepublication Draft: Comments Welcome

KRAFT, Charles H.
        Dynamic Theologizing, Studies in Christian
        Theology from an Anthropological Perspective.
        Pasadena, Fuller Theological Seminary, School of
        World Mission.

205

CHRISTIANITY AND CULTURE II, SWM 731   Second Quarter
Professor Donald McGavran   3 hours credit

Description of the Course

This course explores the relationship of Christianity
to the many cultures as men from each become Christian.
Adjustment, accommodation, syncretism, and possession, in
regard to customs, attitudes, beliefs, rituals, and
institutions, are considered against the authority of the
Bible. The extensive debate between Hinduism and Christianity illustrates the world-wide dimensions of the problem.

Purpose of the Course

206

As Christians of one culture carry their faith to men
of another, the Gospel they present usually has a foreign
aroma. Embodied Christianity is always a mixture of
essential Christianity with cultural Christianity of the
advocate. Hearers often resist it for cultural reasons.
This course is designed to help evangelists and missionaries discriminate between cultural trappings and essential Christian faith and appropriate the riches in other
cultures while remaining faithful to biblical truth. The
course should help Christians steer between the Scylla of
syncretism and the Charybdis of ineffective foreign formu-
lation posing as orthodoxy. Exact discriminating thinking
in light of the complex realities of the situation is encouraged.

As Christianity spreads into the myriad cultures of
Earth, it correctly adjusts to each; but what are the
limits of such adjustment? As Christianity becomes the
religion of increasing numbers in every culture of every
continent how does it influence and change every element
of the culture? These are the two foci around which
this course revolves.

Reading Required

From the bibliography below, select about 1200 pages which suit your interests. Read these saying: As Christianity spreads through the cultures of mankind, it correctly adjusts to each, but what are the limits of such adjustment? Feel free to add to these books and articles, others along similar lines. The sixty volumes of the International Review of Missions are rich in articles on this subject which has always lain at the heart of the missionary enterprise. Look through many volumes and read as many articles as possible. They will be more directly on the subject than many of the books. Asterisked books must be read.

Elenctics (*one book)

THOMAS, Madathilparampil M.
   1969 The Acknowledged Christ of the Indian
         Renaissance. London, S.C.M. Press.

SHARPE, Eric J.
   1965 Not to Destroy but to Fulfil; the contribution
         of J. N. Farquhar to Protestant missionary
         thought in India before 1914. Lund, Gleerup.

NEILL, Stephen Charles
   1961 Christian Faith and Other Faiths; the Christian
         dialogue with other religions. London, New
         York, Oxford University Press.

APPLETON, George
   1958 Christian Approach to the Buddhist. London,
         Edinburgh House Press.

ROGERS, Edward
   1959 The Christian Approach to the Communist.
         London, Edinburgh House Press.

WEST, Charles C.
   1958 Communism and the Theologians; study of an
         encounter. Philadelphia, Westminster Press.

The Authority and Inspiration of the Bible (* one book)

PACKER, J. I.
1965 God Speaks to Man. Philadelphia, Westminster
      Press.

HAMILTON, Kenneth M.
1971 Words and The Word. Grand Rapids, Eerdmans.

HUGHES, Robert John III
1958 An Inductive Inquiry into the Biblical Doctrine
      of the Inspiration of the Scripture. Pasadena,
      Fuller Theological Seminary, Th.M. Thesis.

PINNOCK, Clark H.
1971 Biblical Revelation--The Foundation of Christian
      Theology. Chicago, Moody Press.

WARFIELD, Benjamin Breckinridge
1948 The Inspiration and Authority of the Bible.
      Philadelphia, Presbyterian and Reformed.

208

The Clash of Christianity and Cultures

AJAYI, J. F. Ade
1965 Christian Missions in Nigeria, 1841-1891; the
      making of a new élite. Evanston, Illinois,
      Northwestern University Press.

*BURKLE and ROTH
      Indian Voices in Today's Theological Debate.

DEVANANDAN, Paul David
1944 "Whither Theology in Christian India."
      International Review of Missions, 121.

*HARGREAVES, Cecil
1972 Asian Christian Thinking. Indian SPCK, Delhi-6,
      Lucknow, U. P., Lucknow Publishing House.

HOLLENWEGER, Walter J.
1971 "Flowers and Songs in Mexico." International
      Review of Missions, April.

KRUYT, A. C.
 1924 "Christianity in the Celebes." International
 Review of Missions, 267.

KULANDRAM, Sabapathy
 1964 Grace; A Comparative Study of the Doctrine in
 Christianity and Hinduism. London, Lutterworth
 Press.

McGAVRAN, Donald A., (ed.)
 1969 Church Growth Bulletin: Volumes I to V. South
 Pasadena, William Carey Library. [pp 82-84,
 170-174, 244-250, 263-264].

*MONAHAN, C. Dermott
 1945 "The Christian Church and Indigenous Culture."
 International Review of Missions, 397.

OLDHAM,J. H.
 1920 "Nationality and Mission." International
 Review of Missions, 372.

SCHALWIJK, J. M. W.
 1971 "Mission in the Caribbean." International
 Review of Missions, April.

SHROPSHIRE, Denys
 1942 "Primitive Marriage and European Law."
 International Review of Missions, 211.

SMALLEY, William A.
 1958 "Cultural Implication of the Indigenous Church."
 Practical Anthropology, Volume 5, Number 2,
 pp 51-65.

*SMITH, Edwin W.
 1941 "Association and Assimilation." International
 Review of Missions, 235.

SPEER, Robert Elliott
 1933 The Finality of Jesus Christ. New York,
 Fleming H. Revell Company.

*TIPPETT, Alan R., John MBITI, and Lloyd KWAST
   1972 "Part Two: Anthropological Issues" in
         Crucial Issues in Missions Tomorrow, edited
         by Donald A. McGAVRAN. Chicago, Moody Press.
         [pp 125 - 171]

VISSER'T Hooft, Willem Adolph
   1963 No Other Name; the Choice between Syncretism
         and Christian Universalism. Philadelphia,
         Westminster Press.

Term Papers

1. Due mid-term: "My Major Problems in Christianity and
   Cultures." In the light of the readings, discussion
   and lectures, describe the problems which appear most
   serious for your church planting, your field, your
   training of evangelism.
2. Due end of term: "How I Propose to Use the Bible in
   Judging Whether Cultural Adaptations are Legitimate
   or Not."
Both these papers should be written to fit a cluster of
congregations with which you have worked on the field.

Sequence of Lectures

Week One   Six Beginning Considerations
             The Fundamental Issues (A & B)

Week Two   Can there be "National" Theologies?
             Suggested Guide Lines for Missionary Action

Week Three   Components of Culture One Key to Understanding
             Keeping Backward People Down by Honoring Their
             Culture

Week Four   A Diagramatic Understanding of the Dynamic
             Relationship of Christianity to Cultures
             Applying Biblical Principles to Cultural
             Adaptations

Week Five   The Bible Basis for Evaluating Cultural
             Components
             Needs for Discriminating Thinking

210

Week Six   The Philosophy and Context of Indian
              Christian Theology (R. H. S. Boyd)

Week Seven   The Theological Task of the Church in
              India (J. Russell Chandran)

Week Eight   Modernization of Traditional Societies
              (M. M. Thomas)

Week Nine   Indigenization and Indigenous Theology
              (Asian Christian Thinking, Chapter 9, 10)

              Review and Summary.

CULTURE PERSONALITY AND THE GOSPEL,SWM 732--Spring Quarter
Professor Charles H. Kraft   3 hours credit

Description of Course

Examination of cross-cultural studies in psychological
anthropology, interactions of culture and the thought,
emotions, and actions of individuals, the resulting
culture patterns and configurations, and the bearing of
these on church planting and growth.

Textbooks:

ARONOFF, Joel
    1967 Psychological Needs and Cultural Systems.
          Princeton, New Jersey, D. Van Nostrand Company.

HONIGMANN, John J.
    1967 Personality in Culture. New York, Harper & Row.

212

Course Requirements:
1. Readings as assigned
2. A term project with a twenty-page writeup on:
   a. Culture, Personality and Church Growth Among
      the _____
      (deal with either your own work or that
      described by Aronoff)
   b. Some other appropriate study

Course Outline:

(March 23) - I Introduction
                Course details
                Discuss Honigmann, chapter 1

(March 30) - II The Field of Culture and Personality
                Honigmann, chapters 2-4 (pps. 35-129)

(April 6) -   Honigmann, chapters 5-7 (pps. 130-213)

(April 13) -   Honigmann, chapters 8-10 (pps. 214-319)

(April 20) -   Honigmann, chapters 11-13 (pps. 320-425)

(April 27) -   Session with Professor James A. Oakland
                of Graduate School of Psychology
                (Prepare three questions each concern-
                ing the psychological aspects of the
                subject matter to direct to Dr. Oakland)

(May 4)   - III Case Study in Culture and Personality
                 Aronoff, chapters 1-6 (pps. 1-113)

(May 11) -   Aronoff, chapters 7-10 (pps. 114-222)

(May 18) - IV Discussion of Culture, Personality and
                Church Growth

(May 25) - Term Project Reports and Discussion   213

CONVERSION WITH A MINIMUM OF DISLOCATION, SWM 733
Professor Charles H. Kraft   3 hours credit

Description of Course

   Analysis of the anthropological, theological and
psychological factors relating to conversion, with focus
on distinguishing cultural from supracultural elements,
so that missionaries may encourage conversion truly
Christian, yet culturally appropriate.

Textbooks

BARCLAY, William
   1964 Turning to God: A Study of Conversion in the
         Book of Acts and Today. Grand Rapids, Baker
         Book House.

MASLOW, Abraham H.
   1970 Religions, Values and Peak-Experiences. New York,
         The Viking Press.

PRACTICAL ANTHROPOLOGY
         Volume 10, numbers 4 and 6; Volume 15, numbers
         4 and 5; Volume 16, number 1. Tarrytown, N. Y.,
         Practical Anthropology.

SMALLEY, William A., Editor
   1967 Readings in Missionary Anthropology. Tarrytown,
         N. Y., Practical Anthropology.

TIPPETT, Alan R.
   1970 Church Growth and the Word of God, The Biblical
         Basis of the Church Growth Viewpoint. Grand
         Rapids, Wm. B. Eerdmans.

TIPPETT, Alan R.
 1971   People Movements in Southern Polynesia, Studies
        in the Dynamics of Church-planting and Growth in
        Tahiti, New Zealand, Tonga, and Samoa. Chicago,
        Moody Press.

        "The Role of the Missionary with Relation to
        Conversion Patterns" from Unpublished Manuscript
        For Classroom Use Only.

        "Missionary Attitudes and Church Growth" from
        Unpublished Manuscript For Classroom Use Only.

        "Church Growth and Time Perspective" from
        Unpublished Manuscript For Classroom Use Only.

Course Outline or Sequence of Presentation

Jan. 4 Introduction - Based on SHARPE, "The Problem of
        Conversion..." Reading List, part 1, Biblico-
        Theological Perspectives   215
     9 Skim read BARCLAY, Turning to God.
    11 Read several of the articles on Reading List,
        part 1.
        Psychological Perspectives
    16 Read MASLOW, Religions, Values and Peak-Experiences
        (skim-read).
    18 Discussion Session with Professor Jack W. Rogers
        on Theology of Conversion--Prepare one or more
        questions on this topic to ask him to comment on.
    23 Read articles on Reading List, part 2, plus Kraft's
        reply to Oden lectures.
    25 Discussion session with Professor James A. Oakland
        on Psychology of Conversion--Prepare one or more
        questions on this topic to ask him to comment on.
        Anthropological Perspectives
    30 Read any three articles on your area (or one of
        your choice) from Area Reading List--Discussion
        of these in class.
Feb. 1 Write 2-3 pages listing of questions you want
        answered by this course (outline plus comment
        format)--Discussion of these in class.

Ethnotheological Perspectives
Feb. 6 Christianity and Culture--Read or Review materials
        on Reading List, part 3.
     8 Skim-read TIPPETT, Church Growth and the Word of
        God, especially section II.
    13 Skim-read TIPPETT, People Movements in Southern
        Polynesia--first half.
    20 Skim-read TIPPETT, People Movements in Southern
        Polynesia--last half.
    22 Conversion and Incorporation--Read Reading List,
        parts 6 and 7.
    27 Conversion and Incorporation--Read Reading List,
        parts 6 and 7.
Mar. 1 Conversion, Culture Change and the Missionary--
        Reading List, parts 8 and 9.
     6 Conversion, Culture Change and the Missionary--
        Reading List, parts 8 and 9.

        Putting it All Together
     8 Submit a paper analyzing your own conversion/
        affirmation from this perspective (3-5 pages).
    13 Submit a paper dealing with questions you wrote
        up for February 1 (plus anything else) in terms of
        1. Your (cross-cultural) experience
        2. Insights derived from this course
        (The paper should be a maximum of 15 pages.)

216

Term Papers

    The two papers required for this course are described
above at the conclusion of Course Outline--Putting it All
Together.

Reading List and Bibliography

1. Biblico-Theological Perspective
    *BARCLAY, Turning to God

    *BRANDON, Owen
        1959 The Battle for the Soul; aspect of religious
              conversion. Philadelphia, Westminister Press.
        1965 Christianity from Within; a frank discussion
              religion, conversion, evangelism and revival.
              London, Hodder and Stoughton, (pp. 76-92).

LOEFFLER, Paul
  1967 "Conversion in an Ecumenical Setting,"
        Ecumenical Review, 19:252-260.

NEILL, Stephen Charles
  1950 "Conversion," Scottish Journal of Theology,
        3:352-362.

NOCK, A. D.
  1961 Conversion; the old and the new in religion
        from Alexander the great to Augustine of
        Hippo. London, Oxford University Press. (pp 1-16)

PATERSON, William
  1939 Conversion. London, Hodder and Stoughton,
        (pp. 97-111).

SHARPE, Eric J.
  1970 "The Problem of Conversion in Recent
        Missionary Thought," The Evangelical Quarterly,
        41:221-231.   217

2. Psychological Perspective

HILTNER, Seward
  1966 "Toward a Theology of Conversion in the Light
        of Psychology," Pastoral Psychology, 17:166,
        Sept. pp 35-42.

LLOYD-JONES, Martin
  1959 Conversions: Psychological and Spiritual.
        London, Intervarsity Fellowship Press.

SCROGGS & DOUGLAS
  1967 "Issues in the Psychology of Religious
        Conversion," Journal of Religion and Health,
        6:204-216.

Ethnotheological Perspective

3. Christianity and Culture

KRAFT, Charles H.
1963 "Christian Conversion or Cultural Conversion,"
Practical Anthropology, 10:179-187.

NIEBUHR, Helmut Richard
1951 Christ and Culture. New York, Harper, pp 27-
29, 32-44, 117-123, 149-158, 190-196.
[Reprint in Cell, Religion and Contemporary
Western Culture, pp 47-64]

Cultural and Supracultural Aspects of Conversion/
Incorporation

KRAFT, Charles H.
"Communicating the Supracultural Gospel to
Culture-Bound Man"

SAMARIN, William J.
1954 "Theology and/or Anthropology," Practical
Anthropology, 1:120-121.

SMALLEY, William A.
1955 "Culture and Superculture," Practical Anthropology, 2:58-71.

WONDERLY William L, and Eugene A. NIDA
1963 "Cultural Differences and Communication of
Christian Values," Practical Anthropology,
10:241-258.

4. TIPPETT, Alan R.
1970 Church Growth and the Word of God - (textbook)

5. Group Conversion

PICKETT, Jarrell Waskom, et al.
1956 Church Growth and Group Conversion. Lucknow,
Lucknow Publishing House.

6. Conversion and Incorporation

LOEWEN, Jacob A.
1968 "Socialization and Social Control..."
Practical Anthropology, 15:145-156.

LOEWEN, Jacob A.
  1968 "The Indigenous Church and Resocialization,"
        Practical Anthropology, 15:193-204.
  1969 "Socialization and Conversion in the Ongoing
        Church," Practical Anthropology, 16:1-17.

WIENS, Delbert
  1965 New Wineskins for Old Wine, A Study of the
        Mennonite Brethren Church, Hillsboro, Kansas,
        Mennonite Brethren Publishing House.

7. Conversion/Incorporation and the Indigenous Church

SMALLEY, William A.
  1958 "Cultural Implications of an Indigenous
        Church," Practical Anthropology, 5:51-65.
        [Also in SMALLEY, William A., Readings in
        Missionary Anthropology, pp 147-156 -textbook]

TIPPETT, Alan R.   219
  1969 Verdict Theology in Missionary Theory,
        Lincoln, Ill., Lincoln Christian College
        Press, pp 126-141.

8. Conversion/Incorporation and Culture Change

KIETZMAN, Dale W.
  1958 "Conversion and Culture Change," Practical
        Anthropology, 5:203-210.
        [Also in SMALLEY, William A., Readings in
        Missionary Anthropology, pp 124-131 -textbook]

TIPPETT, Alan R., Verdict Theology, pp 95-125.

9. Conversion/Incorporation and the Advocate

TIPPETT, Alan R.   --from Unpublished Manuscript:
        "The Role of the Missionary with Relation to
        Conversion Patterns,"
        "Missionary Attitudes and Church Growth,"
        "Church Growth and Time Perspective."

General Readings on Conversion

BRANDENFELS, Fred
1963 Some Sociological Factors in Group Conversion
      to Christianity, M.A. Thesis, Hartford
      Seminary Foundation.

KIETZMEN, Dale W.
1958 "Conversion and Culture Change," Practical
      Anthropology, 5:203-210.
      [Also in SMALLEY, William A., Readings in
      Missionary Anthropology, pp 124-131 -textbook]

KRAFT, Charles H.
1963 "Christian Conversion or Cultural Conversion,"
      Practical Anthropology, 10:179-187.

LOEWEN, Jacob, A.
1968 "Socialization and Social Control..."
      Practical Anthropology, 15:145-156.
1968 "The Indigenous Church and Resocialization,"
      Practical Anthropology, 15:193-204.
1969 "Socialization and Conversion in the Ongoing
      Church," Practical Anthropology, 16:1-7.

NEWBIGIN, Lesslie
1969 The Finality of Christ, London, SCM Press Ltd.,
      (pp 88-115).

NOBLE, Lowell L.
1962 "A Culturally Relevant Witness to Animists,"
      Practical Anthropology, 9:220-222.

SMALLEY, William A.
1958 "Cultural Implications of an Indigenous Church,"
      Practical Anthropology, 5:51-65.
      [Also in SMALLEY, William A., Readings in
      Missionary Anthropology, pp 147-156 -textbook]

WALLACE, Anthony F. C.
1956 "Revitalization Movements," American Anthro-
      pology, 58:264-281, Bobs-Merrill Reprint A-230.

220

Latin America

LOEWEN, Jacob A.
1965 "The Way to First Class..." Practical Anthro-
      pology, 12:193-209.

SALER, B.
1965 "Religious Conversion and Self-Aggrandizement..."
      Practical Anthropology, 12:107-114.

WONDERLY, William L and Eugene A. NIDA
1963 "Cultural Differences and Communication of
      Christian Values," Practical Anthropology,
      10:241-258.

Africa

ANDERSON, E.
1968 Churches at the Grass-Roots, London, Lutterworth,
      (pp 44-53, 124-142, 223-227, 248-252).   221

HORTON, R.
1971 "African Conversion," Africa, 41:85-108.

HUTCHINSON, B.
1957 "Some Social Consequences of 19th Century
      Missionary Activity Among the South African
      Bantu," Africa, 27:16-175.
      [reprinted in part in Practical Anthropology,
      6:67-76, 1959]

MESSENGER, John C., Jr.
1959 "The Christian Concept of Forgiveness and
      Anang Morality," Practical Anthropology,
      6:97-103.
      [Also in SMALLEY, William A., Readings in
      Missionary Anthropology, pp 180-186 -textbook]

      "Reinterpretations of Christian and Indigenous
      Belief in a Nigerian Nativist Church," Practical
      Anthropology, 62:268-278.
1955 "Religious Acculturation Among the Anang Ibibio"
      in Bascom and Herskovits, Continuity and Change
      in African Cultures. U. of Chicago, (pp 279-299)

REYBURN, William D.
  1957 "The Transformation of God and the Conversion
        of Man," Practical Anthropology, 4:185-194.
        [Also in SMALLEY, William A., Readings in
        Missionary Anthropology, pp 26-30]
  1958 "Meaning and Restructuring," Practical
        Anthropology, 5:79-82.
        [Also in SMALLEY, William A., Readings in
        Missionary Anthropology, pp 171-173]

ROSS, E.
  1955 "Impact of Christianity in Africa," The Annals
        298:161-169.

SANGREE, W. H.
  1959 "The Structure and Symbol Underlying 'Conver-
        sion' in Bantu Tiriki," Practical Anthropology,
        6:132-134.

SCHAPERA, I.
  1958 "Christianity and the Tswana," Journal of
        Royal Anthropological Institute, 88:1-9
        and OTTENBERG, S. & P, Cultures and Societies
        of Africa, pp 489-503.

TRIMINGHAM, S. S.
  1955 The Christian Church and Islam in West Africa,
        London, SCM Press, pp 30-53.

India-Pakistan

ANNETT, E. A.
  1920 Conversion in India, Madras, Christian
        Literature Society for India.

INNIGER, M. W.
  1963 "Mass Movements and Individual Conversion in
        Pakistan," Practical Anthropology, 10:122-126.

PICKETT, Jarrell Waskom
  1933 Christian Mass Movements in India, Lucknow,
        Lucknow Publishing House, pp 319-348.

222

PICKET, Jarrell Waskom
1960   Christ's Way to India's Heart, Lucknow,
       Lucknow Publishing House, (pp22-32).

SINGH, H. J.
1967   "Christian Conversion in a Hindu Context,"
       Ecumenical Review, 19:302-306.

SAHAY, K. N.
1968   "Impact of Christianity on the Uraon of the
       Chainpur Belt in Chotanagpur: An Analysis
       of Its Cultural Processes," American
       Anthropologist, 70:923-942.

Pacific

BACDAYAN, A. S.
       "Religious Conversion and Social Change: A
       Northern Luzon Case," Practical Anthropology,
       17:119-127.

TIPPETT, Alan R.
1967   Solomon Islands Christianity, A Study in
       Growth and Obstruction. London, Lutterworth
       Press. (pp 42-44, 57-62, 102-111, 319-329)

VICEDOM, G. F.
1962   "An Example of Group Conversion," Practical
       Anthropology, 9:123-128.

223

URBAN ANTHROPOLOGY, SWM (734)   Second Quarter
Professor A. R. Tippett   3 hours credit

Description of Course

A seminar for interaction. Cross-cultural urban and
industrial studies of places open for evangelism today,
the character of religious encounter, sociological and
economic factors, methodological procedures for investigating the possibilities of church planting.

[SWM 634 is the detailed syllabus for SWM (734).]

224

ANTHROPOLOGICAL THEORY, SWM 734   First Quarter
Professor Charles H. Kraft   3 hours credit

Description of Course

Historical development of encounters in anthropological theory as it bears on such matters as the conceptualization of culture, social structure, innovation and
social change, primitive religion, culture and personality, diffusion, function, stress situations, and how this
theory relates to missiological principles and techniques
in cross-cultural religious processes, natural and
directed.

Bibliography: Textbooks (major texts asterisked)   225

BEATTIE, John   --(Be)
  1964 Other Cultures, Aims, Methods, and Achievements
        in Social Anthropology. New York, The Free Press.

BIDNEY, David   --(Bi)
  1967 Theoretical Anthropology. New York, Schocken
        Books.

CALVERTON, V. F.   --(C)
  1931 The Making of Man: An Outline of Anthropology.
        New York, Random House (The Modern Library).

*HARRIS, Marvin   --(Hr)
  1968 The Rise of Anthropological Theory, A History of
        Theories of Culture. New York, Thomas Y. Crowell
        Company.

*HAYS, H. R.   --(Hy)
  1958 From Ape to Angel. New York, Knopf.

*KARDINER, A. and E. PREBLE   --(K&P)
  1961 They Studied Man. Cleveland, World Publishing Co.

KROEBER, A. L. and T. T. WATERMAN   --(K&W)
  1931 Source Book in Anthropology. New York, Harcourt,
        Brace and Company.

*LOWIE, Robert H.   --(L)
  1937 History of Ethnological Theory. New York, Farrar
        and Rinehart.

Course Outline:

Oct. 3, 5   Overview
     10, 12   I   Classical Evolutionism
                 II Reactions to Evolutionism
     17   a. Miscellaneous Critiques
     19, 24, 26   b. Historical Particularism
     31, Nov. 2   c. Diffusionism
Nov. 7, 9   d. French Sociology
     14, 16, 21   e. Functionalism and Social
                       Anthropology
     23, 28   III Culture and Personality
     30   IV Ethnoscience
Dec. 5   V   Neo-evolutionism

Topics, Persons and Readings

Topics	Important Persons	Readings
1. Introduction		Bi 3-53; Be 16-48; Hy vii-xv; K&P 225-37
2. Classical Evolutionism	Spencer, Morgan, Maine, Tylor, Frazer	Hr 108-216; Hy 3-130; K&P 15-94; L 19-127; Bi 183-214; C 168-81, 635-59, 693-713; K&W 388-97, 464-71.
3. Reactions to Evolutionism		
a. Miscellaneous Critiques	Lang, Marett, Briffault	Hy 133-224; C 203-33, 485-564, 761-70.
b. Historical Particularism	Boas	Hr 250-318; Bi 215-23; Hy 227-68, C 113-56; K&W 332-7, 374-87.
	Kroeber, Lowie	Hr 319-72; Bi 252-60, 55-62; K&P 163-77;

226

Topics	Important Persons	Readings
		Hy 329-36; C 714-60; K&W 304-9; 472-88.
c. Diffusionism	G. Elliot Smith, W. Schmidt, Rivers, Wissler	Hr 373-92; L 156-95; Hy 282-93; C 234-48, 393-465, 818-27; K&W 505-11, 524-34.
d. French Sociology	Durkheim, Levi-Strauss	L 196-227; Hr 464-513 K&P 95-116; Hy 294-305, 390-93; C 249-80, 771-804.
e. Functionalism and Social Anthropology	Malinowski, Radcliffe-Brown	Hr 514-67; L 228-47; K&P 140-62; Hy 309-28 Be 49-64; C 565-85; K&W 267-83.
4. Culture and Personality	(Sapir), (Linton), Benedict, Mead, Kluckhohn	Hr 393-463; Hy 336-67 K&P 178-86; C 586-602, 805-17; K&W 317-31, 545-62.
5. Ethnoscience	(Sapir, Whorf), Goodenough, Lounsbury	Hr 568-604.
6. Neo-evolutionism	White, Steward	Hr 634-87.

227

Course Requirements:

1. Reading - Approximately fifty pages per class period
    selected from the above listings.

2. Writing - Each member of the class is to produce one
    in-depth writeup of a given person or theoretical
    school. This is to be dittoed so that each member of
    the class has a copy of the material given in class.
    These writeups should provide such information as
    the following:

    > Person(s) and his/their background(s);
    > The major problem(s) he/they addressed himself/
    > themselves to; Were they reacting against any
    > approach?; Characteristics of their approach;
    > Key ideas and methods of the approach;
    > Contribution to anthropological theory;
    > Contribution (theoretical or actual) to missio-
    > logical theory and/or practice; Bibliography.

ETHNOLINGUISTICS, SWM 735   Spring Quarter
Professor Charles H. Kraft   3 hours credit

Description of Course

A study of the interrelationships between language and
culture. Topics covered include Bible translation, discovery of a culture's values through the study of its
folklore and mythology, language acquisition, bilingualism
and indigenous hymnology.

Textbooks:

BURLING, Robbins
  1970 Man's Many Voices. N.Y., Holt, Rinehart & Winston.

NIDA, Eugene A., and Charles R. TABER
  1969 The Theory and Practice of Translating, Helps
       For Translators. Leiden, Published for the
       United Bible Societies by E. J. Brill.

PRACTICAL ANTHROPOLOGY
       Volume 16, numbers 4 & 5 (Mythology)
       Volume 9, number 6 (Musicology)
       Tarrytown, N. Y., Practical Anthropology.

Course Requirements:

1. Readings as assigned
2. A term project studying either individually or as a
   part of a team:
   a. The 41 problems in NIDA & TABER (answer,
      duplicate and distribute in class on the day we
      discuss the given chapters)
   b. Some aspect of the folklore (or other ethno-
      linguistic material) of your people
   c. The Solomonic (or other) Proverbs in the Bible

d. The Parables from an ethnolinguistic perspective
e. Other Biblical materials
3. Produce a report of your project and duplicate for
each member of the class. Some or all of these
reports will be discussed during the final two
sessions of the class. Some will be due by May 18,
the rest by May 25.

Course Outline or Sequence of Presentation:

Mar. 23 I   Introduction
                 Course Outline, Texts, Term Projects
                 Methodology of Ethnolinguistics, Hausa
                 Folklore
     30 II The Subject Matter of Ethnolinguistics
                 BURLING, chapters 1-7 (pp. 1-102)
Apr. 6   BURLING, chapters 8-13 (pp. 103-200)
     13 III Myth and Mission
                 Practical Anthropology, volume 16,
                 numbers 4 & 5
     20 IV Case Study: Bible Translation
                 NIDA & TABER, chapters 1, 2 (pp. 1-32),
                 Problems 1-7
     27   NIDA & TABER, chapters 3-5 (pp. 33-98),
                 Problems 8-32
May   4   NIDA & TABER, chapters 6-8 (pp. 99-173),
                 Problems 33-41
     11 V   Musicology
                 Practical Anthropology, volume 9, number 6
     18 &
     25   Term Project Reports and Discussion.

229

ANTHROPOLOGICAL BASIS OF LEADERSHIP, SWM 736   2nd Quarter
Professor Alan R. Tippett   3 hours credit

Description of Course

A study in leadership in different societies, the significance of status, roles, authority and decision-making patterns in stable and changing society, the nature and function of education, the justification of directed change, what these concepts mean for the church-planter, and meeting the cultural needs of an indigenous church at different periods of its growth.

Bibliography

TIPPETT, A. R., Compiled by
1971   Bibliography For Cross-Cultural Workers.
       South Pasadena, William Carey Library.

A general bibliography for this course on "Patterns of Leadership and Authority" is found on pages 99 - 107 of the above volume.

Required Reading

Four one-page book reports on four distinct case studies will be required. Choose any four but one from each group:

African Society
COHEN, Ronald
           The Kanuri of Bornu. New York, Holt, Rinehart and Winston, Inc.
GAMST, Frederick C.
           The Qemant: A Pagan-Hebraic Peasantry of Ethiopia. N.Y., Holt, Rinehart and Winston, Inc.

KUPER, Hilda
  1963   The Swazi: A South African Kingdom. New York,
          Holt, Rinehart and Winston, Inc.
MIDDLETON, John
          The Lugbara of Uganda. New York, Holt,
          Rinehart and Winston, Inc.
UCHENDU, Victor C.
          The Igbo of Southeast Nigeria. New York,
          Holt, Rinehart and Winston, Inc.

Asian Society
DENTAN, Robert Knox
          The Semai: A Nonviolent People of Malaya.
          New York, Holt, Rinehart and Winston, Inc.
DOZIER, Edward P.
          The Kalinga of Northern Luzon, Philippines.
          New York, Holt, Rinehart and Winston, Inc.
FRASER, Thomas M., Jr.
          Fishermen of South Thailand: The Malay
          Villagers. N.Y., Holt, Rinehart and Winston   231
VON FURER-HAIMENDORF., Christoph
          The Konyak Nagas: An Indian Frontier Tribe.
          New York, Holt, Rinehart and Winston, Inc.
WILLIAMS, Thomas Rhys
          The Dusun: A North Borneo Society.
          New York, Holt, Rinehart and Winston, Inc.

European and American Society
DUNN, Stephen P. and DUNN, Ethel
          The Peasants of Central Russia. New York,
          Holt, Rinehart and Winston, Inc.
FRIEDL, Ernestine
  1962   Vasilika: A Village in Modern Greece.
          New York, Holt, Rinehart and Winston, Inc.
HOSTETLER, John A., and HUNTINGTON, Gertrude Enders
          The Hutterites in North America. New York,
          Holt, Rinehart and Winston, Inc.
LEWIS, Oscar
          Tepoztlan: Village in Mexico. New York,
          Holt, Rinehart and Winston, Inc.
MADSEN, William
          The Mexican-Americans of South Texas.
          New York, Holt, Rinehart and Winston, Inc.

One of the following societies
BEALS, Alan R.
        Gopalpur: A South Indian Village. New York,
        Holt, Rinehart and Winston, Inc.
DOWNS, James F.
        The Two Worlds of the Washo. New York, Holt,
        Rinehart and Winston, Inc.
DOZIER, Edward P.
        Hano: A Tewa Indian Community in Arizona.
        New York, Holt, Rinehart and Winston, Inc.
HOEBEL, E. Adamson
        The Cheyennes: Indians of the Great Plains.
        New York, Holt, Rinehart and Winston, Inc.
KLIMA, George J.
        The Barabaig: East African Cattle-Herders.
        New York, Holt, Rinehart, and Winston, Inc.
PIERCE, Joe E.
  1964 Life in a Turkish Village. New York, Holt,
        Rinehart and Winston, Inc.
TRIGGER, Bruce G.
        The Huron: Farmers of the North. New York,
        Holt, Rinehart, and Winston, Inc.

232

Examination: There will be no EXAM.

Sequence of Presentation

1. INTRODUCTORY

Scope of the Course: definitions, concepts to be used,
historical and anthropological orientation, periods of
development of leadership training, source material,
course requirements, aims and objects, and application
of field situations.

2. ANTHROPOLOGICAL BASE - Leadership and Social
                                    Organization
Variety of Human Organization from a State to a Stateless
Society, the importance of leadership patterns for the
perpetuity of society, wide differences from our own
patterns. What does this mean with respect to the imposi-
tion of western denominational patterns on such societies?

The Concept of Roles: Analysis of a specific society
demonstrating the various levels where leadership is involved, relationship of leadership roles to social structure. What would this mean to an indigenous church?

Supernatural Sanctions and Leadership: Comparison of
specific patterns. What does this mean when Christianity
is injected into such societies?

The Role of Elders in a Gerontocracy: Using material
from a specific society questions and problems will be
posed to show what this type of situation means with
regard to church leadership.

The Role of the Chief: Various societies with chiefly
patterns will be compared, leading to discussion of
authority and how it bears on the stability and function-
ing of these societies, the significance of group acceptance and what this means for the church-planter. Why
should the missionary understand the authority patterns
of his people?

233

Influence of Acculturation on Leadership. Leadership in
western society, how it compares and differs from that in
communal society, study of the Self Help Program.

Education as Enculturation: Various forms of status,
graduation by initiation, function of initiation, how
society finds, creates and trains its own leaders,
achieved and ascribed status. What does this mean to a
church which aims at being indigenous?

Leadership Roles and Culture Change: How the leaders of
a group meet change, how stability is maintained in spite
of change, meeting the crisis, creation of new leaders to
meet new situations. Specific cases will be considered to
ascertain what this means for changes brought about by
the introduction of a new religion.

Emerging Leadership under Urbanization: Consideration of
the significance of changing authority patterns due to
migrants removing to urban and industrial situations and
other kinds of displacement, the creation of new leader-

ship patterns, new criteria, industrial patterns, housing, gang organization. What does this mean for the Church?

Leadership Patterns in Matriarchal Society: Consideration of the variations of authority, role, status, discipline and organization under matriarchal rule and matriocality. Specific cases of problems this creates for a western missionary.

Leadership and Personality: Using specific documented cases consideration will be given to how societies produce their own natural leaders and structuralize their roles, what this means to a foreign mission, how culture affects personality and what this means for leaders in an indigenous church.

3. THEORY - Education, Social Change and Decision-making.

The Function of Education in Social Change: The justification of 'directed change,' the relation of education to culture, the error of Europeanization, the blending of culture (F. E. Williams, Luzbetak).

234

The Main Tasks of Education: Application of F. E. William's theory to mission situations, maintenance of what is good, expurgation of what is bad or obsolete, incorporation of new elements (enrichment and expansion).

Leadership and Culture Change: Stimuli for change, nature of emergent leadership, co-existence, dysfunctions from leadership change, changes in meaning, resistance and acceptance, dominance towards self-determination (Roland Force).

Structure and Psychology of Decision-making Patterns: the changing situation in time perspective, how decisions are made and what they imply, fixing of social norms (Sherif) with examination of specific data.

4. LEADERSHIP IN THE GROWING CHURCH - Diachronic Case
                                      Study - Fiji
Early Group Action: Introduction to Fiji, class leaders, prayer leaders, stewards, their roles and status and the organization under which they operated, their institutions

and devotional aids.

The Importance of the Institution: What is and is not expected of an institution, the Viwa Plan, the Glasgow
System.

The Function of Devotional Aids, their preparation and use,
how they operate to develop both leadership and congregational participation, the use of Scripture, hymn book,
catechism, lectionary and worship patterns, the role of
the choir and other functional groups, the role of the
Church in education.

The Emergence of the Professional Ministry and Specialized Leadership, industrial, teaching, medical, seminary,
the problem of upgrading standards (how slow, how fast),
the need for balance, professional ministers and lay
representatives in Synod and other meetings.

The Professional Ministry: remuneration or otherwise,
types of ministry required, the ministerial call, a relevant curriculum for ministerial training, Bible School   235
and Seminary levels (at what point are the two needed?)
and the problem of producing a system which can be taken
over and financed by the indigenous church.

Conflicts of Growth (growing pains), professional minister versus profession teacher, missionary obstructions,
the doctrine of the Church.

The Changing Role of the Missionary at different periods
in the emergence of the Church - preacher, pastor,
teacher, itinerant supervisor, translator, medical worker,
writer, administrator - and the need for the missionary
to see himself in relation to his church in time
perspective.

Leadership in a Day of Rapid Change: Acceptance of
structures for youth activity and self-determination, the
emergence of youth leaders with a role in the Church at
large and their relationship with the elders.

Problems of the Contemporary Situation: Post-war conditions, nationalism, inter-racial acceptance, how the
white man is rated, confrontation with social and

political issues and what these mean for leadership today.

Theological Training - Changes in the Contemporary
Situation: Little change in doctrine, except perhaps in
the doctrine of the nature and function of the Church,
but considerable organic change in the structure of
training, bi-lateral training for current local needs,
pan-Pacific provisions.

Survey - The Ministry of the Whole People of God:
Consideration of evangelism, pastorate, class, worship,
youth work, women's work, service projects, training
programs.

INDIGENEITY SWM 737   Second Quarter
Professor Charles H. Kraft   3 hours credit

Description of Course

This course explores the nature of the relationship
of churches to their surrounding cultures and the expression
of churchness in culture. Models of indigeneity are
developed and a variety of mission and independent churches
evaluated in terms of their approximation to the ideal.

Objects of the Course

1. Clarification of Relevant Issues
2. Production of Studies of Indigeneity   237

Assignments

1. Wide reading (approximately 500 pages) in the three
   areas listed on the Reading List.
2. Production of Term Paper to be reported on in class.
   A synopsis of the report is to be duplicated and
   distributed to the class in written form. Students
   may work individually or in groups.
   a. Suggested length of the paper: 15-30 pages
      (per person), double spaced typing.
   b. Suggested Topics for Term Paper:
      1) Description and Evaluation of a specific
         Church (local or denominational) according
         to the Kraft scales or some adaptation of
         them.
      2) A Study of One or More Aspects of the
         Problem of Postulating Dynamic Equivalence
         to Biblical Models (New Testament and/or
         Old Testament) e.g. by answering such a
         question as: "In what ways did/did not
         the people of God (NT and/or OT) manifest
         the ideals of dynamic equivalence implied
         in the Kraft scales?"

3) A Brief Evaluation of a Specific Church
that falls seriously short of Dynamic
Equivalence, followed by the development
of a strategy to move that church toward
Dynamic Equivalence.

Course Outline

1. Introductory Discussions and Reading, Jan. 8, 10.
   15 and 17.
2. Preparation of Term Project Proposals (due: Jan. 29)
   a. Read widely on the three topics listed on the
      Reading List.
   b. Write up Term Project Proposal and Tentative
      Bibliography (2-3 pages) to hand in.
   NO CLASS MEETINGS ON JANUARY 22 and 24.
3. Term Project Proposals Discussed and Report Dates
   Assigned, Jan. 29, 31.
4. Reports and Discussion:
   Feb. 5
        7
       12
       14
       19
       21
       26
       28
   Mar. 5
        7
       12
       14

238

Indigeneity Reading List

A. Indigeneity Theory:

HODGES, Melvin L.
1953   On the Mission Field - The Indigenous Church.
       Springfield, Mo., The Gospel Publishing House.

KRAFT, Charles H.
       "Dynamic Equivalence Churches." (Unpublished
       Manuscript) Pasadena, Fuller Theological
       Seminary.

NIDA, Eugene
1960 Message and Mission: The Communication of the
      Christian Faith. South Pasadena, William
      Carey Library. [Indigenization vs. Syncretism
      pages 184-188]

NIDA, Eugene and Charles R. TABER
1969 The Theory and Practice of Translation. Leiden,
      E. J. Brill for The United Bible Societies.
      [pages 1-32]

SMALLEY, William A.
1958 "Cultural Implications of an Indigenous Church."
      Practical Anthropology, 5:51-65. Reprinted in:
      Readings in Missionary Anthropology, William A.
      Smalley, Editor. Tarrytown, N. Y., Practical
      Anthropology, pages 147-156.
1959 "What Are Indigenous Churches Like?"
      Practical Anthropology, 6:135-139. Reprinted in:
      Readings in Missionary Anthropology, William A.
      Smalley, Editor. Tarrytown, N. Y., Practical   239
      Anthropology, pages 157-161.

TIPPETT, Alan R.
1973 Verdict Theology in Missionary Theory. (second
      edition) South Pasadena, William Carey Library.
      [pages 148-163]

WHIPPLE, N. M., L. L. KING, D. A. McGAVRAN and others
1960 The Indigenous Church. A Report from Many
      Fields. Chicago, Moody Press.

B. Independency: (Choose articles and books on your area.)

BARRETT, David B.
1968 Schism and Renewal in Africa. An Analysis of
      Six Thousand Contemporary Religious Movements.
      Nairobi (etc.), Oxford University Press.

LA BARRE, W.
1971 Bibliography on crisis cults in Current
      Anthropology, 12:3-44 and especially pp 38-44.

4   Kraft, SWM 737

MITCHELL, Robert Cameron, and Harold W. TURNER
1966   A Comprehensive Bibliography of Modern
       African Religious Movements. Evanston,
       Northwestern University Press.

WELBOURN, Frederick Burkewood, and B. OGOT
1966   A Place to Feel at Home: a study of two
       independent Churches in Western Kenya.
       London, Nairobi (etc.) Oxford University Press.

C. Syncretism:

BEEKMAN, John
1959   "Minimizing Religious Syncretism Among the
       Chols." Practical Anthropology, 6:241-250.
       Reprinted in: Readings in Missionary Anthro-
       pology, William A. Smalley, Editor. Tarrytown,
       N. Y., Practical Anthropology, pages 235-244.

*LA BARRE, W.
240   1971   Bibliography on crisis cults in Current
       Anthropology, 12:3-44 and especially pp 38-44.

LUZBETAK, Louis J.
1963   The Church and Cultures; an applied anthro-
       pology for religious worker. Techny, Ill.,
       Divine Word Publications. [See Bibliographies
       on pages 262 and 363, and Index under Syncre-
       tism, page 428.]

*MADSEN, William
1957   Christo-Paganism: A Study of Mexican Religious
       Syncretism. New Orleans, Middle American
       Research Institute. [See review by Wm. L.
       Wonderly, below.]

MESSENGER, John C.
1959   "The Christian Concept of Forgiveness and
       Anang Morality." Practical Anthropology,
       6:97-103. Reprinted in: Readings in Mission-
       ary Anthropology, William A. Smalley, Editor.
       Tarrytown, N. Y., Practical Anthropology,
       pages 180-186.

NIDA, Eugene A.
  1957 "Mariology in Latin America." Practical
        Anthropology, 4:69-82. Reprinted in:
        Readings in Missionary Anthropology, William
        A. Smalley, Editor. Tarrytown, N. Y., Practical
        Anthropology, pages 17-25.

REYBURN, William D.
  1957 "The Transformation of God and the Conversion
        of Man." Practical Anthropology, 4:185-194.
        Reprinted in: Readings in Missionary
        Anthropology, William A. Smalley, Editor.
        Tarrytown, N. Y., Practical Anthropology,
        pages 26-30.
  1957 "Conflicts and Contradictions in African
        Christianity." Practical Anthropology, 4:161-
        169. Reprinted in: Readings in Missionary
        Anthropology, William A. Smalley, Editor.
        Tarrytown, N. Y., Practical Anthropology,
        pages 162-166.
  1958 "Motivations for Christianity: An African
        Conversation." Practical Anthropology, 5:27-
        32. Reprinted in: Readings in Missionary
        Anthropology, William A. Smalley, Editor.
        Tarrytown, N. Y., Practical Anthropology,
        pages 167-170.
  1958 "Meaning and Restructuring: A Cultural
        Process." Practical Anthropology, 5:79-82.
        Reprinted in: Readings in Missionary
        Anthropology, William A. Smalley, Editor.
        Tarrytown, N. Y., Practical Anthropology,
        pages 171-173.
  1959 "The Spiritual, the Material, and the Western
        Reaction in Africa." Practical Anthropology,
        6:78-83. Reprinted in: Readings in Mission-
        ary Anthropology, William A. Smalley, Editor.
        Tarrytown, N. Y., Practical Anthropology,
        pages 174-179.

*WONDERLY, William L.
  1958 "Pagan and Christian Concepts in a Mexican
        Indian Culture." Practical Anthropology,
        5:197-202. Reprinted in: Readings in
        Missionary Anthropology, William A. Smalley,
        Editor. Tarrytown, N. Y., pages 229-234.

241

MISSIONS AND SOCIAL CHANGE, SWM 738
Professor C. Peter Wagner   3 hours credit

Description of Course

The reciprocal effect of missions and changing world
conditions with special emphasis on urbanization,
secularization and liberation movements in The Third
World.

242

700 courses are considered doctoral level.

    IV. Techniques, Organization and Methods in
        Mission

        740 COMMUNICATION, MASS MEDIA AND
             CHURCH GROWTH.

COMMUNICATION, MASS MEDIA AND CHURCH GROWTH, SWM 740
Professor Ralph D. Winter   3 hours credit

Description of Course

    The role of communications in initial evangelism, in
the development of people movements and in church planting
and continuing missions. The actual and potential
contributions of the modern media.   243

700 courses are considered doctoral level.

V. History of Missions and Church Expansion

(754) HISTORY OF EVANGELICAL AWAKENINGS.

756 THE CHURCH GROWTH MOVEMENT IN HISTORICAL
PERSPECTIVE.

HISTORY OF EVANGELICAL AWAKENINGS, SWM (754)
(See following page.)

THE CHURCH GROWTH MOVEMENT IN HISTORICAL PERSPECTIVE, 756
Professor Ralph D. Winter   3 hours credit

Description of Course

The key books and articles of the Church Growth
movement are surveyed and analyzed to familiarize the
doctoral candidate with the documents and their relation
to the historical context and their continuing role in
the movement.

HISTORY OF EVANGELICAL AWAKENINGS, SWM (754) 2nd Quarter
Professor J. Edwin Orr   3 hours credit

Description of Course

Detailed study of the revivals and awakenings of the
19th and 20th centuries, with emphasis upon their
influence upon missionary expansion and upon national
church growth in all the continents.

Bibliography

ORR, J. Edwin
  1965   The Light of the Nations.
         Grand Rapids, Eerdmans.

  1975   The Eager Feet. 1792-
         Chicago, Moody Press.

  1974   The Fervent Prayer. 1858-
         Chicago, Moody Press.

  1973   The Flaming Tongue. 1905-
         Chicago, Moody Press.

245

700 courses are considered doctoral level.

VI. Church Growth

    760 ADVANCED CHURCH GROWTH.

    761 THE PATTERNS OF CHURCH GROWTH.

    (766) STRATEGY OF MISSIONS.

    (767f) CASE STUDIES: THE CHURCH IN INDIA

    767 CURRENT CHURCH HISTORY

246

ADVANCED CHURCH GROWTH SWM 760
Professor Donald A. McGavran

Second Quarter
3 hours credit

Description of the Course

This course assumes (1) that the basic task of the missionary and an important task of the minister is to communicate the Christian Faith in such a way that on-going churches arise, and (2) that the candidates have acquired considerable knowledge of the process. This course, therefore, presents advanced theological, socio-logical, and anthropological, and methodological considerations which affect the theory and practice of establishing churches, helping them to grow into on-going denominations, and developing in them the desire and ability to propagate the Gospel.

247

Purpose of the Course

Any program which presents history, theology, anthro-pology, and past practices of Church and Mission as separate subjects in a curriculum may present these as ends in themselves - good knowledge whether the Christian Faith is reproduced or not. The purpose of this course is to insure that doctoral candidates, as part of essential input, do substantial reading on and hear lectures devoted to current significant problems in church growth. Through discussions, and the writing of essays and term papers the greatly expanded knowledge of many different aspects of reality will thus be harnessed to church growth. Many of the problems in church growth experienced in year one have been solved. Candidates are free to devote their time to the interaction of the various disciplines and theories and bodies of knowledge which the missionary must know.

Reading Required

A. Pre-requisite Reading. It is assumed that the candidate has studied the following books carefully in years
past and has spent some hours with each one recently. He
should own them, know what they say, and be able to find
in them what he wants.

LINDSELL, Harold, Edited by
  1966 The Church's World Wide Mission, an analysis of
        the current state of evangelical missions, and a
        strategy for future activity. Waco, Word Books.

McGAVRAN, Donald A.
  1955 The Bridges of God. London, World Dominion; New
        York, Friendship.

  1959 How Churches Grow. London, World Dominion; New
        York, Friendship.

  1965 Church Growth and Christian Mission. New York,
        Harper and Row, Publishers.

  1970 Understanding Church Growth. Grand Rapids,
        Eerdmans.

  1972 Crucial Issues in Missions Tomorrow. Chicago,
        Moody Press.

NEVIUS, John Livingstone
  1958 Planting and Development of Missionary Churches.
        Philadelphia, Reformed and Presbyterian Publishing.

PICKETT, Jarrell Waskom
  1933 Christian Mass Movements in India. Lucknow,
        Lucknow Publishing House.

  1973 Church Growth and Group Conversion. South
        Pasadena, William Carey Library.

SHEARER, Roy E.
  1966 Wildfire: The Growth of the Church in Korea.
        Grand Rapids, Eerdmans.

248

TIPPETT, Alan R.
1969   Verdict Theology in Missionary Theory. Lincoln,
       Illinois. Lincoln Christian College Press.

1970   Church Growth and the Word of God, The Biblical
       Basis of the Church Growth Viewpoint. Grand
       Rapids, Eerdmans.

1971   People Movements in Southern Polynesia. Chicago,
       Moody Press.

McGAVRAN, Donald A., Edited by
1969   Church Growth Bulletin Volumes I - V. (One
       Volume, 1964 - 1968) South Pasadena, William
       Carey Library.

B. This Quarter's Reading. The candidate should complete
the following books and theses. He may, with the permission of the instructor, substitute. He should do at least
1400 pages of new reading. Double asterisked books he
should own. Single asterisks indicate theses.

249

**BRAUN, Neil Henry
1971   Laity Mobilized, Reflections on Church Growth in
       Japan and Other Lands. Grand Rapids, Eerdmans.

**GERBER, Vergil
1973   A Manual for Evangelism / Church Growth. South
       Pasadena, William Carey Library.

**GREENWAY, Roger S.
1973   Urban Strategy for Latin America. Grand Rapids,
       Baker Book House.

KELLY, Dean M.
1972   Why Conservative Churches are Growing, A Study in
       Sociology of Religion. New York, Harper & Row.

**McGAVRAN, Donald A. and Win C. ARN
1973   How to Grow a Church. Glendale, Regal, A Division
       of G/L Publications.

**McQUILKIN, J. Robert
1973   How Biblical Is The Church Growth Movement?
       Chicago, Moody Press.

*READ, William Richard
1973   "Brazil 1980: a tool for the evangelization of
       Brazil." An unpublished D.Miss. dissertation,
       Pasadena, Fuller Theological Seminary, School of
       World Mission.

*SARGUNAM, M. Ezra
1973   "Multiplying Churches in Urban India, An Experiment
       in Madras." An unpublished M.A. in Missiology
       thesis, Pasadena, Fuller Theological Seminary,
       School of World Mission.

**TIPPETT, Alan R., (ed.)
1973   God, Man and Church Growth. Grand Rapids, Eerdmans.

250   **WAGNER, C. Peter
      1971   Frontiers in Missionary Strategy. Chicago, Moody
             Press.

*YAMAMORI, Tetsunao
1970   "Church Growth in Japan, A Study in the Development
       of Eight Denominations, 1859-1939." An unpublished
       Ph.D. dissertation in the Dept. of Religion in the
       Graduate School of Arts and Sciences of Duke
       University. [Copy at Pasadena, Fuller Theological
       Seminary, School of World Mission.]

C. Day by Day Reading. Reading required for each day's
lessons will be announced from time to time.

D. Independent Reading. The doctoral candidate does
much indpendent reading, following his own interest in
regard to advanced church growth and discovering new bearing of the disciplines on the development of denominations.
He will be following leads in regard to ways in which recruitment of missionaries, training of ministers, ecumenical movement, national-missionary relations, theories of
mission, the revolution, correspondence Bible Schools,
and other activities and fields of knowledge bear on the

Extension of Christianity. All are parts of the context
of church growth. Nothing in that is outside his reading
purposes.

Term Papers

The purpose of this term paper is to give the candidate
an opportunity to develop an aspect of church growth which
to him is new and challenging. He is encouraged to take
actual instances of well-documented church growth and
explore factors which affected the growth, and how the
concepts of mission, history of mission, communication
theory, ethnic insight, sociological or psychological
principles which he has learned operated in that particular
instance to accelerate or retard growth. This paper should
be such that it could be submitted for publication to
Missiology, International Review of Missions, Evangelical
Missions Quarterly, or Denominational missionary magazine -
a thoughtful, well-prepared article. About 2000 words.

Sequence of Lectures   251

Theological Considerations Affecting Church Growth

Massive Reinterpretation of the Purpose of Mission
The Vigorous Attack on Church Growth
Social Action, Mission and Church Growth
The Frankfurt Declaration and Church Growth
Vindicating the Righteousness of God in Resistant
Populations
Proclaiming the Gospel and Discipling the Ethne

Sociological Considerations Affecting Church Growth

Typologies of Latfricasian Churches
Four Roadblocks to Church Growth - Common Law Marriages
Four Roadblocks to Church Growth - Polygamy
Four Roadblocks to Church Growth - Caste
Four Roadblocks to Church Growth - Ancestor Worship
The Relative Importance of Indigeneity and People
Movements in Growth

Methodological Considerations Affecting Church Growth

Sharing Church Growth Insights with Latfricasian
Congregations (Gerber)
American Church Growth
Estimating Responsiveness
Church-Mission Relationships
Responsibility for Churching the Unchurched

THE PATTERNS OF CHURCH GROWTH, SWM 761   Quarter
Professor Ralph D. Winter   3 hours credit

Description of Course

Typical growth patterns of non-western churches.
Histories of denominations in process of formation,
focusing on the social contexts, graphs of growth and
potential for further communication of a vital Christian
faith.

STRATEGY OF MISSIONS, SWM (766)   Second Quarter   253
Professor C. Peter Wagner   3 hours credit

Description of Course

Investigates ways in which a sound theory and theology
of mission is being put into effect by missions and
churches. What missionary structures, ministerial training, patterns of church growth and advanced education for
missionaries best serve the unchanging mandate.

[SWM 666 is the detailed syllabus for SWM (766).]

CASE STUDIES IN CURRENT CHURCH HISTORY:
THE CHURCH IN INDIA, SWM (767f)   Second Quarter
Professor Donald A. McGavran   3 hours credit

Description of the Course

This course describes the socio-ecclesiastical
realities which compose the Church in India. It
distinguishes four main types of church - Syrian,
Conglomerate, People Movement from Caste, and People
Movement from Tribe. It shows the varied forms of each
which develop in different environments and suggests
how ministers, missionaries, and other leaders of the
Church should understand and use these forms in nurturing
existing congregations and extending the Christian
movement.

[SWM 667f is the detailed syllabus for SWM (767f).]

254

CURRENT CHURCH HISTORY, SWM 767
Professor Ralph D. Winter   3 hours credit

Description of Course

Case studies in current church history involving
denominations, churches and missions in the Third World,
Europe and North America. Special attention on spiritual
and environmental factors in growing and non-growing
movements.

VII.   The World Church--Ecumenics

   770   HERMENEUTICS, ECCLESIOLOGY, ECUMENICS AND
         MISSION.

HERMENEUTICS, ECCLESIOLOGY, ECUMENICS AND MISSION, SWM 770
Professor Arthur F. Glasser   3 hours credit

Description of Course

   The interrelation of contemporary patterns of biblical
interpretation, the Church's understanding of herself and
ecumenical theology and practice and their impact on
Great Commission missions.

255

VIII.   Biblical Studies and Theology

   (780-789)

(IX.) Research

    (790) RESEARCH.

    (791) READING AND CONFERENCE.

    (793) SPECIAL PROJECTS.

    (795) FIELD RESEARCH IN PROPAGATING THE GOSPEL.

RESEARCH, SWM (790)   Quarter
Faculty   Hours as arranged

Description of Course

    Guidance provided to individual missionaries or small groups pressing forward with research on their own problems in mission. Special attention paid to problems assigned to a missionary by his church or mission. Hours as arranged.

    SWM (790) may be used for credit in any section of the curriculum I to VIII for special work or for thesis.

READING AND CONFERENCE, SWM (791)   Quarter
Faculty   Hours as arranged

Description of Course

    Reading, report and discussion designed to cover areas of special interest or those in which the student is weak. Hours as arranged.

[See detailed description of this course under SWM 691 (791).]

SPECIAL PROJECTS, SWM(793)   Third Quarter
MISSIONARY EDUCATION OVERSEAS   3 hours credit
Professor Ralph D. Winter

Description of Course

   In connection with one of the eight branches of the
discipline, graduate students under faculty guidance pursue an investigation of substance. Hours as arranged.

FIELD RESEARCH IN PROPAGATING THE GOSPEL, SWM (795)
Faculty   Hours as arranged

Description of Course

   Directed research abroad, in accordance with plans and
programs worked out and approved during residence at SWM-
ICG, probing some aspect of mission which cannot be known
from lectures and books. Prerequisites required. Hours
as arranged.

4. SWM MISSIOLOGICAL LITERATURE

MISSIOLOGICAL RESEARCH IN THE
FULLER SEMINARY SCHOOL OF MISSIONS

C. Peter Wagner
Associate Professor of Latin American Affairs

The purpose of this section is to describe a research program in missiological studies which has been operating since 1960, and which has begun to make a rather substantial contribution to world-wide missionary thinking and practice. Although admittedly there is nothing new under the sun, it does seem that in several aspects missiological research at Fuller Seminary is breaking sufficient new ground to attract serious attention of churchmen, missionaries and theological faculties in the United States, Europe and the Third World.

Through the years, I have observed mission studies at Fuller Seminary from three perspectives: first as a ministerial student and missionary alumnus, then as an M.A. candidate in the School of World Mission itself, and finally as a member of the faculty. I confess that I have been fascinated by this development and ask the indulgence of my friends if my enthusiasm for the program seems excessive.

Feedback from others to the School of Missions has not all been equally enthusiastic. As the July 1968 issue of *International Review of Missions* shows, strong criticism has been aroused by the persistent articulation of the framework in which all SWM research is conducted. This is known, in the words of the founder of the school and its guiding light, Donald McGavran, as "church growth

261

eyes." Its missiological implications are brought out in our other papers, but here it must be admitted that the context of SWM research is not a neutral one. All that is involved in what is now known technically as church growth theology and theory is brought to bear on research. Through a core course structure, all degree candidates receive a thorough introduction to the various facets of church growth thinking as they launch out on their research work.

Research at SWM is in essence goal-oriented. Research as an academic exercise, only marginally related to the live issues of the day, is discouraged. Our common goal is the faithful completion of the Great Commission, interpreted as making Christian disciples and multiplying congregations of worshiping and witnessing believers. SWM men do not apologize for the pragmatic flavor of their research work. In the drive toward discovering and classifying missiological theory, strategy, and methods that God has blessed, inevitably other activities turn up which, for one reason or another, God has *not* blessed. Myths evaporate when plotted on logarithmic graph paper. Our research knows no sacred cows enshrined in expensive trappings of promotional material. If the Spirit of God has used a given method of evangelistic ministry, our research attempts to find out just what is being done right, and how this might be effective in other places, cultures, and times (if in fact it is not culture-bound). If another program has been fruitless, research aims at finding the reasons why, so that errors of the past will not be uncritically perpetuated in the future.

It does not follow that the spirit of SWM research is iconoclastic. Some have misinterpreted it as such saying, for example, that the SWM is automatically opposed to the "school approach" in evangelism. We are not. The SWM applauds the school approach as well as other missionary methods *where they have been used to bring people to a commitment to Christ.* But where they have not, there is no hesitancy in suggesting that evangelistic resources might be better invested in different methods or in different places. Research carried out in many cultures shows that the world is full of barren missiological fig trees. They have been planted, branches and foliage have sprouted in abundance. The trees should bear fruit. But they don't. When SWM researchers in their conclusions suggest, as did the owner of the fig orchard in the parable, that the barren tree be cut down so that something more productive can be put in its place, predictable negative feelings are produced. Those who feel threatened by such recommendations often overgeneralize their reactions. One critic, after accusing church growth theology as being a syncretism of capitalistic technology and Christianity, ended by calling the church growth point of view "numerolatry"!

Naturally, this goal-centered orientation creates limits. The fact that SWM research has many limitations is recognized, but it is considered the prerogative of any academic discipline to define its own parameters. Some friends, for example, have told us they have been disappointed not to find in the SWM curriculum stronger emphasis on comparative religions or the social implications of Christianity. While it is fully acknowledged that such fields of study and activity are good, and that many consider them even central to the Christian mission, experience has shown us that involvement in these fields has been somewhat noncontributory to the missionary goal of discipling the nations. A great deal of excellent research on these and other subjects is being carried out in sister graduate schools and we rejoice in what is being done there. In short, while we claim the whole field of classical missions, our research believes that mission thinking should be done "against the graph of growth," i.e. in the light of the actual facts concerning the communication of the Gospel.

The Researchers

After these introductory remarks, designed to convey some of the feeling behind SWM missiological research, I turn to a description of the type of person engaged in the research work itself. Enrollment in the School of Missions this past academic year was ninety-nine. Conventional terminology would label these ninety-nine as "students," but we hesitate to use the word because we feel these mature men (nationals and missionaries) have much to teach as well as to learn. We therefore call them "research associates."

263

Since the scope of SWM research is intentionally limited, the number of persons qualified to do such research is correspondingly limited. Field experience is one of the most essential qualifications. This restricts the admission of candidates who have had no previous missionary experience. In-service, rather than pre-service training is stressed. This brings to the SWM a more mature student, seasoned by one, two, three or more terms of missionary service.

The SWM has defined missions to include the cross-cultural dimension. The focus is on the Third World. Missionary associates must have made a successful cross-cultural adjustment in their ministry to qualify for admission. They must demonstrate fluency in the language of their second culture before they can be awarded a degree. This, by definition, excludes such people as pastors of North American churches who may be as experienced and as interested in the dynamics of church growth as any missionary, but who have not acquired the cross-cultural perspective. SWM people fully recognize that church growth insights could and should be applied to the North American scene, but can only hope that some other graduate institution will assume the burden of establishing a church growth institute with that goal in mind.

Since the Third World is so vigorously stressed in SWM, it is to be expected that Third World Christian workers will be welcomed. Some twenty per cent of the typical student body are nationals from the Third World. The cross-cultural dimension is preserved by the fact that these men must make a linguistic and cultural adjustment to the USA in order to study with us. Recognizing the special needs of these men, however, the SWM attempts to create an atmosphere in which they can conduct relevant research without the deculturation process which occurs in so many North American graduate schools, followed by what has been called the "brain-drain." In some cases papers are written in their vernacular languages, and one doctoral candidate is preparing his dissertation in Spanish, since it deals with Latin American issues. Another is working in Indonesian. In admission procedures for Third World men, considerable weight is attached to maturity, leadership qualities and future potential for aggressive activities in fulfilling the Great Commission in their regions. Some of these men, through no lack of intellectual ability or initiative of their own, have not had opportunities for theological training on exactly the North American model. Consequently, where consonant with maintaining academic excellence in SWM, allowances are made.

For the past two years, a rather unique combination of associates has been conducting research. Teams composed of a top-level missionary and a top-level leader of the Asian Church have conducted joint research in the expansion of Christianity in their part of the world. Thus such one team from Viet Nam and another from Indonesia have studied, planned and written together. They have returned to their fields of service, equipped with new tools and insights to be shared with fellow workers and which will increase the fruitfulness of the ministry of a large number of missionaries and national workers alike.

Research Programs

While research in the School of Missions is conducted on a graduate level, and is geared to accredited degree programs, we constantly stress that the objective of research is not the degree, but rather effectiveness in making disciples and multiplying churches. Every effort is made to prevent research becoming simply a device for academic advancement. We find that Christian workers are more than willing to invest nine months to two years of their best energies and abilities whether they get a degree or not. While perhaps nine-tenths of the researches have been submitted in partial fulfillment of degree requirements, a significant few have not. Several outstanding books in the field of missions such as Shearer's *Wildfire, The Growth of the Church in Korea* and Read, Monterroso and Johnson's *Latin American Church Growth* have been produced at SWM in non-degree research programs.

At the present time, the degree programs include two M.A.s and a Doctor of Missiology (D.Miss.).

The M.A. in Missions is a pre-M.Div. (B.D.) degree. It requires two years of residence with a schedule of studies in the Fuller School of Theology along with the missiological input from the SWM.

The M.A. in Missiology is a post-M.Div. (B.D.) degree and ordinarily involves one academic year of residence for completion. This degree is considered equivalent to a Th.M.

Research for either of the M.A. programs may eventuate in a thesis or a project, depending on the nature of the subject to be treated and the needs of the researcher. Projects are classified as "research in progress" and are bound and placed in the SWM research library, but neither polished to meet thesis requirements nor cataloged in the McAlister Library of the Seminary. A project is not an inferior piece of research, it is simply reported in a different style.

The D.Miss. is also a post-M.Div. degree. Research is directed toward the production of a doctoral dissertation through two years of residence work.

Although no definite dates have been set for its inauguration, it might be mentioned that the SWM faculty will begin a Ph.D. program of missiological studies soon. Unlike the D.Miss. which is a "professional" degree, like the Ed.D. the M.D. etc., prepares a man better to serve in mission work. The Ph.D. will prepare a person as an academic professor in the field of missiology.

Research Models

Research projects over the years have begun to form certain patterns which might be described as models for missiological research. The complete list of researches done to date is found in the Appendix to this article, therefore mention of specific works will be kept to a minimum, but examples of outstanding work in each category will be mentioned. Six general categories can be discerned at the present time.

1. *Church Growth Area Surveys.* These research projects give a general picture of the Church in an area of the world. The principal example of this kind of research is *Latin American Church Growth,* a book by William Read, Victor Monterroso, and Harmon Johnson published by Eerdmans in 1969. It has subsequently been published in both Spanish and Portuguese and has been widely read by Christian workers.

2. *Church Growth National Surveys.* These projects record the history of the Church in a given nation, attempting to interpret history in terms of the dynamics of growth and non-growth of the Churches. As do most SWM research projects, these end with a concluding section on "hard, bold plans for church growth." Published examples include Grimley and Robinson on Nigeria, Olsen on Sierra Leone, Wagner on Bolivia, Tuggy and Toliver on the Philippines, and Enns on Argentina.

3. *Church Growth Denominational Surveys.* These projects have been conducted on both international and national bases. They are perhaps the most popular type of research since they provide the student an opportunity to analyze the work with which he is most familiar and make projections for future strategy on the basis of his research. This has been exceedingly helpful to mission management even though it has caused some dismay. When personalities and contemporary issues are involved, it is often difficult to strike a balance between courage and frankness on the one hand and discernment and tact on the other. Conrad's survey of Nazarene missions world-wide is an example of the international model. Nationally, Shearer on the Presbyterians in Korea and Kwast on the Baptists in West Cameroon are examples of what can be done.

4. *Analysis of Missionary Methodologies.* This type of study zeroes in on a particular missionary method or the method of a particular society. It tests its effectiveness against the goals that have been set by workers using it, and makes suggestions for reinforcement or modification as the case may be. Some outstanding examples are Bradshaw on Evangelism-in-Depth, Voelkel on Latin America, Chua on Asian student work and Braun's significant book *Laity Mobilized.*

5. *Biblical and Theological Principles.* Interest in research in this area is growing in SWM. Murphy's thesis on Spiritual Gifts and Evans on Spirit Possession are examples of the application of church growth principles to theology and biblical studies. Research in progress in this field includes Professor Norvald Yri on The Principle of Religious Authority in the Norwegian Lutheran Church and the Faith and Order Movement; Dagfinn Solheim on The Theology of Missions in the Confessional Lutheran Tradition; Professor Edward Pentecost on The Theology of Missions in the Dispensational Tradition and Pablo Perez on Latin American Theology.

6. *Elenctics or the science of bringing peoples of non-Christian religiosity to repentance and faith.* Non-Christian religions become the subjects of research in order to be able to present convincingly to their devotees the claims of Christ. Examples of this kind of research include Gustafson on Thai Buddhism, Gates on Chinese Animism, Johnson on Brazilian Spiritism and Nordyke on Aymara Animism.

267

As time goes by, undoubtedly new models for missiological research will be added to this list. Every attempt is made to be flexible enough to allow each associate freedom in selecting an area of research that will meet his particular needs and be most helpful in his future work.

Faculty Research and Publication

During the course of the academic year, each faculty member supervises from four to seven research programs, and serves on the committees of several others. This not only provides guidance to the church leaders studying there, but also strengthens the faculty member by giving him insight into many actual cases of church growth — geographical area, denominational emphases, and missionary methods with which he might not otherwise have come into contact. Our "associates" educate us! Faculty members thus do their own thinking, teaching and writing on expanding data bases, reinforced by missionary associates with first-hand knowledge of many of the mission fields of the world.

All SWM faculty members have themselves been missionaries. They know by personal experience what is involved in cross-cultural ministry, and therefore can enter sympathetically into the struggles of the missionary associates. Each professor has specialized not only in his own area of the world, but also in certain fields of missiological thought and activity and in at least one ethnic religion.

Donald McGavran is the prophet and the father of the Church Growth Movement. He draws on thirty years' experience in India as well as extensive world travels to further refine the classic principles of church growth. The most complete statement of these is found in *Understanding Church Growth* (Eerdmans). Other recent literary works include *The Eye of the Storm* (Word) and *Crucial Issues in Missions Tomorrow* (Moody), both of which McGavran has edited.

Arthur Glasser, formerly of China, is McGavran's successor as Dean of the School of Missions. His field is theology of mission, and recent contributions include chapters on Religious Encounter, the Cultural Mandate, Communism, Old Testament Mission Themes, etc.

Alan Tippett, a social anthropologist, has produced some of the finest area studies available, such as *Solomon Islands Christianity* (Lutterworth) and *People Movements in Southern Polynesia* (Moody). He makes a special effort to bring the religious dimension to secular anthropology by full participation in professional meetings. At present he is preparing a major paper for the forthcoming meeting of the World Conference on Science and Religion on "A Taxonomy of Glossolalia and Spirit Possession," attempting to design it for application to both pagan and Christian forms.

Ralph Winter is making a major attempt to reconstruct the history of missions on the church growth model. His widely-circulated book, *The Twenty-Five Unbelievable Years* (William Carey Library) is a prototype of things to come. In the meantime he has made outstanding contributions to missions as one of the architects of the Latin American extension seminary movement (his anthology, *Theological Education by Extension* published by the William Carey Library, is the classic work on the subject), and with his introduction of the concept of vertical and horizontal structures in missions in *The Warp and the Woof* (William Carey Library).

Charles Kraft has just published what may become the definitive English-language textbook on the Hausa language. He is making a valuable contribution to missiological research with his development of a discipline called Christian Ethnotheology. A book on the subject of Culture and Christianity is projected for late 1973, and will include his findings on ethnotheology as well as insights into other missiological matters.

J. Edwin Orr, the world's chief authority on Christian awakenings and revivals has produced a definitive account of *Evangelical Awakenings in India,* a second *Campus Aflame: Awakenings in Collegiate Communities Throughout the World* and has one in press on *Evangelical Awakenings in Africa.*

As the newcomer to the faculty, and a former mission administrator, I have concentrated on some areas of methodology. Moody Press is this month publishing my *Frontiers in Missionary Strategy.* I have attempted to record some insights from first-hand experience in Latin America in *An Extension Seminary Primer,* and have edited *Church Mission Tensions Today,* a symposium produced by thirteen delegates to the recent IFMA/EFMA Green Lake Conference on church-mission relationships.

Publication and Dissemination of Research

Goal-oriented SWM research demands that the results not be buried in library stacks, but used by the men who are making decisions and forming opinions in the world of missions today.

269

A "Common Room" is the center of SWM activities. Here students and professors circulate throughout the day, sipping coffee, discussing issues, and enjoying fellowship. Prominent in the Common Room are the convenient shelves holding the many volumes of SWM research. Whereas a black-bound copy of each thesis and dissertation is presented to the Fuller Seminary McAlister Library, another copy, bound in color, is shelved in the Common Room. The visitor will see at once the 19 works on Latin America in green, the 28 on Asia in red, the 22 on Africa in blue, the 8 on Oceania in beige, and several other minor classifications. With the addition of the 1972 production (approximately 20) the total of bound works has now passed the 100 mark. These are available on a reserve basis. They are constantly used, but are not removed from the room.

We are aiming for a thousand factual studies of young churches in all parts of the world. We want to put a foundation of fact under the vast missionary program of the Church.

Also prominently shelved, are samples of the published versions of the researches, both those which come from missionary and national associates and from professors. As the Appendix shows, about one third of our researches have been published. Whenever possible, this is the goal. Missionary associates are encouraged to produce research reports which multiply the usefulness of their insights and thus merit publication. Several religious publishers have expressed interest in producing church growth books, but first Eerdmans and more recently Moody Press have done the most along this line.

Perhaps the most significant vehicle for the publication of SWM research is the William Carey Library. Burdened with the need for a publishing house which could handle low volume publications at reasonable prices without disastrous delays, Professor Ralph Winter began a study of the publishing business in 1968. He located the bottlenecks of the traditional publishers, and devised ways and means to break them. The result was the William Carey Library, a private business enterprise dedicated to the publication of missionary literature.

This venture in so-called "mini-publishing" has been highly successful. By using typewritten copy, the barrier of high composition cost has been surmounted. Another distinctive contribution has been describing the market for each book. The William Carey Library, together with the author, analyze the market and sales potential for the book. Advance orders are secured. Production capital is sought from the outside. On this basis production costs are calculated. The William Carey Library is not a vanity press. Books are not subsidized. But in the three years of operation, 37 missionary works have been published and distributed to the markets where they have been most needed. Currently, 30 others are in one stage or another of production.

Among William Carey Library titles which already have exercised a measurable influence on the missionary world and which have been widely reviewed are *Theological Education by Extension, Church Growth Though Evangelism in Depth, Missions in Creative Tension, The Twenty-Five Unbelievable Years,* and others.

Soon after the William Carey Library began, complaints started to arrive from missionaries on the field disturbed by the fact that they were not being kept infomed as to what new literature was available. With the number of SWM alumni swelling in all parts of the world, demand for missionary literature was on the increase. This led Winter to take another bold step and set up the Church

Growth Book Club. Making use of the distribution network of the *Church Growth Bulletin,* Winter made arrangements with the publishers of the *Church Growth Bulletin* to include a Church Growth Book Club insert with each issue. A subscription to the *Church Growth Bulletin* now includes membership in the Church Growth Book Club, a bargain package at only $1.00 per year. The book club offers discounts of 40% on most books. Over half the selections are from publishers other than William Carey Library, so the range of missionary literature offered at the club is wide. Over 50,000 volumes were distributed through the club during 1971.

The William Carey Library and the Church Growth Book Club are now expanding their offerings into the field of cassettes. They are also concerned for the need of distributing smaller research documents, and plans for the publication of "separates" are on the drawing board.

It might be helpful to stress again that William Carey Library and Church Growth Book Club are private undertakings, only tangentially related to the School of Missions. The same is true of the *Church Growth Bulletin,* a bi-monthly publication with a circulation of 6,000 to 7,000. This is edited by Donald McGavran, and has proved to be one of the most effective tools for the dissemination of insights gained through SWM research. But it is the property and responsibility of Overseas Crusades of Palo Alto, California, one of America's most creative and avant-garde inter-denominational missionary societies.

271

More directly related to the School of Missions are the annual church growth lectures. Distinguished leaders in world missions are invited to deliver series of lectures to all three faculties of the seminary: theology, psychology and missions. Subsequent publication of these lectures is encouraged. Books such as Bishop Pickett's *Dynamics of Church Growth* (Abingdon), Dr. David Stowe's *Ecumenicity and Evangelism* (Eerdmans), and Dr. Peter Beyerhaus' *World Missions: The Theological Dimension* (Zondervan) were all developed as part of the Church Growth Lectureship.

Current Research

To describe all current research in the School of Missions would be excessively tedious. I will, therefore, select only one model, a project in which I have been directly involved and which may have broken some new ground.

At the beginning of the past academic year, announcement was made of a research seminar on Third World missions. The need for this had been exposed through contacts I had made with David Barrett and Edward Dayton, two of the co-editors of the current *World Christian Handbook.* The data being gathered for that publication included missionary sending agencies from the Western world, but efforts were not projected for reporting similar agencies originating in the Third World. The principal reason for this was that the data was thought to be unavailable.

Enrollment for the seminar was limited to three. Peter Larson, a Baptist missionary to Argentina and a doctoral candidate, agreed to head the research team. Edward Pentecost, one of seven professors of missions from sister institutions currently taking doctoral work at SWM, and James Wong, an Anglican minister from Singapore, joined Larson.

Research extended through the entire school year. 697 letters of introduction and questionnaires were mailed to a list of contacts compiled from various sources. Independent financing for this was secured through the initiative of the team itself. A bibliography of 165 entries was compiled. With the assistance of technicians in The Missions Advanced Research and Communications division of World Vision, data classification systems were developed. Full use was made of the human resources represented by the 99 SWM residence students.

The report of the year's project has just been submitted. It covers 375 pages, and contains data unavailable from any other source. Identified to date as a result of a 34.1% response to questionnaires, are 209 agencies originating in the Third World and sending 2,994 missionaries either cross-culturally or cross-geographically in evangelistic and church-planting missions. Patterns of recruitment, organization, and support are often vastly different from Western models.

Much refinement needs to be done. Questions as to whether some of these agencies deserve to be called missionary societies remain unanswered. Are these 209 agencies a complete list or do they represent just the tip of an iceberg? Is the Spirit of God moving in the Third World in ways we are only beginning to discover? Can western missions learn something about missionary financing, for example, from a Nigerian mission agency currently sending out 97 couples on a budget of $20,000 per year?

Questions like these simply underscore the exciting potential this research presents. New dimensions of missiological theory and activity may be opening up. Continuing schedule of research seminars has been developed to follow through on Third World missions and to keep the data current.

This type of research, multiplied many times over, creates a general atmosphere of expectation and optimism at Fuller Seminary's School of World Mission and Institute of Church Growth. Long ago we became convinced that rather than living in a post-Christian age, we live in the time of the most rapid expansion of the Kingdom of God in recorded history. To a man, the faculty and associates of the community of missionary scholars called the School of World Mission rejoice at the privilege of being on the front lines of God's work at a time like this. We are awed on one hand by the evident fulfillment of the signs of the times in world history, and the approaching of the eschatological Kingdom. On the other hand, we joyfully put our hand to the plow and work while it is yet day. As we toil, we look with the Prophet Isaiah toward that day when all the escaped of the nations shall turn from the wood and stone of their carved images, bow the knee, and confess with the tongue that Jehovah is God and "there is none else" (Isa. 45).

Missiological Research Conducted by Students at
the Fuller Theological Seminary School of World Mission,
1966-1972

PUBLISHED WORKS
(Published titles, rather than thesis titles given)

BENNET, Charles (MA '71) — *Tinder in Tabasco: A Study of Church Growth in Mexico* (Eerdmans)

BRADSHAW, Malcolm R. (MA '69) — *Church Growth Through Evangelism-in-Depth* (William Carey Library)

BRAUN, Neil (MA '66) — *Laity Mobilized: Reflections on Church Growth in Japan and Other Lands* (Eerdmans)

COX, Emmett D. (MA '69) — *The Church of the United Brethren in Christ in Sierra Leone* (William Carey Library)

EDWARDS, Fred E. (MA '69) — *The Role of the Faith Mission: A Brazilian Case Study* (William Carey Library)

ENNS, Arno (MA '67)	*Man, Milieu and Mission in Argentina* (Eerdmans)
ENYART, Paul C.	*Friends in Central America* (William Carey Library)
GAXIOLA, Manuel	*La Serpiente y la Paloma* (William Carey Library)
GRIMLEY, John and ROBINSON, Gordon E.	*Church Growth in Central and Southern Nigeria* (Eerdmans)
HAMILTON, Keith	*Church Growth in the High Andes* (Institute of Church Growth)
HEDLUND, Roger (MA '70)	*The Protestant Movement in Italy: Its Progress, Problems and Prospects* (William Carey Library)
HILL, Leslie (MA '73)	*Designing a Theological Education by Extension Program* (William Carey Library)
JOHNSON, Alfred E.	*Venezuela Survey Report, Potential for Revolutionary Church Growth* (Worldwide Evangelization Crusade)
KWAST, Lloyd E. (MA '68)	*The Discipling of West Cameroon: A Study of Baptist Growth* (Eerdmans)
LIAO, David (MA '69)	*The Unresponsive, Resistant or Neglected?* (Moody)
MALASKA, Hilkka O. (MA '70)	*The Challenge for Evangelical Missions to Europe. A Scandinavian Case Study.* (William Carey Library)
MITCHELL, James E. (MA '70)	*The Emergence of a Mexican Church* (William Carey Library)
OLSEN, Gilbert (MA '66)	*Church Growth in Sierra Leone* (Eerdmans)
PENTECOST, Edward (MA '72), WONG, James (MA '72), and LARSON, Peter (D.Miss. '73)	*Missions from the Third World* (Church Growth Study Center — Singapore)

274

RANDALL, Max Ward (MA '69)	*Profile for Victory: New Prospects for Missions in Zambia* (William Carey Library)
READ, William R. (D.Miss. '73)	*Brazil 1980* (MARC)
READ, William R. (D.Miss. '73)	*New Patterns of Church Growth in Brazil* (Eerdmans)
READ, William R., MONTERROSO, Victor, and JOHNSON, Harmon	*Latin American Church Growth* (Eerdmans)
SHEARER, Roy E. (Ph.D. '72)	*Wildfire: The Church in Korea* (Eerdmans)
SHEWMAKER, Stanford (MA '70)	*Tonga Christianity* (William Carey Library)
SMITH, Ebbie C. (MA '70)	*God's Miracles: Indonesian Church Growth* (William Carey Library)
SUBBAMMA, B.V. (MA '70)	*New Patterns for Discipling Hindus* (William Carey Library)
SUNDA, James	*Church Growth in New Guinea* (Institute of Church Growth)
SWANSON, Allen (MA '68)	*Taiwan: Mainline Versus Independent Church Growth* (William Carey Library)
TREVOR, Hugh	*Church Growth and the O.M.F. in the Philippines* (Overseas Missionary Fellowship)
TUGGY, Arthur (MA '68)	*The Philippine Church: Growth in a Changing Society* (Eerdmans)
TUGGY, Arthur (MA '68), and TOLIVER, Ralph	*Seeing the Philippine Church* (Overseas Missionary Fellowship Publishers)
VOUGHT, Dale (MA '73)	*Protestants in Modern Spain*
WAGNER, C. Peter (MA '68)	*The Protestant Movement in Bolivia* (William Carey Library)
WELD, Wayne C. (D.Miss. '73)	*An Ecuadorian Impasse* (Institute of Church Growth)

275

WELD, Wayne C. (D.Miss. '73)   *The World Directory of Theological Education by Extension* (William Carey Library)

WOLD, Joseph   *God's Impatience in Liberia* (Eerdmans)

UNPUBLISHED RESEARCH

ALEXANDER, Frank (MA '69)   *Missions in Malawi*

ASPINALL, H. Raymond (MA '73)   *The Brethren Church in Argentina: A Church Growth Study*

AVERY, Allen W. (MA '69)   *African Independency: A Study of the Phenomenon of Independency and the Lessons From It for Greater Church Growth in Africa*

BALISKY, Paul (MA '72)   *African and Other Studies*

BROOM, Wendell W. (MA '70)   *Growth of Churches of Christ Among Ibibios of Nigeria*

BROUGHAM, David R. (MA '70)   *The Training of the Chinese in Indonesia for the Ministry*

BUEHLER, Herman (MA '73)   *Nominality Considered: A Survey of Contemporary Thinking*

276

CARR, Lucille (MA '66)   *A Seminary and Church Growth, a Critical Analysis on the Taiwan Conservative Baptist Theological Seminary from the Church Growth Viewpoint*

CARVER, E. Earl (MA '72)   *Evangelical Church Growth in Puerto Rico*

CHAE, Eun Soo (MA '73)   *Receptivity of Korea-Taiwan Mountain People*

CHANDLER, Thomas W. (MA '73)   *A Statistical Study of Short Term Missionaries*

CONLEY, William W. (D.Miss. '73)   *The Kalimantan Kenyah*

CONRAD, William H. (MA '67)   *A Report to the Department of Missions of the Church of the Nazarene Concerning Growth on Its Mission Fields*

CORNELIUS, Gollapalli (MA '71)	*Urban Church Growth – South India*
CURRY, Michael W. (MA '72)	*Mission Institutions of the Churches of Christ in Southern Tanzania*
DANIEL, K.C. (MA '71)*	*Indian Church Growth Dynamics*
DAVIS, Linnell (MA '68)	*The Use of the Bible in the Kamba Tribal Setting*
DILWORTH, Donald (MA '67)	*Evangelization of the Quichuas of Ecuador*
ELLISTON, Edgar J. (MA '68)	*An Ethnohistory of Ethiopia, A Study of the Factors which Affect the Planting and Growing of the Church*
ERICKSON, Edwin (MA '73)	*Training of Ethiopian Rural Church Leadership*
EVANS, Melvin O. (MA '71)	*Spirit Possession in Certain Southern Bantu Tribes*
FRIEND, Leslie A. (MA '71)	*The Contribution of Mission Schools to Church Growth in Sub-Saharan Africa*
FUGMANN, Gernott (MA '69)	*Church Growth and Urbanization in New Guinea*
GAMALIEL, James C. (MA '67)	*The Church in Kerala: A People Movement Study*
GATES, Alan (D.Miss. '71)	*Christianity and Animism: China and Taiwan*
GATES, Alan (D.Miss. '71)	*Church Growth in Taiwan*
GROVER, Jeanne	*Church Growth in Eastern Peru*
GUSTAFSON, James W. (MA '70)	*Syncretistic Rural Thai Buddhism: Its Complications for Christian Mission in Thailand*
HENNEBERGER, James (MA '68)	*Quo Vadis IELU? A Case Study of the Iglesia Evangelica Unida in Argentina*
HIAN, Chua W. (MA '72)	*Out of Asia: A Study of Asian Christian Students*

277

HILL, James (MA '69) *Theological Education for the Church in Mission*

HILL, Robert W. (MA '69) *The Christianization of the Central African Republic*

HUDSPITH, J. Edwin (MA '69) *Tribal Highways and Byways: A Church Growth Study in North Thailand*

JACOBSEN, Leonard (MA '68) *Church Growth on the Island of Madagascar*

JOHNSON, Harmon A. (MA '69) *Authority over the Spirits: Brazilian Spiritism and Evangelical Church Growth*

JONES, Rex R. (MA '71) *A Strategy for Ethiopia*

KAMASI, Frans Lawrence (MA '73) *Church Growth Lessons for the Indonesian Church (written in Indonesian)*

KAY, Richard W. (MA '72) *Church Growth and Renewal in the Bahamas*

KJAERLAND, Gunnar (MA '71) *Planting the Church Among Nomads*

278 KWAST, Lloyd E. (D.Miss. '72) *Protestant Christianity in West Cameroon 1841-1886*

LARSON, Peter A. (D.Miss. '73) *Migration and Church Growth in Argentina*

MAST, Michael M. (MA '72) *An Approach to Theological Training Among the Tobas of Argentina*

MATHEWS, Edward F. (MA '70) *Planting of the Church in Honduras: The Development of a Culturally Relevant Witness*

MICHELSEN, Clifford S. (MA '69) *The Evangelical Lutheran Church of East Cameroun*

MIDDLETON, Vernon J. (MA '72) *A Pattern of Church Growth for Tribal India*

MONTGOMERY, Jim *Why They Grow*

MURPHY, Edward (MA '72)   *Gifts of the Spirit and the Mission of the Church*

NORDYKE, Quentin H. (MA '72)   *Animistic Aymaras and Church Growth*

OLIVER, Dennis (D.Miss. '73)   *Make Disciples: The Nature and Scope of the Great Commission*

PENTECOST, Edward C. (MA '72)   *Mexican Indian Church Growth Study*

PEREZ, Pablo (D. Miss. '73)   *Mision Y Liberacion* (The theology of the mission of the Church in Latin America in the light of the current debate on revolution. Written in Spanish.)

PHILIP, Puthuvail T. (MA '73)   *Growth of Baptist Churches of Tribal Nagaland*

RADER, Paul (D.Miss. '73)   *The Salvation Army in Korea After 1945*

RAMBO, David (MA '68)   *Training Competent Leaders for the Christian and Missionary Alliance Churches of the Philippines*

REED, Grady Q. (MA '71)   *Strategizing Church of Christ Missions*

REIMER, Reginald E. (MA '72)   *The Protestant Movement in Vietnam: Church Growth in Peace and War Among the Ethnic Vietnamese*

RIDDLE, Norman (MA '71)   *Church Growth in Kinshasa*

RO, Sang Kook (MA '73)   *Pauline Missiology and the Church in Korea*

ROMERO, Joel E. (MA '70)   *Church Planting Evangelism: An Argentine Case Study*

ROSS, Charles   *The Emergence of the Presbyterian Church in the Kasai, Congo*

SAMUEL, George (MA '73)   *Growth Potential of Urban Churches: A Study in Bombay*

SARGUNAM, Ezra (MA '73)   *Multiplying Churches in Urban India: An Experiment in Madras*

SAUDER, James (MA '73)   *Planning for Church Growth*

SAVAGE, Peter   *The Ministry in the Iglesia Evangelica Peruana*

SAWATZKY, Sheldon V. (MA '70)   *The Gateway to Promise: A Study of the Taiwan Mennonite Church*

SCHWARTZ, Glenn J. (MA '73)   *Crucial Issues of the Brethren in Christ in Zambia*

SHEARER, Roy E. (Ph.D. '72)   *Animism and the Church in Korea*

SHEWMAKER, Stanford (MA '69)   *Church Growth in Butonga*

SHUMAKER, John T. (MA '72)   *Church Growth in Paraguay*

SKIVINGTON, S. Robert (MA '70)   *Baptist Methods of Church Growth in the Philippines*

SPRUTH, Erwin L. (MA '70)   *The Mission of God in the Wabag Area of New Guinea: A Preliminary Study of Church Growth Among the Enga and Ipili Peoples*

STOCK, Fred   *Church Growth in West Pakistan*

TAI, James (MA '73)   *Church Growth Principles for Chinese Christians* (in Mandarin)

TAKAMI, Toshihiro (MA '69)   *Concepts of Leadership and Their Meaning for the Growth of Christian Churches*

TATE, Francis V. (MA '70)   *Patterns of Church Growth in Nairobi*

TAUFA, Lopeti (MA '68)   *Change and Continuity in Oceania*

TEGENFELDT, Herman (D.Miss. '73)   *The Kachin Baptist Church of Burma*

THOTTUNGAL, Abraham (MA '67)   *History and Growth of the Mar Thoma Church*

TOLIVER, Ralph   *A Preliminary Inquiry into the History and Growth of the Church in the Philippines*

VENBERG, Rodney W. (MA '70)   *The Lutheran Brethren Church in Chad and Cameroun*

VOELKEL, Janvier W. (MA '71)	*The Eternal Revolutionary: Evangelical Ministry to the University Student in Latin America*
WARNER, Bruce M. (MA '72)	*Missions as Advocate of Cultural Change Among the Batak People, Sumatra*
WATSON, Leslie (MA '68)	*Conserving the Converts in the Japanese Church*
WATSON, Helen T. (MA '68)	*Revival and Church Growth in Korea 1884-1910*
WEERSTRA, Hans M. (D.Miss. '72)	*Maya Peasant Evangelism: Communication, Receptivity and Acceptance Factors Among Maya Campesinos*
WONG, James Yui Kok (MA '72)	*Singapore: The Urban Church in the Midst of Rapid Social Change*

RESEARCH IN PROGRESS

ACTON, Lawrence	*Growth of the Cumberland Presbyterian Church in Colombia*
AIER, Imotemjen	*The Growth of Garo Baptist Churches of Meghalaya in Northeast India*
BANDELA, Yesupadam	*Lay Movements in Northern Circars, India*
BENNETT, David and MURPHY, Edward	*Church Growth in the San Gabriel Valley of California*
BOLTON, Robert	*Church Growth Among Taiwan's Urban Minnan Chinese*
BUCKMAN, Allan	*Introducing Christianity to the Yala People of Southeast Nigeria*
CHAN, Wilson	*An Introduction to Missiology from the Chinese Perspective* (in Chinese)
CHANG, Joseph	An adaptation of *Church Growth and the Word of God* (Tippett) for the Korean Church

281

COOK, Clyde	*Selected Case Studies in Evangelism as Related to Cross-cultural Communication*
CUNVILLE, Robert	*A Study of the Growth of the Presbyterian Church in the Khasi and Jaintia Hills of North East India*
CYSTER, Graham	*The Coloureds of South Africa*
DRETKE, James	*A Christian Approach to Muslims in Ghana*
ENNS, C. Marlin	*Church Planting in a Middle Class Area of Mexico City*
GANT, Edwin	*Church Growth in the Mountains of Tucuman, Argentina*
GAXIOLA, Manuel	*The Growth of the Apostolic Church of the Faith in Mexico*
HEDLUND, Roger	*The Conservative Baptist Movement in the U.S.A.: A Study in Self-Understanding*
HERENDEEN, Dale	*Conversion Receptivity and Church Growth Among the Ethnic Vietnamese*
HETRICK, Paul	*Nazarene Church Growth in Swaziland*
HOLLAND, Clifton	*The Religious Dimension in Spanish Los Angeles: A Protestant Case Study*
HOOGSHAGEN, Searle	*A Descriptive Study of Little People Movements Generated Through Wycliffe Bible Translators*
HUTCHENS, James	*A Case for Messianic Judiasm*
IWABUCHI, Hiro	An adaptation of *Church Growth and the Word of God* (Tippett) for the Japanese church (in Japanese)
KIM, Samuel	*Christian Encounter in Thailand: The Growth of the Church of Christ in Thailand After World War II*

282

KLASSEN, Jacob	*Fire on the Patamo: Church Growth in the High Andes of Ecuador*
LENNING, Larry	*Training for Christian Leadership in the Cameroons*
MARTIN, Alvin	*Missiology Today: A Study in Contemporary Development*
MASIH, Rehmat	*Theological Education and Church Growth: A Case Study of the Gujranwala Theological Seminary in Pakistan*
MONTERROSO, Vicotr	*Evangelism-in-Depth and Church Growth in Paraguay*
NANFELT, Peter	*Christian and Missionary Alliance Church Growth in Indonesia*
NELSON, Amirtheraj	*Church Growth in Madras City, India*
OLSEN, Walther	*An Investigation of Foreign Missionary Strategy for the French Urban Context*
PHILIP, Abraham	*Mobilizing the Laity in the Mar Thoma Church for Evangelism*
PINOLA, Sakari	*Church Growth Insights: A Descriptive and Evaluative Study*
REED, Jerold	*The Dynamics of the Growth of the Hispanio Churches in Ecuador*
ROEDA, Jack	*The Role of Communications Media in Church Growth*
ROSS, Charles	*The Christian Movement Among the Kuba-Kete Tribes of Central Zaire*
SEATON, Dr. Ron	*Health Education by Extension*
SOLHEIM, Dagfinn	*Theology of Mission in the Lutheran Tradition*
STOCK, Fred	*Church Growth in Pakistan with Special Emphasis upon the United Presbyterian Church*

283

STEYNE, Philip	*The Flock and the Fold in South Africa*
TAI, James	*The Gospel and Culture* (in Chinese)
THANNICKAL, John	*Communication of the Gospel in Indian Culture*
THOMAS, Harold	*Factors of Church Growth Among the Chorti Indians of Guatemala*
VILLEGAS, Cerefino	*Annotated Bibliography on Lay Training*
WANG, John C.	An adaptation of *Frontiers of Mission Strategy* (Wagner) for the Chinese Church and her world-wide mission
YANG, Bill	An adaptation of *Church Growth and the Word of God* (Tippett) for the Chinese church
YOUNG, Joseph	*Chinese Reflections on the Expansion of the Christian Movement Among the Chinese People*
YRI, Norvald	*Biblical Authority: The Crucial Issue for Church and Mission in the Ecumenical Movement from 1910-1973*

284

PUBLISHED WORKS OF SWM FACULTY
(Books and Chapters only)

ARTHUR F. GLASSER, Dean and Associate Professor Theology of Missions.

And Some Believed, Chicago, Moody Press, 1946.

"Communism," chapter in *Religions in a Changing World*, Howard Vos, ed., Chicago, Moody Press, 1959.

Missions in Crisis (with Eric S. Fife), Chicago, Inter-Varsity Press, 1961.

"Confession, Church Growth, and Authentic Unity in Missionary Strategy," chapter in *Protestant Crosscurrents in Mission*, Norman A. Horner, ed., Nashville, Abingdon Press, 1968.

"The Evangelicals: World Outreach," chapter in *The Future of the Christian World Mission*, William J. Danker and Wi Jo Kang, eds., Grand Rapids, Eerdmans, 1971.

"Mission and Cultural Environment," *Toward a Theology for the Future*, David F. Wells and Clark H. Pinnock, eds., Carol Stream, Creation House, 1971.

Crossroads in Missions, (editor), South Pasadena, William Carey Library, 1971.

"Salvation Today and the Kingdom," chapter in *Crucial Issues in Mission Tomorrow*, Chicago, Moody Press, 1972.

DONALD A. MCGAVRAN, Dean Emeritus and Senior Professor of Mission and Church Growth.

How to Teach Religion in Mission Schools, Lucknow, Lucknow Publishing House, 1930.

Church Growth and Group Conversion (with Wascomb Pickett and others), Lucknow, Lucknow Publishing House, 1936, revised 1955.

The Bridges of God, New York, Friendship Press, 1955.

Multiplying Churches in the Philippines, Manila, United Church of Christ in the Philippines, 1958.

How Churches Grow, London, World Dominion Press, 1959.

Church Growth in Jamaica, Lucknow, Lucknow Publishing House, 1962

Church Growth in Mexico (with John Huegel and Jack Taylor), Grand Rapids, Eerdmans, 1963.

Church Growth and Christian Mission (editor), New York, Harper & Row, 1965.

Church Growth Bulletin, Volumes I-V (editor), South Pasadena, William Carey Library, 1969.

Understanding Church Growth, Grand Rapids, Eerdmans, 1970.

Principles of Church Growth, (with Wayne Weld), South Pasadena, William Carey Library, 1971.

Eye of the Storm, The Great Debate in Mission (editor), Waco, Word Books, 1972.

Crucial Issues in Missions Tomorrow (editor), Chicago, Moody Press, 1972.

J. EDWIN ORR, Visiting Professor, History of Mission.

Can God?, London, Marshall, Morgan & Scott, 1934.
The Church Must First Repent, London, Marshall, Morgan & Scott, 1938.
Through Blood and Fire in China, London, Marshall, Morgan & Scott, 1940.
I Saw No Tears, London, Marshall, Morgan & Scott, 1948.
Full Surrender, London, Marshall, Morgan & Scott, 1951.
The Second Evangelical Awakening in America, London, Marshall, Morgan & Scott, 1952.
Faith That Makes Sense, London, Marshall, Morgan & Scott, 1960.
The Second Evangelical Awakening in Britain, London, Marshall, Morgan & Scott, 1949.
The Light of the Nations, Grand Rapids, Eerdmans, 1965.
Evangelical Awakenings in India in the Early Twentieth Century, New Delhi, Christian Literature Institute, 1970.
Campus Aflame, Dynamic of Student Religious Revolution, Glendale, Regal Books, 1971.
The Flaming Tongue: The Impact of Twentieth Century Revivals, Chicago, Moody Press, 1973

ALAN R. TIPPETT, Professor of Missionary Anthropology.

The Christian: Fiji 1835-67, Auckland, Institute Printing & Publishing Co., 1954.
Solomon Islands Christianity, London, Lutterworth Press, 1967.
Fijian Material Culture: Culture Context, Function and Change, Honolulu, Bishop Museum, 1968.
Verdict Theology in Missionary Theory, 1st Edition, 1969; 2nd Edition, South Pasadena, William Carey Library, 1973.
Church Growth and the Word of God, Grand Rapids, Eerdmans, 1970.
Peoples of Southwest Ethiopia, South Pasadena, William Carey Library, 1970.
People Movements in Southern Polynesia, Chicago, Moody Press, 1971.
Bibliography for Cross-Cultural Workers, South Pasadena, William Carey Library, 1971.
"Possessing the Philosophy of Animism for Christ" and "The Holy Spirit and Responsive Populations," chapters in *Crucial Issues*

in Missions Tomorrow, Donald McGavran, ed., Chicago, Moody Press, 1972.

"For Uppsala to Consider" in *Eye of the Storm,* ed., D.A. McGavran, Waco, Word Books, 1972.

Religious Experience: Its Nature and Function in the Human Psyche, by Clark, Maloney, Daana and Tippett, Springfield, Illinois, C.C. Thomas, 1973.

God, Man and Church Growth, ed., A.R. Tippett, Grand Rapids, Wm. B. Eerdmans, 1973.

"Situational *Givens* in Frontier Missions" in *The Gospel and Frontier Peoples,* South Pasadena, Wm. Carey Library, 1973.

"Conceptual Dyads in the Ethnotheology of 'Salvation Today' " from *IRM,* reprinted in *The Evangelical Response to Bangkok,* ed., R.W. Winter, 1973.

Articles on "Animism", "Cannibalism", "Missions", "Patricide", "Suttee" and "Widow-strangling" in *Baker's Dictionary of Christian Ethics,* ed., C.F.H. Henry, Grand Rapids, Baker Book House, 1973.

Aspects of Pacific Ethnohistory, South Pasadena, Wm. Carey Library, 1973.

RALPH D. WINTER, Professor of the Historical Development of the Christian Movement

"A New Approach to the Hebrew Lexical Problem," chapter in *Doran: Hebraic Studies,* Naamani and Rudarsky, eds., New York, National Association of Professors of Hebrew, 1965.

"Reading in the Guatemalan Environment," chapter in *New Frontiers in College-Adult Reading,* George B. Shick and Merrill M. Hay, eds., National Reading Conference, 1966.

Theological Education by Extension (editor), South Pasadena, William Carey Library, 1969.

The Twenty-Five Unbelievable Years, 1945-1969, South Pasadena, William Carey Library, 1970; revised and reissued, Glendale, Regal Books, 1972.

The Warp and the Woof, Organizing for Mission (with R. Pierce Beaver), South Pasadena, William Carey Library, 1970.

"Quantity or Quality?" chapter in *Crucial Issues in Missions Tomorrow,* Donald McGavran, ed., Chicago, Moody Press, 1972.

"Planting Younger Missions," chapter in *Church/Mission Tensions Today*, C. Peter Wagner, ed., Chicago, Moody Press, 1972.

"Organization of Missions Today," chapter in *Mission Handbook: North American Protestant Ministries Overseas*, Monrovia, MARC, 1973

The Evangelical Response to Bangkok, (editor), South Pasadena, William Carey Library, 1973

C. PETER WAGNER, Associate Professor of Latin American Affairs.

The Condor of the Jungle (with Joseph S. McCullough), Old Tappan, Fleming Revell, 1966.

Defeat of the Bird God, Grand Rapids, Zondervan, 1967.

"The Crisis in Ministerial Training in the Younger Churches," chapter in *Theological Education by Extension*, Ralph D. Winter, ed., South Pasadena, William Carey Library, 1969.

Latin American Theology: Radical or Evangelical?, Grand Rapids, Eerdmans, 1970.

The Protestant Movement in Bolivia, South Pasadena, William Carey Library, 1970.

An Extension Seminary Primer (with Ralph Covell), South Pasadena, William Carey Library, 1971.

A Turned-on Church in an Uptight World, Grand Rapids, Zondervan, 1971.

"What is Evangelism?", chapter in *Christ the Liberator*, Downer's Grove, Inter-Varsity Press, 1971.

Frontiers in Missionary Strategy, Chicago, Moody Press, 1972.

"Pragmatic Strategy for Tomorrow's Mission," chapter in *God, Man and Church Growth*, Alan R. Tippett, ed., Grand Rapids, Eerdmans, 1973.

Look Out! The Pentecostals Are Coming, Carol Stream, Creation House, 1973.

"Disneyland at Bangkok?" and "Two Evangelicals Look at Bangkok," chapters in *The Evangelical Response to Bangkok*, Ralph D. Winter, ed., South Pasadena, William Carey Library, 1973.

Stop the World, I Want to Get On, Glendale, Regal Books, 1974.

Fifty articles for *Diccionario Ilustrado de la Biblia*, Miami, Editorial Caribe, for 1974.

CHARLES H. KRAFT, Associate Professor of Missionary Anthropology and African Affairs

A Study of Hausa Syntax (3 volumes), Hartford, Hartford Studies in Linguistics, volumes 8, 9, and 10, 1963.

Where Do I Go From Here? (with Marguerite E. Kraft), Washington, United States Peace Corps, 1966.

Teach Yourself Hausa, London, English Universities Press, 1973.

Spoken Hausa, Introductory Course (with Marguerite E. Kraft), Berkeley, University of California Press, 1973.

Cultural Materials in Hausa (editor), Berkeley, University of California Press, in press for 1974.

Chadic Word Lists (3 volumes), Ibadan, Institute of African Studies, in press for 1974.

African Linguistic Classification (editor), Bloomington, Indiana University, for 1974.

Higi Ethnography (3 volumes), New Haven, HRAFlex Books, for 1974.

289

MILESTONE BOOKS IN THE CHURCH GROWTH MOVEMENT

Ralph D. Winter
Professor of the Historical Development
of the Christian Movement
Fuller School of World Mission and
Institute of Church Growth

The list of books chosen to be annotated below is by no means exhaustive. The Church Growth movement derives from a broad spectrum of keen observers who have now and then, here and there, studied how societies are structured, how men and groups actually become Christian, how churches multiply, how movements to Christ are arrested or obstructed, how evangelism develops, etc. This is not the place to try to give credit to all whose thinking has contributed to the movement. Time would fail us to tell how Lorimer Fison, the Methodist missionary anthropologist 80 years ago saw accurately the social structure of Fijian tribes and how this affected the growth of the church among them, how G.W. Vicedom explored the encounter of the church with the people of New Guinea, how Christian Kaiser, also in New Guinea, Bruno Gutmann in Tanzania, and Warneck in Sumatra wrote down observations in a similar vein. Certain writers did their work in some pocket of the mission movement so that their thinking did not contribute to the growth of the Church Growth movement until much later. Others' writings are not in English or are out of print. Our desire here is to list books which are immediately available so that readers can evaluate the Church Growth movement for themselves.

In any list of books on Church Growth, one is almost forced to tip his hat to William Carey's 1972 booklet, *An Enquiry,* as the first statistical, historical, Biblical, evangelistic and organizational thrust that could be regarded to have set the pace for modern Church Growth studies. We look forward to its reissuance soon by the William Carey Library.

1910 to 1930

Roland Allen is the restless, indefatigable missionary, Bible-scholar, high-church Anglican whose writings almost single hand-edly in this period built up significant pressure for radical re-thinking about missionary strategy. Not the same at all as the infamous *Rethinking* (1932) done by Hocking et al, Allen's works were highly spiritual and Biblical but unfortunately did not gain a wide audience in the USA until the 60s, when with the help of Eerdmans, they splashed down as a triumvirate: *Missionary Methods: St Paul's or Ours?, The Spontaneous Expansion of the Church and the Causes Which Hinder It,* and *The Ministry of the Spirit* (selections from his writings), all currently in print, comment-ed on below.

1930-1955

In 1933 *Christian Mass Movements in India* appeared, and its author, J. Wascom Pickett, immediately became a trail blazer for the study of group conversion phenomena in India. Later he became a professor of missions and the author of a second book to be mentioned in the next section. *Christian Mass Movements* is a book of 382 pages jammed with the data of real experience. McGavran, who shortly afterwards worked with Pickett in further studies, says that this book was "epochal" and "marked a turning point in mission history." "To leaders convinced that Christianiza-tion is necessarily a very slow and difficult process, Dr. Pickett's accounts of the triumphs of the Gospel . . . in the people movement fashion caused a revolution in thinking."

The collaboration of Pickett, McGavran and Singh produced a second book in 1936, later to be reissued under the title *Church Growth and Group Conversion.* Echoing similar sentiments, and also in 1936, Latourette's prophetic world-wide summary *Missions Tomorrow* appeared, in which he wrote

"More and more we must dream in terms of winning groups, not merely of individuals. Too often, with our Protestant, nineteenth-century individualism, we have torn men and women, one by one, out of the family or village or clan, with the result that they have been permanently deracinated and maladjusted. To be sure, in its last analysis conversion must result in a new relation between the individual and his Maker — in radiant, transformed lives. Usually the group, if won, is brought over by a few of its members who have found, singly, the truth of the gospel and have begun the new life. Experience, however, shows that it is much better if an entire natural group — a family, a village, a caste, a tribe — can come rapidly over into the faith. That gives reinforcement to the individual Christian and makes easier the Christianization of the entire life of a community."

While this book is not available today, others of his are. Latourette produced almost one book a year during this whole period, including his seven volume *History of the Expansion of Christianity*, which elaborately investigates the spread of Christianity, the reasons why, the processes and methods, noting in detail the influence of the environment on Christianity and vice versa. In the introduction to the largest single volume he produced, *A History of Christianity (1953)*, he spoke of "taking account of the forms of the faith which spread, the reasons for the expansion, and the methods, agents, and agencies through which the spread took place." (In 1963 he agreed to be one of the sponsors of the Institute of Church Growth, which McGavran had established in Eugene, Oregon, and in 1968, three weeks before his death in a car accident, he agreed to deliver a series of lectures on "European People Movements," at the new location of that institute in Pasadena, California.)

A significant development throughout this period was the growth of interest among American evangelicals in the concept of the indigenous church, much earlier advanced by men like Henry Venn and Rufus Anderson. Highly strategic was the decision of the Assemblies of God Foreign Department to pull off the field one of their most productive missionaries, Melvin L. Hodges, and ask him to blend his experience with research in what others were doing and thinking. The resulting book *The Indigenous Church* shows that he really did his home work, and it also shows the affinity between many different writers in different quarters. His book is peppered with references to World Dominion publications, to Allen's writings specifically as well as to Herbert Kane's, John Ritchie's, and to documents reflecting advanced thinking in the Conservative Baptist Foreign Mission Society. Moody for a time published a special edition entitled *On the Mission Field.* We will see this man again.

1955-1965

This is the period of initial institutionalization: the founding of the Institute of Church Growth at Northwest Christian College in Eugene, and the inauguration of the *Church Growth Bulletin* in 1964.

McGavran's *The Bridges of God, A Study in the Strategy of Missions* (1955) pulled it all together at that point in time. Latourette wrote the introduction. The book was published originally by the World Dominion Press, which in England had sponsored Roland Allen's writings, thus showing the affinity between the two. The same press came out with McGavran's *How Churches Grow, The New Frontiers of Mission* in 1959.

Presently the Roland Allen triumvirate of books mentioned above came booming in on the American scene, thanks to Eerdmans. *Church Growth and Group Conversion* also appeared again, reprinted from 1936, under this new title. Ending the period there appeared under Harper's imprint *Church Growth and Christian Mission* (1965) which brought under one cover four leading mission thinkers, from widely separated quarters: McGavran, Cal Guy (Southern Baptist, professor of missions at Fort Worth), Melvin L. Hodges, whom we have seen in the previous period, and Eugene Nida, that most widely travelled missionary in history, of the American Bible Society.

293

1965 to the Present

This new period begins with the expansion and re-establishment of the Institute of Church Growth. Now appeared the first fruits of a significant decision by the Eerdmans Publishing House — to start a *Church Growth Series* of books. Eight of the fifteen appearing through 1973 are reports of studies done at Eugene:
Church Growth in Mexico: Donald McGavran, John Huegel, Jack Taylor

Wildfire − Church Growth in Korea: Roy E. Shearer
New Patterns of Church Growth in Brazil: William R. Read
Church Growth in Central and Southern Nigeria: John B. Grimley,
  Gordon E. Robinson
God's Impatience in Liberia: Joseph Conrad Wold
Tinder in Tabasco: Charles Bennett
Church Growth in Sierra Leone: Gilbert W. Olson
*Laity Mobilized: The Growth of the Church in Japan and Other
  Lands:* Neil Braun

Another six have already appeared, which were studies done at
Pasadena:

Latin American Church Growth: William R. Read, Victor M.
  Monterroso, Harmon A. Johnson
Understanding Church Growth: Donald McGavran
Church Growth and the Word of God: Alan R. Tippett
Man, Milieu, and Mission in Argentina: Arno W. Enns
The Philippine Church: Growth in a Changing Society: Arthur L.
  Tuggy
The Discipling of West Cameroon: A Study of Baptist Growth:
  Lloyd E. Kwast
God, Man, and Church Growth: Alan R. Tippett

294   Most of these are studies in specific regions, and all but two
were done at least in part, by missionary research associates rather
than by one of the Institute's faculty members. The authors
represent a wide spectrum of different church communions. One of
the two exceptions referred to is McGavran's definitive work,
Understanding Church Growth (1970), which is the best single
book representing his thinking. A close second, of a very different
type, is the volume which brings together the first five years of the
Church Growth Bulletin. This is fascinating to browse through.
More recently McGavran has edited *Crucial Issues in Missions
Tomorrow* (Moody) and *Eye of the Storm* (Word).

This brings us to a second publisher that has begun a *Church
Growth Series:* Moody Press. Five books have now appeared in this
series: *Crucial Issues,* mentioned just above, *Historic Patterns of
Church Growth* by Harold R. Cook, *The Unresponsive, Resistant or
Neglected* by David C.E. Liao, *Frontiers of Mission Strategy* by C.
Peter Wagner, and *People Movements in Southern Polynesia* by
Alan R. Tippett, a profoundly significant work, almost half of
which is devoted to general Church Growth theory.

The latter author, Tippett, produced two of the Eerdmans series as well, one of which, *God, Man and Church Growth,* is the largest, most comprehensive anthology of Church Growth writings yet to appear. His earlier *Solomon Islands Christianity* (1967) has set the pace for regional studies more than any other single-country study, displaying the full range of Biblical, theological, ecclesiastical, historical, political and, above all, anthropological factors involved in Church Growth theory and practice. He has also given us *Peoples of Southwest Ethiopia, Bibliography for Cross-Cultural Workers,* and *Verdict Theology in Missionary Theory,* all of which are under the William Carey Library imprint.

The most recent institutional phenomenon in the Church Growth movement is the founding of the William Carey Library in 1969 and the Church Growth Book Club in 1970. The William Carey Library is designed to publish, whether by book, microfilm, tape, or film, materials that bear on the strategic aspects of the Christian World Mission. Its 55 books as of this date (1973) are too numerous to list. [You may request a list from the William Carey Library, 533 Hermosa Street, South Pasadena, Calif. 91030.] The Church Growth Book Club does not publish books but edits a section in each issue of the *Church Growth Bulletin* (which goes bi-monthly to 8,000 people) highlighting books which it makes available (but does not send automatically) at a 40% discount to subscribers. It stocks all the William Carey Library books plus more than 100 others from 34 publishers including virtually all the books mentioned in this article. Its larger list is available from the same address above. The Club and the William Carey Library together have sold more than 100,000 Church Growth books in the past three years. This, in addition to the Church Growth books that have been sold directly by the various publishers like Eerdmans and Moody, is a significant measure of the present momentum of the movement.

295

Those who wish to follow the Church Growth movement will also want to know about new ideas and new books as they constantly stream forth. Overseas Crusades has made this easy, and has put us all in their debt, by shouldering the publishing of the *Church Growth Bulletin* (Box 66, Palo Alto, Calif., $1 per year). It's edited by Donald A. McGavran and carries in each issue the section mentioned above on new books as they become available.

Brief abstracts of dissertations, theses or projects
presented to the faculty of the School of World Mission
and Institute of Church Growth, Fuller Theological Seminary,
Pasadena, California, are given alphabetically according to
the surname of the associates. The associate's SWM number
(see DIRECTORY OF SWM ASSOCIATES), precedes the name.

290
AIER, K. IMOTEMJEN. THE GROWTH OF THE GARO BAPTIST CHURCHES
OF MEGHALAYA IN NORTH EAST INDIA. SWM, M.A. THESIS,
PASADENA, 1974.

THIS THESIS AIMS TO GIVE HISTORICAL BACKGROUND OF
THE GARO TRIBE AND THE COMING OF THE BAPTIST MISSION.
DEALS WITH THE STAGES OF CHURCH GROWTH THROUGH THE
YEARS AMONG THE GAROS. EVALUATES CRITICALLY THE
METHODS AND PROGRAMMES THAT AFFECTED THE GROWTH AND
NON-GROWTH. MAKES SOME POSSIBLE SUGGESTIONS AND
RECOMMENDATIONS FOR SPEEDY GROWTH.

400
ALEXANDER, FRANK. MISSIONS IN MALAWI. SWM, M.A. THESIS,
300 pp. PASADENA, 1969.

THE LAND AND HISTORY OF BANTU PEOPLE IN MALAWI.
ANTHROPOLOGICAL INFORMATION CONCERNING BANTU
RELIGION AND WORLD-VIEW. ACCULTURATION AND
URBANIZATION DISCUSSED AS WELL AS PRESBYTERIAN
MISSIONS AND SEVERAL OTHERS. SPECIAL COVERAGE
OF MISSIONS OF THE CHURCHES OF CHRIST.
PROPOSALS MADE FOR INCREASED CHURCH GROWTH.

910
ALSOP, ALBERT A. A NEW BEGINNING - THE UNITED EVANGELICAL
        LUTHERAN CHURCH OF ARGENTINA. SWM, M.A. PROJECT
        REPORT TO THE LUTHERAN CHURCH IN ARGENTINA--SOME
        OBSERVATIONS. 35 pp. PASADENA, 1974.

        AFTER SPENDING TWENTY YEARS IN LATIN AMERICA, WITH
        THE MAJOR EMPHASIS IN ARGENTINA AND CHILE, AND
        AFTER ACQUIRING CHURCH GROWTH INSIGHTS FOR ASSESSING
        PAST EFFORTS IN THE EXPANSION OF THE CHURCH, THE
        NEED FOR APPRAISAL WITH THE IDEA TOWARDS MAKING A
        NEW BEGINNING WAS BORN.

910
ALSOP, ALBERT A. A TRANSLATION FROM ENGLISH TO SPANISH
        OF THE BOOK BY ALAN R. TIPPETT, CHURCH GROWTH AND
        THE WORD OF GOD. SWM, M.A. WORK PROJECT, 80 pp.
        PASADENA, 1974.

1700
ASPINALL, H, RAYMOND. THE BRETHREN CHURCH IN ARGENTINA:
        A CHURCH GROWTH STUDY. SWM, M.A. THESIS, 128 pp.
        PASADENA, 1973.

297

        A CHURCH GROWTH STUDY OF A SMALL CHURCH (LESS
        THAN 1000) IN ARGENTINA INCLUDING COMPARISONS
        WITH NAZARENE CHURCH, MENNONITE CHURCH AND THE
        ASSEMBLIES OF GOD. INCLUDES A STRATEGY OF
        REVITALIZATION FOR CHURCH GROWTH. INCLUDES MAPS,
        FIGURES, TABLES AND BIBLIOGRAPHY.

1900
AVERY, ALLEN W. AFRICAN INDEPENDENCY. SWM, M.A. THESIS
        157 pp. PASADENA, 1973.

        THE NATURE OF THE PHENOMENON OF AFRICAN INDEPENDENT
        CHURCHES IS DISCUSSED. THERE ARE BETWEEN 5000 AND
        6000 OF THESE MOVEMENTS. CAUSES, TRENDS, AND
        ORGANIZATIONAL DEVELOPMENT ARE TRACED. CHURCH
        GROWTH ANALYSES OF SOME CHRISTIAN AND CHRISTO-PAGAN
        MOVEMENTS ARE INCLUDED. THREE SYNCRETISTIC CHURCHES
        ARE STUDIED.

2200
BALISKY, E. PAUL. AFRICAN AND OTHER STUDIES. SWM, M.A.
RESEARCH PROJECT, 142 pp. PASADENA, 1972.

A SERIES OF ARTICLES ON AFRICAN HYMNOLOGY, CHURCH
GROWTH IN SOUTHERN ETHIOPIA, BENGT SUNDKLER--THE
MISSIOLOGIST, AND ENCOUNTERING ANIMISTIC BELIEF
AND PRACTICE.

2800
BENNETT, CHARLES T. TINDER IN TABASCO. EERDMANS, GRAND
RAPIDS, 213 pp. 1968.

A STUDY OF CHURCH GROWTH IN TROPICAL MEXICO.
PRESBYTERIAN CHURCH DEVELOPMENT IN TABASCO ANALYZED
FROM EARLIEST BEGINNINGS IN THE 1880's UNTIL THE
PRESENT. PERIODS OF GROWTH AND STAGNATION ARE
PROBED FOR REASONS AND RECOMMENDATIONS ARE MADE
FOR THE FUTURE.

3600
BOLTON, ROBERT J. TREASURE ISLAND: CHURCH GROWTH AMONG
TAIWAN'S URBAN MINNAN CHINESE. SWM, M.A. THESIS,
PASADENA, 1974.

298

DESCRIBES THE MINNAN CHINESE, THEIR HISTORY, SOCIAL
STRUCTURE AND RELIGION. GIVES A HISTORY OF
CHRISTIAN MISSION AMONG THEM IN CHINA AND TAIWAN.
A CHAPTER IS DEVOTED TO URBANIZATION. CASE STUDIES
OF CONVERSION AND URBAN CHURCHES ARE WRITTEN FROM
FIELD DATA. CONCLUDES WITH A STRATEGY OF MISSIONS.

4000
BRADSHAW, MALCOLM. CHURCH GROWTH THROUGH EVANGELISM-IN-
DEPTH. WILLIAM CAREY LIBRARY, SOUTH PASADENA,
127 pp. 1969.

THE FIRST EFFORT OF ITS KIND TO BRING TOGETHER
TWO PERVASIVE MOVEMENTS OF REVITALIZATION IN THE
CHURCHES OF THE LATTER HALF OF THE 20TH CENTURY.
EXCELLENT CONCISE DEFINITIONS OF BOTH CHURCH
GROWTH AND EVANGELISM-IN-DEPTH ARE GIVEN. INCLUDES
CONCLUSIONS OF SEVERAL STUDIES DONE ON EID. ALSO
GIVES SYNOPSES OF NEW LIFE FOR ALL AND CHRIST FOR
ALL.

4300
BRAUN, NEIL H. LAITY MOBILIZED: REFLECTIONS ON CHURCH
      GROWTH IN JAPAN AND OTHER LANDS. EERDMANS,
      GRAND RAPIDS, 244 pp. 1971.

      THESIS BASED ON THE QUESTION "HOW CAN THE WHOLE
      PEOPLE OF GOD IN JAPAN BE MOBILIZED FOR
      EVANGELISM AND CHURCH PLANTING IN OUR DAY?"
      SYNCHRONIC AND DIACHRONIC STUDIES OF CHURCH
      GROWTH ARE MADE AND CONCLUSIONS FORMED FOR GREATER
      EFFECTIVENESS. INCLUDES A CHAPTER ON "THE LAOS
      OF GOD." APPENDICES AND BIBLIOGRAPHY.

*
BRIDGES, JULIAN C. A STUDY OF THE NUMBER, DISTRIBUTION,
      AND GROWTH OF THE PROTESTANT POPULATION IN MEXICO.
      UNIVERSITY OF FLORIDA, M.A. THESIS, 108 pp.
      GAINESVILLE, 1969.

      PROTESTANT GROWTH PATTERN EXAMINED FROM 1860 TO
      PRESENT WITH PARTICULAR EMPHASIS ON THE PERIOD
      FROM 1940-1960. ALSO DEALS WITH INTERRELATEDNESS
      OF NUMBER, DISTRIBUTION AND GROWTH AND REASONS
      FOR THIS.

299

4500
BROOM, WENDELL W. GROWTH OF CHURCHES OF CHRIST AMONG
      IBIBIOS OF NIGERIA. SWM, M.A. THESIS, 268 pp.
      PASADENA, 1970.

      DISCUSSES ESTABLISHMENT OF OTHER CHRISTIAN MISSIONS
      BEFORE AND AFTER LAUNCHING OF CHURCH OF CHRIST IN
      1948 WITH A VIEW TO UNDERSTANDING REASONS FOR
      GROWTH AND NON-GROWTH. THE FANTASTIC GROWTH OF
      THE CHURCHES OF CHRIST IS ANALYZED. LEADERSHIP
      TRAINING AT SEVERAL LEVELS, PRIORITY ON EVANGELISM
      AND CONGREGATIONAL AUTONOMY ARE FACTORS CAUSING
      GROWTH.

---

*
Absence of a number signifies that the writer of this
thesis (or dissertation) is not a SWM associate. The (*)
thesis or dissertation has been added to the SWM shelves
for missiological research purposes.

4600
BROUGHAM, DAVID R. THE TRAINING OF THE CHINESE IN
      INDONESIA FOR THE MINISTRY. SWM, M.A. THESIS,
      188 pp. PASADENA, 1970.

      "THE PURPOSE OF THIS STUDY IS TO EXAMINE THE
      ROLE OF THE CHINESE IN INDONESIA AS POTENTIAL
      CARRIERS OF THE GOSPEL OF CHRIST FOR INDONESIA,
      FOR SOUTHEAST ASIA, AND FOR CHINA, AND TO
      DISCOVER THOSE TRAINING PATTERNS THAT ENABLE
      CHINESE TO BECOME CHURCH PLANTERS AND TO
      CONTRIBUTE TO THE GROWTH AND MULTIPLICATION
      OF EXISTING CHURCHES."

5000
BUEHLER, HERMAN G. NOMINALITY CONSIDERED: A SURVEY
      OF CONTEMPORARY THINKING. SWM, M.A. THESIS,
      200 pp. PASADENA, 1973.

      A COMPREHENSIVE STUDY OF NOMINAL CHRISTIANITY
      WITH HISTORICAL, ANTHROPOLOGICAL, AND THEOLOGICAL
      CONSIDERATIONS. INCLUDES A CASE STUDY OF THE
      TRUKESE CHURCH. BIBLICAL NORMS AND HUMAN
      RESPONSES ARE COMPARED AND RELATED TO PRESENT
300 DAY MISSIOLOGICAL RESEARCH AND ANALYSIS.

5300
BUTLER, CHARLES O. CHURCH GROWTH IN PANAMA. SOUTHERN
      METHODIST UNIVERSITY, S.T.M. THESIS, 80 pp.
      DALLAS, 1964.

      A STUDY OF FOURSQUARE GOSPEL AND METHODIST
      PATTERNS OF GROWTH IN A CHANGING PANAMA.
      CHURCH GROWTH PRINCIPLES UNDERLIE THIS STUDY.

5500
CARR, LUCILLE. A SEMINARY AND CHURCH GROWTH IN TAIWAN.
      SWM, M.A. THESIS, 235 pp. PASADENA, 1966.

      A CRITICAL ANALYSIS OF THE TAIWAN CONSERVATIVE
      BAPTIST THEOLOGICAL SEMINARY FROM THE CHURCH
      GROWTH VIEWPOINT.

5600
CARVER, E. EARL. SHOWCASE FOR GOD: A STUDY OF EVANGELICAL
    CHURCH GROWTH IN PUERTO RICO. SWM, M.A. THESIS,
    254 pp. PASADENA, 1972.

    STUDY OF THE DEVELOPMENT OF THE EVANGELICAL
    DENOMINATIONS OF PUERTO RICO. THE GROWTH OF
    THESE DENOMINATIONS COMPARED AMONG THEMSELVES
    AND TO THE REST OF LATIN AMERICA. ETHNIC GROUPS
    WITHIN THE COUNTRY DISCUSSED. EXTENSIVE USE OF
    CHARTS, GRAPHS, STATISTICS.

5800
CHAE, EUN SOO. RECEPTIVITY OF KOREA-TAIWAN MOUNTAIN
    PEOPLE. SWM, M.A. RESEARCH PROJECT, 133 pp.
    PASADENA, 1973.

    DESCRIBES RELIGIOUS LIFE AND RECEPTIVITY IN KOREA
    TO CHRISTIANITY. A 109 PAGE PAPER INCLUDES
    HISTORICAL AND NATIONAL CHARACTERISTICS. A SECOND
    PAPER OF 25 PAGES IS A STUDY OF INDIGENOUS MOUNTAIN
    PEOPLE OF TAIWAN. IT INCLUDES A STUDY OF SOCIAL AND
    RELIGIOUS LIFE WITH REFERENCE TO A PEOPLE MOVEMENT
    DURING THE DUTCH PERIOD OF OCCUPATION.

301

6000
CHANDLER, THOMAS W. A STATISTICAL STUDY OF SHORT TERM
    MISSIONARIES. SWM. M.A. PROJECT, PASADENA, 1973.

    AN ANALYSIS OF SHORT TERM MISSIONARY ACTIVITY
    INCLUDING REASONS FOR SHORT TERMS, PROBLEMS OF
    ADJUSTMENT AND INTERPERSONAL RELATIONSHIPS.
    INCLUDES APPENDICES AND BIBLIOGRAPHY.

7100
CONLEY, WILLIAM W. THE KALIMANTAN KENYAH. SWM, DOCTORAL
    DISSERTATION, 444 pp. PASADENA, 1973.

    A STUDY OF TRIBAL CONVERSION IN TERMS OF DYNAMIC
    CULTURAL THEMES. OPLER'S CULTURAL THEMES ARE
    COMPARED AND RELATED TO SOCIAL CHANGE IN A
    CHRISTIANIZED SOCIETY. A STUDY OF THE CHRISTIAN
    AND MISSIONARY ALLIANCE CHURCH IN INDONESIA
    (90,000 MEMBERS).

7200
CONRAD, WILLIAM H. A REPORT TO THE DEPARTMENT OF MISSIONS
    OF THE CHURCH OF THE NAZARENE CONCERNING GROWTH
    ON ITS MISSION FIELDS. SWM, M.A. THESIS,
    PASADENA, 1967.

7500
CORNELIUS, GOLLAPALLI. URBAN CHURCH GROWTH AMONG
    TELUGU BAPTISTS IN SOUTH INDIA. SWM, M.A. THESIS,
    173 pp. PASADENA, 1971.

    INVESTIGATES THE GROWTH OF BAPTIST CONGREGATIONS
    IN FOUR INDIAN CITIES--MADRAS, VISAKHAPATNAM,
    KURNOOL, AND KAKINADA. A CAREFUL LOOK AT THIS
    GROWTH TO DISCOVER ITS ORIGIN AND VERACITY.
    ETHNIC CONGREGATIONS ARE ENCOURAGED TO PROMOTE
    CONTINUED CHURCH GROWTH.

302 7700
COX, EMMETT D. THE UNITED BRETHREN IN CHRIST IN SIERRA
    LEONE. WILLIAM CAREY LIBRARY, SOUTH PASADENA,
    171 pp. 1970.

    A CHURCH GROWTH STUDY OF A CHURCH OF LESS THAN
    3000 IN WEST AFRICA. INCLUDES GEOGRAPHY, OTHER
    RELIGIONS, FACTORS INFLUENCING GROWTH OF THE
    CHURCH AND PROSPECTS FOR FUTURE GROWTH. THE
    PARISH PLAN OF EVANGELISM IS GIVEN AS A
    POSSIBILITY FOR MOBILIZATION. MAPS, CHARTS,
    AND BIBLIOGRAPHY INCLUDED.

7900
CURRY, MICHAEL W. MISSION INSTITUTIONS OF THE CHURCHES IN
    SOUTHERN TANZANIA. SWM, M.A. THESIS, 256 pp.
    PASADENA, 1972.

    A STUDY OF MODERN MISSIONS WITH THEIR RELATION TO
    CHURCH INSTITUTIONS. BASED ON FIELD RESEARCH WITH
    ANTHROPOLOGICAL DATA. DEALS WITH TRADITIONAL RELIGION,
    EVANGELISTIC STRATEGY AND RECOMMENDATIONS.

8000
DANIEL, KURUMANASSERIL C. INDIAN CHURCH GROWTH DYNAMICS.
SWM, M.A. THESIS, 161 pp. PASADENA, 1971.

A DESCRIPTION OF THE MAR THOMA CHURCH AND ITS
PROBLEMS OF NON-GROWTH. PROPOSES THE DEVELOPMENT
OF ETHNIC CONGREGATIONS IN WHICH NEW BELIEVERS
CAN FEEL AT HOME. IN-DEPTH LOOK AT A CHURCH
CAUGHT IN A VERY DIFFICULT SOCIAL MILIEU.

8300
DAVIS, LINNELL E. THE USE OF THE BIBLE IN THE KAMBA
TRIBAL SETTING. SWM, M.A. THESIS, 241 pp.
PASADENA, 1968.

THOROUGH ANTHROPOLOGICAL TREATMENT OF THE KAMBA
PEOPLE OF KENYA, THEIR RELIGIOUS CONCEPTS, AND
THEIR REACTIONS TO SOCIAL CHANGE. SPECIAL
TREATMENT GIVEN TO MAKING THE BIBLE COMMUNICATE
TO THESE PEOPLE IN THEIR CULTURAL MILIEU.

8800
DILWORTH, DONALD R. THE EVANGELIZATION OF THE QUICHUAS
OF ECUADOR. SWM, M.A. THESIS, 124 pp. PASADENA,
1967.

303

HISTORICAL, ETHNOLOGICAL AND SOCIOLOGICAL FACTORS
AFFECTING THE EVANGELIZATION OF THE QUICHUAS ARE
DISCUSSED. LIFE, CHRISTIANITY, MISSIONS AND
MISSIONARIES SEEN THROUGH THE EYES OF THE QUICHUA.

*DYCK, PAUL I. EMERGENCE OF NEW CASTES IN INDIA.
UNIVERSITY OF MANITOBA, M.A. THESIS, 120 pp.
WINNIPEG, 1970.

AN ANTHROPOLOGICAL ANALYSIS OF SOCIAL CHANGE IN
MODERN INDIA. STUDIES THE PROCESSES BY WHICH NEW
CASTES EMERGE. COVERS AN HISTORICAL PERIOD FROM
APPROXIMATELY 1850-1950. THIS HISTORICAL SURVEY
IS USED TO PROJECT THE FUTURE OF SOCIAL CHANGE IN
INDIA. BASED UPON LIBRARY RESEARCH, QUESTIONNAIRES
AND PERSONAL OBSERVATIONS IN INDIA.

9400

EDWARDS, FRED E. THE ROLE OF THE FAITH MISSION: A
        BRAZILIAN CASE STUDY. WILLIAM CAREY LIBRARY,
        SOUTH PASADENA, 1971.

        STUDIES BRAZILIAN MAINLINE PROTESTANT MISSIONS
        AND FAITH MISSIONS IN GENERAL, THEN TAKES A CLOSER
        LOOK AT DIFFERENT TYPES OF FAITH MISSIONS. THE
        INTER-AMERICAN MISSIONARY SOCIETY, OF WHICH THE
        AUTHOR IS A PART, IS ANALYZED IN DEPTH.

9900

ELLISTON, EDGAR J. AN ETHNOHISTORY OF ETHIOPIA. SWM,
        M.A. THESIS, 177 pp. PASADENA, 1968.

        COMPREHENSIVE ETHNOHISTORY INCLUDING POLITICAL,
        CULTURAL AND RELIGIOUS FACTORS. RELEVANCE OF THE
        RESEARCH TO THE CHRISTIAN MISSIONARY FELLOWSHIP.
        INCLUDES MAPS, APPENDIX, GLOSSARY, AND BIBLIOGRAPHY.

10000

ENNS, ARNO W. MAN, MILIEU, AND MISSION IN ARGENTINA,
        A CLOSE LOOK AT CHURCH GROWTH. EERDMANS, GRAND
        RAPIDS, 1971.

304

        DESCRIBES THOSE FACTORS WHICH HAVE CAUSED GROWTH
        AND NON-GROWTH IN ARGENTINE EVANGELICAL CHURCHES.
        PUTS FORTH THE THEORY THAT BOTH EXTERNAL ENVIRON-
        MENT AND INTERNAL DEVELOPMENTS OF THESE CHURCHES
        AFFECTED CHURCH GROWTH. SPECIAL ATTENTION TO
        FORMATION OF NATION, RELIGION AND PERSONALITY OF
        THE ARGENTINE.

10500

ERICKSON, EDWIN. TRAINING OF ETHIOPIAN RURAL CHURCH
        LEADERSHIP. SWM,M.A. THESIS, 276 pp. PASADENA,
        1972.

        ATTEMPT TO DESIGN A CULTURALLY RELEVANT PROGRAM
        OF THEOLOGICAL EDUCATION FOR ETHIOPIA IN GENERAL
        WITH SPECIAL REFERENCE TO THE EASTERN MECHA GALLA
        PEOPLE. THEOLOGICAL EDUCATION BY EXTENTION (TAKING
        BIBLE TRAINING TO THE PEOPLE), AND CREATING AN
        INDIGENOUS THEOLOGY ARE PRIME CONCERNS.

11000
EVANS, MELVIN O. SPIRIT POSSESSION IN CERTAIN SOUTHERN
    BANTU TRIBES. SWM, M.A. THESIS, 171 pp. PASADENA,
    1971.

    TREATS THE BIBLICAL UNDERSTANDING OF SPIRITS AND
    THE PSYCHOLOGICAL AND MEDICAL BACKGROUND OF SPIRIT
    POSSESSION. ANALYZES THE EFFECTS OF SPIRIT
    POSESSION IN THREE BANTU TRIBES AND THE INFLUENCE
    CHRISTIAN MISSIONS HAS HAD UPON SUCH BONDAGE.
    CHURCH GROWTH PRINCIPLES ARE APPLIED.

11600
FRIEND, L. ANDREW. THE CONTRIBUTION OF MISSION SCHOOLS
    TO CHURCH GROWTH IN SUB-SAHARAN AFRICA. SWM, M.A.
    THESIS, 259 pp. PASADENA, 1971.

    DISCUSSES THE ENORMOUS COMMITMENT OF MEN AND MONEY
    TO INSTITUTIONS DEVELOPED BY CHURCHES AND MISSIONS
    IN SUB-SAHARAN AFRICA. SEEKS TO SHOW HOW MISSION
    INSTITUTIONS HAVE DIVERTED MISSIONARIES FROM THEIR
    TRUE TASK OF EFFECTIVE EVANGELISM.

11700
FUGMANN,GERNOT. CHURCH GROWTH AND URBANIZATION IN NEW   305
    GUINEA. SWM, M.A. THESIS, 244 pp. PASADENA, 1969.

    A PRELIMINARY EMPIRICAL-CRITICAL STUDY IN AN AREA
    OF YOUNG CHRISTIANITY. HISTORY OF THE NEW GUINEA
    CHURCHES IS EXPLORED. REASONS ARE GIVEN FOR
    INCREASED URBANIZATION WITHIN THE SOCIETY. IN-DEPTH
    STUDY OF URBAN CHURCHES, THEIR PECULIAR FEATURES
    AND THEIR NEEDS.

12000
GAMALIEL, JAMES C. THE CHURCH IN KERALA: A PEOPLE
    MOVEMENT STUDY. SWM, M.A. THESIS, 170 pp.
    PASADENA, 1967.

    A STUDY OF THE GROWTH PATTERNS OF KERALA CHURCHES,
    WITH SPECIAL EMPHASIS GIVEN TO REASONS FOR SLOW
    GROWTH. THE PROBLEMS OF CASTE ARE DISCUSSED AS THEY
    RELATE TO THE CHURCH. PROPOSALS ARE MADE FOR MORE
    EFFECTIVE INDIGENIZATION AND EVANGELISM.

12200
GATES, ALAN F.   CHRISTIANITY AND ANIMISM: CHINA AND
        TAIWAN.   SWM, DOCTORAL DISSERTATION, 262 pp.
        PASADENA, 1971.

        A COMPREHENSIVE AND CAREFULLY PREPARED WORK ON
        CHRISTIANITY IN CONFRONTATION WITH ANIMISM.
        INCLUDES STUDIES OF WORLD VIEWS, SHAMINISM AND
        THE POWER ENCOUNTER APPROACH TO ANIMISTIC PRACTICES.
        APOSTLE PAUL'S THEOLOGY OF "THE POWERS" STUDIED.

12200
GATES, ALAN F.   CHURCH GROWTH IN TAIWAN.   SWM, M.A.
        THESIS, 251 pp.   PASADENA, 1966.

        STUDIES THE LESSONS OF HISTORY FOR THE GROWTH OF
        THE CHURCHES IN TAIWAN 1622-1965.   INCLUDES A
        COMPREHENSIVE ANALYSIS OF SOCIAL STRUCTURES IN BOTH
        URBAN AND RURAL TAIWAN.   BIBLIOGRAPHY.

*GREENWAY, ROGER S.   THE DUTCH REFORMED CHURCH IN CEYLON
        1642-1796.   CALVIN SEMINARY, Th.M. THESIS, 219 pp.
        GRAND RAPIDS, 1963.

306   HISTORICAL TREATMENT OF SUBJECT.   DEALS WITH
        RELIGIOUS AND POLITICAL FORCES WHICH HINDERED
        SPREAD OF PROTESTANTISM, THE CONTINUING EFFORTS
        OF THE DUTCH TO ESTABLISH THE CHURCH THROUGH
        CHRISTIAN SCHOOLS, LITERATURE WORK, THEOLOGICAL
        EDUCATION AND COERCION: AND THE EVENTUAL COLLAPSE
        OF THE DUTCH REFORMED CHURCH IN CEYLON.

*GREENWAY, ROGER S.   AN URBAN STRATEGY FOR LATIN AMERICA.
        SOUTHWESTERN BAPTIST THEOLOGICAL SEMINARY, DOCTORAL
        DISSERTATION, 392 pp.   FORT WORTH, 1972.

        "THE PURPOSE OF THIS DISSERTATION IS TO EXPLAIN
        AND DEMONSTRATE THE OPPORTUNITY PROVIDED BY MODERN
        URBANIZATION FOR THE SPREAD OF THE GOSPEL IN LATIN
        AMERICA.   A BASIC ASSUMPTION UNDERLYING THIS STUDY
        IS THAT GOD CONTROLS HISTORY AND USES HISTORICAL
        MOVEMENTS IN THE ACCOMPLISHMENT OF HIS REDEMPTIVE
        PURPOSE."

13200
GROVER, JEANNE. CHURCH GROWTH IN EASTERN PERU. SWM,
RESEARCH PROJECT, 62 pp. PASADENA, 1966.

A LOOK AT THE ROMAN CATHOLIC MISSION WORK IN
LATIN AMERICA, ITS SUCCESSES AND FAILURES. AN
ANALYSIS OF THE EVANGELICAL MISSION OUTREACH IN
PERUVIAN JUNGLES SINCE 1888. CHARTS AND BIBLIOGRAPHY.

13300
GUSTAFSON, JAMES W. SYNCRETISTIC RURAL THAI BUDDHISM.
SWM, M.A. THESIS, 272 pp. PASADENA, 1970.

A STUDY OF THE ORIGIN AND GROWTH OF THAI BUDDHISM
INCLUDING WORLD-VIEW AND SYNCRETISM. ALSO A
HISTORY OF PROTESTANT MISSIONS IN THAILAND WITH
SEVERAL CHAPTERS DEVOTED TO RETHINKING MISSIONARY
METHODS. INCLUDES BIBLIOGRAPHY.

*HAINES, JOSEPH H. A HISTORY OF PROTESTANT MISSIONS IN
MALAYA DURING THE NINETEENTH CENTURY. PRINCETON
THEOLOGICAL SEMINARY, DOCTORAL DISSERTATION,
372 pp. PRINCETON, 1962.

307

DEALS WITH THE YEARS 1815-1881. A STUDY OF THE
RELIGIOUS ENVIRONMENT OF MALAYA INCLUDING EARLY
ATTEMPTS TO EVANGELIZE. COMPREHENSIVE ANALYSIS OF
RELATIONSHIPS INCLUDING AMERICAN BOARD OF
COMMISSIONERS, CHURCH MISSIONARY SOCIETY, PRESBYTERIAN
CHURCH AND THE LONDON MISSIONARY SOCIETY.

14000
HEDLUND, ROGER E. CONSERVATIVE BAPTISTS IN MID-PASSAGE:
THE STUDY OF A MOVEMENT, ITS GROWTH AND SELF-
UNDERSTANDING, ITS PRESENT CRISIS OF UNCERTAINTY.
SWM, DOCTORAL DISSERTATION, 300 pp. PASADENA, 1974.

DESCRIPTIVE ANALYSIS OF AN AMERICAN DENOMINATION
TO DETERMINE THE CAUSES OF ITS PRESENT MALAISE AND
TO SET FORTH REALISTIC, PRAGMATIC SOLUTIONS.
ILLUSTRATED WITH 71 GRAPHICS.

14200
HENNEBERGER, JAMES E. QUO VADIS IELU? SWM, M.A. THESIS,
      401 pp. PASADENA, 1968.

      A CASE STUDY OF THE IGLESIA EVANGELICA LUTERANA
      UNIDA OF ARGENTINA. SHOW THE HISTORICAL SETTING
      OF LUTHERANS IN ARGENTINA WITH THE BASIC PRINCIPLES
      OF CHURCH GROWTH THEORY AND THE IELU IN AN
      EVALUATIVE STUDY. INCLUDES PROPOSALS FOR INCREASED
      CHURCH GROWTH. MAPS, TABLES, GRAPHS, APPENDIX, AND
      BIBLIOGRAPHY.

*HIAN, CHUA W. OUT OF ASIA. SWM, M.A. THESIS, 175 pp.
      PASADENA, 1972.

      A STUDY OF ASIAN CHRISTIAN STUDENTS AND THEIR
      CONTRIBUTION TO THE WORLDWIDE CHURCH. THE BURDEN
      AND VISION OF THESE STUDENTS IS BOTH COMMENDED AND
      CALLED FOR. PROPOSES A STRONG ROLE FOR PARA-CHURCH
      ORGANIZATIONS SUCH AS STUDENT VOLUNTEER GROUPS IN
      EVANGELISM.

14700
308 HILL, D. LESLIE. DESIGNING A THEOLOGICAL EDUCATION BY
      EXTENSION PROGRAM. WILLIAM CAREY LIBRARY, SOUTH
      PASADENA, 1973.

      DESIGNING A THEOLOGICAL EDUCATION BY EXTENSION
      PROGRAM FOR THE PHILIPPINE BAPTIST MISSION.
      INCLUDES CHARTS AND GRAPHS WITH PLANS FOR STARTING
      LEARNING CENTERS AND WRITING THE PROGRAMS.
      COMPARISONS ARE MADE TO CONVENTIONAL THEOLOGICAL
      TRAINING.

14600
HILL, JAMES E. THEOLOGICAL EDUCATION FOR THE CHURCH IN
      MISSION. SWM, M.A. THESIS, 265 pp. PASADENA, 1969.

      A CASE HISTORY OF THE BAPTIST, METHODIST AND FREE
      BRETHREN CHURCHES IN THE ARGENTINE REPUBLIC.
      ATTEMPT TO DISCOVER THOSE FACTORS IN THEOLOGICAL
      EDUCATION WHICH HAVE HAD A SPECIAL INFLUENCE UPON
      THE RATE AND EXTENT OF GROWTH ACHIEVED IN THESE
      THREE EVANGELICAL CHURCHES.

14800
HILL, ROBERT W. THE CHRISTIANIZATION OF THE CENTRAL
    AFRICAN REPUBLIC. SWM, M.A. THESIS, 301 pp.
    PASADENA, 1969.

    COMPREHENSIVE SURVEY OF THE LAND, PEOPLE, HISTORY
    OF THE CENTRAL AFRICAN REPUBLIC. THE BRETHREN
    MISSION PROGRAM IS ANALYZED IN DETAIL AS IS THE
    BAPTIST MID-MISSION, THE SWEDISH BAPTIST MISSION,
    AFRICA INLAND MISSION, OTHER PROTESTANT MISSIONS
    AND THE ROMAN CATHOLIC MISSIONS. INCLUDES MAPS,
    TABLES, FIGURES, AND BIBLIOGRAPHY.

*HOKE, WILLIAM R. THE BRETHREN IN CHRIST CHURCH, NORTH
    BIHAR, INDIA. ASHLAND THEOLOGICAL SEMINARY, 143 pp.
    ASHLAND, 1971.

    A STUDY OF CHURCH GROWTH IN BIHAR REGION OF INDIA.
    INCLUDES A DESCRIPTION OF CHRISTIAN COMMUNITIES
    AMONG URAON AND SANTAL TRIBES. STUDY BASED UPON
    AUTHOR'S WORK AS A MISSIONARY IN INDIA AND HIS
    STUDY AT ASHLAND THEOLOGICAL SEMINARY. INCLUDES
    BIBLIOGRAPHY.

                                                        309

15700
HUDSPITH, J. EDWIN. GROWTH STUDY IN NORTH THAILAND.
    SWM, M.A. THESIS, 363 pp. PASADENA, 1969.

    A COMPILATION OF CULTURAL AND CHURCH GROWTH DATA
    RELATING TO NINE DIFFERENT TRIBAL PEOPLES OF NORTH
    THAILAND. CHURCH GROWTH EVALUATION OF TOTAL STUDY
    CONCLUDES THESIS. GRAPHS AND MAPS.

16000
HUTCHENS, JAMES M. A CASE FOR MESSIANIC JUDAISM. SWM,
    DOCTORAL DISSERTATION, 275 pp. PASADENA, 1974.

    DEALS WITH THE DEVELOPMENT OF THE SALIENT FEATURES
    OF MESSIANIC JUDAISM. THE CENTRAL THRUST OF THE
    STUDY ENCOURAGES AND ALLOWS FOR THE ACCEPTANCE OF
    JESUS AS LORD, REDEEMER AND PROMISED MESSIAH, BY
    THE JEWISH PEOPLE, WHILE MAINTAINING THEIR CULTURAL
    AND RELIGIOUS IDENTITY AS JEWS.

16100
JACOBSEN, LEONARD D. CHURCH GROWTH ON THE ISLAND OF
    MADAGASCAR. SWM, M.A. THESIS, 105 pp. PASADENA,
    1967.

    A STUDY OF THE MALAGASY LUTHERAN CHURCH AT THE
    TIME OF ITS CENTENARY. CAREFULLY CONSIDERS
    EVANGELISM UNDER AN EVALUATION OF EFFECTIVENESS.
    INCLUDES MAPS, CHARTS, AND GRAPHS OF SEVERAL OTHER
    CHURCHES IN THE AREA. BIBLIOGRAPHY.

16500
JOHNSON, HARMON A. AUTHORITY OVER THE SPIRITS: BRAZILIAN
    SPIRITISM AND EVANGELICAL CHURCH GROWTH. SWM,
    M.A. THESIS, 136 pp. PASADENA, 1969.

    A MOST COMPETENT THESIS SURVEYING BRAZILIAN
    SPIRITISM WITH ITS AFRICAN AND MOSLEM BACKGROUND.
    PROPOSES THAT SERIOUS RECOGNITION OF EVIL SPIRITS
    AND DIRECT CONFRONTATION IN POWER ENCOUNTER WITH
    THE HOLY SPIRIT IS THE REASON FOR SUCCESS OF
    PENTECOSTAL MOVEMENTS.

310 *JOHNSON, NORBERT E. THE HISTORY, DYNAMIC AND PROBLEMS OF
    THE PENTECOSTAL MOVEMENT IN CHILE. UNION
    THEOLOGICAL SEMINARY, Th. M. THESIS, 132 pp. NEW
    YORK, 1970.

    A SKETCH OF EARLY PROTESTANT MISSION FOLLOWED BY
    THE DEVELOPMENT OF CHILEAN PENTECOSTALISM. SHOWS
    THE PHENOMENAL GROWTH AND ECUMENICAL BREAKTHROUGH
    WITH THE SIGNS OF CHANGE IN LATIN AMERICA'S WAVE
    OF THE FUTURE. CONCLUDES WITH A "POTPOURI OF
    OBSERVATIONS."

*JOHNSTON, ARTHUR P. A STUDY OF THE THEOLOGY OF EVANGELISM
    IN THE INTERNATIONAL MISSIONARY COUNCIL, 1921-1961.
    UNIVERSITY OF STRASBOURG, DOCTORAL DISSERTATION,
    311 pp. STRASBOURG, 1969.

    A COMPREHENSIVE STUDY TRACING THE THEOLOGY OF
    EVANGELISM BEGINNING BRIEFLY WITH THE REFORMATION
    BUT CENTERING MAINLY ON THE DEVELOPMENT OF THE
    WORLD COUNCIL OF CHURCHES BEGINNING AT EDINBURGH.

17100
JONES, REX R. A STRATEGY FOR ETHIOPIA. SWM, M.A. THESIS
341 pp. PASADENA, 1971.

A STUDY OF THE WORK OF THE CHRISTIAN MISSIONARY
FELLOWSHIP IN ETHIOPIA WITH AN ATTEMPT TO BRING
TOGETHER THE BEST FROM MISSION THEORY AND
CULTURAL ANTHROPOLOGY. INCLUDES A STRATEGY FOR
PLANTING CHURCHES AMONG THE GALLA TRIBE IN THE
WELLEGA PROVINCE OF SOUTHERN ETHIOPIA.

17300
KAMASI, LAWRENCE. CHURCH GROWTH LESSONS FOR THE
INDONESIAN CHURCH. SWM, RESEARCH PROJECT,
100 pp. PASADENA, 1973.

A SERIES OF LESSONS WRITTEN IN THE INDONESIAN
LANGUAGE FOR USE IN THE THEOLOGICAL EDUCATION
BY EXTENSION PROGRAM OF THE CHRISTIAN AND
MISSIONARY ALLIANCE CHURCH IN INDONESIA.
PARTICULARLY DESIGNED FOR PASTORS AND LAY-PREACHERS.
CENTERED ON THE PRINCIPLES OF CHURCH GROWTH.

17400
KASDORF, HANS. A DECADE OF EVANGELISM-IN-DEPTH IN   311
LATIN AMERICA. MENNONITE BRETHREN BIBLICAL
SEMINARY, M.R.E. THESIS, 296 pp. FRESNO, 1972.

BRIEF BIOGRAPHICAL SKETCH OF R. KENNETH STRACHAN,
ORIGINATOR OF EID. ANALYZES THE NATURE, PHILOSOPHY
AND PROGRAM OF EID. ONE CHAPTER DEVOTED TO ACCOUNTS
OF EACH CAMPAIGN HELD THROUGHOUT LATIN AMERICA.
EID IS EVALUATED IN TERMS OF STRENGTHS, WEAKNESSES
AND DIRECTION FOR THE FUTURE.

17500
KAY, RICHARD W. CHURCH GROWTH AND RENEWAL IN THE BAHAMAS.
SWM, M.A. THESIS, 282 pp. PASADENA, 1972.

A COMPREHENSIVE STUDY OF OLDER AND NEWER
DENOMINATIONS IN THE BAHAMAS. BEGINS IN 1731 WITH
ANGLICAN WORK TO THE PRESENT. DISCUSSES NOMINALITY
IN THE OLDER CHURCHES AND SLOW GROWTH IN THE NEWER
ONES. PROPOSES DEVELOPMENT OF A TRULY BLACK
CHRISTIANITY WITH NEW PATTERNS OF INCREASED CHURCH
GROWTH. INCLUDES INDEX AND BIBLIOGRAPHY.

17800
KIM, SAMUEL I. THE UNFINISHED MISSION IN THAILAND.
SWM, DOCTORAL DISSERTATION, 300 pp. PASADENA, 1974.

A GENERAL SKETCH OF CHRISTIAN MISSION IN THAILAND
WITH ANALYTIC APPROACH ON THE CHURCH GROWTH OF
THE C.C.T. AFTER THE SECOND WORLD WAR. THE PRIME
FOCUS IS IN POINTING OUT THE MAJOR CAUSES FOR
SLOW GROWTH: HUMANIZATION OF MISSION WHICH IS
BASED ON LIBERALISM, AND POPULAR ECUMENICAL ETHOS
OF W.C.C., RATHER THAN SPIRITUAL PRIORITY OF THE
CHURCH.

*KING, CHRISTOPHER R. THE EMERGENCE OF NAGALAND.
UNIVERSITY OF WISCONSIN, M.A. THESIS, 168 pp.
MILWAUKEE, 1969.

A SOCIAL AND POLITICAL STUDY OF IMPERIAL
ADMINISTRATION, MISSIONARY INFLUENCE, AND NAGA
RESPONSES. APPENDICES AND EXTENSIVE BIBLIOGRAPHY.

17900
312 KJAERLAND, GUNNAR. PLANTING THE CHURCH AMONG NOMADS.
SWM, M.A. THESIS, 309 pp. PASADENA, 1971.

AIMS TO DESCRIBE THE SOCIAL LIFE OF THE FORANA
NOMADS OF SOUTHERN ETHIOPIA UNDER THE IMPACT OF
CORRECT ACCULTURATION. DISCUSSES THE WORK OF THE
NORWEGIAN LUTHERN MISSIONSOMBAND. AUTHOR CONSIDERS
THE TASK ENORMOUS AND THIS WORK, RESEARCH IN PROGRESS.

18800
KWAST, LLOYD E. THE DISCIPLING OF WEST CAMEROON.
EERDMANS, GRAND RAPIDS, 205 pp. 1971.

"TELLS THE EXCITING STORY OF A RAPIDLY GROWING
CHURCH IN A SMALL, OFTEN OVERLOOKED, CORNER OF
WEST AFRICA--THE STORY OF WEST CAMEROON BAPTIST
CHURCH GROWTH." DELVES INTO HISTORY. POINTS
OUT SOME MISSION POLICIES INFLUENCING CHURCH
GROWTH. APPENDICES.

18800
KWAST, LLOYD E. PROTESTANT CHRISTIANITY IN WEST CAMEROON
1841-1886. SWM, DOCTORAL DISSERTATION, 406 pp.
PASADENA, 1972.

AN ETHNOHISTORICAL STUDY OF THE ORIGINS AND
NINETEENTH CENTURY DEVELOPMENT OF PROTESTANT
CHRISTIANITY IN CAMEROON, WEST AFRICA, COVERING
SPECIFICALLY THE PERIOD 1841-1884.
EARLY DIMINUTATIVE GROWTH IS ANALYZED.
EXTENSIVE BIBLIOGRAPHY AND APPENDICES.

19100
LARSON, PETER A. MIGRATION AND CHURCH GROWTH IN ARGENTINA.
SWM, DOCTORAL DISSERTATION, 492 pp. PASADENA, 1973.

A CHURCH GROWTH SURVEY OF CULTURAL CHANGE RELATED
TO THE PREACHING OF THE GOSPEL. THE INFLUENCE OF
MIGRATION ON SOCIAL CHANGE AND ITS IMPLICATIONS
FOR CHURCH PLANTING. INCLUDES TABLES, CHARTS AND
BIBLIOGRAPHY.

19350
LENNING, LARRY G. NEEDS ASSESSMENT IN THEOLOGICAL EDUCATION 313
IN AFRICA. SWM, M.A. THESIS, 100 pp. PASADENA, 1974.

A FOCUS ON NEEDS AS THE FIRST BASIC ELEMENT IN A
TOTAL EVALUATION PROCESS IN THEOLOGICAL EDUCATION.
A STUDY OF CHURCH AND MINISTRY, THE AFRICAN PASTOR,
AND THEOLOGICAL EDUCATION IN THE EVANGELICAL LUTHERAN
CHURCH OF CAMEROUN, SERVES AS GROUNDWORK FOR DESIGNING
A PLAN TO FOLLOW IN DOING A NEEDS ASSESSMENT IN
THEOLOGICAL EDUCATION IN AFRICA.

19500
LIAO, DAVID. THE UNRESPONSIVE, RESISTANT OR NEGLECTED?
MOODY, CHICAGO, 1972.

A DESCRIPTION OF TAIWAN'S INDIGENOUS PEOPLE WITH
IMPLICATIONS OF CULTURE FOR CHURCH PLANTING. INCLUDES
HAKKA ANCESTOR WORSHIP AND VALIDITY OF ETHNIC CHURCHES.
OPTIMISM IS EXPRESSED IN A CHAPTER ENTITLED "OPEN
DOORS." HAKKAS NUMBER 1,700,000--13% OF TAIWAN'S
POPULATION. INCLUDES APPENDICES AND BIBLIOGRAPHY.

20200

MARTIN, ALVIN. MISSIOLOGICAL EDUCATION: AN APPRAISAL OF
THE 1972-74 CURRICULUM OF THE SCHOOL OF WORLD MISSION.
DOCTORAL DISSERTATION, 550 pp. PASADENA, 1974.

PART ONE--ACADEMIC MANUAL: FULL DESCRIPTION OF THE
SWM CURRICULUM INCLUDING SPECIFIC COURSE SYLLABI AND
REQUIRED TEXTBOOKS, COMPREHENSIVE EXAMINATIONS AND
PROCEDURES GOVERNING THE DEGREE DOCTOR OF MISSIOLOGY.
SWM MISSIOLOGICAL LITERATURE AND ABSTRACTS, MANUAL
ON TECHNICAL WRITING AND DIRECTORY OF SWM ASSOCIATES
ALSO INCLUDED. PART TWO--APPRAISAL AND SUGGESTIONS
FOR EXPANDING MISSIOLOGICAL EDUCATION THROUGH THE
EXTENSION OF SWM CURRICULUM.

20600

MAST, MICHAEL M. AN APPROACH TO THEOLOGICAL TRAINING
AMONG THE TOBAS OF ARGENTINA. SWM, M.A. THESIS,
165 pp. PASADENA, 1972.

"THE PURPOSE OF THIS STUDY PRECISELY STATED IS
TO DETERMINE WHAT APPROACH, IF ANY, WOULD BE MOST
FEASIBLE FOR INTRODUCING INTENSIVE THEOLOGICAL
EDUCATION INTO TOBA CHRISTIANITY." A LOOK AT THE
PEOPLE THEMSELVES AND AT THEORETICAL CONSIDERATIONS.
PRACTICAL PROPOSALS MADE.

314

20700

MATHEWS, EDWARD F. PLANTING THE CHURCH IN HONDURAS:
THE DEVELOPMENT OF A CULTURALLY RELEVANT WITNESS.
SWM, M.A. THESIS, 260 pp. PASADENA, 1970.

DEALS WITH THE DEVELOPMENT OF A CULTURALLY
RELEVANT WITNESS, PROBLEMS OF CULTURE CONTACT,
PRINCIPLES OF CROSS-CULTURAL COMMUNICATION, AND
THE PHENOMENA OF CULTURE CHANGE. ALSO PROPOSES
STRATEGY FOR THE PLANTING OF AN INDIGENOUS CHURCH
IN HONDURAS.

21000
MICHELSON, CLIFFORD S. THE EVANGELICAL LUTHERAN CHURCH
    OF EAST CAMEROUN. SWM. M.A. THESIS, 226 pp.
    PASADENA, 1969.

    DESCRIBES THE LAND, PEOPLE AND POLITICAL HISTORY
    OF CAMEROUN. INCLUDES A STUDY OF THE EVANGELICAL
    LUTHERAN CHURCH WITH THE CULTURAL SETTING OF THE
    GBAYA AND DOWYO TRIBES. CONCLUDES WITH ONE
    SECTION ON THE DYNAMICS OF CHURCH GROWTH AND
    ANOTHER ON RECOMMENDATIONS TO AID CHURCH GROWTH.

21100
MIDDLETON, VERNON J. A PATTERN OF CHURCH GROWTH FOR
    TRIBAL INDIA. SWM, M.A. THESIS, 223 pp.
    PASADENA, 1972.

    A PRELIMINARY STUDY OF CHURCH GROWTH AMONG THE
    KORKU AND KOND PEOPLES. SUGGESTS POSSIBILITIES
    OF MAKING CHRISTIANITY RELEVANT TO CULTURE. POINTS
    OUT PROBLEMS WHEN THIS IS NOT DONE. "A CONSIDERED
    POLICY OF DISCIPLING THE TRIBES (MATTHEW 28:19,20)
    IS SET FORTH."

21500   315
MONTGOMERY, JIM. WHY THEY GROW. SWM, RESEARCH PROJECT.
    322 pp. PASADENA.

    A DESCRIPTION OF THE FOURSQUARE CHURCH IN THE
    PHILIPPINES. STORIES OF PHENOMENAL GROWTH AMONG
    BAPTISTS AND PENTECOSTAL CHURCHES RELATED. INCLUDES
    A PROGNOSIS FOR THE FOURSQUARE CHURCH IN THE
    PHILIPPINES.

*MULHOLLAND, KENNETH B. HONDURAS THEOLOGICAL EDUCATION
    BY EXTENSION. LANCASTER THEOLOGICAL SEMINARY OF
    U.C.C., S.T.M. THESIS, 241 pp. LANCASTER, 1971.

    A COMPREHENSIVE ANALYSIS OF THEOLOGICAL EDUCATION
    BY EXTENSION IN HONDURAS. INCLUDES COMPARISON OF
    RESIDENCE AND EXTENSION CONCEPTS. SHOWS ROLE OF
    TEACHER IN TEE AND RELATIONSHIP OF THE MOVEMENT TO
    CHURCH GROWTH. INCLUDES GLOSSARY AND BIBLIOGRAPHY.

22000
MURPHY, EDWARD F. THE GIFTS OF THE SPIRIT AND THE MISSION
OF THE CHURCH. SWM, M.A. THESIS, 171 pp.
PASADENA, 1971.

A CAREFUL AND TIMELY STUDY OF THE GIFTS OF THE
SPIRIT. TOUCHES SUCH IMPORTANT SUBJECTS AS
"BAPTISM OF THE HOLY SPIRIT," "CHARISMATIC
ENDOWMENTS," "PASTORAL MINISTRY," AND "EQUIPPING
OF THE SAINTS." PROPOSES RECEPTOR ORIENTED
COMMUNICATION AND DEVELOPMENT OF GIFTED LEADERSHIP
IN THE CHURCHES.

23000
NELSON, AMIRTHARAJ. LIFE AND GROWTH OF THE PROTESTANT
CHURCHES IN MADRAS, INDIA. SWM DOCTORAL DISSERTATION,
416 pp. PASADENA, 1974.

DEALS WITH THIRTY PROTESTANT DENOMINATIONS AND THEIR
ONE HUNDRED AND TWENTY-EIGHT CONGREGATIONS. ANALYZES
TYPICAL CONGREGATIONS AND DESCRIBES TRENDS AND
PATTERNS OF GROWTH. PROBES INTO NON-CHRISTIAN
SOCIETY, SOCIAL STRUCTURE, WAYS OF THINKING AND
CASTES INSOFAR AS THESE BEAR UPON ESTABLISHING
CHURCHES AND INFLUENCING THEIR LIFE AND DEVELOPMENT.

316

23300
NORDYKE, QUENTIN H. ANIMISTIC AYMARAS AND CHURCH GROWTH.
THE BARCLAY PRESS, NEWBERG, OREGON, 1972.

THE AYMARA SEEN IN LIGHT OF HIS ENVIRONMENT
HISTORICALLY, GEOGRAPHICALLY AND CULTURALLY. AN
IN-DEPTH LOOK AT THE AYMARA AS AN ANIMIST. FINALLY,
THE AYMARA AS A CHRISTIAN CONSIDERED, HIS
CONVERSION, HIS CHURCH AND ITS GROWTH.

23500
OLIVER, DENNIS M. MAKE DISCIPLES: THE NATURE AND SCOPE
OF THE GREAT COMMISSION. SWM, DOCTORAL DISSERTATION,
150pp. PASADENA, 1973.

THE GREAT COMMISSION IS ANALYZED EXEGETICALLY AND
SET IN A FRAMEWORK OF MODERN MISSIOLOGY. ANCIENT
MODELS OF EVANGELISM AT JERUSALEM, ANTIOCH AND IN
ASIAN CHURCHES ARE ANALYZED. PEOPLE MOVEMENTS AS
VALID MODES OF EVANGELIZATION ARE DISCUSSED.

23700
OLSEN, GILBERT W. CHURCH GROWTH IN SIERRA LEONE.
EERDMANS, GRAND RAPIDS, 222 pp. 1969.

A DETAILED ANALYSIS OF SEVERAL CREOLE CHURCHES,
TWO AFRICAN INDEPENDENT CHURCHES AND NINE OTHER
MISSION-RELATED CHURCHES WITH SPECIAL INTEREST
IN GROWTH OR NON-GROWTH PATTERNS. CONCLUDES WITH
A PLAN FOR WINNING THE MENDE TRIBE. MAPS AND GRAPHS.

24800
PENTECOST, EDWARD C. MEXICAN INDIAN MISSION CHURCH GROWTH
STUDY. SWM, M.A. THESIS, 291 pp. PASADENA, 1972.

A STUDY OF SEVERAL INDIAN ETHNIC GROUPS IN SPANISH
MEXICAN SURROUNDINGS. INCLUDES STUDIES OF CHRISTO-
PAGANISM AND THE ESTABLISHMENT OF THE MEXICAN
INDIAN MISSION. PROPOSES PLANS FOR INCREASED
CHURCH GROWTH AND AN APPENDIX ENTITLED MANUAL
FOR MISSIONARIES. INDEX AND BIBLIOGRAPHY.

24900
PEREZ, PABLO M. MISION Y LIBERACION. SWM, DOCTORAL
DISSERTATION, 224 pp. PASADENA, 1973.   317

WRITTEN IN SPANISH AND DISCUSSES LIBERATION
MOVEMENTS FROM EARLY EXPLORERS TO LATIN AMERICAN
INDIAN TRIBES TO MODERN POLITICAL MOVEMENTS.
COMPARING EVANGELISTIC AND SOCIAL MANDATES IN
EVANGELICAL CHRISTIANITY.

25300
PHILIP, ABRAHAM. MOBILIZING THE LAITY IN THE MAR THOMA
CHURCH FOR EVANGELISM. SWM DOCTORAL DISSERTATION,
250 pp. PASADENA, 1974.

A STUDY OF THE POTENTIAL OF THE LAITY IN THE MAR
THOMA CHURCH IN INDIA. INCLUDES A STUDY OF THE
SOCIO-CULTURAL POSITION OF THE SYRIAN CHRISTIANS OF
INDIA. SUGGESTS WAYS AND MEANS TO MOBILIZE THE
LAITY FOR EVANGELIZATION AND CHURCH PLANTING.

25400
PHILIP, PUTHUVAIL T. GROWTH OF BAPTIST CHURCHES OF TRIBAL
     NAGALAND. SWM, M.A. THESIS, 200 pp. PASADENA, 1972.

     A CAREFUL STUDY OF BAPTIST CHURCHES IN INDIA'S
     NAGALAND INCLUDING BOTH FOREIGN AND NATIONAL BAPTIST
     ASSOCIATIONS. CONCLUDING THESIS IS THAT MISSIONS
     MUST BE ESTABLISHED BY THE NATIONAL CHURCHES. THE
     BRIGHT FUTURE OF NAGA CHURCHES INCREASES THE
     RESPONSIBILITY OF THE NATIONAL CHURCHES. INCLUDES
     MAPS, GRAPHS, CHARTS AND BIBLIOGRAPHY.

25420
PINOLA, M. SAKARI. CHURCH GROWTH, A PRACTICAL MISSIONARY
     METHODOLOGY (IN FINNISH). SWM, M.A. PROJECT, 195 pp.
     PASADENA, 1974.

     A GENERAL STUDY OF THE CHURCH GROWTH MOVEMENT, ITS
     THEOLOGICAL AND ANTHROPOLOGICAL PERSPECTIVES FOR
     MISSION, KEY FACTORS OF ITS METHODOLOGY AND AN
     APPLICATION OF ITS PRINCIPLES TO PRACTICAL
     MISSIONARY WORK INCLUDING ITS CRITICS.

26300
318 RADER, PAUL A. THE SALVATION ARMY IN KOREA AFTER 1945.
     SWM, DOCTORAL DISSERTATION, 317 pp. PASADENA, 1973.

     DISCUSSES SALVATION ARMY WORK IN KOREA WITH
     COMPREHENSIVE ANALYSIS OF THEOLOGY AND MANDATES FOR
     MISSION. CAREFUL SURVEY OF FACTORS RELATED TO SELF-
     IMAGE AND SELF-UNDERSTANDING OF A NATIONAL CHURCH.
     SALVATION ARMY ECCLESIOLOGY IS DISCUSSED IN LIGHT
     OF KOREA TODAY WITH STRATEGIC PLANNING FOR TOMORROW.

26400
RAMBO, DAVID L. TRAINING COMPETENT LEADERS FOR THE
     CHRISTIAN AND MISSIONARY ALLIANCE CHURCHES OF THE
     PHILIPPINES. SWM, M.A. THESIS, 205 pp. PASADENA,
     1968.

     DISCUSSES HISTORY AND DEVELOPMENT OF THE CHRISTIAN
     AND MISSIONARY ALLIANCE CHURCH THROUGHOUT THE
     PHILIPPINES, BUT PRIMARILY SEEKS TO ANALYZE THE
     LEADERSHIP WITHIN THIS CHURCH. IN-DEPTH LOOK AT
     TWO LEVELS OF TRAINING LEADERSHIP. GRAPHS, APPENDICES.

26600
RANDALL, MAX W.   PROFILE FOR VICTORY: NEW PROPOSALS FOR
    ZAMBIA. WILLIAM CAREY LIBRARY, SOUTH PASADENA,
    204 pp. 1970.

    THOROUGH TREATMENT OF SOCIAL AND ANTHROPOLOGICAL
    CONCERNS OF ZAMBIA AND ITS PEOPLE. DISCUSSES
    INFLUENCE OF COLONIALISM, EDUCATIONAL AND MEDICAL
    APPROACHES UPON MISSION, AND POINTS OUT THE NEED
    FOR CHANGE IF ZAMBIA IS TO BE DISCIPLED.

26900
READ, WILLIAM R.   BRAZIL 1980. MARC, MONROVIA, 1973.

    A CHURCH GROWTH ANALYSIS BASED UPON 4800 PAGES OF
    COMPUTER PRINTOUT ABOUT SOCIAL AND RELIGIOUS CHANGE
    IN BRAZIL. IT SHOWS THE INFLUENCE OF ROAD BUILDING
    UPON CHRISTIANIZATION IN MODERN TIMES. THIS PROJECT
    WON THE DONALD A. McGAVRAN RESEARCH AWARD FOR 1973.

27100
REED, GRADY WOOD.   STRATEGIZING CHURCH OF CHRIST MISSIONS
    IN THE LIGHT OF VARYING RECEPTIVITY. SWM, M.A.
    THESIS, 182 pp. PASADENA.

319

    AN EVALUATION OF RECEPTIVITY TO THE GOSPEL, AND CASE
    STUDIES OF CHURCHES OF CHRIST (IN EIGHT OF TEN SUB-
    SAHARAN AFRICA), THAT HAVE WITNESSED VARYING
    RECEPTIVITY. INCLUDES THE HISTORICAL, SOCIO-CULTURAL,
    AND MISSION-CHURCH FACTORS THAT HAVE EITHER
    EXPEDITED OR IMPEDED THE GROWTH IN CASE STUDY.

27200
REED, JEROLD F.   THE DYNAMICS OF THE GROWTH OF THE SPANISH-
    SPEAKING PROTESTANT CHURCHES IN ECUADOR. SWM,
    DOCTORAL DISSERTATION, 200 pp. PASADENA, 1974.

    A COMPUTERIZED COMPONENTIAL ANALYSIS OF OVER FIFTY
    GROWTH INFLUENCING FACTORS FROM EDUCATIONAL LEVEL
    AND VOCATIONS TO CONVERSION FACTORS AND PASTORAL
    ATTENTION. INCLUDES BREAKDOWN OF ALL THE PROTESTANT
    GROUPS AND CHURCHES BY COUNTRY, REGIONS, PROVINCES,
    MAJOR CITIES AND DENOMINATIONS.

27400
REIMER, REGINALD E. THE PROTESTANT MOVEMENT IN VIETNAM.
SWM. M.A. THESIS, 320 pp. PASADENA, 1972.

A DESCRIPTION OF CHURCH GROWTH IN PEACE AND WAR
AMONG THE ETHNIC VIETNAMESE. SHOWS THAT THE YOUNG
CHURCH HAD A HIGH RATE OF GROWTH BUT WAS DECIDEDLY
SLOW WHEN IT GOT LARGER. BASED UPON CAREFUL
STATISTICAL ANALYSIS WITH GRAPHING. CATHOLIC
PRESENCE IS STUDIED.

27700
RIDDLE, NORMAN G. CHURCH GROWTH IN KINSHASA. SWM, M.A.
THESIS, 196 pp. PASADENA, 1971.

DESCRIBES PROBLEMS OF KINSHASA. PRESENTS ACTUAL
CASE STUDIES OF INDIVIDUAL CONGREGATIONS. IN-DEPTH
STUDY OF THE INDEPENDENT KIMBANGUIST CHURCH AND
FOUR MISSION-RELATED CHURCHES. DISCUSSES QUESTIONS
OF COMMUNICATION AT LENGTH. MAPS, GRAPHS, AND PLATES
INCLUDED.

28000
320 RO, SANG KOOK. PAULINE MISSIOLOGY AND THE CHURCH IN KOREA.
SWM, M.A. THESIS, 257 pp. PASADENA, 1973.

PAUL'S PRACTICE AND THEOLOGY OF MISSION WITH
PARTICULAR REFERENCE TO THE CHURCH AT ROME AND
THEIR BEARING ON THE CHURCH IN KOREA TODAY.
DISCUSSING PAUL, THE MISSIOLOGIST, AND KOREA'S
PRESENT DAY CHURCH AND MISSION.

28500
ROMERO, JOEL E. CHURCH PLANTING EVANGELISM: AN ARGENTINE
CASE STUDY. SWM, M.A. THESIS, 238 pp. PASADENA, 1970.

A CAREFUL LOOK AT CHURCH-PLANTING MINISTRIES IN
ARGENTINE. "THE BASIC EMPHASIS WHICH UNDERLIES THIS
INVESTIGATION IS THAT THE GROWTH SECURED BY EACH
CHURCH IS IN DIRECT PROPORTION TO THE EFFORT
EMPLOYED IN CHURCH-PLANTING EVANGELISM."

28800
ROSS, CHARLES. THE EMERGENCE OF THE PRESBYTERIAN CHURCH
     IN THE KASAI, CONGO. SWM, M.A. THESIS, 230 pp.
     PASADENA, 1973.

     A CRITICAL APPRAISAL OF THE EGLISE PRESBYTERIENNE
     AU CONGO, ITS HISTORY, CHANGING STRATEGY,
     INSTITUTIONS AND CHURCH GROWTH. CHARTS AND
     BIBLIOGRAPHY.

29000
SAMUEL, GEORGE. GROWTH POTENTIAL OF URBAN CHURCHES: A
     STUDY IN BOMBAY. SWM, M.A. THESIS, 230 pp.
     PASADENA, 1973.

     A COMPREHENSIVE ANALYSIS OF ETHNIC GROUPS IN
     BOMBAY. REFLECTS 100% RESPONSE TO QUESTIONNAIRES
     DEALING WITH CHURCH PLANTING, PATTERNS OF GROWTH,
     NON-CHRISTIAN PEOPLES, URBANIZATION AND CHURCH
     GROWTH STRATEGY. INCLUDES 42 RECOMMENDATIONS
     CONCERNING DISCIPLING AND CROSS-CULTURAL
     COMMUNICATION OF THE GOSPEL.

29100
SARGUNAM, M. EZRA. MULTIPLYING CHURCHES IN URBAN INDIA: 321
     AN EXPERIMENT IN MADRAS. SWM, M.A. THESIS, 230 pp.
     PASADENA, 1973.

     A STUDY OF MADRAS, INDIA, WITH PARTICULAR
     REFERENCE TO CONTEMPORARY MOVEMENTS OF URBANIZATION,
     EVANGELISM AND TRADITIONAL CHURCH PROGRAMS. INCLUDES
     ORIENTAL MISSIONARY SOCIETY'S ENTRY INTO MADRAS.
     PROPOSALS FOR INCREASED CHURCH GROWTH IN A MULTI-
     ETHNIC SOCIETY. INCLUDES MAPS, GRAPHS, AND
     BIBLIOGRAPHY.

29200
SAUDER, JAMES. PLANNING FOR CHURCH GROWTH. SWM, M.A.
     THESIS, 184 pp. PASADENA, 1971.

     CASE STUDY USED TO ILLUSTRATE THE PRINCIPLES AND
     PROCEDURES OF CHURCH GROWTH PLANNING. THE
     HONDURAS MENNONITE CHURCH USED FOR BACKGROUND OF
     RESEARCH. EVALUATION OF MISSION, PROBLEMS,
     RESOURCES AND GOALS.

29300
SAVAGE, PETER. THE MINISTRY IN THE IGLESIA EVANGELICA
        PERUANA. SWM, RESEARCH PAPER, 89 pp. PASADENA,
        1967.

        DISCUSSES THE GEOGRAPHICAL, ETHNIC, SOCIOLOGICAL
        AND ANTHROPOLOGICAL FACTORS INFLUENCING THE MINISTRY
        IN THE I.E.P. ASSESSES THE MINISTRY AND ITS
        TRAINING. MAKES PROPOSALS FOR MAKING THE MINISTRY
        MORE RELEVANT, REALISTIC AND CREATIVE.

29400
SAWATZKY, SHELDON V. THE GATEWAY OF PROMISE: A STUDY OF
        THE TAIWAN MENNONITE CHURCH. SWM, M.A. THESIS,
        238 pp. PASADENA, 1970.

        A STUDY OF THE FACTORS AFFECTING THE GROWTH OF THIS
        CHURCH, "AND IN THE LAST FEW YEARS, ITS LACK OF
        GROWTH." IN-DEPTH LOOK AT MEDICAL WORK AND ITS
        RELATIONSHIP TO CHURCH BUILDING. ANTHROPOLOGICAL
        FACTORS TREATED. MISSION STRATEGY FOR THE FUTURE
        PROPOSED.

322   *SEAMANDS, JOHN T. METHODIST CHURCH GROWTH IN SOUTH INDIA
        AND HYDERABAD CONFERENCES. SERAMPORE UNIVERSITY,
        DOCTORAL DISSERTATION, 278 pp. SERAMPORE, 1969.

        INCLUDES STUDIES OF CHURCH GROWTH FROM 1885-1967
        WITH ANALYSIS OF SLOW GROWTH AND PEOPLE MOVEMENTS.
        INCLUDES OBSERVATIONS ON METHODIST CHURCH WITH
        RECOMMENDATIONS FOR INCREASED GROWTH OF THE CHURCH.

30000
SCHWARTZ, GLENN. CRUCIAL ISSUES OF THE BRETHREN IN CHRIST
        IN ZAMBIA. SWM, M.A. RESEARCH PROJECT, 125 pp.
        PASADENA, 1973.

        A SERIES OF STUDIES POINTING TO SOME OF THE CRUCIAL
        ISSUES FACING THE CHURCHES OF CENTRAL AFRICA TODAY.
        PARTICULAR REFERENCE TO WAYS THE MISSIONS MIGHT
        INDIGENIZE THE FAITH FOR AFRICA'S PRESENT NEED.
        INCLUDES AN APPENDIX ON THE FELLOWSHIP OF
        EVANGELICAL BELIEVERS IN SOUTHERN ETHIOPIA.

*SEMA, NAJEKHU Y. NAGALAND CHURCH GROWTH. BETHEL
    THEOLOGICAL SEMINARY, Th.M. THESIS, 127 pp.
    ST. PAUL, 1972.

    A STUDY OF THE GROWTH AND EXPANSION OF THE BAPTIST
    CHURCH IN NAGALAND WITH SPECIAL REFERENCE TO THE
    MAJOR TRIBES. DISCUSSES NAGA SOCIETY AND
    TRADITIONS, THE PAST AND PRESENT POLITICAL
    SITUATION, THE MISSIONARIES' CONTRIBUTION TO
    NAGALAND, AND THE PROBLEMS CONFRONTING THE CHURCH.

30300
SHEARER, ROY E. ANIMISM AND THE CHURCH IN KOREA. SWM
    THESIS, 153 pp. PASADENA, 1968.

    DESCRIBES HOW ANIMISM IS RELATED TO RECEPTIVITY
    TO THE GOSPEL. POINTS OUT THAT UNDERSTANDING OF
    CULTURAL AND RELIGIOUS FACTORS IN A SOCIETY IS
    NECESSARY TO EFFECTIVE CHURCH PLANTING AND GROWTH.

30400
SHEWMAKER, STAN. TONGA CHRISTIANITY. WILLIAM CAREY
    LIBRARY, SOUTH PASADENA, 199 pp. 1970.

323

    THOROUGH COVERAGE OF TONGA ANIMISTIC PHILOSOPHY,
    SOCIAL STRUCTURE AND REACTION TO CULTURE CHANGE.
    HISTORY OF THE CHURCH OF CHRIST IN ZAMBIA IS
    DISCUSSED AS WELL AS PRESENT STRATEGY. AN IN-
    DEPTH LOOK AT A TONGA VILLAGE GIVES IMPETUS TO
    NEW DIRECTIONS AND IDEAS FOR THE FUTURE. PATTERNS
    OF GROWTH AND NON-GROWTH ARE DISCUSSED.

30400
SHEWMAKER, STAN. CHURCH GROWTH IN BUTONGA. SWM, RESEARCH
    PROJECT, 59 pp. PASADENA, 1970.

    A STATISTICAL SURVEY OF EACH AREA AND EACH CHURCH
    WHERE THE CHURCH OF CHRIST ARE REPRESENTED IN
    SOUTHERN ZAMBIA. AUTHOR PERSONALLY COLLECTED ALL
    THE DATA. ATTEMPTS TO POINT OUT REASONS FOR
    GROWTH OR NON-GROWTH. REPLETE WITH CHARTS.

30630
SHINDE, BENJAMIN P. THE CONTRIBUTION OF THE ASSEMBLIES OF
     ASSEMBLIES OF GOD TO CHURCH GROWTH IN INDIA. SWM
     M.A. THESIS, 200 pp. PASADENA, 1974.

     THE PURPOSE OF THIS THESIS IS TO TRACE THE
     HISTORICAL DEVELOPMENT OF THE PENTECOSTAL REVIVAL
     OF THE TWENTIETH CENTURY WITH THE SPECIAL EMPHASIS
     ON THE RISE AND GROWTH OF THE ASSEMBLIES OF GOD
     WORK IN INDIA AND ITS CONTRIBUTION TO THE CHURCH
     IN INDIA. IT INCLUDES A CHAPTER ON THE GENERAL
     FACTORS WHICH CAUSED GROWTH AND ALSO FACTORS WHICH
     CAUSED LACK OF GROWTH.

30800
SHUMAKER, JOHN T.   CHURCH GROWTH IN PARAGUAY. SWM, M.A.
     THESIS, 158 pp. PASADENA, 1972.

     ANALYZES HISTORY AND CULTURAL SETTINGS OF THE
     PROTESTANT CHURCHES IN PARAGUAY IN ORDER TO
     UNDERSTAND AND FURTHER THEIR GROWTH. FACTORS
     INFLUENCING CHURCH GROWTH ARE EXAMINED WITH A
     VIEW TO THE FUTURE. CHARTS AND GRAPHS INCLUDED.

324 31400
SKIVINGTON S. ROBERT.   BAPTIST METHODS OF CHURCH GROWTH
     IN THE PHILIPPINES. SWM, M.A. THESIS, 326 pp.
     PASADENA, 1970.

     DESCRIBES AND MEASURES GROWTH OF SEVEN MISSION-
     RELATED BAPTIST CHURCHES IN PHILIPPINES, FOCUSING
     ON METHODS, POLICIES AND PRACTICES EACH USES TO
     ACIEVE GROWTH. ALSO IN-DEPTH LOOK AT ROMAN CATHOLIC
     SUCCESSES. CHARTS, GRAPHS, APPENDICES.

32500
SPRUTH, ERWIN L.   THE MISSION OF GOD IN THE WABAG AREA
     OF NEW GUINEA. SWM, MA.A THESIS, 471 pp. PASADENA,
     1970.

     A PRELIMINARY STUDY OF CHURCH GROWTH AMONG THE
     ANIMISTIC, PRELITERATE ENGA AND IPILI PEOPLES OF
     NEW GUINEA. ASKS HARD QUESTIONS SUCH AS THESE:
     "HOW CAN A CHURCH AND/OR MISSION SUSTAIN A PEOPLE
     MOVEMENT UNTIL THE ENTIRE ETHNOS HAS COME TO ITS
     LORD?"

33000

STOCK, FREDERICK E. CHURCH GROWTH IN WEST PAKISTAN. SWM
RESEARCH SEMINAR THESIS, 252 pp. PASADENA, 1968.

SPECIAL EMPHASIS UPON THE UNITED PRESBYTERIAN CHURCH
IN WEST PAKISTAN, WITH BRIEF SKETCHES OF OTHER
MISSION. A PLAN FOR PLANTING NEW CHURCHES. MANY
GRAPHS INCLUDED.

33400

SWANSON, ALLEN J. TAIWAN: MAINLINE VERSUS INDEPENDENT
CHURCH GROWTH. WILLIAM CAREY LIBRARY, 300 pp.
SOUTH PASADENA, 1970.

A STUDY OF INDEPENDENCY IN TAIWAN CHURCHES BEGINNING
WITH THE SETTING ON THE MAINLAND AND THEN COMPARING
FOUR MAINLINE CHURCHES OF TAIWAN: PRESBYTERIANS,
SOUTHERN BAPTISTS, ASSEMBLIES OF GOD AND THE TAIWAN
LUTHERAN CHURCH. NEARLY 75 PAGES GIVEN TO NEW
DIRECTIONS FOR A NEW DAY. APENDICES AND BIBLIOGRAPHY.

33600

TAI, JAMES S. CHURCH GROWTH PRINCIPLES FOR CHINESE
CHRISTIANS. SWM, MASTERS PROJECT, 153 pp.
PASADENA, 1973.   325

TEN CHAPTERS OF UNDERSTANDING CHURCH GROWTH BY
DONALD A. McGAVRAN TRANSLATED INTO MANDARIN. FIRST
PUBLISHED AS A SERIES OF ARTICLES IN A MONTHLY
MAGAZINE OF CHINESE OVERSEAS MISSIONS IN TAIPEI.

33700

TAKAMI, TOSHIHIRO. CONCEPTS OF LEADERSHIP AND THEIR
MEANING FOR THE GROWTH OF CHRISTIAN CHURCHES. SWM,
M.A. THESIS, 128 pp. PASADENA, 1969.

PARTICULARLY DESCRIBES THE GROWTH OF CHRISTIAN
CHURCHES IN INDIA. SHOWS THE RELATIONSHIP OF CHURCH
LEADERSHIP WITH SOCIAL STRUCTURES. INCLUDES
RELIGION AS AN INNOVATOR OF SOCIAL CHANGE. PARTICULAR
EMPHASIS IS GIVEN TO THE TELEGU TRIBE WITH PEOPLE
MOVEMENTS AND THEIR LEADERSHIP.

33800
TATE, FRANCIS V. PATTERNS OF CHURCH GROWTH IN NAIROBI.
SWM, M.A. THESIS, 210 pp. PASADENA, 1970.

DESCRIBES TEN REPRESENTATIVE NAIROBI CONGREGATIONS
AND ANALYZES GROWTH IN TERMS OF TYPES, CAUSES AND
PATTERNS. INCLUDES MAPS, CHARTS, GRAPHS AND
BIBLIOGRAPHY.

34100
TAUFA, LOPETI. CHANGE AND CONTINUITY IN OCEANIA. SWM,
MA.A. THESIS, 248 pp. PASADENA, 1968.

ATTENTION IS PAID TO SOCIAL AND RELIGIOUS
STRUCTURE IN THREE SPECIFIC CASE STUDIES--
POLYNESIAN, MICRONESIAN AND MELANESIAN CULTURES.
CHURCH IN THE ISLANDS EVALUATED FOR STRENGTHS
AND WEAKNESSES. UNEVANGELIZED FIELDS POINTED OUT.
RECOMMENDATIONS TO HELP THE ISLAND CHURCHES GROW
ARE PROPOSED.

34200
TEGENFELDT, HERMAN G. THE KACHIN BAPTIST CHURCH OF BURMA.
326   SWM, DOCTORAL DISSERTATION, 496 pp. PASADENA, 1973.

A GEOGRAPHICAL AND HISTORICAL SURVEY OF A CHURCH
OF 50,000 (AMERICAN BAPTISTS). RAPID GROWTH IS
SURVEYED BETWEEN THE WORLD WARS AND ANALYSIS OF
THE GROWTH FACTORS GIVEN. MISSIONARY METHODS IN
AN ANIMISTIC SOCIETY ARE DISCUSSED.

34900
THOTTUNGAL, ABRAHAM J. THE HISTORY AND GROWTH OF THE
MAR THOMA CHURCH. SWM, M.A. THESIS, 171 pp.
PASADENA, 1967.

ATTEMPT MADE TO FIND CAUSES FOR RAPID GROWTH OF
THE MAR THOMA CHURCH IN EARLY DECADES AND
DECLINING GROWTH IN RECENT DECADES.

35100
TOLIVER, RALPH. A PRELIMINARY INQUIRY INTO THE HISTORY
     AND GROWTH OF THE CHURCH IN THE PHILIPPINES.
     SWM, RESEARCH PROJECT, 185 pp. PASADENA.

     ANALYSIS OF GROWTH IN SEVERAL MISSION-RELATED
     CHURCHES AS WELL AS AN IN-DEPTH STUDY OF THE
     PHILIPPINE INDEPENDENT CHURCH. APPENDIX, MAPS
     AND GRAPHS.

35200
TREVOR, HUGH. CHURCH GROWTH AND O.M.F. IN JAPAN.
     OVERSEAS MISSIONARY FELLOWSHIP, 153 pp. 1972.

     A GENERAL OVERVIEW OF THE FOUNDING AND GROWTH
     OF THE PROTESTANT CHURCH IN JAPAN. GROWTH OF
     OMF CHURCHES IN PARTICULAR ARE THEN EXAMINED AND
     PROPOSALS AND SUGGESTIONS ARE MADE FOR THE
     FUTURE.

35400
TUGGY, ARTHUR L. THE PHILIPPINE CHURCH: GROWTH IN A
     CHANGING SOCIETY. EERDMANS, GRAND RAPIDS, 1971

     INVESTIGATES IN DEPTH THE RELATIONSHIP BETWEEN   327
     THE SOCIAL STRUCTURE AND THE GROWTH OF CHRISTIANITY
     IN THE PHILIPPINES SEEN IN HISTORICAL PERSPECTIVE.

35400
TUGGY, A. LEONARD. THE PHILIPPINE IGLESIA NI CRISTO. SWM,
     DOCTORAL DISSERTAION, 320 pp. PASADENA, 1974.

     THIS VERY LARGE, HIGHLY STRUCTURED, TIGHTLY
     DISCIPLINED, INDIGENOUS AND INDEPENDENT CHURCH IS
     PORTRAYED AS AN ILLUMINATING ASIAN EXAMPLE OF THE
     WORLDWIDE INDEPENDENT CHURCH PHENOMENON. ITS
     HISTORY, TEACHINGS, ORGANIZATION, LIFE AND
     PROPAGATION METHODOLOGY ARE INVESTIGATED. IMPORTANT
     IMPLICATIONS FOR OTHER CHURCHES ARE DRAWN.

35400

TUGGY, A. LEONARD, and TOLIVER, RALPH. SEEING THE CHURCH
    IN THE PHILIPPINES. OVERSEAS MISSIONARY FELLOWSHIP,
    MANILA, 290 pp. 1970.

    A CHURCH GROWTH ANALYSIS OF CHRISTIAN MISSION IN
    THE PHILIPPINES. ATTENTION IS GIVEN TO MAINLINE
    DENOMINATIONS AND SOME FAST GROWING SMALLER GROUPS.
    URBAN CHURCH GROWTH, SPECIFIC PROBLEMS AND
    STRATEGIES ARE CONSIDERED THEOLOGICALLY,
    ANTHROPOLOGICALLY AND MISSIOLOGICALLY. CHARTS,
    GLOSSARY, BIBLIOGRAPHY AND INDEX.

36100

VENBERG, RODNEY W. THE LUTHERAN BRETHREN CHURCH IN CHAD
    AND CAMEROUN. SWM, M.A. THESIS, 178 pp. PASADENA,
    1970.

    DESCRIBES TRIBAL PEOPLE OF CHAD AND CAMEROUN, THEIR
    SOCIAL STRUCTURE AND RELIGIOUS BELIEFS. ESTABLISH-
    MENT AND GROWTH OF LUTHERAN BRETHREN MISSION AND OF
    THE RESULTANT NATIONAL CHURCH ARE DISCUSSED. CHURCH
    GROWTH PRINCIPLES ARE APPLIED TO THE ISSUES WITHIN
    THE NATIONAL CHURCH.

328

36300

VOELKEL, J. W. THE ETERNAL REVOLUTIONARY: EVANGELICAL
    MINISTRY TO THE UNIVERSITY STUDENT IN LATIN AMERICA.
    SWM, M.A. THESIS, 224 pp. PASADENA, 1971.

    DISCUSSES THE EVANGELICAL STUDENT AS AN ETERNAL
    REVOLUTIONARY. INCLUDES STUDIES OF STUDENT MOVEMENTS
    SUCH AS CAMPUS CRUSADE, NAVIGATORS AND OTHERS. GIVES
    INFORMATION ON LEADERSHIP TRAINING, SOCIAL CONCERN,
    SPIRITUAL RENEWAL AND ORGANIZATIONAL STRUCTURES.

36400

VOUGHT, DALE G. PROTESTANTS IN MODERN SPAIN. WILLIAM
    CAREY LIBRARY, SOUTH PASADENA, 153 pp. 1973.

    A SURVEY INCLUDING HISTORICAL CONSIDERATIONS, THE
    LAW OF RELIGIOUS LIBERTY OF 1967 IN SPAIN AND
    PROTESTANT CHURCH AND PARA CHURCH STRUCTURES.
    EVANGELICAL CHRISTIAN IMPERATIVES ARE SET FORTH AS
    VIABLE OPPORTUNITIES FOR PROTESTANT CHURCHES AND
    MISSIONS IN SPAIN TODAY.

36600
WAGNER, C. PETER. THE PROTESTANT MOVEMENT IN BOLIVIA.
WILLIAM CAREY LIBRARY, SOUTH PASADENA, 240 pp. 1970.

THOROUGH ANALYSIS OF PROTESTANT MAINLINE CHURCHES
AND MISSIONS IN BOLIVIA. DISCUSSES NEWER GROUPS
SUCH AS THE PENTECOSTALS. INCLUDES ONE CHAPTER ON
INTERDENOMINATIONAL COOPERATION WITH GROWTH RATES
AND STRATEGY FOR THE NEW DAY. INCLUDES APPENDICES
AND BIBLIOGRAPHY.

36900
WARNER, BRUCE M. MISSIONS AS ADVOCATE OF CULTURAL CHANGE
AMONG THE BATAK PEOPLE, SUMATRA. SWM, M.A. THESIS,
187 pp. PASADENA, 1972.

ETHNOHISTORICAL SURVEY OF INDONESIAN PEOPLE IN
GENERAL AND THE BATAK PEOPLE IN PARTICULAR.
ADVOCACIES OF CHRISTIAN MISSIONS ARE CRITICALLY
EXAMINED AND RESULTING RESPONSIBILITIES DEFINED.
THE FINAL SECTION "SEEKS TO TIE TOGETHER THE ROLE
OF MISSION THEOLOGY WITH ANTHROPOLOGY."

36990
WATSON, HAZEL T. REVIVAL AND CHURCH GROWTH IN KOREA 1884- 329
1910. SWM, M.A. THESIS, 290 pp. PASADENA, 1969.

DEALS WITH THE REVITALIZATION OF THE CHRISTIAN
CHURCHES IN KOREA TOUCHING ON SUCH SUBJECTS AS
TRAINING A NATIONAL MINISTRY, PERFECTION GROWTH
AND REVIVAL BEYOND THE BORDERS OF KOREA. REASONS
ARE GIVEN TO SHOW THAT REVIVAL DOESN'T ALWAYS
RESULT IN CHURCH GROWTH. APPENDICES AND BIBLIOGRAPHY.

37000
WATSON, LESLIE. CONSERVING THE CONVERTS IN THE JAPANESE
CHURCH. SWM, M.A. THESIS, 220 pp. PASADENA, 1968.

A TREATMENT OF JAPANESE CULTURE, RELIGIONS AND
MODERN LIFE-STYLE AND THE RELATIONSHIP THIS HAS TO
CHRISTIAN DEDICATION OR LACK OF IT. SUGGESTIONS
OFFERED FOR KEEPING CHRISTIANS IN THE CHURCH.

37200
WEERSTRA, HANS. MAYA PEASANT EVANGELISM. SWM, DOCTORAL
      DISSERTATION, 393 pp. PASADENA, 1972.

      DISCUSSES COMMUNICATION, RECEPTIVITY AND ACCEPTANCE
      FACTORS AMONG MAYA PEASANTS. SOCIAL AND RELIGIOUS
      LIFE OF THE "CAMPESINOS" SEEN AS BACKGROUND FOR
      THEIR RECEPTIVITY TO THE GOSPEL. AUTHOR TAKES A
      CLOSE LOOK AT THE PROCESS OF GOSPEL COMMUNICATION.

37300
WELD, WAYNE C. AN ECUADORIAN IMPASSE. EVANGELICAL
      COVENANT CHURCH, CHICAGO, 135 pp. 1968.

      SEEKS TO EXAMINE AND IN PART TO STATE THE REASONS
      FOR THE RELATIVE LACK OF GROWTH OF THE ECUADORIAN
      CHURCHES. GIVES SOCIAL, ECONOMIC, RELIGIOUS AND
      HISTORICAL FACTORS INFLUENCING THESE CHURCHES.
      THREE CASE STUDIES ARE PRESENTED. STRATEGY
      PROPOSED FOR THE DISCIPLING OF THE PEOPLES OF
      ECUADOR.

37300
330   WELD, WAYNE C. THE WORLD DIRECTORY OF THE THEOLOGICAL
      EDUCATION BY EXTENSION. WILLIAM CAREY LIBRARY,
      SOUTH PASADENA, 374 pp. 1973.

      FIRST WORLD DIRECTORY OF TEE. SERIES OF ESSAYS
      ON THE CONCEPT OF THEOLOGICAL EDUCATION BY
      EXTENSION FOLLOWED BY PRACTICAL CONSIDERATION SUCH
      AS FACTORS INVOLVED IN PRODUCING PROGRAMMED
      MATERIALS IN WORKSHOPS. WORKSHOPS ARE LISTED
      PLUS NEARLY 200 PAGES OF INSTITUTIONS SHOWING
      THEIR STATISTICAL INVOLVEMENT IN TEE.

38600
WONG, JAMES, LARSON, PETER, AND PENTECOST, EDWARD. MISSIONS
      FROM THE THIRD WORLD. CHURCH GROWTH STUDY CENTER,
      SINGAPORE, 135 pp. 1973.

      A STATISTICAL SURVEY REVEALING FOR THE FIRST TIME
      SOME THIRD WORLD MISSIONARY AGENCIES. TO
      QUESTIONNAIRES SENT OUT 44 COUNTRIES RESPONDED
      REVEALING 196 MISSIONARY SOCIETIES FROM THE THIRD
      WORLD. MOST OF THESE SOCIETIES STARTED IN THE LAST
      10-20 YEARS. INCLUDES INDICES AND BIBLIOGRAPHY.

38600
WONG, JAMES. SINGAPORE: THE URBAN CHURCH IN THE MIDST
OF SOCIAL CHANGE. SWM, M.A. THESIS, 285 pp.
PASADENA, 1972.

A STUDY OF SINGAPORE CHURCH GROWTH INCLUDING TWO
MODELS--SOUTHERN BAPTIST AND ANGLICAN. INCLUDES
STRATEGY FOR URBAN CHURCH GROWTH, DEVELOPMENT OF
LAY LEADERSHIP TRAINING FOR THE MINISTRY AND
MISSION AS THE KEY TO THE GROWTH OF ALL CHURCHES.
INCLUDES APPENDICES, MAPS, CHARTS AND BIBLIOGRAPHY.

38800
WORKS, HERBERT M. THE CHURCH GROWTH MOVEMENT TO 1965: AN
HISTORICAL PERSPECTIVE. SWM, DOCTORAL DISSERTATION,
PASADENA, 1974.

AN HISTORICAL STUDY OF THE ROOTS AND EARLY DEVELOP-
MENT OF THE CHURCH GROWTH SCHOOL OF THOUGHT IN
MODERN MISSIONS. NOTES EARLY OBSERVERS OF CHURCH
GROWTH PHENOMENA, BUT CONCENTRATES ON THE DEVELOP-
MENT OF CHURCH GROWTH CONCEPTS BY DONALD A. McGAVRAN.
DESCRIBES THE INSTITUTE OF CHURCH GROWTH IN EUGENE,
OREGON.

331

38900
YAMAMORI, TETSUNAO. CHURCH GROWTH IN JAPAN. DUKE
UNIVERSITY, PH.D. DISSERTATION, 262 pp. DURHAM, 1970.

A STUDY IN THE DEVELOPMENT OF EIGHT DENOMINATIONS
IN JAPAN BETWEEN 1859 AND 1939. AIMS TO SCRUTINIZE
FACTORS CAUSING CROWTH AND NON-GROWTH. HISTORICAL
AND SOCIOLOGICAL STUDY OF JAPANESE PROTESTANTISM.

38950
YANG, BILL T. C. THE BIBLICAL BASIS OF THE CHURCH GROWTH--
FOR THE CHINESE CHURCHES IN TAIWAN. SWM, M.A. PROJECT,
150 pp. PASADENA, 1974.

THIS PROJECT SEEKS TO CLARIFY THE ISSUES INVOLVED IN
THE SLOW GROWTH OF THE CHINESE CHURCHES IN TAIWAN
AND TO SHOW THE BIBLICAL BASIS OF THE CHURCH GROWTH
VIEWPOINT. IT IS AN ADAPTATION OF ALAN R. TIPPETT'S
CHURCH GROWTH AND THE WORD OF GOD FOR THE CHINESE
CHURCHES.

39150
YOUNG, JOSEPH. A CHINESE REFLECTION ON THE CHRISTIAN
    MOVEMENTS AMONG THE CHINESE PEOPLE. SWM, M.A.
    THESIS, 195 pp. PASADENA, 1974.

    A GENERAL SURVEY AND EVALUATION OF CHRISTIAN
    MISSIONS IN CHINA PRIOR TO 1949, WITH A CASE STUDY
    OF PHILIPPINE CHINESE CHURCHES TODAY. PROPOSAL
    FOR OVERSEAS CHINESE TO EVANGELIZE 800 MILLION
    COUNTRYMEN. (THESIS DONE IN CHINESE.)

5. GUIDELINES FOR RESEARCH

A. "Manual on Technical Writing"

B. "How to Do a Survey of Church Growth"
   by Donald A. McGavran 433

CHURCH GROWTH RESEARCH AND WRITING, SWM 692a,b.--1 & 2 Qs.
Professor Arthur F. Glasser and faculty--1 hour credit ea.

Description of Course

An analysis of research methodology for the planning and construction of the thesis or dissertation, resources in the Los Angeles area, appraising source materials, note taking and documentation organization of materials with particular attention given to graphs of growth during the winter quarter. 692a offered fall quarter and 692b winter quarter. Both are required for degree candidates.

COURSE REQUIREMENTS for 692a

Key Assignments:

1. The VITA must be submitted by end of the 2nd week.

2. The THESIS PROPOSAL must be submitted by end of the 6th week.

334 3. The METHODOLOGY must be submitted by end of the 8th week.

4. The PRELIMINARY BIBLIOGRAPHY must be submitted by end of the term: for inspection along with a sample of two pages of bibliographical entries typed out in the form in which they will ultimately appear in your thesis.

NOTE: In this course no attempt will be made to critique the content of your project, thesis or dissertation. Nothing will be said about the manner in which you handle either your data or your argument. Our only object will be to facilitate the work of your mentor. Remember that the thesis proposal, methodology and bibliography must be worked out with and approved by your mentor before they will be accepted by the faculty.

Class Exercises:

1. Introduction: What this course is all about.

2. VITA!
   Discussion: The subject, its presuppositions and
                  supporting data.

3. STRUNK:*   Elementary Rules of Usage (1-9).
   Discussion: The tentative bibliography and Los
                  Angeles area resources.

4. Discussion: Gathering and classifying the data.

5. STRUNK: Elementary Principles of Composition
                  (10-27).
   Discussion: Methodology.

6. THESIS PROPOSAL!
   Discussion: Organization.

7. STRUNK: A Few Matters of Form (28-32).
   Discussion: The Outline.

8. METHODOLOGY!
   Discussion: Theology and Theoretical Depth.

9. STRUNK: Words and Expressions Commonly Misused
                  (33-51).   335
   Discussion: Reading as research.

10. STRUNK: Style.
    Discussion: Gathering Loose Ends.

End of Term: PRELIMINARY BIBLIOGRAPHY!

*STRUNK, Jr., William
   1972 The Elements of Style. With Revisions, an Intro.
         and a Chapter on Writing by E. B. White. Second
         Edition. New York, The Macmillan Company.

THESIS PROPOSAL

1. The Suggested Title.

2. The Problem:

   (a) State briefly and clearly the major problem
       to be investigated or the hypothesis to be
       tested.
   (b) List any secondary problems you intend to
       investigate.

3. The Methodology:

   Outline briefly the methods you plan to use (inter-
       views, questionnaires, observation, archival
       research and so forth).
   (a) to collect your data.
   (b) to test your data.
   (c) to classify your data.
   (d) to draw your conclusions.

4. The Sources:

   What sources are available and where? What types of
       material will you be using--statistics, reports,
       correspondence, notes of interviews, question-
       naire returns, archival and library reading
       notes, etc.?
   (a) brought from the field
   (b) from resources at Fuller
   (c) at other repositories in the Los Angeles area
   (d) from elsewhere in the U.S.A. (e.g. Board or
       Church headquarters)
   (e) from correspondence with missionaries
   (f) any other

5. The Table of Contents:

   Prepare a table of contents with heads and sub-heads,
       as you see it at the present time, showing how
       you intend to present your case.

336

6. The Evaluation:

    State in a short paragraph why this research
    interests you, what you consider to be its
    contribution to knowledge and what value should it
    have to any who may use it afterwards.

                    THESIS FLOW CHART

PHASE ONE

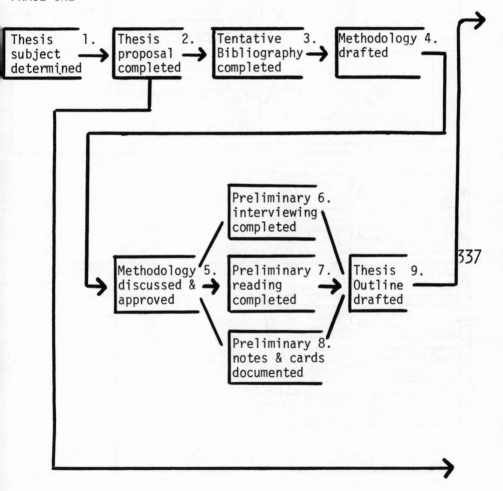

337

PHASE TWO

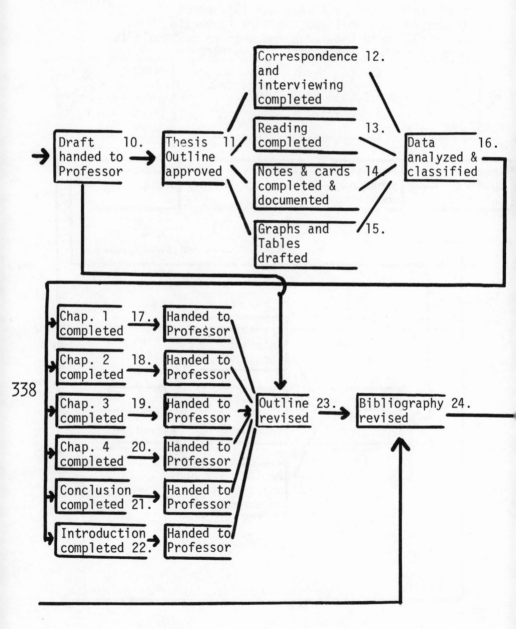

338

PHASE THREE

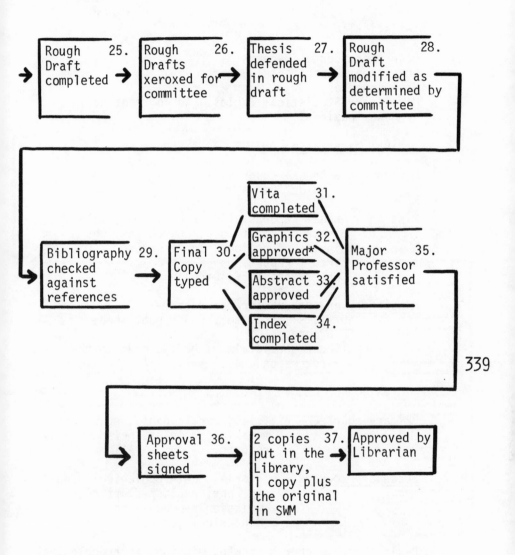

Rough 25. Draft completed → Rough 26. Drafts xeroxed for committee → Thesis 27. defended in rough draft → Rough 28. Draft modified as determined by committee

Bibliography 29. checked against references → Final 30. Copy typed

Vita 31. completed

Graphics 32. approved*

Abstract 33. approved

Index 34. completed

Major 35. Professor satisfied

339

Approval 36. sheets signed → 2 copies 37. put in the Library, 1 copy plus the original in SWM → Approved by Librarian

* Graphics must be approved by Professor Ralph D. Winter.

RESOURCES FOR THESIS RESEARCH

1. Statistical:

    Government Census Reports
    Government Departmental Reports
    Encyclopedias
    Missionary Statistical Tables - world, regional,
        denominational.

2. Archival Materials:

    Government - Annual Reports
                 "Blue" Books

    Mission - Annual Reports of home office or field
              Minute books of local church meetings
              Minutes of regional conferences
              Circuit reports
              Conferences (TEF, etc.)

    Missionary and other correspondence -
              Official, private (Mss or published)
              journals
              (There should always be two ends to the
                  correspondence.)

3. Printed Books, etc.:

    Primary sources - official, participants, observers,
                      magazine articles, newspaper
                      reports.

    Secondary sources - histories, anthropological mono-
                        graphs, published articles,
                        missionary magazines,
                        technical journals.

    Basic theory - church growth, mission, anthropological.

340

4. Unpublished MSS, University Theses, etc.:

    These may have to be used at the repository, or may
    be borrowed by interlibrary loan, or perhaps
    a microfilm obtained.

5. Interviews:

    With old missionaries, with old residents, with men
    in executive positions. Correspond after
    interviews.

6. Your own correspondence, and, if need be, questionnaire:

    With people whom you cannot interview, in other parts
    of the country and on the field.

7. Your own field notes and journals.

REFERENCE WORKS AT FULLER LIBRARY

1. Main Library Reading Room:

    Index to Religious Periodical Literature
    Union list of Periodicals in Libraries of So. Calif.
    Reader's Guide to Periodical Literature
    Catholic Periodicals Index   341
    Social Sciences and Humanities Index (formerly
        International Index)

2. Office:

    Library of Congress authors and subjects and supplements
    Union Theological Seminary Library
    Subject Headings (Dictionary Catalogs of Library of
        Congress)

STATISTICAL TABLES IN FULLER LIBRARY

BLISS, Edwin Munsell
1891   The Encyclopaedia of Missions. Descriptive,
       historical, biographical, statistical... 2 vols.
       New York, Funk & Wagnalls Co. [Ref. NJ/B649 v 1, v 2]

1904   The Encyclopedia of Missions. Second edition edited
       by Henry O. Dwight, H. Allen Tupper, and Edwin M.
       Bliss, New York, Funk & Wagnalls. [Ref. NJ/D992 2]

STRONG, Esther Boorman, A. L. WARNSHUIS (eds.)
1933   Directory of Foreign Missions. New York, Inter-
       national Missionary Council. [Ref. NJ2/D598]

PARKER, Joseph I. (ed.)
1938   Directory of World Missions. New York, Inter-
       national Missionary Council. [Ref. NJ2/D598]

World Missionary Atlas: 1911 [NJ4/S933w]; 1916 [NJ2/F714W];
                         1925 [NJ4/159W]; The Atlas appeared
                         first with a geographical volume in
                         1901 [NJ4/B365g], Beach, ed.

BEACH, Harlan P., Charles H. FAHS, (eds.)
1925   World Missionary Atlas. New York, Institute of
       social and religious Research. [Succeeds World
       Atlas of Christian Missions, 1911, and World
       Statistics of Christian Missions, 1916.]

342

BEACH, Harlan P., Burton St. JOHN, (eds.)
1916   World Statistics of Christian Missions. New York,
       The Committee of Reference and Counsel of The
       Foreign Missions Conference of North America.

DENNIS, James S., Harlan P. BEACH, Charles H. FAHS, (eds.)
1911   World Atlas of Christian Missions. New York,
       Student Volunteer Movement for Foreign Missions.
       [Succeeds H. P. BEACH, A Geography and Atlas of
       Protestant Missions, vol. 1, 1901, & vol. 2, 1903.]

FREITAG, Anton, (et al.)
1963   The Twentieth Century Atlas of the Christian World.
       The Expansion of Christianity through the Centuries.
       New York, Hawthorn Books, Inc., Publishes [NN3/F866]

STATISTICAL TABLES IN FULLER LIBRARY, Contd.

PARKER, Joseph I.
1938 Interpretative Statistical Survey of The World
Mission of The Christian Church. New York,
Internal Missionary Council. [NJ2/I61i]

World Christian Handbook: 1949 [Ref. IT/G855W];
1952; 1957; 1962; 1968.

GRUBB, Kenneth G. (ed.)
1949 World Christian Handbook. London, World
Dominion Press. [Ref. IT/G885W]

BINGLE, E. J. and Kenneth G. GRUBB (eds.)
1952 World Christian Handbook. London, World
Dominion Press.

1957 (Same title and publisher.)

COXHILL, H. Wakelin, and Kenneth G. GRUBB, (eds.)
1962 World Christian Handbook. London, World
Dominion Press.

1968 (Same title and publisher.)

Miscellaneous Handbooks:

1903 Missionary Atlas and Handbook. Westminster, S.W. 343
Published by the Society for the Propagation of
the Gospel in Foreign Parts. [Ref. NJ4/M678]

DWIGHT, Henry Otis
1905 The Blue Book of Missions for 1905. New York,
Funk & Wagnalls Co. [Ref. NJ2/B658]

BEACH, Roderich, (ed.)
1920 Foreign Missions Year Book of North America.
New York, Committee of Reference and Counsel of
the Foreign Missions Conference of North
America, Inc. [Ref. NC/F714/G]

1933 (See STRONG, E. B. above, Directory of Foreign
Missions.)

1938   (See PARKER, Joseph I. above, <u>Directory of World Missions.</u>)

Fifth Edition
1962   <u>North American Protestant Foreign Mission Agencies.</u> New York, Missionary Research Library.

Sixth Edition
1964   (Same title and publisher.) [Ref. NJ2/D5985]

Seventh Edition
1966   (Same title and publisher.)

GODDARD, Burton L. (et al.)
1967   <u>The Encyclopedia of Modern Christian Missions. The Agencies.</u> Camden, N. J., Thomas Nelson & Sons. [Ref. NJ/E56/v.1]]

Eighth Edition
1968   <u>North American Protestant Ministries Overseas.</u> Missionary Research Library in Cooperation with Missions Advanced Research and Communication Center. Waco, Published by Word Books.

Ninth Edition
1970   <u>North American Protestant Ministries Overseas.</u> Compiled and written for the Missionary Research Library by Missions Advanced Research and Communication Center. Monrovia, Calif. MARC.

Tenth Edition, DAYTON, Edward R., (ed.)
1973   <u>North American Protestant Ministries Overseas.</u> Monrovia, Calif., MARC.

<u>World Dominion Series of Regional Surveys:</u> e.g. <u>The Pacific Islands,1930.</u>

344

MISSIONARY JOURNALS IN THE FULLER LIBRARY

International Review of Missions. Geneva, World Council
     of Churches. [A complete set: vol. 1, 1911--
     1969 the "s" in Missions was dropped.]

The Missionary Review of the World. Princeton, N. J., The
     Princeton Press. [Though not in the catalogue there
     are about 55 volumes: Vol. 10, 1887 -- Vol. 62,
     1939.]

The Missionary Herald. [There are about 70 volumes: Vol.
     17, 1821 -- Vol. 118, 1922.]

The East and The West, A Quarterly Review of the Study of
     Missions. [The collection covers about 20 years,
     from the beginning of the century, with a few odd
     extras of a later period: Vol. 1, 1903 -- Vol. 16,
     1918, part of Vol. 17, 1919, and Vol. 18, 1920.]

Moslem World (Muslim World). Hartford, Hartford Seminary
     Foundation. [Listed in the catalogue only since
     1963; but there is a fairly complete holding from
     1920.]

Allgemeine Missions-Zeitschrift. Berlin, Verlag von
     Martin Warneck. Vols. 1-44, 1874-1917. [German
     series edited by D. Gustav Warneck.]

345

More recently added subscriptions with no back numbers:

1. Worldmission. New York, Published under the
     sponsorship of the National Office of the Society
     for the Propagation of the Faith. Sept., 1950, v.1--

2. Evangelical Missions Quarterly. Wheaton, Evangelical
     Missions Information Service, Inc. Vol. 1, 1964--

3. East Asia Millions. Philadelphia, Overseas Missionary
     Fellowship. From Vol. 56, 1948-- [Started as
     China's Millions by China Inland Mission.]

4. Frontier. London, Published on Behalf of World
     Dominion Press and Christian Frontier Council.
     Vol. 1, 1958--

5. Missionary Research Library. Occasional Bulletin.
    New York, Missionary Research Library. Vol. 1, 1950--

Other Repositories:

A.B.M. Review   from 1935 to date is at U.C.L.A.
Missionary Review (Aust) Good but not complete sequence
                     from 1891, fairly complete since 1934,
                     at U.C.L.A.
Missionary Herald, fair assortment from 1826, at U.C.L.A.
C.M.S. Quarterly Paper, 1816-35, at U.C.L.A.
C.M.S. Proceedings from 1801 to date, at U.C.L.A.
Missionary Register, 1813-1855 numerous odd volumes, at
                     U.C.L.A.

REGIONAL MATERIAL ON AFRICA AND ASIA IN FULLER LIBRARY

All these items are recent subscriptions. We have no back
numbers or extensive holdings of any regional material.

Southeast Asia Journal of Theology (much on training the
        Ministry, etc.) Singapore, Association of Theological
        Schools in South East Asia. [Began publication in
        1960. We have it except for Vol. 1, nos. 1 and 2.]

Religion and Society. Bangalore, Christian Institute for
        the Study of Religion and Society. [Held since 1959.]

346 Commenced more recently:

Journal of African History. London, Cambridge University
        Press.

Journal of African and Asian Studies.

Journal of Modern African Studies. London, Cambridge
        University Press.

Pacific Affairs. Vancouver, University of British
        Columbia. (SE Asia mainland and islands)

Modern African Studies.

African Report

Japan Studies

Japan Christian Quarterly

Other Repositories for Larger Holdings:

African Affairs at U.C.L.A. and Occidental

Africa at U.C.L.A., Occidental and Riverside

African Abstracts at U.C.L.A.

Journal of African History at L.A. Public Library.
      (Check U.C.L.A.)

RESEARCH METHODS, ETC., IN FULLER LIBRARY

American Journal of Sociology. Chicago, Chicago University
      Press. [The catalogue shows holdings only since 1963,
      but the material in the stacks is complete from 1948.

American Sociological Review. Washington, D.C., American
      Sociological Association. [17 odd copies on the
      shelves.]

Other Repositories:

American Journal of Sociology is at Claremont (H), U.C.L.A.
      and U.S.C. but also at Pasadena and Glendale Public 347
      Libraries.

American Sociological Review - Claremont (H), U.S.C.,
      U.C.L.A., Pasadena Public Library.

American Behavioral Scientist is at Claremont (H).

Human Organization is at U.S.C., U.C.L.A. & Claremont (H).

Human Relations is at Claremont (H).

British Journal of Sociology is at U.S.C. and U.C.L.A.

American Catholic Sociological Review is at U.S.C.

Basic articles on Research Method are scattered through
the anthropological and sociological journals. THere is
a scarcity of text books in this area.

ANTHROPOLOGICAL MATERIAL IN FULLER LIBRARY

Practical Anthropology. Tarrytown, Practical Anthropology.
    1955 to date. Complete. [This relates anthropology
    to Mission.]

Missiology, An International Review. South Pasadena,
    American Society of Missiology. Continuing
    Practical Anthropology. Vol. 1, January, 1973--

Other Repositories:

American Anthropologist, at U.C.L.A. or Claremont (H)

Oceania, at U.C.L.A., 1956-58, 1961 to date

Current Anthropology, at Claremont (H)

Journal Royal Anthropological Institute of Great Britain
    and Ireland. Claremont (H) and U.S.C.

Eastern Anthropologist (India), at Claremont (H) and L.A.
    Public Library

348

Journal of Polynesian Society, U.C.L.A. and L.A. State
    College

Man (Great Britain), at Claremont (H) and U.C.L.A.

Man in India, at Claremont (H), U.C.L.A. and U.S.C.

Anthropos, U.C.L.A. and U.S.C.

Southwestern Journal of Anthropology, at U.C.L.A. and
    U.S.C. and Claremont (H)

HISTORY OF RELIGIONS MATERIAL IN FULLER LIBRARY

Revue de 1 histoire des religions. We have a sequence
       since 1956.

History of Religions. Chicago, University of Chicago
       Press. [Recent publication - We have complete set.]

Contemporary Religions of Japan. [New subscription -
       1964 only.]

Other Repositories:

Archives de Sociologie des Religions. Paris, Groupe de
       Sociologie des Religions. [at U.C.L.A.]

UNIVERSITY OF CALIFORNIA, LOS ANGELES (U.C.L.A.)

This is the best research library in the area. A library
card is available and should be obtained so that admission
can be had to the stacks. The library is good in
anthropology, sociology and history. It has a wide
coverage in regional studies and in missions. Some valuable
mission series are there, bound journals over the years
and reports of missionary societies.

UCLA has a special concentration in African studies. The
African Studies Center issues a handbook with all information
and the names of professors, and so forth. This partici-   349
pating faculty in cross-departmental African studies numbers
46 persons. There are 16,000 volumes on Africa alone, and
these are increasing by 2000 a year.

UCLA also has a department of Latin American Studies.

UCLA also issues a Library Catalog and a handbook called
A Guide to Research Materials for Graduate Students. This
includes information about bibliographies available, and
bibliographies of bibliographies, catalogues of special
collections at the university and national catalogues, also
bibliographies of dissertations. It also has a list of
guides to newspapers, government publications, manuscripts,
and special files.

The Periodical Room beside the circulation desk has the
current numbers of the most important technical journals.

Dissertations Abstracts are found in the main reference
room to the left of the entrance in the research library.
Z/5055/U5D57

American Anthropologists are found in the stacks GN1 on
the 3rd floor.

Visit the Student Book Store when you go to UCLA. The
turn-over is rapid and new items are coming out all the
time. It is the best textbook shop in the area.

UNIVERSITY OF SOUTHERN CALIFORNIA (USC)

This is a little nearer than UCLA. It has a good library
but not nearly as good as UCLA. Nevertheless it has some
books that are not available at UCLA. You should visit
the place at least to check on the cards. It is strong
on Psychology and has devoted some attention to religion.

The most important resource for us at USC is the Human
Relations Area Files, classified after Murdock's system.
We have the key to this in our library so you can get your
reference numbers before you go. I have a record of the
breakdown of countries and tribes, so if you see me before
you go, I can tell you if they have anything of interest
to you. Miss Wishard is the curator of this collection
and is very cooperative.

Also at USC is the Population Research Laboratory with its
program in research and training. This is part of the
Dept. of Anthropology and Sociology. It works on population distribution and mobility, urbanization community
structure and social disorganization. They have done a
good deal of original work on the utility of urban typology.
It just may be that one of you is working along these lines.

Another resource here is the Von Kleinsmid Library of
World Affairs, research library in international relations.
It is rich in current and recent material, government
material, reports of conferences, etc. It is in a
different building, in the basement and has open stacks.
Visit the Book Store while you are there.

PASADENA PUBLIC LIBRARY

This not a very extensive collection, but I consider it
worth having a card. It has a small selection on missions,
anthropology, sociology and is good in history and travel.

The library subscribes to a number of useful journals:

Pacific Affairs
Pacific Historical Review
Hibbert Journal
Asia 1933-46
Sociology and Social Research
Social Forces
American Sociological Review
American Journal of Sociology
American Historical Review

Just recently it has commenced taking American Anthropologist.

The library has facilities for xeroxing material.

- - - - - -

Other libraries in the district which may be visited are at:

Pasadena City College
California State College
Los Angeles Public Library
Claremont
Etc.

351

THESIS STYLE INSTRUCTIONS

compiled by Alvin Martin

for
CHURCH GROWTH RESEARCH AND WRITING COURSE, SWM 692

CONTENTS

CHURCH GROWTH RESEARCH AND WRITING, SWM 692
Professor Arthur F. Glasser

THESIS STYLE INSTRUCTIONS

The writer of the thesis should familarize himself with
these rules and build them into his rough draft and fair
as well as final copy. This will simplify and speed up
the final typing to his own benefit and satisfaction.

The system of documentation and bibliography is that
approved for writing in anthropological journals. When
instructions in this manual are not explicit, the American
Anthropologist may be taken as a model.

This manual should be given to the person who types the
final copy of the thesis or dissertation. Ask the typist
to study the manual carefully and observe it scrupulously.

FORMAT

The elements of the thesis will consist of the following:* 353

1. Approval Sheet signed by examining professors.

2. Title page set out as per specification.

3. Table of Contents.

4. Table of Figures (including charts, maps, etc.).

5. Glossary (if required).

6. Introduction.

7. Methodology (if this has not been included in the
   Introduction).

* For a fuller description see pages 19-22, and 25-44.

8. Chapters of the thesis text.

9. Bibliography (set out in the prescribed form).

10. Any appendices (including Index, Abstract and Vita).

These ten items should be checked before handing the thesis,
(the original plus three copies) to the SWM secretary.

METHODOLOGY

Methodology concerns your method of research, your manner of
attacking the problem and presentation of the argument. It
covers sources, research tools and data-collection. The
section on methodology is essential and normally should be
located in the introduction (under a special subheading), in
the chapter where it is being employed (again with a heading),
or in a chapter by itself. Sometimes it may be given an
appendix, but this usually deals with technical problems of
testing, measurement, calculations or debatable issues. In
any case, methodology is not something thrown in with
acknowledgments or as an afterthought. It is essentially
part of the structure and validation of the thesis.

REFERENCES

The anthropological system of reference will be used. It
consists of:

1. Author's surname, year, volume number (if any) and
    page numbers in parentheses within the text. If
    author has already been named in the sentence, do
    not put his name in parentheses: e.g., These are
    Latourette's figures for all Protestants in Japan
    (1944:390-399).

2. Examples:

    a. Reference to whole book: (Jones 1948)

    b. Reference to page(s) in book: (Jones 1948:124)

c. Reference including volume number: (Jones
    1948: Vol. 2, 98-100). If volume number is
    Roman in source, use Roman; if Arabic, use
    Arabic.

d. Multiple-source references. If you feel that
    you must mention two or three sources, separate
    them by semicolons.

e. In bibliography, surname in solid caps. (JONES
    1958:2). In text, name in mixed caps (Jones
    1958:2).

f. Bibliography. When unsigned, official journals
    and reports are used, the creating agency
    should be listed in place of the author's name.
    E.g., India, Government of; London Missionary
    Society; Department of Health.

g. The writer of the thesis is free to use a
    system of abbreviations (e.g., L.M.S. for
    London Missionary Society), provided he sup-
    plies an alphabetical table either at the
    beginning of the thesis or immediately prior
    to the bibliography.

BIBLIOGRAPHY

355

The following examples demonstrate variations of biblogra-
phy listings:

1. A book by one author:

    JONES, Paul
        1960 Church Practices. Garden City, N.Y.,
              Doubleday.

2. A book by two authors:

    JONES, Paul, and SMITH, Ralph (or Ralph SMITH)
        1960 Changing World. New York, Macmillan.

3. Author of a magazine article:

> JONES, Paul
> 1960 "Moral Stability in an Unstable
>   Society," Christian Outlook, 17: 9-11
>   (meaning vol. number or issue and page
>   numbers).
>   or (Summer) 9-11
>   or (June) 9-11.

4. Author of a report:

> JONES, Paul
> 1960 Training Missionaries for Primitive
>   Areas. Fuller Theological Seminary,
>   Pasadena, California. National Con-
>   ference of Evangelicals. (Mimeographed)

5. Editor of a book:

> JONES, Paul, ed.
> 1960 Survey of Protestant Missions. London,
>   Oxford University Press.

6. Book (which is a translation of one in another
    language):

> HELLER, Karl
> 1960 Church and Mission. Maryknoll, N.Y.,
>   Maryknoll Publications. (Translated
>   by A. V. Littledale from the original
>   German.)

7. Book (in a foreign language):

> CASTRO, Juan
> 1960 El Final de la Vida. Mexico City,
>   Publicaciones de la Fuente.

8. Author of one book in a series which has volumes
    numbered:

JONES, Paul
    1960 <u>History of Missions</u>. Vol. 10 of Brown
           <u>Commentary</u>. New York, World Publishers.

9. Author of one article in an encyclopedia or
    commentary:

        SMITH, Andrew
        1960 "Animism," New York, <u>Encyclopedia</u>
            <u>Britannica</u>.

10. Interviews:

        JONES, Paul
        1960 Interview with author, June 15, 1960.

11. Correspondence:

        JONES, Paul
        1960 Letter to author, June 15.

12. Correspondence, Collection of:

        JONES, Paul
        1958-65 Private Correspondence.

13. One section of book which contains writings of
    several authors:

357

        JONES, Paul
        1960 "The Church and Society" in R. Brown
            (ed.) [N.B. This presupposes that
            the full entry of Brown is given
            under "B" in the bibliography].

14. Lectures or Sermons:

        JONES, Paul
        1960 "The Great Commission and You."
            Sermon (printed) delivered at Colonial
            Church, Pasadena, California.

15. Unsigned documents (Church Mission Society, Committee) annual reports, typescripts, committee reports, field reports:

     PRESBYTERIAN CHURCH IN U.S.A.
     1960 Annual Report Congo Mission.

16. One author citing another:

     list by author who cites, <u>not</u> by author cited.

17. Unpublished dissertations:

     JONES, Paul
     1960 "Christianity and Syncretistic
           Societies." An unpublished Ph.D.
           dissertation, University of Minnesota.
           [If a microfilm is used add the
           phrase - (m/f used).]

18. Old document republished in recent work:

     The writer of the thesis may wish to preserve
     the antiquity of the source he quotes. The
     following entry would be in order:

     TYLOR, Edward B.
     1873 "Animism" from Primitive Culture,
           London Murray, cited from The Making
           of Man, Ed. V.F. Calverton, New York,
           The Modern Library, 1931.

     In this case the entry in the text of the
     thesis should read (Tylor, 1873) <u>not</u> (Tylor,
     1873:645).

     The preferable form is to word the text of the
     thesis like this: In 1873 Tylor said of
     animism (Calverton, 1931:645) that ...

     The bibliographical entry would then appear
     under Calverton not under Tylor.

When the writer of the thesis desires to
preserve the original date of the statement
cited he would normally cite from the original
edition (giving the page), but if he cited
from a later edition this should be shown in
the bibliography. See the entries under Boas
in Keesing (1971:424).

Remember the reference system and bibliography
together comprise a working tool, a finding
aid, so the reader knows precisely where you
got your information.

The bibliography may be defined as an accurate list of all
books, articles in journals, and other written material or
sources from which you have derived useful information.
It should be arranged alphabetically according to the
surnames of the authors; several books or articles by one
author should be arranged chronologically according to the
year of publication. If Jones has published more than one
book or article in 1960, the second citation should be
designated 1960b.

Primary sources (e.g., original documents, newspaper
accounts, letters, etc.) should be listed separately from
secondary sources (such as second-hand accounts, translations, and paraphrases).

A sample page of a bibliography with frequently occurring   359
types of entries is included in the appendix. Special
problems can usually be solved by applying the principles
evident in typical examples. Be consistent. All titles
of books and journals should be italicized (underlined).

The growing trend in formats is toward brevity; however,
be sure that all facts given in the bibliography concerning any book or article are accurate and sufficient to be
readily identifiable. The complete title, including the
subtitle as it appears on the title page, should be given.
Identify the publisher by copying the name as it is on the
title page. Prevailing practice is to modify the name
according to a consistent pattern as found in indexes
(e.g., Cumulative Book Index) or anthropological journals.

Although several references to a single work may be made
in a chapter or chapters, there is only one entry for it
in the bibliography. The full description of each work is
to be recorded not in the first reference but only in the
bibliography.

QUOTATIONS

A quotation of less than three lines shall be regarded as
short and may be included within quotation marks within
the normal text. If a quotation requires three or more
lines it should be indented, block style, without any
quotation marks, like the following:

> To a large extent all religious work is with
> individuals. In group conversions, the individual
> is still as important as ever. The mistake occurs
> when the object is only the individual, who is
> separated from the group. Instead of separating
> him from the group, the individual should lead the
> way into the group (Warnshuis, 1955:17).

Interpolations should be enclosed in brackets or may be
footnoted. Always give references for direct quotations.
Be meticulous about crediting sources for all material
that is not expressed in your own words. Failure to do
this constitutes plagiarism.

360 Normally express as much as possible in your own words.
An exception to this rule will be a discussion of debatable
points and controversial issues, when the specific view-
points of various writers are being examined or compared.
Quotations from a single writer should be limited. If you
are dependent on a single source for a great deal of
material, reduce it as a precis or paraphrase into a
paragraph or two, or discuss its use under "Methodology."

Avoid creating the impression that you are writing from
library research cards splicing one quotation into another.
Use your quotations judiciously so that the basic writing
is your own.

At the same time you need a number of select quotations

to demonstrate that you have studied the subject and have
some theoretical and theological depth in the thesis and
can discuss critical issues.

STYLE AND PREPARATION

Paper, Format and Number of Copies

The school requires three copies of your thesis plus the
original. If you want one yourself prepare five. Use the
thesis paper available at the seminary bookstore. The original
or ribbon copy is to be presented unbound for SWM archival use.
The first copy for the Library must be 100 per cent rag content paper on 20 or 16 lb. bond. The second Library copy may
be on 13 lb. rag paper; it may be Xeroxed from the original
if you so desire. The third copy, which is for the SWM-ICG
dissertation shelves, may be on any type of paper and reproduced by carbon, Xerox or Minolta. The first and second copies
must be on a permanent paper - not corrasable or ezerase.

The Library has agreed to accept whatever format is necessary
when publication is contemplated. This last phrase includes
both commercial book publishing and also private two-pages-
per-page Xeroxing of multiple copies. The format is thus
determined by the reproduction process, not vice versa.

Where publication is expected, or hoped for, or planned, the
Library will accept two Xeroxed copies so long as they are
100% rag bond. That means the original or ribbon copy will be   361
kept by SWM for possible subsequent reproduction purposes, the
ribbon copy being for reproduction far superior to any kind of
Xerox or carbon copy. However, not just the quality of image
is important, the very size and shape of the column of print
is to be considered.

One example, Dr. Winter relates: "A man came to my office a
few minutes ago with a double-spaced 200-page project. He
now wants to make 50 copies by a two-page-per-page Xeroxing
procedure. But he cannot do this unless he reduces the
pages to 65% of the original size (due to the wide column
of his 8 1/2 x 11 double-spaced sheets). If he had only
thought ahead he could have put the same amount of words into
a single-spaced longish format (4 3/4 x 7 3/4 for example)
and easily gotten two pages on one without reduction.

Furthermore, it is that "longish" format which is necessary for a reproduction in book form. But let's take up all these questions one at a time. I attach a preliminary version of a brochure for people doing MSS for the William Carey Library."*

Pages

Number pages in upper right-hand corner, or for publishing number pages alternately in upper right-hand and upper left-hand corner. Chapter titles are always on the odd-numbered pages, i.e. always on the right-hand side.

Paragraphs

Indent all paragraphs.

Margins

Margin: 1 1/2 inches from the left margin, 1 inch for the right and bottom margins, and 3/4 of an inch for the top margin. (Alternative book format margins: 1 7/8 inches for the left and right margins, 1 5/8 inches for the top and bottom margins. The writing area, 4 3/4 x 7 3/4, similar to this page, is centered on an 8 1/2 x 11 page.) (See Appendix for sample guide sheets for typist.)

Titles

Underline book titles; put titles of chapters, articles, published or unpublished theses, lectures and sermons in quotation marks.

Headings

All chapter headings in straight caps and centered. Triple space below chapter headings.

All sub-heads of chapters in mixed caps and centered.

All smaller sectional headings in mixed caps, flush with the left margin.

---

*See Appendix for this brochure, p. 45.

A paragraph heading may be used if required. It is part
of the paragraph and is placed as the paragraph indentation.

Subheadings (centered) and sectional headings (against
margin) should have a triple space above and a double
space below.

If the centered subheadings are more than four inches in
length they should be broken into two lines in single space.

Do not underline headings and subheadings unless you want
them to be italicized.

Footnotes

Footnotes should normally contain writer's comments only.
(See "References").

Separate footnotes from text by a one-inch line, two
spaces below last line.

Use asterisks (*) or (**) instead of numbers.

Italics

Underline foreign words and phrases to indicate italics.

Do not translate foreign book titles.   363

Underline or italicize key terms and concepts only when
used for the first time.

Corrections

Typographical errors in the final manuscript of your thesis
which have been corrected must be inconspicuous and
expertly centered. With any correction of more than a word
the page should be retyped. The obliteration of whole
phrases and clauses by means of correcting fluid is not
approved. Remember the writer of the thesis is responsible
for delivering to the Library a neat and respectable manuscript, and he may meet with rejection at the last minute
if his manuscript is classified as untidy typing.

Alternative Format for Thesis

Theses in other schools are usually double spaced. SWM faculty is often called upon for copies of SWM theses, and is thus concerned about economical reproduction. For this reason they have approved single-spaced theses. Since every thesis may be subject to requests for reproduction, the faculty suggests that the instructions given in the William Carey Library brochure (included in Appendix) be followed even where no arrangement with the WCL or any other publishers has yet been made. Advise the Library that you have followed this procedure when you deposit the two approved Xerox copies. The original, which will be used for reproduction, is to be deposited with the faculty secretary; it will be retained by the SWM.

CAPITALIZATION

Caps: Bible

Christian (noun and adjective)

Church (Church Universal, a denomination, proper
                                        name)
Communion

Deity (all names or titles of God and Jesus Christ.
        Personal pronouns [He, Him, His] Holy Spirit
        - Spirit of God)

Fraternal or Monastic orders, denominations, political parties, whether nouns or adjectives

Geographic zones and regions
        e.g., Central States, East (section of
        country), East Side (section of city),
        Promised Land, the North

God's Word

Gospel (noun)

Headings (capitalize all words except prepositions,
        conjunctions and articles.)

Lord's Day

Mission (mission board or society of a foreign Church
    or the mission organization within a country.)

Passover

Protestant

Reformation

Scripture

Sunday School

Titles (capitalize all academic, governmental,
    judicial, military, political and religious
    titles preceding a proper name; also titles
    of nobility and royalty preceding proper
    name.)

Lower Case

biblical

church (adjective) when used as an adj. or to
    indicate individual congregations, or the
    building.   365

deity, relative pronouns (who, whom, whose)

directions (where term is used as a common noun or
    common adj.) east, easterly, eastern,
    easternmost, eastward.

gospel (adjective)

government

institute (except when part of title)

kingdom

mission (a particular field within a country, or an adjective.)

missionary

pastor (unless a title)

pre-Christian

presbytery (except when specific)

school (except when part of title)

scriptural

seasons of the year

PUNCTUATION

No attempt will be made to cover all punctuation rules. Those listed are merely a few that seem to be common problems. It should be noted, too, that there are often options in punctuation and that some of the "rules" given are not so much for the sake of purity as for consistency.

apostrophe Avoid triple sibilants (hissing sounds) either in one word (Jesus' - not Jesus's) or in more than one word (goodness' sake - not goodness's sake).

brackets Brackets are used to enclose interpolations or editorial comments upon the word(s) immediately preceding them.

comma A comma before the last item of a series and preceding the conjunction may or may not be used, according to the writer's preference. However, CONSISTENCY in this matter is important.

dash Use two hyphens to represent the dash -- (never follow a comma with a dash).

ellipsis This is used to denote the omission of
      words, sentences, or paragraphs from a
      quotation. It consists of three periods
      preceded and followed by one space. Any use
      of this devise for shortening a quotation
      obligates the writer to preserve the basic
      meaning of the passage. Be careful about
      eliminating qualifying clauses.

exclamation point Excessive use is the mark of the
      amateur. Use it sparingly, relying on words
      to convey emphasis.

parentheses Material enclosed in parentheses
      qualifies the phrase or sentence immediately
      preceding, and no punctuation marks should
      intervene. Any necessary punctuation marks
      following the qualified clause or phrase
      should be inserted after the passage enclosed
      in parentheses. The material enclosed is
      understood to have originated with the writer
      of the passage.

quotation marks Place all commas or periods inside
      quotation marks. Place the question mark,
      colon, semicolon, and exclamation point inside
      the quotation marks if they belong to the
      quoted part; otherwise, place them outside the
      quotation marks.

367

word division If a word cannot be included in its
      entirety or properly syllabified within the
      established margins, the entire word should be
      placed on the next line. The set of rules for
      dividing words at the end of the line are set
      out in the U.S. Government Printing Office
      Style Manual Supplement. When in doubt refer
      to the dictionary. Do not guess.

worthy rules Enclose parenthetical phrases in commas.

      Use a comma before a conjunction introducing
      an independent clause.

MISCELLANEOUS

Time

In reading matter: 12 o'clock, 1 o'clock.

In tabular matter: 8:45 P.M., 12:00 P.M.

Per Cent (%)

In reading matter, spell out: 10 per cent (two words).

In tabular matter, use sign: 10%.

Titles

As a general rule, it is better to omit all titles
such as "Dr." and "Rev." in the bibliography
because it is so easy to blunder in these areas.

B.C. - A.D.

A.D. goes before the figures: e.g., Josephus was
born at Jerusalem A.D. 37.

B.C. goes after the figures: e.g., Brutus dies in
42 B.C.

368 ABBREVIATIONS

(The common abbreviations are not included.)

c.   circa = about

ed.   editor

et al. and others

n.d.   no date

Abbreviations are ordinarily not used in formal
writings (except Mr., Messrs., Mrs., Ms. and their foreign
equivalents; Dr., St., Rev., and Hon., preceding proper
names; and Esq., Sr., and Jr. following proper names).

Abbreviations of the Names of Biblical Books (with the Apocrypha)

Gen	Nah	Add Esth	Acts
Exod	Hab	Bar	Rom
Lev	Zeph	Bel	1-2 Cor
Num	Hag	1-2 Esdr	Gal
Deut	Zech	4 Esdr	Eph
Josh	Mal	Jdt	Phil
Judg	Ps (pl.: Pss)	Ep Jer	Col
1-2 Sam	Job	1-2-3-4 Mac	1-2 Thes
1-2 Kgs	Prov	Pr Azar	1-2 Tim
Isa	Ruth	Pr Man	Tit
Jer	Cant	Sir	Phlm
Ezek	Eccl (or Qoh)	Sus	Heb
Hos	Lam	Tob	Jas
Joel	Esth	Wis	1-2 Pet
Amos	Dan	Matt	1-2-3 John
Obad	Ezra	Mark	Jude
Jonah	Neh	Luke	Rev
Mic	1-2 Chr	John	

Journal of Biblical Literature - Supplement

HOW TO GET YOUR THESIS ACCEPTED FOR LIBRARY ACCESSION

Have it signed by your Advisors (Get approval sheets from Registrar to give to your Mentor). Signatures are to be in black ink only.

369

Deliver two boxed copies to the Library Order Department after paying Business Office for binding. The cost to bind extra personal copies is also $7.50 each. All copies of one's thesis are to be given to the Library at one time. If Index is desired, it must be included at the time thesis is handed in.

If thesis is to be microfilmed, it is to be done before handing the unbound copies to the Library. Allow six weeks.

Use pica or elite type. For other type faces see Librarian. Use double or single space.

Use Greek or Hebrew typewriter in preference to handwriting.

Good typing form should be used. Do not begin a new
paragraph or outline heading at the bottom of the page.
Consult standard typing manual.

The typist's and writer's responsibilities are discussed
in chapter eight of Form and Style, Theses, Reports,
Term Papers / 4th edition, by William Giles Campbell and
Stephen Vaughan Ballou, (Boston: Houghton Mifflin
Company), 1974.

For help with such punctuation as quotation marks,
parentheses, and commas consult P. G. Perrin, Writer's
Guide and Index to English, or other standard books of
good English usage.

For instructions not included in this "Thesis Style
Instructions," the Library recommends that you use
A Manual for Writers of Dissertations by Kate L. Turabian
(Chicago, University of Chicago Press). Paperback edition
is on sale in the bookstore. The 4th edition of Form and
Style, by Campbell and Ballou (1974), is comprehensive
and very helpful. Old theses are not acceptable as form
authorities.

For abbreviation of Dead Sea Scrolls, early Christian
literature and periodicals, see list at circulation desk.
Fine points in footnoting, works of composite authorship
and corporate body entries can be established by the Head
370 Cataloger. The Library uses Library of Congress form.

Xerox may be used for all copies (except approval sheet).
Approved lithographed, lithoprinted and letter press
copies are also accepted. They must equal the physical
appearance of original typed copy. The weight of stock
of the first copy submitted must be 16 lbs. or heavier
and the second copy may be 13 lbs.; both must be 100 per
cent rag content paper. The original ribbon copy of the
thesis or dissertation is to be turned over to the School
of World Mission and Institute of Church Growth. One copy
of the thesis or dissertation to be bound for the SWM
dissertation/thesis shelves is to be submitted along with
the original.

DEFINITION AND/OR FACSIMILE OF THESIS ELEMENTS

A dissertation or thesis includes three categories of
materials: the preliminaries, the body of the thesis or
the text, and the reference materials. Not all the
elements here defined are included in every thesis; but
the various components occur in the approximate order in
which they are presented. See Campbell / Ballou
(1974:15-20) for additional information on each element,
and the APPENDIX for a facsimile of each element. The
source (dissertation writer) of each "sample page" is
given in the upper right corner.

1. Approval Sheet - SWM facsimile, Appendix, p. 25.
    (The signatures of the thesis committee
    are to be in black ink only.)

2. Title Page - dissertation sample, p. 26.

    The designation of the faculty and the
    institution, the degree sought (or granted), the
    full name of the candidate, and the month and
    year in which the degree is to be (or was) granted
    follow the title of thesis or dissertation. Note
    the number of single spaces between each line.

3. Copyright Page - facsimile, Appendix, p. 27.

    Even though most theses or dissertations   371
    are not registered with the Copyright Office, a
    page for copyright notice is of value. Simply
    add a page after the Title page and put:
    "   ©Copyright 1974 by (your name)."
    Special copyright instructions for theses to be
    published or microfilmed should be followed.
    Consult your mentor.

4. Abstract - facsimile in Appendix, p. 28.

    A 200-300 word thesis abstract or 500-600
    word dissertation abstract should include:

    1. A definitive statement of the problem.

    2. A brief description of research method.

3. Major findings and significance or
   lack of conclusive evidence.

4. Conclusions.

The abstract is not one of the preliminaries.
It is not included in the page numbering even
though it is bound into the dissertation. The
abstract is usually placed after the last page of
the appendix or before the title page.

5. Preface

Turabian (1967:3-4) defines this element
as follows:

> Included in the preface (or foreward) are
> such matters as the writer's reasons for
> making the study, its background, scope,
> and purpose, and acknowledgment of the aids
> afforded him in the process of the research
> and writing by institutions and persons.

6. Acknowledgments - facsimile attached, p. 30.

If a section contains only expressions of
appreciation, it is designated ACKNOWLEDGMENTS.
Individuals who have given valuable assistance
and to whom the writer is indebted are recognized.
Acknowledgments are expressed simply and tactfully.

7. Table of Contents - facsimile attached, p. 32.

The major divisions of the thesis are all
included in the table of contents with their
respective page numbers. It includes an introduction, the chapters or their equivalents, which
are not always designated as chapters, the
appendix, bibliography and index if one has been
prepared. The table of contents gives the reader
an analytical overview of the material included
in the study, and indicates the order of
presentation.

Lowercase Roman numerals (e.g., ix, x), are
used for pagination of preliminary matters; these
are all included in the table of contents. The
first page is the title page; it and the table of
contents are not marked with a Roman numeral, but
are included in the sequence of Roman numerals.
Arabic numerals in sequence are used for each
page of the text (the body of the thesis); this
sequence begins with the first page of the introduction or the first page of chapter one if the
introduction is part of that first chapter.

8. Table of Figures (including charts, graphs) p. 35.

If three or more charts or figures are
used, a table should be added. See the sample
page in Appendix. If the table of figures must
include a variety of charts, maps and tables,
see Campbell / Ballou (1974:17,18) for additional
guidance.

9. Glossary (if required) - see Appendix, p. 40.

The nature of the glossary will determine
the best format to be used.

10. Introduction

The introduction, whether designated as   *373*
Chapter I or Introduction, is the first major
division of the text. It begins with page 1
(Arabic numeral) and is not the last of the
preliminaries (Roman numerals) as is sometimes
supposed.

The introduction is one of the most
important chapters. According to Campbell /
Ballou (1974:18), the introduction should include
the following:

1. An introduction of the problem, an
indication of its importance and validity,
together with suitable background information,
should be incorporated.

2. A sharply defined statement of the problem, plus an analysis and acknowledgment of delimitations.

3. The theoretical framework, review of related literature and design or procedure of research should also be included.

11. Methodology (if this has not been included in the Introduction).

See Kwast (1972:8-26) for an example of historical methodology, and Conley (1973:30-42) for a description of the anthropological method followed by him in pursuing and presenting his investigation.

12. Chapters of the thesis or dissertation text.

A format should be adopted and followed consistently. Examine a few dissertations like Rader (1973), Conley (1973) and Kwast (1972) and then discuss with your mentor the format you plan to follow.

13. Bibliography - facsimile in Appendix, p. 42.

In addition to specific instructions already given, use Bibliography for Cross-Cultural Workers, compiled by A. R. Tippett as your model. (Note new directive on page 42.)

14. Appendix - facsimile of Index in Appendix, p. 43.

The appendix may be placed before or after the bibliography. If an index has been prepared it should be included in the appendix. See Campbell / Ballou (1974:19-20) for more on the purpose and content of an appendix.

15. Vita - facsimile attached, p. 44 in Appendix.

The vita is a brief biographical sketch. It is the last page of the dissertation (no number)

BIBLIOGRAPHY

AMERICAN ANTHROPOLOGIST. Washington, D.C., American
        Anthropological Association.

CAMPBELL, William Giles and Stephen Vaughan BALLOU
    1974   Form and Style, Theses, Reports, Term Papers.
           4th ed., Boston, Houghton Mifflin Company.

CHANDLER, Thomas W.
    1973   "A Statistical Study of Short Term Missionaries."
           An unpublished M.A. thesis, Fuller Theological
           Seminary, School of World Mission.

CONLEY, William Wallace
    1973   "The Kalimantan Kenyah: A Study of Tribal
           Conversion in Terms of Dynamic Cultural Themes."
           An unpublished D.Miss. dissertation, Fuller
           Theological Seminary, School of World Mission.

CUMULATIVE BOOK INDEX
    1973   A World List of Books in the English Language.
           New York, The H. W. Wilson Company.

KEESING, Roger M., and Felix Maxwell KEESING
    1971   Cultural Anthropology. New perspectives in
           cultural anthropology. New York, Holt, Rinehart
           and Winston.

HINKLE, George and Francis R. JOHNSON
    1964   "The Form for the Term or Research Paper."
           Prepared for use in courses in the Department of
           English, Stanford, Stanford University Press.

KWAST, Lloyd Emerson
    1972   "The Origins and Nineteenth Century Development
           of Protestant Christianity in West Cameroon,
           1841-1886." An unpublished D.Miss. dissertation,
           Fuller Theological Seminary, School of World Mission.

MODERN LANGUAGE ASSOCIATION OF AMERICA
    1970   The MLA Style Sheet. 2nd. ed., New York,
           Modern Language Association.

375

OLIVER, Dennis Mackintosh
  1973 "Make Disciples! The Nature and Scope of Great
        Commission Mission." An unpublished D.Miss.
        dissertation, Fuller Theological Seminary, School
        of World Mission.

PERRIN, Porter Gale
  1950 Writer's Guide and Index to English. Rev. ed.,
        Chicago, Scott, Foresman.

RADER, Paul Alexander
  1973 "The Salvation Army in Korea after 1945; A Study
        in Growth and Self-Understanding." An unpublished
        D.Miss. dissertation, Fuller Theological Seminary,
        School of World Mission.

STRUNK, William Jr., and E. B. WHITE
  1972 The Elements of Style. With Revisions, an
        Introduction, and a Chapter on Writing, by E. G.
        White. 2nd. ed., New York, Macmillan Company.

TIPPETT, Alan R.
  1970 Peoples of Southwest Ethiopia. South Pasadena,
        William Carey Library.

  1971 Bibliography for Cross-Cultural Workers.
        South Pasadena, William Carey Library.

376 TURABIAN, Kate L.
  1967 A Manual for Writers of Term Papers, Theses, and
        Dissertations. 3d. ed., Chicago, University of
        Chicago Press.

U.S. GOVERNMENT PRINTING
  1970 Word Division, Supplement to Office Style Manual.
        Washington, D.C., For sale by the Superintendent
        of Documents, Washington, D.C., 20402.

WAGNER, C. Peter, and Ralph COVELL
  1971 An Extension Seminary Primer. South Pasadena,
        William Carey Library.

WATKINS, Floyd C., William B. DILLINGHAM, Edwin T. MARTIN
  1970 Practical English Handbook. 4th ed., Boston,
        Houghton Mifflin Company.

WEERSTRA, Hans
  1972 "Maya Peasant Evangelism: Communication
        Receptivity and Acceptance Factors Among Maya
        Campesinos." An unpublished D.Miss. dissertation,
        Fuller Theological Seminary, School of World Mission.

WINTER, Ralph D.
  1970 The 25 Unbelievable Years 1945 - 1969.
        South Pasadena, William Carey Library.

  1972 "Minipublishing: New Hope for Strategic
        Dialogue." Occasional Bulletin. Vol. 23:3, Feb.

APPENDIX

Graduate Schools of
THEOLOGY
PSYCHOLOGY
WORLD MISSION

(Conley 1973)

Thesis Approval Sheet

This thesis, entitled

The Kalimantan Kenyah:

A Study of Tribal Conversion

in Terms of Dynamic Cultural Themes

written by

William Wallace Conley

and submitted in partial fulfilment of the

requirements for the degree of

Doctor of Missiology

has been read and approved by the undersigned members of the Faculty of Fuller Theological Seminary.

378

Date May 15, 1973

26

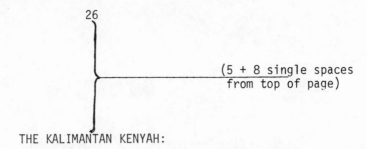

(5 + 8 single spaces
from top of page)

THE KALIMANTAN KENYAH:

A Study of Tribal Conversion

in Terms of Dynamic Cultural Themes

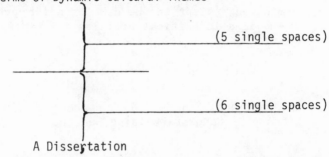

(5 single spaces)

(6 single spaces)

A Dissertation

Presented to the Faculty of

The School of World Mission and Institute of Church Growth

Fuller Theological Seminary

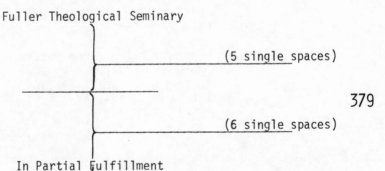

(5 single spaces)

379

(6 single spaces)

In Partial Fulfillment

of the Requirements for the Degree

Doctor of Missiology

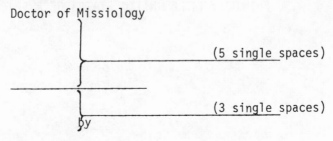

(5 single spaces)

(3 single spaces)

by

William Wallace Conley

May 1973

International Standard Book Number: 0-87808-102-X
Library of Congress Catalog Number: 73-1254459

Third Printing

Published by the William Carey Library
533 Hermosa Street
South Pasadena, Calif. 91030
Telephone 213-682-2047

380

ABSTRACT   28   (Conley, 1973)

The Kenyah are a Dayak tribe numbering about
35,000 in Indonesian Kalimantan with 8-10,000 more in
Sarawak. Between 1930, when an American missionary
first contacted them in the interior of East Kalimantan,
and 1965, the Kalimantan Kenyah converted to Christianity. This study is an attempt to analyze the conversion process in terms of dynamic cultural themes.

Using Opler's approach six different themes
have been identified and described: Supernaturalism,
Communalism, Children, Status and Rank, Rice Agricul-
ture and Riverine Orientation. Supernaturalism is the
central theme, supporting and giving direction to the
other five themes. Each of these themes is balanced by
certain limiting factors which operate for equilibrium   381
in the society.

During the process of tribal conversion
Christians experienced some opposition and overt
persecution. This developed particularly in situations
where the believers were a minority group. In other
cases strong people movements resulted in a relatively
smooth transition from paganism to Christianity. The
major strength of the conversion process, in respect
to the stability of a Kenyah community, is the fact
that as Christianity replaced the Animistic core of
Supernaturalism the new religious faith has been able
to maintain the other dynamic cultural themes relatively
or wholly undisturbed. These themes are compatible
with Christianity and thus the Christian Kenyah

Abstract   29   (Conley, 1973)

remained in fact Kenyah culturally.

        The history of the Kenyah Church is traced
and significant events which predisposed the tribe
toward change are described. Finally, suggestions are
offered to the leadership of the Church (KINGMI) and
to the mission (The Christian and Missionary Alliance)
as well as to church planters who might find in the
Kenyah situation some ideas appropriate to the
evangelization of tribal peoples elsewhere.

Acknowledgments

It would be impossible to include in this brief acknowledgment all the people who should justly be recognized. I have mentioned by name a number of informants in the Appendix but I am indebted to many kind and patient people in the KINGMI Church of East Kalimantan who never begrudged time and consideration in response to my questions. Rev. P.N. Potu and Rev. PeBaya' Jalong deserve special mention. The Christian and Missionary Alliance in Indonesia were cooperative in every respect; especially are we grateful to Rev. and Mrs. Larry Bell for their hospitality in Long Bia, and to Rev. and Mrs. Ken Riggenback for the use of their home while they were on furlough. The Foreign Department of the C&MA provided generous assistance for transportation and field expenses for this study. The Missionary Aviation Fellowship, and in particular pilot Jerry Reeder made trips to the interior possible. Dr. Sieswanpo, a friend from student days at the University of Minnesota, now director of the *Yayasan Ilmu Sosial dan Budaya*, a foundation for the advancement of social studies in Indonesia, was most gracious in offering his help.

I am grateful to the St. Paul Bible College for granting me a year of sabbatical study, and to Fuller Theological Seminary for tuition scholarship assistance. Arthur F. Glasser and Donald A. McGavran, dean and senior professor in the School of World Mission at Fuller provided more encouragement than they may realize in urging that this research be undertaken.

Charles H. Kraft and Clifford E. Larson, professors at
Fuller, read the rough draft and offered useful suggestions. Personal correspondence with Herbert and
Patricia Whittier of the department of anthropology at
Michigan State University enabled me to profit from
their own field research among the Kenyah of the Kayan
river area.

       The facilities of the McAlister Library at
Fuller Seminary, the U.C.L.A. Research Library in Los
Angeles, and the Rutenber Memorial Library of St. Paul
Bible College in Minnesota were utilized. Finally, I
must acknowledge two people without whose assistance
this study would never have been written: Dr. A.R.
Tippett, my mentor, professor of missionary anthropology in the School of World Mission at Fuller, who
directed my approach to the problem from the beginning,
supervised my field work, and made many vital suggestions during the entire course of the writing, and to
Anita, my wife, who not only typed the material in the
rough and final copies, made the six drawings illustrat-
ing the cultural themes, but never wearied of providing
the support that kept the project from bogging down in
the "Slough of Despond" that crops up in this kind of
an undertaking. I thank you, one and all.

TABLE OF CONTENTS (Oliver, 1973)

386

CONTENTS

387

35   (Chandler, 1973)

FIGURES

388

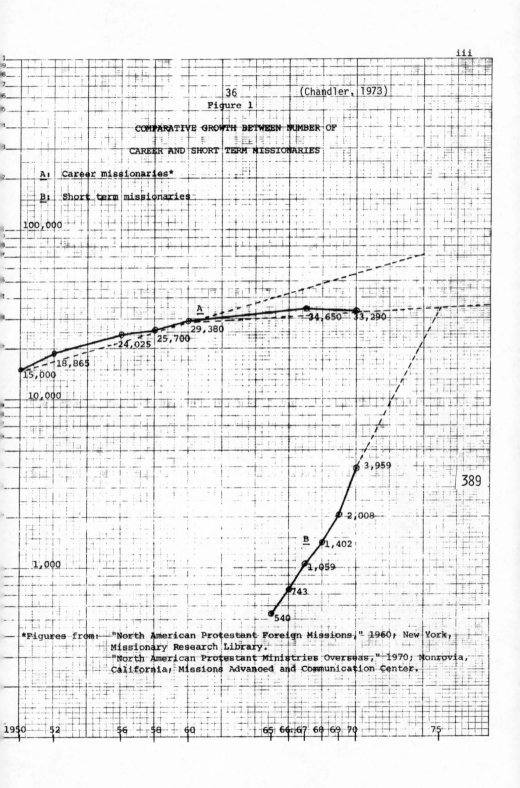

36   (Chandler, 1973)

Figure 1

COMPARATIVE GROWTH BETWEEN NUMBER OF

CAREER AND SHORT TERM MISSIONARIES

(Rader, 1973)

390

Presbyterian Groups

Methodist Groups

Holiness Groups

Seventh Day Adventist

Korea Baptist Convention

Assemblies of God

The Salvation Army

Anglican

Nazarenes

Others

Figure I
Selected Protestant Denominations
in Korea — Number of Churches

(For numerical data see Table A
in Appendix B)

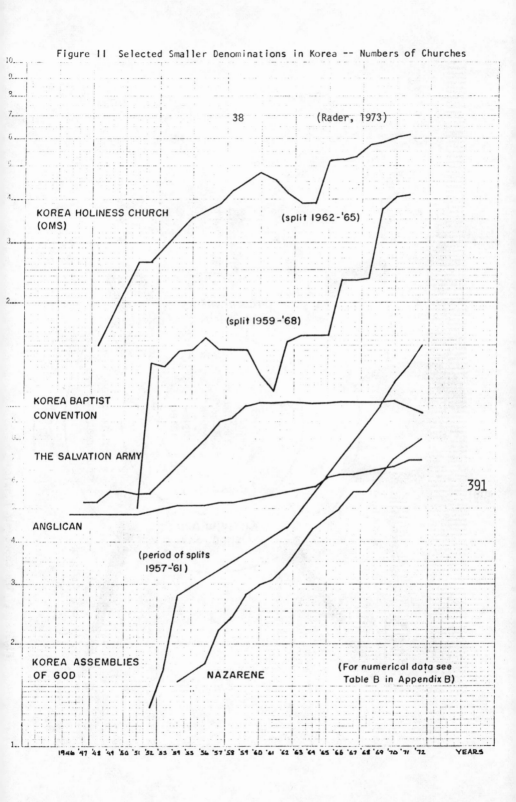

Figure II Selected Smaller Denominations in Korea -- Numbers of Churches

38   (Rader, 1973)

KOREA HOLINESS CHURCH
(OMS)   (split 1962-'65)

(split 1959-'68)

KOREA BAPTIST
CONVENTION

THE SALVATION ARMY

391

ANGLICAN

(period of splits
1957-'61)

KOREA ASSEMBLIES
OF GOD   NAZARENE   (For numerical data see
                                        Table B in Appendix B)

1946 '47 '48 '49 '50 '51 '52 '53 '54 '55 '56 '57 '58 '59 '60 '61 '62 '63 '64 '65 '66 '67 '68 '69 '70 '71 '72   YEARS

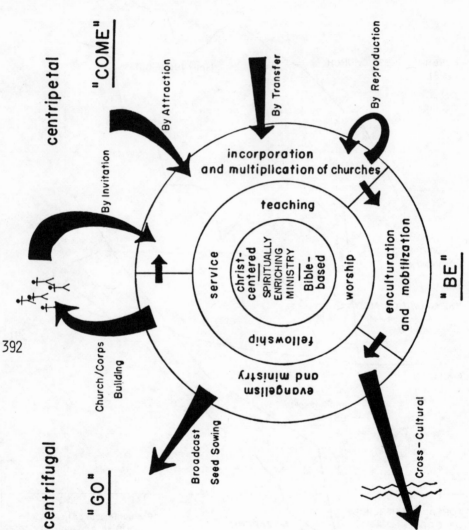

Figure IX The Church in Mission

GLOSSARY

Words Defined According to Local Usage

ción Católica - Catholic Action; a growing Catholic lay movement in Latin America.

ción de Gracia - Special service of thanksgiving

uardiente - Liquor; usually beer; literally, "burning water"

dea - Village; scattered rural settlement

igo - Friend

igo del Pueblo - Friend of the community

mpesino - Rural peasant

ntina - Saloon

ntón - Rural township

iman - Mam shaman

fradía - Civil-religious leadership guild

frado - A member of the cofradia

lonia - District of a town or city; suburb   393

mandante - Police

misario - Village mayor

misario Ejidal - Director of land distribution of government controlled property.

mpadre - Godfather; family friend

nsejo - Advice; counsel

nquistador - (Spanish) Conqueror

stumbre - Pagan rituals performed by shaman; animistic religion

"at home" and "abroad." Peripheral discussion has been largely
confined to footnotes. The advantage is that the development of
the central theme might be more easily grasped. The disadvantage
is that the implications and justifications of many statements
might not be immediately apparent.

Introducing Some Key Terms

The author's central thesis is grounded in a few biblical
concepts. These are tied to words which have been variously defined and which are used today with many different meanings. The
following terms are derived from a careful exegesis of the Scriptures. They are technically correct. However, this does not
prejudice those who would pour different meanings into the same
words. Though the following concepts will be more fully explicate
in the body of this study, it is useful to introduce them with
their essential biblical meaning.

Disciple: one who follows Jesus Christ as Lord.

Discipleship: the disciple's continuing obedience and
                         growth. (Note: This is not a biblical term

Discipling or
disciple-making: leading men and women to the point of whole
                         heartedly yielding themselves to Jesus Chri
                         as Lord.

Maturity: the type of relationship with God, that ex-
                         presses itself in single-minded obedience.

Perfection: a synonym of maturity.

394   Only one of the above terms, *as presently defined,* describes
the continuing growth of the believer. The writer would not deny
the need for such "qualitative growth." Nor would he underestimat
the value of those ministries which encourage it. The reader
should note, however, that *in this study* the terms discipling,
maturity and perfection do not refer to the Christian's continuing
walk.

Further Research Needed

If the central thesis of the work is valid, it needs further
exploration and testing. Many more historical models need to be
researched. Even more important, the theological base needs to be
expanded. The Matthean emphasis upon discipling needs to be related to the Scriptures' broad teaching of conversion. The two
Church mandates, evangelistic and pastoral, need to be more fully
related to the apostolic ministry, and to that of our Lord. Further, there is a great need for exploring the biblical data

NEW DIRECTIVE: Improve the bibliographic apparatus!

Presently we have no way, scanning a man's bibliography, to check
on how (or if!) a man makes use of a given source document.   We
cannot readily turn to the page in his thesis when he cites the
document to see how he handles it.   Therefore, in the bibliograhic
section of a thesis, each source cited should be followed by the
page number(s) in the thesis where that source is cited.   This
will produce in effect an author index automatically.   Whenever
an author index is supplied, this directive is not needed.

AICHNER, P.
   1956   "Adat Bungan," *Sarawak Museum Journal*
          7:476-477

ARENSBERG, Conrad M. and Arthur N. Niehoff
   1964   *Introducing Social Change: A Manual for
          Overseas Americans.*   Chicago, Aldine

ARNOLD, Guy
   1959   *Longhouse and Jungle.*   London, Chatto
          and Windas

BARNETT, Homer G.
   1953   *Innovation: Basis of Cultural Change.*
          New York, McGraw-Hill   395

BARNEY, G. Linwood
   1957   "The Meo--an Incipient Church," *Practical
          Anthropology* 4:31-50

BAVINCK, J.H.
   1961   *An Introduction to the Science of Missions.*
          Grand Rapids, Baker

BEALS, Ralph L., and Harry Hoijer
   1971   *An Introduction to Anthropology*   (4th ed.).
          New York, MacMillan

William Wallace Conley was born on October 31, 1917 in Rutherford, N.J., of Alexander Francis Conley (deceased in 1962) and Sarah Hill Conley, nee Patrick. Six years later the family, including one brother, Richard, moved to Scranton, Pa. where he finished high school. The family was nominally religious but not until age 20 did he come to know Christ as his personal Savior. This took place in Erie, Pa., in The Christian and Missionary Alliance Church.

He graduated from Nyack College, married Mae Stolz of Erie, Pa., and became the first pastor of an extension project church in Spartansburg, Pa., all in the month of June, 1941.

In February 1944 he entered the army as a chaplain and volunteered for paratroop duty. He served in the Philippines and Japan with the 11th Airborne Division. After separation from active duty the family, now including two children, Diana and William, Jr., went to Indonesia as missionaries under The C & M A where they lived until Mrs. Conley's health required them to return to the United States in 1961. During this time two more children were born, Stephen and Michael. He joined the faculty of the St. Paul Bible College in Minnesota where he presently teaches missions and anthropology. Mrs. Conley died in March 1971 after some years of serious illness. In May 1972 he was married to Anita S.Y. Goo, of Honolulu, at Fuller Theological Seminary in Pasadena.

397

He has the B.S. in Theology degree from Nyack College, and the M.A. in anthropology from the University of Minnesota.

"A preliminary ... brochure for people doing MSS for WCL."

MEMO:

To: All SWM Associates writing theses.
From: Ralph D. Winter, April 4, 1973
Subject: Questions people ask the William Carey Library.

What paper do I use?

Anyone who would like to prepare his thesis for possible publication as a book, should use for his ribbon copy a special kind of paper designed for photographic reproduction. To those who will be publishing under the William Carey Library, this paper is furnished free. (It is 8 1/4 X 12" but is acceptable by both J & T and the Copy Shoppe for making xerox [1:] copies at 4¢ each.) This paper is not essential; cheap, smooth Sub. 20 spirit-duplicator paper will do, but 100% rag and mimeo bond are almost hopelessly rough-surfaced for use as "camera-ready" copy.

What kind of typewriter do I use?

You need a good typewriter but not a special one to type for reproduction. (Dr. Tippett's book Peoples of Southwest Ethiopia was done on an ordinary portable). But you must watch the ribbon to make sure it is fairly new; silk is best because it gives a clean impression. There are some new space-age ribbons that are almost as good as a carbon ribbon.

398

If you can get a typist who owns an IBM Selectric, so much the better, because this will allow the "running heads" at the top of each page to be put into italics and, more important, will allow for proper italicization all the way through the text.

Warning: if you rent a Selectric, make sure it is a Selectric designed originally to be used with a carbon ribbon. A cloth-ribbon Selectric will hold a special carbon ribbon cartridge, but the ribbon moves faster and ends up costing twice as much for ribbons. Worse: it

reverses automatically before you realize it and a line or
two will be spotty.

You will probably want an elite type size, which is
"12 pitch" in IBM terminology (e.g. 12 letters per inch).

What format do I use?

Follow An Extension Seminary Primer as an example.
Be sure your chapter titles are on the odd-numbered pages,
etc. and that your numbers alternate right and left etc.
A 65¢ manual is available from the William Carey Library,
but you can simply follow the format of the book mentioned.
That is, count the letters per line and lines per page and
you'll come out O.K. Be very, very sure, for example,
that you use a "drop format" on the first page of each
chapter title. Begin with page one on the first page of
Chapter One (or Introduction).

The main idea, however, is to use a compact single
spaced format which is a long rectangle rather than the
nearly-square variety that eventuates usually in the use
of 8 1/2 X 11" double spacing. (Each line is 4 3/4" long;
total number of lines to a page [7 3/4" long] is 46).

It is best to type one or two pages and check with
Roberta Winter (of WCL) than to have to do many pages
over again later.

399

How do I know if my thesis will be publishable as a book?

Most theses done here at Fuller, being built on field
experience (unlike most theses) and being written by mature
people, deserve to be published. That is, they have a real
contribution to make, and are effective in presenting their
material.

Very, very few theses done here will likely be
publishable by a standard publisher (who deals mainly
through bookstores in America) since our subjects are
specialized and of special interest to a clientele that
does not crowd U. S. bookstores in droves.

However, so long as a thesis is well-written and valuable, it is often possible to build the special marketing machinery to enable enough copies to be sold to repay the production of the book.

How many copies must be sold in order for a book to be publishable?

If you expect the book to have a conventional price (e.g. 1 1/2 to 3¢ per page) it must (through William Carey Library at least) have a guaranteed sale of 700 copies, and 1,000 is much safer.

This means not only mission leaders and missionaries on the field must get it (this can be called the primary market) but also people back home must take many of the copies (this is the secondary market and is usually much larger, though less important than the primary market.)

It will be very helpful to get all the missionaries you know to agree to send home in their prayer letters a little brochure (you will supply them) which has a coupon to fill out and mail in with their money. Suppose 20 missionaries sent out 200 each - that is 4,000 copies going out.

One missionary may size up his potential market as follows:

400

100 copies - personal friends and relatives and special supporters.
100 copies - to one large supporting church.
150 copies - or 50 to each of three other supporting churches.
150 copies - or 30 to each of five other supporting churches.
300 copies - to some of 4,000 people who get a brochure along with a prayer letter from some 20 missionaries on the field and send their order in.
 50 copies - sold through Fuller bookstore to next 3 years of students.
150 copies - sold through Church Growth Book Club.
 50 copies - sold to miscellaneous requests to WCL.
1,000 Total

It goes without saying that this type of "custom marketing" cannot be devised by any publisher. Thus far the William Carey Library is the only publisher that will work with you in this way. Call this "cooperative publishing" or whatever, it is apparently essential for the author and/or his mission agency to shoulder the major responsibility for the marketing of the book.

How does the price of a book become established?

The more copies sold the lower the cost can be. But let's take the case of a 192 page book printed at 1,000 copies. Here are the costs (beyond a typed, camera-ready text):

```
$    35 - Cover design.
     35 - Interior artwork (title pages, chapter
          titles in display lettering, etc.).
     50 - Organization of manuscript for printer.
    814 - Printing cost.
     80 - Transportation to publisher.
 $1,014
```

If 50 are used for review copies, and another 100 are unsold, this means 850 are sold. Thus you divide the cost ($1,014) by 850 and get $1.20 as the production cost per book sold. Now this is put into the inevitable industry price structure as follows:

401

```
Production cost          1.20 = 30% of retail.
Author's royalty          .40 = 10% of retail.
Distribution overhead     .80 = 20% of retail.
Bookstore margin         1.60 = 40% of retail.
                        $4.00
```

That is, the retail price is what people pay in the theoretical bookstore. In the Church Growth Book Club this is eliminated, and the book is sold for $4.00 - 1.60 = $2.40. The entire machinery for warehousing, handling orders, shipping etc. is the next 20%, and the 10% is the amount paid to the author.

If enough copies are sure to be sold to be able to print 2,000 safely, the production cost would drop down to about 80¢ a copy, and this would leave a 40¢ margin with which to do some advertising or to pay for losses on another book or to pay an outside agency for its trouble in helping to market the extra 1,000 copies.

Does the author ever have to put up any money?

Assuming a book is in every other way acceptable, and if the marketing plans are shaky, or if the publisher has no available capital at the moment, this is necessary. Or it may be that the author or his agency would like to put up the capital and receive whatever profits there might be between the production cost and the 30% of retail (first line above). As the William Carey Library gets more and more books under its roof, it is more and more likely that outside financing will be necessary.

In many cases, mission agencies have put up 1/2 the funds and have been willing to receive their 1/2 back last. Then if the last 100 books are sold, this extra income (100 X $1.20) is divided equally between the two, or in whatever proportion the agency provides. It could be 100%.

How does this differ from the so-called Vanity Press?

402

The difference is that the Vanity Press will print any book the customer will pay for, whereas the William Carey Library will print only those books which William Carey Library would have been willing to print. Perhaps it is the difference between accepting a child just because the State will pay you to keep it and adopting a child whom you will be proud to bear your own name.

Course Title and Number   (50)   Ray Davis, 00518, 73a
Professor's Name   February 16, 1973

(drop 10 single spaces)

NEW DEVELOPMENTS IN THE
SCHOOL OF WORLD MISSION ARCHIVAL PROGRAM

Much of the research done by missionary associates
at the School of World Mission is of a very high standard
and will be very helpful to others. However, much of the
value of such papers is lost in that at present these are
not readily accessible for others to build upon. For
this reason, and with a view to establishing a more permanent archive of term papers, a standardized format in
all courses for typed term papers is now required, as
follows:

A. The first page.
  1. Shall include the following information
     (similar to the heading of this page):
     a. course title and number
     b. professor's name
     c. missionary associate's name, index
        number, year number (73a) + letter
     d. date
     e. paper title - centered, capitalized
  2. The body of the paper shall begin one third
     of the distance from the top to the bottom,
     but shall otherwise conform to the dimensions
     of subsequent pages.
B. All subsequent pages.
  1. Page numbers shall appear in the center of
     the top space, followed by name and number.
  2. Double-space from page number to first line.
  3. Page 3 illustrates dimensions and position
     of writing area.
C. Entire paper shall be single-spaced, indenting
   the first line of each paragraph 5 spaces, and
   double spacing between paragraphs.

403

D. There shall be <u>no</u> face sheet.
E. There shall be <u>no</u> extra binding or folder
included with the paper.
F. Pages should be stapled in upper left corner.

Many missionary associates are either not aware of
or are not making use of all the existing resources.
Some, by using only the standard sources of information,
i.e., library books, encyclopedias, magazines, ignore the
more valuable sources:

A. SWM theses and other thesis-length researches
B. Term papers written in other years, soon to be
available in the common room
C. Other published and unpublished articles.

Before commencing a paper the missionary associate
must ascertain what research has previously been done on
the topic or related topics. He can then make use of the
material by building upon it. Failure to take note of
this may result in duplication of subject matter, the
presentation of a paper of little value, and a significant
waste of time.

The following page gives the dimensions and position
of the writing area, and the page may be used as a backing
sheet to outline the margins for your typing of papers and
thesis or dissertation for publication.

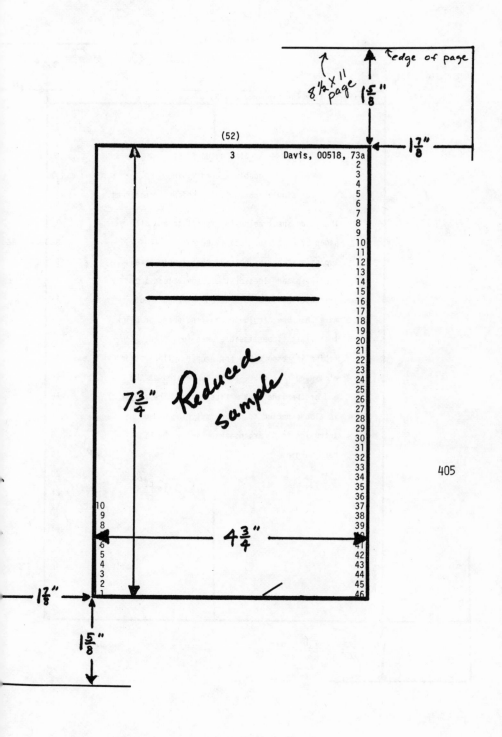

edge of page

8½ x 11 page

1⅝"

1⅞"

(52)

3   Davis, 00518, 73a

7¾"

Reduced Sample

4¾"

1⅞"

1⅝"

405

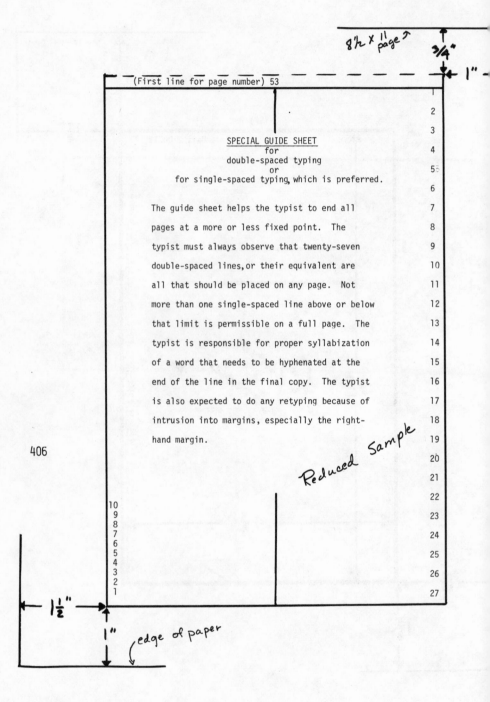

406

HOW TO USE JONING SHEETS AND BAR TAPE

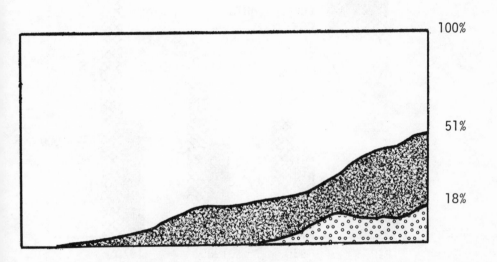

100%

51%

18%

HOW TO DO IT:

1. Place tone sheet over area to be covered.

2. Scratch slightly larger area and peel up from tone backing.

3. Place over area.

4. Scratch outline.

5. Peel up excess. Note: better not to cut tone backing because then it is hard to peel apart.

407

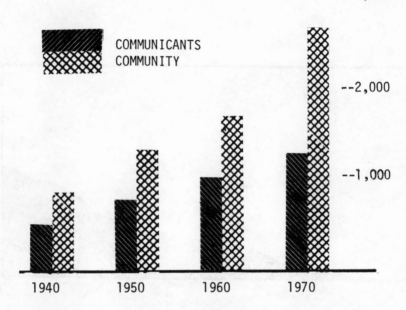

6. It is best not to letter by hand unless you are very good at it, or have no typewriter.

7. There is no need to plaster a graph with detailed raw data. The visual impact is as reliable as the psychological / logical impact of a lot of numbers. Numbers (raw data) ought to be in a table in the appendix to "back up" this particular chart. At that location you should indicate source(s) of raw data.

(1)   Cut slight excess.

(2)   Scratch on line with sharp edge and peel away excess.

(3)   Writing under toning doesn't work well.

(4)   (Double-bar system is easier and better than two pies.)

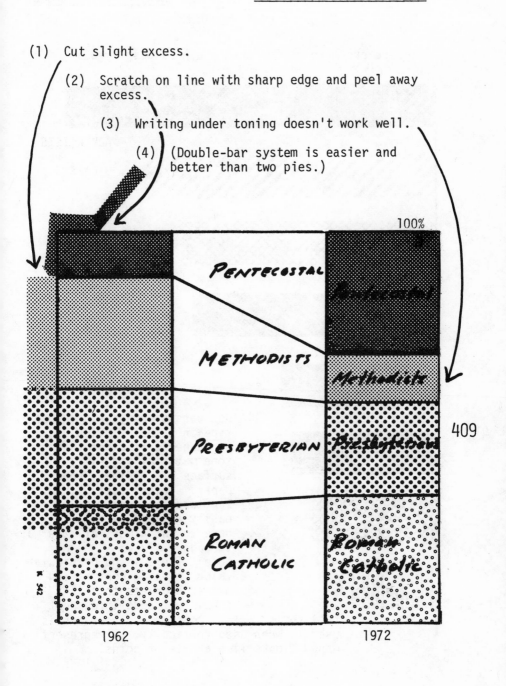

100%

PENTECOSTAL

METHODISTS

PRESBYTERIAN

ROMAN CATHOLIC

Methodists

Presbyterian

Roman Catholic

409

K 542

1962   1972

(There are more styles than are here displayed.)

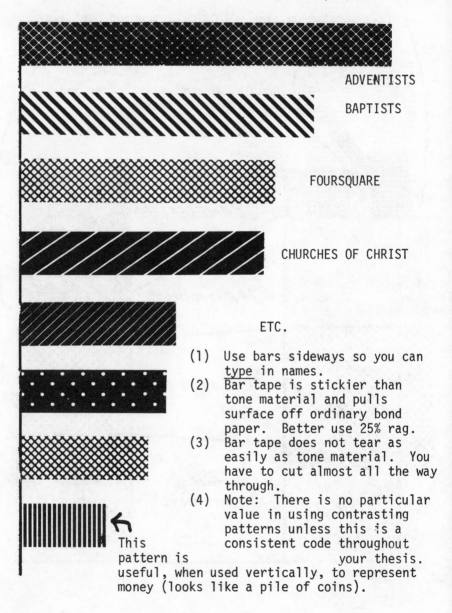

ADVENTISTS

BAPTISTS

FOURSQUARE

CHURCHES OF CHRIST

ETC.

410

(1) Use bars sideways so you can type in names.
(2) Bar tape is stickier than tone material and pulls surface off ordinary bond paper. Better use 25% rag.
(3) Bar tape does not tear as easily as tone material. You have to cut almost all the way through.
(4) Note: There is no particular value in using contrasting patterns unless this is a consistent code throughout your thesis.

This pattern is useful, when used vertically, to represent money (looks like a pile of coins).

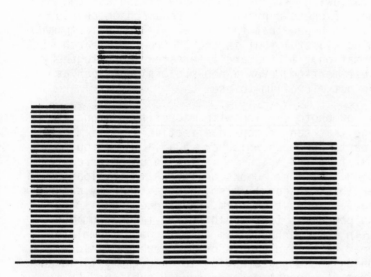

This pattern is useful, to represent money (looks like a pile of coins), or other facts in a vertical bar graph.

RULES FOR THE USE OF THE ART MATERIALS.

These are for the use, exclusively, of School of World Mission Research Associates and Faculty.

See rate sheet in green folder for costs. Do not leave cash; rather, mark down your name, date, and amount. You will be billed later.   411

Materials and tools are not to be taken from research room.

SUGGESTIONS

Additional tools and materials will be acquired as suggestions point the way. Give your ideas to the Research Associates Committee or to Professor Winter.

PHOTO-COPYING FOR CHURCH GROWTH RESEARCH by Roy E. Shearer

The following is a brief summary of the use and limitations of photo-copying in my research on church growth. It is hoped that the reader will be able to make microfilming a useful tool in church growth research with this information. If you are interested in photography and in experimenting, even a non-professional such as myself can put microfilm to use.

Uses for photo-copying with microfilm. Among the many things that can be copied effectively on film are books or parts of books which are available to you only for a short time and which will need to be referred to again and again later. Books on inter-library loan would come under this category. Also, I have taken my camera into libraries and put on film, reference books, rare books, and pamphlets that could not be taken from the library. In this manner I was able to get a complete, year-by-year narrative report on my overseas field -- by photographing those pages having to do with my field and subject from the annual mission survey published by my denomination. So from our Board headquarters in New York I was able to get onto one roll of film a picture of the mission work from its beginning, in this case 1885, until the present.

On that same trip to New York, I used photography in another way that proved invaluable. The files of the personal reports of missionaries on my field down through the years were opened to me. These files, had they been stacked up one on top of another, would have risen eight or ten feet high. Since I was in New York for only a few days and had to absorb a lot of information fast, I quickly glanced through these reports. Any time I caught a glimpse of something that looked valuable for my study of church growth, I placed the report under the camera and snapped the picture of that part or of the whole report. So at the time I did not have to stop, think through the ideas and facts presented in order to make notes, but could continue on my search and have recorded on film the next interesting fact before I could have digested the previous one. Later, I studied the films and had quotes from original sources in the environment in which they were written, not isolated notes. In ten days I was able to collect enough material on film to keep me busy for a month of analyzing in New York.

412

I believe the most important use of photo-copying is that of copying statistics. On my overseas field I found complete statistical records of the national Church for 40 years in the back of official minutes of the annual General Assembly. But there are only four or five copies of these minutes in existence so they could not be kept for any lengthy study. Also it would have been impossible for me to try to copy these over 20,000 entries or to select the right ones to copy, until I had become acquainted with the principles and precedures in the study of church growth. Even with proper selection I would be subject to scribal error, so I put the annual statistics of the Church on film and brought them home for continued study. Now I have available a full set of statistics that were exactly as printed in the church records, and as I study I can check statements of missionaries and nationals against the statistical record.

Limitations of photo-copying. Photo-copying on microfilm should not be thought a substitute for taking notes out of books and articles with the expectation of later organizing the film to write. When material is set down on film, it is even less accessible than in a book. The reel of film is put onto the microfilm reader and the film wound through the reader in order to go from one page to another. I found microfilm useful only for recording and preserving material such as statistics and literature which I had no time to study thoroughly when it was in my possession. I had to take notes later on all of my microfilm material in order to organize and present it in my research paper.

413

Equipment. There are now many new dry copying machines such as Xerox copying available in the United States, but at the cost of about ten cents a sheet their extensive use is prohibitive. But if this kind of equipment is available, some use of the dry copy will certainly facilitate organization of material for study. Material on film cannot be as easily organized as Xeroxed material.

Professional microfilm equipment under the hand of an experienced operator is the best and ultimately cheapest way to collect material on film. I found a university on the field which had an army surplus microfilmer and they

did excellent work for me on some of my material for about
three cents a frame. However, if this equipment is not
available, a good camera will serve you just as well but
will take a little more time in taking and splicing the
pictures. With the camera you are limited by a 36 exposure
roll, while a professional microfilmer can take a 100-foot
roll of film.

I used a Pentax single lens reflex 35mm camera with
the normal 55mm lens. A camera that has a separate view-
finder could be used but the problem of parallex must be
overcome since in microfilm-copying you are working at
close range. A piece of ground glass placed on the film
plane will give you a picture of the area that you will be
taking. A single lens reflex camera, however, eliminates
the problem of parallex and is superior to any other
camera for this work. As well as a 35mm camera, a 16mm
movie camera that will shoot one frame at a time with
through-the-lens viewing, can also be used.

A tripod or copy stand is needed for best results
because it is best to use a slow shutter speed. At this
close range any movement in your camera may cut off part
of the material you want to photograph. I used the tripod
with a pan head that could be raised and lowered. I
turned the head upside down so that the camera was placed
down between the legs. It still could be raised and lowered
on the track. I have had fair results for a few frames
hand-held when I was in a hurry. A cable release is
essential when the camera is used with the tripod. A yellow
filter with proper exposure compensation will give better
contrast when photographing old, yellowed documents.

While ordinary black and white film can be used, I buy
Kodak high-contrast copy 35mm film (M417) in 100-foot rolls
and hand-load it into cassettes. This is quite a bit
cheaper than buying it already loaded in cassettes. This
film is made for copying and will reproduce blacks and
whites with no shades of gray in between. This is what
you want for easy reading. Plux X film will work in a
pinch but not give you a vivid black on white or white on
black, only a picture of light gray on dark gray or vice
versa. I have collected all of my material using simply
the negative and not getting a positive copy made of the

414

film. I find reading a negative in a microfilm reader
just as hard on my eyes as reading a positive film.

If you use your own camera, you will want to have
some way to splice your film to put it on 100-foot rolls
for use on the reader. I found some milar splicing
material for 35 movie film in New York, but had to ask at
several photographic supply houses before I could find it.
The trademark is quik splice and the code number is T35-DP.
It is manufactured by Hudson Photographic Industries, Inc.,
Irvington-on-Hudson, New York.

You will need lights to illuminate the material. Two
light sources of any type with a wide reflector will do
the job. The light does not have to be strong but the two
lights should be equal in strength. Two desk lamps will
work.

Process. Now with your equipment ready you are prepared to begin shooting pictures. Place your camera with
the cable release attached onto the tripod (or copying
stand) and then focus on the material to be copied and
fill the frame with the page or pages to be copied. Then
place two lamps on either side of the camera, pointing
down to the material at a 45° angle. Any light shining
from directly above the camera will shine onto the paper
and give a reflection directly into the camera lens which
will burn out the image. This reflection can be seen
through a single lens reflex camera. Then, check the
illumination to see that the light intensity is equal on
all parts of the page. A check can be made by placing
a pencil in the center of the page and noting the shadows
it casts. A darker shadow on one side means that the
light on that side is weaker and should be moved closer
to the page to be copied.

415

A detachable exposure meter can be used to examine
each part of the page to make the correct exposure. Then,
take an exposure meter reading on a piece of dull, white
paper placed over top of the material to be copied. If
this is done, the exposure index for Kodak M417 film is
12. If, however, you use a gray, 18% reflective card to
read the exposure (as is sometimes recommended), then the
exposure index for this particular film will be 64. Set
the shutter speed at 1/2 of a second and then close down

the iris diaphragm accordingly. The reason for the low
shutter speed is so that the iris diaphragm may be closed
down as far as possible, giving a greater depth of field.
At the close range which you will be copying, the depth
of field is very slight and so the higher f stop will
give you more margin of error and also give better contrast on the film. I found that developing ONE ROLL or
a few frames gave me a good check on exposure. Inciden-
tally, I did my own developing, which is easy in a day-
light tank and easier on the budget. Any film developer
will work. Instructions come with the film.

You will want to hold the material flat so that the
plane of the paper is parallel to the plane of the film
to prevent distortion on a book that tends to curl; a
piece of glass can be placed on the book to hold it down
(reflection won't bother if the lights are at a 45°
angle). Most of the time I was in a hurry and instead of
using glass I used my thumb to hold down the corner of
the page on books that tended to round in the middle. By
now I have a highly photographed thumb.

Now with the camera properly set for exposure, the
lights turned on, and the film in place, you are almost
ready to take the first exposure. But take it from a
person who has had 20 rolls of film at one time out on
the table, trying to edit and splice this into one continuous roll, the next thing you would do is shoot the first
frame of this and every following roll of a big identifying
number. This numbers the film in order so that when it is
developed you can quickly splice No. 1 film to No. 2, etc.
Otherwise you will spend hours editing the film, putting
it on the reader to find out where you are, and then taking
it out again trying to splice it. Now, after you have shot
one frame with the identifying number on it, go ahead and
take pictures of the rest of your material.

I went further in microfilming the statistics and
instead of merely numbering each roll, numbered each frame
with a small number out at the edge of the page of statistics. This proved invaluable, as I had 5 x 7 prints made
on the field (which there were only ten cents apiece, while
in the U.S. would be 75¢ apiece). This numbering gave me
statistics in a useable form which I could shuffle and
compare fairly easily, even though I had to use a small

16

magnifying glass for some of the pages. If you can get prints made of the statistics you gather on microfilm, it will be much to your advantage. There may be other ways of getting cheap black and white pictures from microfilm negatives, but I don't know of them.

If you plan to read the 35mm film on a microfilm reader such as is used at the School of World Mission at Fuller Theological Seminary in Pasadena, then a frame that includes both pages of an ordinary opened book will appear on the reader, slightly larger than the original. Typewritten theses appear quite large if you fill the frame with just one page. In order to save film in one case, an assistant put two theses side by side and turned the pages as I was cocking the camera after each exposure. This was quite satisfactory. You will want to keep a record of the material you photograph, particularly if you are photographing only parts of books, in order to identify these parts later. Even better, if you have the time, write or type out the identification on a little piece of white paper and place it at the edge of the frame so that your identification will always be on that picture. Materials can be lost in a roll of film if it is not properly identified.

The gist of all this is: get a camera, bring home lots of facts for a good study of church growth.

417

THE USE OF THE SLIDE RULE   Ray Davis

A. Multiplication.   example (1): 2.50 x 3.50
   1. Set left index of C-scale opposite 2.50 on D-scale.
   2. Set hairline on 3.50 of C-scale.
   3. Read answer under hairline on D-scale: 8.75

                        example (2): 3.65 x 7.12
   1. Set right index of C-scale opposite 3.65 on D-scale.
   2. Set hairline on 7.12 of C-scale.
   3. Read answer under hairline on D-scale: 26.0

B. Division.   example (1): $\frac{5.60}{4.25}$
   1. Set the hairline on 5.60 of the D-scale.
   2. Move slide so that 4.25 on the C-scale is under
      hairline.
   3. Move hairline to C-scale index and read answer
      on D-scale: 1.318

                        example (2): $\frac{4.25}{5.60}$

   1. Set 5.60 of C-scale opposite 4.25 of D-scale.
   2. Read answer on D-scale opposite C-scale index:
      0.759 (or 0.760)

C. Practice problems

418
   1. Multiply: 2. Divide:
      a. (1.199) (9.65)   a. $\frac{7.75}{3.76}$ b. $\frac{44.3}{3.11}$
      b. (4.01) (3.66)
      c. (9.56) (6.23)
      d. (23.9) (5.44)   c. $\frac{12.95}{27.8}$ d. $\frac{38,941}{6,217}$
      e. (0.892) (7.27)
      f. (3.19) (0.235)
                           e. $\frac{560,000}{42,000}$ f. $\frac{112,500}{98,200}$
D. Answers
   1. a. 11.56   2. a. 2.06
      b. 14.69   b. 14.22
      c. 59.6   c. 0.466
      d. 130.0   d. 6.26
      e. 6.49   e. 13.32
      f. 0.750   f. 1.146

E. Computing Growth Rates.
    1. Determine the 2 points in time and subtract to
        obtain the difference in years (sorry, this
        operation is beneath the level of the slide rule).
    2. Determine the 2 figures of population and divide
        the larger one by the smaller.

        example: A church had 900 members in 1860
                    and 1250 members in 1868.
                  step 1: 1868 - 1860 = 8 years
                  step 2: $\frac{1250}{900}$ = 1.39

    3. Locate answer from step 2 on the LL-scale and
        set hairline there.
    4. Move slide until number of years (8) on the
        C-scale is under the hairline.
    5. Move hairline to index of C-scale and read answer
        on LL1-scale: 1.0420.
    6. Since we want a percentage, move the decimal
        point 2 places to the right and we get 104.2.
        Last year was 100 per cent, this year is 104.2
        per cent. Therefore subtract 100% and we have
        4.2% more members than the previous year. The
        average annual growth rate is 4.2%.

Important note: How do you know which LL-scale to
read?
    1. If you are reading opposite the left index:
        a. if the number of years is between 1 and 10,
            then read the answer on the same scale.   419
        b. if the number of years is between 10 and
            100 years, then drop to the next scale down
            to read the answer.
    2. If you are reading opposite the right index:
        a. if the number of years is between 1 and 10,
            then drop to the next scale down to read
            the answer.
        b. if the number of years is between 10 and
            100, then drop 2 scales down to read your
            answer.

F. Practice Problems

1. The Methodist church in Ghana had 6217 communicants
   in 1907 and 38,941 communicants in 1925. Compute
   the annual growth rate.
2. The same church had 58,725 in 1955. What was the
   annual growth rate in the 30 year period?
3. By 1961 the C&MA had baptized 1222 and 1967, 6000
   had been baptized. Compute the annual growth rate.
4. There were 2 believers in the Bahama Pentecostal
   church in 1910. By 1970 there were 14,000. What
   is the average annual growth rate for that period?
5. In 1920 the same church had 900 believers. Compute
   the annual growth rates for the two periods
   (a) 1910 to 1920, and (b) 1920 to 1970.

G. Answers

1. 10.75% per year
2. 1.38% per year
3. 30.4% per year
4. 15.95% per year
5. (a) 84.2% per year
   (b) 5.64% per year.

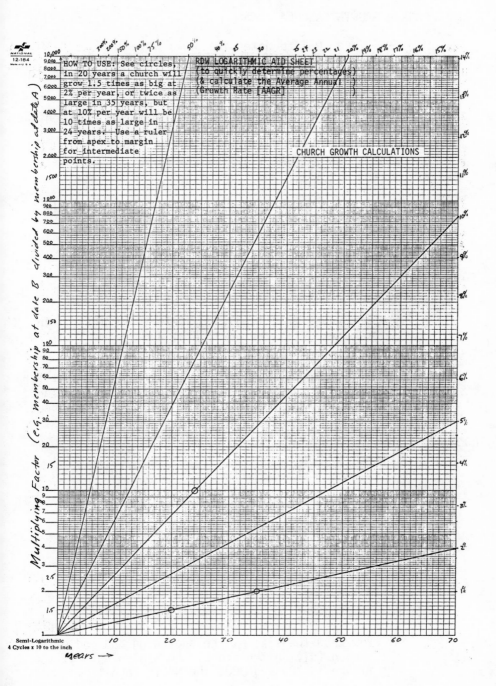

RDW LOGARITHMIC AID SHEET
(to quickly determine percentages)
(& calculate the Average Annual)
(Growth Rate [AAGR])

HOW TO USE: See circles, in 20 years a church will grow 1.5 times as big at 2% per year, or twice as large in 35 years, but at 10% per year will be 10 times as large in 24 years. Use a ruler from apex to margin for intermediate points.

CHURCH GROWTH CALCULATIONS

Multiplying Factor (e.g. membership at date B divided by membership at date A)

years →

Semi-Logarithmic
4 Cycles x 10 to the inch

CHURCH GROWTH CALCULATIONS

How to determine percentages

If a church had 11,500 communicants in 1938 and 24,600 in 1961, is this good growth or not?

Use RDW's LOGARITHMIC AID SHEET to determine percentage of annual growth by taking the following steps:

1. Divide the latter figure by the former, (24,600 -÷- 11,500 = 2.14).

2. Look up the left hand scale of RDW LOGARITHMIC AID SHEET to 2.14 (the multiplying factor).

3. Subtract 1938 from 1961 = 29 years.

4. Find this figure (29) on the scale across the bottom (marked years).

5. Run across on 2.14 line (from left to right) and up on 29 years until the horizontal and the vertical lines converge on a point (and make a dot).

6. Lay a sheet of paper (like a ruler) from the apex (the lower left-hand corner of the page) to the dot; the right-hand edge of the sheet or ruler falls at about 2.7%. This represents the annual growth rate of the above church, which is not very spectacular.

Problems everyone must know how to solve

I. How to find percentage increase per year

   A. If there are 15 new members starting with a congregation of 100, 50, 20%

   B. Note that you cannot do this if you have more than one year.

II. How to find the "multiplying factor"

   A. You know the size at the beginning and end of a period (divide the end by the beginning) If the figure is 200 and 300, the MF is then 1.5.

B. What if a church of 300 members becomes 2.5 times
    as big, how many members will it then have? Same
    for a whole denomination of 30,000?

C. If a church of 200 members grows to 700 members,
    how many times bigger (e.g. MF) will it then be?

D. Suppose a denomination of 200,000 grows to
    700,000, how many times bigger (e.g. MF) will
    it then be?

III. Given two of three: a) growth rate (in % increase per yr.)
                         b) multiplying factor
                         c) number of years of growth

A. a + c, seek b:

   1. If a church adds 2 new members for each 100
       (e.g. 2%) each year, how much bigger will it
       be in 35 years?

   2. In 5 years how many times bigger will a church
       be that each year adds 20 new members per
       hundred members?

   3. Same, but only 10 per hundred?

   4. In 5 years, what will happen if every 20
       members bring in one new contact per year?   423

B. a + b, seek c:

   1. If a church grows at 5% per year (e.g. adds
       5 per 100) how long will it take to double?

   2. If it grows at 10% how soon will it triple?

   3. If a church adds 20 new members each year per
       100 members, how long will it take to be 10
       times as large? In this case how many
       believers are necessary to reach each new
       convert, on the average?

   4. How long will it take for a church to double
       in size if it grows at 2%, 5%, 10%, 20%, 50%
       per year?

5. How long will it take for a church to triple
    if every 20 members win one per year?

C. a + c, seek a:

1. If a church grows from 150 members to 650
    in 14 years, what is the percentage growth
    rate average per year?

2. If a denomination in 1900 was 300,000 and
    is now 2.5 million, what was the average
    annual percentage growth rate? Is this at
    all like a biological average?

3. What if a church doubles in 2 years? What is
    the annual growth rate?

4. Pick out three examples of this type of a
    problem from real statistics available to
    you, and ascertain the growth rate. Assume
    that new members will help to win new members
    rather than assuming that old members will
    become increasingly more effective.

Thus far we have covered the important matter of
calculating the Average Annual Growth Rate (AAGR) where
you begin by knowing only the length of time and the
beginning and the ending size of a group of people. By
using the RDW LOGARITHMIC AID SHEET, you can quickly
determine percentages or the AAGR.

What we have not done is to show why this is all
necessary, why you cannot approach the problem by a more
simple method, which for our purposes here we may call the
BOOBY TRAP METHOD.

Suppose a church grows by 300 members during a three
year period. It is easy and obvious to say that they gained
a hundred new members per year, on the average. And this
is a true statement. But of course it does not tell us
anything about how many believers were necessary to win
this many new people, and unless we know this we lack an
important piece of information.

424

Thus, let us further suppose that the church which
gained 300 members in 3 years was a church that started
the period with 1,000 members and ended it with 1,300.
Now what? That is, now what can we say about the situation
if we want to talk about the <u>rate of growth</u>. Here is where
the booby trap comes in. The temptation is to divide the
300 increase by 3 and say that the church grew by 10% per
year. The trouble with this method is that you cannot
verify it by a straightforward method. For example, if
you add 10% each year, here is what you get:

$$
\begin{array}{ll}
1,000 & \\
\underline{100} & (+10\%) \\
1,100 & \text{at the end of the 1st year} \\
\underline{110} & (10\%\text{ more}) \\
1,210 & \text{at the end of the 2nd year} \\
\underline{121} & (10\%\text{ more}) \\
1,331 & \text{at the end of the 3rd year}
\end{array}
$$

In other words the church did not quite grow at the rate of
10% per year (it was really closer to 9%).

When you are working with decades the booby trap is even
more serious. Suppose a church grew from 1,000 to 3,000
in two decades. Again it would be a temptation to say
that it added an average of 1,000 each decade. This is, so
far, true to say, but it is not true to life, since it could
easily have grown faster, not in rate, but in raw increase,
during the second decade because it had by that time a much 425
larger base. It all depends upon what we want to know. If
we want to know the percentage increase per decade which will
render 3,000 starting from 1,000 then it surely is not going
to be 100% per decade, which is what you would get if you
divided the increase by 2 and expressed the result as a percentage of the beginning membership. Let's try 100% percent
to see if it works:

$$
\begin{array}{ll}
1,000 & \\
\underline{1,000} & (100\%\text{ added}) \\
2,000 & \text{at the end of the 1st decade} \\
\underline{2,000} & (100\%\text{ added}) \\
4,000 & \text{end of the second decade}
\end{array}
$$

In other words the church did not grow 100% per year--it really only grew 73% per decade. It would indeed be possible to say that the church did grow 100% of its beginning membership each decade, referring not to the membership at the beginning of each decade, but to the membership at the beginning of the first decade. This would seem to be an unusual figure to deal with and therefore is not often used in this manner.

The way to calculate decadal growth using the RDW LOGARITHMIC AID SHEET is to figure out the AAGR for the whole period, and on that same slant line read the multiplying factor at the ten-year mark. This will be 1.73, which means that in 10 years the increase is 73%.

- - - - - -

From: C. Peter Wagner
Subject: Church Growth Calculations

1. The other day, Ralph Winter "casually" asked me to answer an apparently simple church growth problem: If a missionary goes to a village with a population of 1,000 and leaves two years later having planted a church of 200 members, how much of the population is Christian?

I quickly said 20%. Wrong!

426

2. Just yesterday, I was composing this news item for Today's Christian:

> According to Australian Baptist Missionary Noel Melzer, 98% of the Dani tribespeople in Irian Jaya are "definitely interested in the Christian faith." Already of the estimated 34,000 Danis, 13,000 have been baptized.

What part of the tribe is Christian? Anyone who has not talked recently with Winter would be likely to say 38.2%.

WRONG!

Here's the problem: When you count Danis or village populations, you count all the people, including babies and children. But when you count church members, you count only adults, perhaps 15 years of age and over.

It is clearly not accurate to compare adult Christians to entire populations.

The solution probably is not to use "community" since this category has its own built-in set of problems.

It seems to me that the best way to figure the percentage of Christians is to compare communicant members to the population 15 years of age or over. But how do we get such figures? Providentially, the Population Reference Bureau charts (which I distributed to all of you a month ago)* has this piece of data for each country. Even though it might differ from homogeneous unit to homogeneous unit, I suggest we start using the national figure as a rule of thumb.

In other words, in Indonesia 44% of the population is under 15 years of age. That means that roughly we are dealing with 25,000 Danis, not 34,000; and instead of 38.2% Christian, we have 52%.

If the hypothetical village were in Burundi, where 47% of the population is under 15, planting a church of 200 members in a village of 1000 would mean that not 20% but 38% were won. You would need only 265 members to have won half the population.

427

Worldwide this means that instead of comparing adult Christians to 3,860,000,000 people (PRB) we do better to compare them to the adults (63%) or 2,431,800,000.

This blows your mind! It has all kinds of implications, but the simplest and most obvious one is that the job is further along than we might have thought, and it may also mean that Christ's coming is all the nearer. Thanks to Winter (who may or may not agree with those eschatological conclusions) we can turn up the volume on our Maranathas a few more decibels . . . And our theses will be more accurate in the meantime.

---

*Obtainable from: Population Reference Bureau, Inc. 1755 Massachusetts Ave., N.W., Washington, D. C. 20036.

NOTES ON CHURCH GROWTH TERMINOLOGY

"Numerical": Let us not use the phrase numerical growth. It belongs to the kindergarten, to an elementary, defective understanding of what growth is. All growth is increase or decrease in something, and is always referred to in quantitative terms, either literal or metaphorically. Almost any kind of growth of anything can be expressed in measurable quantities. Take Tippett's example of measuring piety in Solomon Island congregations (Tippett, 1967: 308-318). Since quantities are expressed numerically, the expression "numerical growth" is a tautology.

Furthermore, despite all the other kinds of growth (which are numerical), what people usually mean by the unwanted phrase, numerical growth, is simply membership growth, either communicant or community, and if so, why not say so?

428

There are three kinds of growth to which, classically, Tippett has referred: growth in size of a church, in its spiritual quality, and in its organizational structure. All three can be measured, and thus expressed numerically. Size can be measured by a hundred different direct and indirect measures of different kinds (e.g. average attendance at a certain kind of service, at an annual meeting of some kind, in terms of number of congregations, pastors, hymn books purchased per year, seating space in all church buildings, etc.). But none of these measurements made merely at any one point in time will tell you anything whatsoever about growth in size. To do that you have to have the same measurement at two different points, and so we ultimately must deal with 1) size at one point, and 2) amount of growth (in absolute or percentage figures between two points, e.g. change in size), and 3) this change compared to the amount of time, which introduces the concept of the rate of change, or rate of growth.

If you look closely at the size of membership, and the
second item above, namely, amount of membership growth
(that is, change of size), you must remember that there are
three kinds of change that add to membership, and three
that subtract:

    1. Positive Components of Membership Growth
       1. born in   ("biological growth")
       2. converted in ("conversion" growth)
       3. transferred in ("transfer" growth)

   11. Negative Components of Membership Growth
       1. Die out   (negative biological growth)
       2. Revert out   (negative conversion growth)
       3. Transfer out   (negative transfer growth)

  (Note 1.1. - 11.1 = "net biological";
       1.2. - 11.2 = net conversion; and
       1.3. - 11.3 = net transfer)

Since any one of these factors can jostle the membership
totals very extensively, it is folly to put too much weight
on any one or two without the others; it is even more incorrect
(and yet common) to suppose that the overall net growth
(e.g. the algebraic sum of all six factors--which is all
most churches record) is clearly the result of any one factor,
say conversion.

For example, often we read that a certain church has grown 429
from, say, 1800 to 14,000 in 65 years. Biological factors
alone would account for most of this, and since they are the
kind we can guess at, we can subtract this "expected" amount
of net biological growth from the overall net growth. What
we have left has got to be the sum of net conversion and net
transfer, and often is no longer so impressive, especially
if it is well known that many members of this church grew
up in other churches.

  (Note: Overall net is 3.1 per year average; if biological
    were 3%?)

There is still another kind of componential awareness.
The overall growth of a church (denomination) may be the
result (and usually is) of uneven growth between regions,
areas, congregations. The poor growth of one area is often
lumped together with good growth elsewhere and thus disguised.
This is the danger of "area lumping." But even the expansion

of a single congregation can be the result of an internal
lumping: perhaps the good overall growth of the congregation
has derived mainly from the growth of the young couples belt
on the Christmas tree chart, or perhaps older people moving
into a nearby retirement center, etc., etc. Thus poor growth
or high loss in another belt may be obscured.

In order to differentiate between the growth of a single
congregation, the growth of the number of congregations, and
the special kind of growth that takes place when Christians
of one culture help to establish a new congregation in another
culture, we may speak of expansion growth, (how the membership
of a congregation gets larger), multiplying growth or
extension growth (how fast new congregations are being
planted), and bridging growth, where congregations in new
cultures (near and far) are established.

As the membership of a congregation gets larger, especially
if its attendance also gets larger (not to be assumed!), it
is desirable for its internal structure to become more
elaborate. Large groups do not minister to people in the
same way smaller groups do, etc. How to do this is the most
crucial unsolved mystery in the U.S. today. It is a problem
of proper structural, organizational growth (or, to use
Tippett's phrase, organic growth).

The same is true as related congregations multiply:
their relationship cannot remain the same, and most church
movements in one way or another elaborate their structure
to deal with this. This is another kind of organic or
structural growth. There are fascinating unsolved problems
in this realm also.

Still another kind of structural phenomenon is the
development of sodalities within a congregation (e.g.
women's meetings, young people, etc.) or church movement
(e.g., mission societies, Campus Crusade, etc.). This too
is organic growth and is little understood.

In some ways the least tangible aspect of growth is the
spiritual aspect. It seems to me that we ought not use
quality as the designation for this, because all growth
of any kind involves various qualities. The size of membership, for example, is a quality. Furthermore, all measurements of any quality are inevitably qualitative measurements,

430

and thus we see the parallel undesirability of labelling any one kind of growth "quantitative."

As I have written in a recent paper, all growth of any kind has both quantitative and qualitative aspects. Thus no one kind or type of growth should be called quantitative growth or qualitative growth. All growth is both quantitative and qualitative.

Calculations:

Suppose you have a congregation of 100 communicants. A year later it has grown to 115 communicants. You can say it has grown an additional 15 persons to arrive at a total of 115 persons. You can also note that it has grown an additional 15% to become 115% of what it was. This latter percentage is the same as a multiplying factor of 1.15. That is, if you multiply 1.15 by 100 you get 115. You get the multiplying factor by dividing the total at the end of the period by the total at the beginning of the period (e.g. 115/100 = 1.15). It is called the multiplying factor because if you multiply the starting total by this number you get the ending number (e.g. 100 x 1.15 = 115).

Other terms are as follows: The absolute increment in this case is 15 persons, while the percentage increment is 15 per cent. The cumulative absolute growth is 115 persons, while the cumulative percentage growth is 115%. Since the time unit involved here is the passage of one year--and this 431 is a common unit of measurement of rate of growth--we can say that when one year is involved the percentage increment is the same as the growth rate per year. That is, the church grew literally "15% per year."

Now suppose another congregation twice as large at the beginning (i.e. 200) ends up with 215 at the end of a year. What is the absolute increment? The percentage increment? The cumulative absolute growth? The cumulative percentage growth? And the growth rate per year?

Now suppose these two churches continue to grow with the same absolute increment per year, what will their cumulative absolute growth be after five years? You can figure this as follows:

	Congregation A	Congregation B
Increment 1st year	15	15
" 2nd year	15	15
" 3rd year	15	15
" 4th year	15	15
" 5th year	15	15
	75	75
Base	100	200
End	175	275

Using our terminology above we can say the following:

	A	B
Absolute increment	75	75
Cumulative absolute growth	175	275
Percentage increment	75%	37-1/2%
Cum. percentage growth	175%	137-1/2%
Multiplying factor	1.75	1.375

Let's not bother at this point to explain how these
numbers were calculated. Just note that the same
absolute increment for the larger congregation does not
produce the same percentage increment. Also, for our
purposes, note that we might expect a larger congregation
to have a larger absolute increment since it has more
people potentially witnessing--assuming that the surrounding
society has additional winnable people in it. HOWEVER,
if this is often true (that a larger congregation may be
432   expected to win more people) then this leads us to observe
that the kind of growth which we have calculated above is
somewhat strange and unusual. That is, in both cases
as the congregations get bigger they do not seem to have
grown with a larger absolute increment. In other words,
it is more likely, if you have to guess, that the
percentage increment would be the same as the absolute
increment.

Ralph D. Winter, November 13, 1972

HOW TO DO A SURVEY
OF CHURCH GROWTH

Donald A. McGavran

Dean Emeritus

School of World Mission

and

Institute of Church Growth

How To Do A Survey Of Church Growth

Leaders of world mission in increasing numbers are realizing that the growth of the Churches, older as well as younger, must be taken with renewed seriousness. It is not sufficient to do excellent mission work in the hope that it will, somehow and sometime, lead to the multiplication of churches. The sheer physical expansion of soundly Christian churches is a central and continuing part of mission. There is a rising interest in it. We must push on through promotional commendations, encouraging generalities and the scaffolding of mission work to *the churches actually being planted and see them clearly.*

People often ask us how to discover and describe church growth. This pamphlet is written in answer. Obviously no one way will fit all Churches.* Describing the growth of the Church of 1,100 members in a pagan population of 500,000 is a different task than describing one of 150,000 in a population of 280,000. Each Church grows out of its own environment. Those studying church growth will, therefore, expect to fit the procedures outlined herein to their own circumstances.

We recommend that any missionary or graduate national coming as a student to the Fuller Seminary School of World Mission investigate membership increase in his own and other denominations. It will make his work here more fruitful and meaningful. It will set before him (and us, when he arrives) his real problems — the real problems confronting his Church. Until Christian Mission discerns the tasks of highest priority, it cannot make the most effective disposition of its resources. "Where to press for church growth and where to hold the line," a most important question in mission, can only be answered after carefully investigating the degree and kind of growth God is granting His churches.

433

How to do this careful investigation is described in four steps following.

FIRST STEP: DEFINING THE STUDY

1. *State carefully the purpose and scope of your study.* For example:
   To study the membership increase of the
   Churches in Land X, or
   To study the relationship between ways
   of training the pastorate and the growth
   of the Church.

2. *Determine the area and Churches to be covered by your study.* It will give you more light to study several denominations working in one general kind of population than to confine yourself to your own. While you may study your own denomination more thoroughly than you do others, comparisons with others are invaluable for understanding.

3. *Determine the kind of population or populations involved.* Are you going to study church growth among:
   Indians or Mestizos?
   rural tribes or city masses?
   the intelligentsia or the illiterate?
   one caste or tribe or many?
   lowlanders or highlanders?
   Kikongo or Lonkundo speakers?

4. *Set down the Churches and populations to be studied.* For example:
   The Church of the Brethren working on
   Western Kenya among the Masai.
   The Presbyterian Church working in all
   Korea among high school and college students.

SECOND STEP: FINDING THE MEMBERSHIP FACTS

1. *Determine the* **field totals** *for each denomination at three or five year intervals from the beginning of the Church till the present.* This is not easy. But by writing to your friends, consulting mission histories and reading old reports, you can dig up the facts. Secure as much information as you can. Sometimes there will be gaps of several years. You may get the full picture only for your own Church or mission, while information for the others will be sketchy — when they began, what their membership is now and a few points in between.

Secure as much information as you can. Sometimes there will be gaps of several years. You may get the full picture only for your own Church or mission, while information for the others will be sketchy — when they began, what their membership is now and a few points in between.

2. *Determine* **membership totals for each homogeneous unit** *in the denomination.* A homogeneous unit is simply a section of society in which all the members have some characteristic in common. If the Methodists in Bolivia number 2,000, discover how many of the 2,000 are Aymara Indians, how many Quechua Indians and how many Mestizos. If the Congregationalists in Polynesia number 67,000, how many live in the Society Islands, the Cook Islands and the Austral Islands? If the Lutherans in Taiwan number 5,000, how many speak Mandarin and how many Amoy?

3. *Determine* **individual church totals** *over as many years as possible.* Nothing grows but local churches. Which congregations are growing, standing still or diminishing? If local church memberships are obtainable, you will find these figures most revealing.

4. *Church and Mission year books for each denomination give membership by "fields" or countries.*

These field totals are compiled from annual reports from parish, diocese or station. Church headquarters, central mission offices or board headquarters usually file these reports. From them you can easily compile membership totals for each homogeneous unit of the Church being studied. (See *How Churches Grow*, pages 35 ff.)

Individual congregation memberships are more difficult to find. Search individual church and mission station records or prior studies of Church or mission.

Mission secretaries, bishops and headquarters' staff are usually helpful in digging out such facts.

5. *Draw a graph for each "homogeneous unit Church."* You may have several graphs for your own denomination and several for others.

You will then have true pictures of what church growth has taken place. Keep refining these. Redraw graphs whenever you have information which leads to major corrections. You are then ready for a most important section of the study.

435

THIRD STEP: ASCERTAINING CAUSES OF GROWTH AND NON-GROWTH

1. *Referring constantly to the graphs, begin asking what caused sudden rises, long plateaus, gradual declines, little mission work and much growth, much mission work and little church growth.* What happened in 1926, for example, which arrested great growth?

Look for *causes* — striking conversions, beliefs and traditions of the tribe, oppression, wars, the work of certain men, or their death or retirement. Consider what policies the Church or mission has followed in times of membership increase or decrease. Did what was "adopted in hope" deliver church growth?

Until you complete the graphs you cannot tell what bearing a given church or mission action had on church growth. You will read an enthusiastic defense of the action, how necessary and wise it was — but you will know whether it *in fact* led to a growth or a decline of the church!

Learn to be ruthless with alleged reasons. You are searching for the *truth*. Much writing and thinking in missions is really a defense of "whatever is." It shies away from admitting defeat. It champions "little growth" as really the best thing that could have happened. Shun such thinking.

Compare your membership increase with that enjoyed by other Churches. A mission in Zaire planted a Church which by 1958 numbered 20,000 — the biggest Church in that board's seven younger Churches. The Zaire mission was quite pleased with itself until it compared its Church with others in Zaire. Then it saw its Church was experiencing growth incommensurate with conditions.

2. *Where do you find what caused church growth or stagnation?* Consult the sources named below, but remember that most answers will be mistaken or partial. Some will be based on misinformation and prejudice — "the accumulated debris of defeat and resignation." Some will be genuine insights. Some will lead you to insight, though themselves faulty. You may be the first to do a serious study of your Church from the point of view of its growth. An exciting exploration in uncharted territory lies before you.

SOURCES OF INFORMATION FOR DOING A CHURCH GROWTH STUDY

A. *The leaders who were there (nationals and missionaries).* Place your graphs before them and ask particular questions. If the graph below were your graph of growth, ask some of those involved the following kinds of questions:

What caused the surge of growth in 1965 after a year of sharp decline?

What stopped growth here in 1968 after those promising years?

What were we doing during this long period when our neighbor Church was growing in New Testament fashion?

Expect to dig. Not every interview will yield information. Missionaries and churchmen, for example, who during their active lives were not interested in the growth of the Church will in retirement remember little about it. Yet their testimony has a negative value — it helps explain why there was little growth or why there was only 100% a decade growth when there might have been 500%. 100% per decade means doubling every decade; 500% per decade means that there are five times as many people as at the beginning of the ten-year period.

Beware of facile explanations. (i) "This was a very difficult field. The Church simply could not grow there." If no denomination in their country was growing, that explanation may be accurate; but frequently it is tendered when next door Presbyterians, Adventists or Roman Catholics are seeing increase. (ii) Or someone says, "After each surge of growth there must be a time for consolidation. This is a natural rhythm of the Gospel." Is it? Or is "consolidation" in this case an excuse for little growth? (iii) "My friend, you have no idea of the Roman Catholic pressure here." Is the real trouble lack of Protestant pressure — or a ministry so highly trained (and paid) that new churches cannot start?

Consult men in *their* language. Talk about church growth to older members, recent converts, national ministers, missionaries now in the field and retired persons. Make the growth of the Church a frequent topic of conversation.

437

B. *Mission histories, church records, baptismal registers, magazine articles and old reports* In these is much chaff and little information about the physical increase of the churches. But if you will patiently winnow the chaff, you will find the wheat. Learn to skim "inspirational" or promotional articles, written to commend mission to supporters, for the sentence or phrase which tells something as to the size, shape or nature of the Church at a given time.

Look for information about "homogeneous units." Figures of church growth for "all Brazil" are not nearly as revealing as those for "the rural communities in the Rio Doce Valley" or those "in the city of Rio de Janeiro." Totals for "our Church in India" will tell you far less than those pertaining to a sudden surge of growth "in the Dacca District."

C. *Government statistics, censuses, anthropological studies, sociological expositions, handbooks for social workers, surveys of the Church, its medical or educational institutions, its giving, the education of its pastors and other material.* Here again you will have to pan a lot of gravel to get an ounce of gold. Do not get wrapped up in panning gravel! A book on theological education may be interested chiefly in lifting the standard of theological education and care little or nothing for the discipling of the nations. It may be concerned entirely with perfecting rather than discipling. Even so, it may throw both positive and negative light on church growth.

Similarly, anthropological treatises should be perused, not for intellectual interest, but to discover how the Church has grown or has not — and how it can grow in accordance with God's will.

3. *Read all you can find on how churches multiply.* The following books set forth theories of church growth which will illumine your situation and stimulate your insights. Read these books several times. In the beginning they help you see what has happened in your churches. During your study they raise fruitful questions. After your study they yield far more understanding than was possible at first. All are available from:

The Church Growth Book Club
305 Pasadena Avenue
South Pasadena, Calif. 91030
U.S.A.

438

	Retail Price	Book Club
AFRICA		
Wold—God's Impatience in Liberia	$2.95	$1.77
Kwast—Discipling of West Cameroun	3.45	2.07
Shewmaker—Tonga Christianity	3.45	2.07
ASIA		
Liao—The Unresponsive: Resistant or Neglected	2.95	1.77
Shearer—Church Growth in Korea	2.95	1.77
Tippett—Solomon Islands Christianity	4.95	2.97
Tuggy—Seeing the Philippine Church	2.50	1.50
LATIN AMERICA		
Read, Monterroso and Johnson—Latin American Church Growth	8.95	5.37
Greenway—An Urban Strategy for Latin America	4.95	2.97
Nordyke—Animistic Aymaras	3.45	2.07
Wagner—Protestant Movement in Bolivia	3.95	2.37
Read—New Patterns of Church Growth in Brazil	2.45	1.47
GENERAL		
McGavran—Understanding Church Growth	7.95	4.77
Braun—Laity Mobilized	3.95	2.37
Wagner—Look Out! The Pentecostals Are Coming	4.95	2.97
Tippett—Verdict Theology in Mission Theory, 2 ed.	2.95	1.77
Winter—Twenty-five Unbelievable Years	1.95	1.17
McGavran—How Churches Grow	2.50	1.50
McGavran—Church Growth and Christian Mission	5.00	3.00
Gerber—Manuel for Evangelism/Church Growth	1.45	.87
Winter—Theological Education by Extension	4.95	2.97
McQuilken—How Biblical Is Church Growth	1.95	1.17

We shall be glad to hear from any who are doing a serious study of the increase of the Church. When you complete the first and second steps let us know the facts revealed. We shall then be able to advise on procedure.

FOURTH STEP: WRITING AND PUBLISHING THE CASE STUDY

1. *The purpose of your study is to give a true account of the physical expansion of a section of the Church.* Your account will likely have the following main divisions.

The Background. Include brief descriptions of populations, social structure, beliefs, culture, custom and history concerned. Incorporate only as much as is necessary to understand the church growth or lack of growth.

The Actual Growth of the Churches. Show tables and graphs of what growth or non-growth has occurred. The value of your study begins in the accuracy and comprehensiveness of this section.

Reasons for Growth or Non-Growth. This section furnished great opportunity for variety of handling. Chronological treatment, taking up typical sections and telling how and why churches multiplied (or did not) is a common and effective procedure. Selecting a few crucial aspects of church growth and discussing these in depth is another beneficial method. Thomas, for example, took those seven years in Japan when the Congregational Church multiplied ten-fold and examined these minutely, dissecting the factors which contributed to the growth of the churches. Other ways to discuss reasons for growth will occur to you.

Actions Essential to Sound and Rapid Growth in the Future. This section is the ultimate justification for the study, that Christ's liberating reign may come in the population with which you are concerned. You recount what has happened in the past in order that you may judge what should happen in the future. Think carefully and courageously. Renounce promotional thinking (defense of what has been done). If the Church has grown 100% a decade, promotional thinking says, "How wonderful." Diagnostic thinking says, "With a ripe population, we should not limit ourselves to a mere 100%. How can we lift our expectation to God's level as we press forward with His command to disciple the nations?"

440

Many Churches and Missions in the past have grown accustomed to coming empty-handed out of ripe fields, or to coming out rather pleased with a few sheaves. In the many responsive sections of mankind—both in Eurica and in Africasia—a new level of expectation is often possible. A few denominations hold such expectations and many more should. The "actions" you will describe are *not* those required to carry on good missions, but those demanded *to carry out the Great Commission.*

2. *Polish your final draft.* Since publication costs are high, *eliminate every spare word, every side issue, every unnecessary story.* Scan every sentence to see if it cannot be stated in simpler, clearer fashion. Ask an experienced writer to condense your manuscript. Pruning may hurt, but the study will

benefit. Busy men and women will be reading your research. Give them the gist of the matter in as few words as possible.

3. *Publication.* A study worth making is worth publishing. At least a few hundred copies should be printed. On the flyleaf should be stated the address from which copies can be ordered, as well as the price. In many cases, the William Carey Library can offer publication facilities not available elsewhere.

4. *Distribution.* Deposit one copy with each of the following:

School of World Mission & Institute of Church Growth
Fuller Theological Seminary
135 N. Oakland Ave., Pasadena, Calif. 91101

The Missionary Research Library
3041 Broadway, New York, N.Y. 10027

The Commission of World Mission and Evangelism
World Council of Churches
475 Riverside Dr., New York, N.Y. 10027

The Secretary, Research Dept. CWME
150 Route de Ferney
1211 Geneva 20, Switzerland

The Evangelical Foreign Missions Assn.
1405 G St., N.W., Washington, D.C. 20005

Interdenominational Foreign Mission Association
54 Bergen Avenue, Ridgefield Park, N.J. 07660

441

Similar associations in Germany, Sweden, Britain, India, Africa, Japan, the Philippines, etc.

Notice that the book is available and should be given to all theological seminaries or English-speaking theological training schools in the continent concerned. Notice or paid advertisement of the book should be placed in Christian weeklies or monthlies of the land.

Send review copies to:
Church Growth Bulletin
135 N. Oakland Avenue
Pasadena, Calif. 91101

The International Review of Missions
150 Route De Ferney
Geneva, Switzerland

Christianity Today
1019 Washington Blvd.
Washington, D.C. 20005

Missiology
135 N. Oakland Ave.
Pasadena, Calif. 91101

Dr. Andrew Wall
Scottish Institute of Missionary Studies
Department of Religious Studies
Kings College, University of Aberdeen
Aberdeen, Scotland   AB9 2UB

Your Own Denominational Magazines

442

# 6. DIRECTORY OF SWM ASSOCIATES

The directory contains an alphabetical list of each SWM associate. The associates assigned number, country where the missionary or national leader serves, church or mission, and years in attendance at the School of World Mission, are given in the first group of names.

In the second group of names, the present mailing address is given. It is impossible to keep this list current; further assistance may be secured by writing to the School of World Mission. Associates are requested to keep the SWM informed every time their address changes.

A. The first group of names is found on pages 444-456.

B. The second group giving the address of each associate is found on pages 457 to 471.

Earl Ackland 100

William Anderson 1200
Uganda
UPC
9-12/71

Yesu Bandela 2300
India
Baptist
71/72/73/74

Larry Acton 200
Colombia
Cumberland Pres. Church
71/72

Egbert Andrews 1300
Taiwan
Orthodox Presbyterian
66/67

Dr. David Barrett 2400
Nairobi, Kenya
CMS

Elwood Bartlett 2500
Zaire
Methodist United Ch.
68/69

Ted Ailanjian 300
Ivory Coast
CBFMS
67/68, 9-12/72

Paul Ariga 1400
Japan
Gospel Crusade
71/72

G. Frank Alexander 400
Zambia
Church of Christ
68/69

Joseph Arthur 1500
Philippines
CMA
72/73/74

Ronald Beech 2600
Philippines
Nazarene
72/73

Merton Alexander 500
Rwanda
Fr. Methodist
68/69

Cecil Ashley 1600
Brazil
Mennonite
72/73

William Bengston 2700
Peru
Lutheran Church of America
71/72

Alfred Allin 600
New Guinea
Highland Christ Mission
72/73

Raymond Aspinall 1700
Argentina
Brethren
72/73

Charles Bennett 2800
Mexico
MAF
65/66, 70/71

Bob Alliston 700

444

John Astleford 1800
Guatemala, C.A.
Friends
9-12/70

Mary Bensick 2900

Assem. of God
71/72

Charles Altig 800

Baptist
1-6/70

Allen Avery Jr. 1900
Zambia
Church of Christ
68/69

Stanley Benson 3000
Indonesia
Lutheran Miss.
68/69

Howard Altig 900

WBT
66/67/68

James Baker 2000
China, Taiwan
Assemblies of God
68/69

Keith Bentson 3100
Argentina
Overseas Crusades
67/68

Bert Block 3200
Mexico
Wycliff
72/73

Eleanor Anderson 1000
Taiwan
LCA
9-12/71

Bruce W. Baillie 2100

Loren Anderson 1100
Guatemala
Primitive Methodist
9-12/68

Paul Balisky 2200
Ethiopia
SIM
71/72

Clarence Boehm 3300
Alaska
FEGC
70/71

Ernest Boehr 3400 Taiwan TEAM 70/71	Don Bray 4410 New Guinea Wesleyan 73	Mrs. D.L. Carr 5500 Taiwan CBFMS 65/66
Harvey Boese 3500 Thailand CMA 9-12/69	Wendell St.Broom 4500 Nigeria Church of Christ 69/70	Earl Carver 5600 Puerto Rico C of G 71/72
Robert Bolton 3600 Taiwan Assembly of God 67/68	David Brougham 4600 Indonesia Go Ye Fellowhip 69/70	Lew Cass 5700 Indonesia Inter.Chris.Miss. 67/68
Miss Ladell Bones 3700 Venezuela TEAM 68/69	Keith Brown 4700 Overseas Crusades 72	Eun Soo Chae 5800 Korea Korea Pres. Ch. 71/72/73
Paul Boschman 3800	Elden Buck 4800 Marshall Islands United Ch. B./World Miss.	Victor Chamberlin 5900 Haiti & New Guinea Wesleyan 70/71
Rolla Bradley 3900 Korea S. Bapt. 67/68	Allan Buckman 4900 Nigeria LCA 71/72	Tom Chandler 6000 Indonesia Overseas Crusades, Inc. 70/71/72/73
Malcolm Bradshaw 4000 Singapore EID 67/68/69	Herman Buehler 5000 Micronesia Liebenzell Miss. of USA 71/72/73	Joseph Chang 6100 Korea OMS 72
John Branner 4100 Taiwan CBFMS 70/71	Harry Burke 5100 Mexico LAM 69/70	Robert Chapman 6200 Ethiopia Chr. Missy. Fellow. 63/64
Eugene Braun 4200	Donald Burns 5200 Peru WBT 71/72	Tiao Him Chion 6300 Philippines Evang. United Ch. 70/71
Neil Braun 4300 Japan American Advent. 65/66	Charles Butler 5300 Panama	Warren Christianson 6400 Japan C of C 70/71/72/73
William Braun 4400 Costa Rica Latin American Mission	Ray Canfield 5400 Guatemala Friends 71/72	Wee Hian Chua 6500 Singapore IVCF 71/72

445

Paul Chung Korea Korea Holiness Ch. 72/73	6600	Basil Costerisan Indonesia Overseas Crusades 70/71	7600	Jacob Deshazer Free Methodist Bd.	8700
Leon Clymore Zambia Ch. of Christ 67/68	6700	Emmett Cox Sierra Leone Ch. of the Brethren 68/69	7700	Dr. Donald Dilworth Ecuador Gp. Miss. Union 66/67	8800
Bruce Colson Brazil United Ch. of Christ 71/72/73	6800	Norman Cummings Overseas Crusades 63	7800	Lee Roy Donnell	8900
Marshall Combs Brazil Chris. Miss. Fellow. 67/68	6900	Michael Curry Tanzania Ch. of Christ 69/70/71/72	7900	Patricia Donnell	9000
Eugene Congdon Mexico MAF 70/71	7000	K.C. Daniel India Marthoma Ch. 70/71	8000	Cecelia Drenth Argentina Chr. Ref. 71/72	9100
William Conley Indonesia C & MA 71/72/73	7100	Rameschandra Dass India U. Methodist 72/73	8100	James Dretke Ghana Lutheran 72/73	9200
William Conrad Costa Rica & Peru Nazarene 66/67	7200	Frank Daugherity Japan Ch. of Christ 72/73	8200	James Duren CBHMS 65/66	9300
Clyde Cook 446 73	7210	Linnell Davis Kenya AIM 66/67	8300	Fred Edwards Brazil OMS 67/68/69, 72/73	9400
Norman Cook Overseas Crusades	7300	Ray Davis Kenya AIM 72/73	8400		9500
Gary Copeland ECC 66/67	7400	Keith Dawson Ivory Coast Wycliff 70/71	8500	Eddie Eggerichs Baptist 72	9600
Gollapalli Cornelius India Telugu Bapt. 70/71	7500	Charles Derr Columbia LAM 66/67	8600	Daniel Ellis Ethiopia Ch. of Christ 71/72	9700

MATERIALS FOR THEOLOGICAL EDUCATION BY EXTENSION

AN EXTENSION SEMINARY PRIMER
Covell & Wagner, WCL. . . . . . .2.45(1.47)
DECIDE FOR YOURSELF: A THEOLOGICAL
WORKBOOK, Lewis, IVP. . . . . . .2.25(1.35)
DEVELOPING PROGRAMMED INSTRUCTIONAL
MATERIALS, Espich & Williams, Fearon
(no discount) . . . .(3.00)
A HANDBOOK OF NEW TESTAMENT GREEK
LaSor, Eerdmans & WCL
(short discount) . . . . 8.95(7.16)
INDUCTIVE STUDY OF THE BOOK OF
JEREMIAH (Programmed), Kinsler,
WCL, 580 pp. . . . . .4.95(2.97)
INDUCTIVE STUDY OF THE BOOK OF MARK
(Programmed), Kinsler, 400 pp.,
WCL. . . . . 3.95(2.37)
PREPARING INSTRUCTIONAL OBJECTIVES
(Programmed), Mager, Fearon, (no
discount). . . . . (3.00)
PRINCIPLES OF CHURCH GROWTH,
(Programmed), Weld & McGavran, WCL,
400 pages. . . . . 3.95(2.37)

PROGRAMMED INSTRUCTION FOR THEOLOGICAL
EDUCATION BY EXTENSION, Ward & Ward,
Urbanus . . . . 4.95(2.97)
THEOLOGICAL EDUCATION BY EXTENSION
(3 books in 1), Winter, WCL,
3rd edition . . . . .5.95(3.57)
THEOLOGICAL EDUCATION BY EXTENSION SLIDES
WITH COMMENTARY. . . . . 2.95(1.77)

NEWSLETTERS

EXTENSION, BY air monthly 5.00
EXTENSION SEMINARY BULLETIN 1.00
PROGRAMMING NEWS (air $2) 1.00
THEOLOGICAL NEWS (air $2) 1.00
The above are annual subscription rates.
---JUST OFF THE PRESS---
DESIGNING A THEOLOGICAL EDUCATION BY
EXTENSION PROGRAM, Hill. . . . . 3.95(2.37)
THE WORLD DIRECTORY OF THEOLOGICAL EDUCATION
BY EXTENSION, Weld, WCL. . . . . 5.95(3.57)

VERY SPECIAL

VERY SPECIAL BARGAINS--Greater than 40% discounts

ARCTIC BUSH MISSION, Chambers, Superior 12.95(3.95)
BEYOND THE RANGES (Latourette's Auto-
biography), Eerdmans. . . . . . . 3.95(.99)

HISTORY OF THE EXPANSION OF CHRISTIANITY,
Latourette, Zondervan = Latourette 7 vol.
set. . . . . 22.95(10.00)
P & H for 7 vol.=2.35, tot. price   12.35

ABC's of Ordering

If you are ordering less than 10 books, please use a separate sheet of paper. Let the upper 1/3 of your order be your shipping label, and send order in duplicate if possible. This gives us a record of your order in case of lost shipments. If ordering more than 10 books, use the order lable on the back, coded according to the word underlined in each entry. Detach the entire order label and mail, printing your address clearly.

We find that it saves us both time and money if you send your order in duplicate. Write "TO" next to your name and address and leave at least an inch of space all around it. Type or print clearly since this will be your shipping label. We will continue to send you a copy of this book list with each mailing so you will be sure to have the most recent list. TAKE ADVANTAGE OF THESE PRICES WHILE THEY LAST. COSTS ARE RISING FOR POSTAGE AND HELP.

ADD UP PRICES IN PARENTHESIS, add 5% tax if to be shipped to a California address, and 35¢ postage and handling per item (books or cassettes). IF ORDERING LESS THAN THREE ITEMS, ADD AN ADDITIONAL 50¢, PLEASE.

The two small items, SAY YES TO MISSION and REVOLUTIONARY AND CHRIST'S WILL do not require any postage and handling if ordered ONE AT A TIME along with a book. If ordering two or more of either, or one of each together, add 35¢ p & h.

You'll note most prices are 40% off, or more. Two or three special cases are less than 40%.

Send payment in U.S. dollars with your order. The Church Growth Book Club operates on a prepaid basis only.

It is not that we do not trust you; it's that we want (for your sake eventually) to avoid the extra cost of getting your payment, which arrives separately, applied against your order. Sounds simple, but it isn't. There are well over 8,000 subscribers. They may order under their own names; separate payment often comes under the name of a mission agency, a school, or what not. If your payment must come separately, try sending your order to that place and have the payment forwarded to us with the order! If all else fails, we'll do our best. But it takes longer to process and lends itself to errors.

WARNING: 1) Do not expect special services such as having packages mailed air freight--which necessitates our taking them personally to the airport one hour away--without paying for the cost of time and gas for such a service. 2) There is no 2nd class air rate from the U.S. If the pkg. is small, the cheapest rate is A.O air mail. 3) We also have to charge an extra fee for "chamberization," etc.

BOOKSTORES, LIBRARIES, AND INSTITUTIONS MAY ORDER ONLY FROM THE CHURCH GROWTH BOOK DEPOSIT (AT COMMERCIAL DISCOUNT SCHECULES) IF THEY EXPECT TO BUY ON CREDIT. LIBRARIES AND INSTITUTIONS MAY BE MEMBERS OF THE CLUB IF THEY BUY ON A PREPAID BASIS AND FOLLOW THE ORDERING PROCEDURES OUTLINED ABOVE.

479

AMERICAN SOCIETY OF MISSIOLOGY

ASM NEWSLETTER

January 1973, No. 73:1, EDITORS: Herbert Kane, John T. Boberg, Roland Scott

MISSIONS JOURNAL BEGUN...CONCORDIA TO HOST CONSTITUTIONAL MEETING

The American Society of Missiology, an organization bringing together professors of mission and others interested in studying the missionary dimension of the Christian Church, was formally proposed June 9-10, in an ad-hoc gathering at Scarritt College for Christian Workers in Nashville. The 45 who attended the meeting approved a statement of purpose and named a Continuation Committee to draft a constitution, solicit additional members, publish a newsletter, explore the feasibility of launching a scholarly journal, and call a constituent assembly set for 8th, 9th and 10th of June, 1973.

The new organization is not intended to take over the functions of two existing groups with similar purposes: The Association of Professors of Mission and the more recent Association of Evangelical Professors of Missions. The presidents of both, James Pyke of Wesley Theological Seminary and Herbert Kane of Trinity Evangelical Divinity School participated in the meeting and joined the A.S.M. as Charter Members.

480

Perhaps the key issue of debate concerned the purpose. Some felt that the A.S.M. should declare as its goal the fulfillment of the Great Commission, others that it should fix as its end the study of missiology but without doctrinal overtones, thus bringing itself more into line with the outlook of the American Council of Learned Societies. As the discussion progressed, the participants, who represented conservative evangelicals, ecumenicals, and Roman Catholics, reached the mutual agreement that

Also, *PRACTICAL ANTHROPOLOGY* will merge with the new ASM journal which will be called simply *MISSIOLOGY, An International Review*. This new, formidable combination will begin with the first quarter of 1973 and will be accompanied with the final, token issue of the former, as it begins its 20th year of publication.

William J. Danker and Wi Jo Kang, professors at Concordia, St. Louis, are hosts as well as co-chairmen of planning and program. The meeting will begin at 5 PM Friday, June 8, and end Sunday afternoon about 5 PM. Program details in our next Newsletter.

While the editorial board of the society's journal has not been finally settled, the following persons have been invited to be members and have agreed to do so:

Eugene Hillman	Katharine B. Hockin	George W. Peters
Louis Luzbetak	R. Pierce Beaver	Cal Guy
Wi Jo Kang	Gerald H. Anderson	Wm. A. Smalley
James A. Scherer	Jack Shepherd	Chas. W. Forman

Dr. Alan R. Tippett has accepted the position of editor. He has behind him some twenty years of missionary service in the Fiji Islands, ten years of missionary research and lecturing, graduate degrees in history and anthropology and five years of cross-cultural editorial experience. He has done missiological research and served as a consultant for the Presbyterians, Episcopalians, Baptists, Mennonites and the World Council of Churches in ten or twelve countries. During his missionary days he wrote a number of Christian textbooks in the Fijian language. He is an expert in Oceanic studies, which qualifies him for comparative research in view of the great diversity of missiological situations in Oceania. You may have seen his critical articles in the *International Review of Mission*, the *Evangelical Missions Quarterly, Practical Anthropology*, and in several dictionaries and symposia. His books are too numerous to list.

Note: Information of interest to those desiring Charter membership is found on page four.

the A.S.M. should be strictly academic. The conservatives in particular expressed the feeling that only as such could they continue to participate.

An International
Review
Volume I
Number 2
April, 1973

*Missiology

481

PUBLISHED QUARTERLY
January, April, July, October

SUBSCRIPTIONS
$8.00 per year.
$3.00 for single copy, $2.50 if payment
accompanies order.

All correspondence concerning
subscriptions should be directed to:
Lorraine Pellon, Business Manager
P.O. Box 1041
New Canaan, Connecticut 06840

All editorial correspondence should be
directed to:
Alan R. Tippett, Editor
American Society of Missiology
135 N. Oakland Avenue
South Pasadena, California 91101

Advertising correspondence, address to:
The Iversen-Norman Associates
175 Fifth Avenue,
New York, New York 10010
(212) 477-3006

PUBLISHERS
American Society of Missiology
Ralph D. Winter, Secretary/Treasurer
135 N. Oakland Avenue
South Pasadena, California 91101

482

Missi*ology

An International Review

Continuing
Practical Anthropology
July, 1973
Volume I, No. 3

Contents

Contributors

483

BIBLIOGRAPHY

Many useful bibliographies are included in several sections of the academic manual.

Section III COURSES OF STUDY, includes a bibliography in each of the many course syllabi. Instead of giving just the title and author of textbooks and references, nearly all entries have been checked and completed, thereby making this a more valuable publication for SWM associates, faculty and other research missiologists.

In Section II, limited bibliographies are given for the following GENERAL AREAS OF STUDY CONSTITUTING MISSIOLOGY:

A. Theory and Theology of Missions
B. Apologetics of the Christian Mission vis á vis non-Christian religions
C. Mission Across Cultures
D. Techniques, Organization and Methods in Mission
E. History of Missions and Church Expansion
F. Church Growth
G. The World Church--ecumenics

A brief list of general textbooks is also included in this section.

The books and articles referred to in the compilation of the "Manual on Technical Writing," are given in the syllabus for the thesis writing course (SWM 692a,b), and on pages 23-24a of the expanded Thesis Style Instructions, Section V GUIDELINES FOR RESEARCH.

APPENDICES

ABBREVIATIONS AND LETTER DESIGNATIONS

AAGR	Average Annual Growth Rate
AATS	American Association of Theological Schools
ABCFM	American Board of Commissioners for Foreign Missions
AEPM	Association of Evangelical Professors of Missions
AFG	Arthur F. Glasser
AM.	American
APM	Association of Professors of Missions
ART	Alan R. Tippett
CAMEO	Committee to Assist Missionary Education Overseas
CGB	Church Growth Bulletin
CGBCM	Church Growth Book Club Member
CHK	Charles H. Kraft
CMS	Church Missionary Society
CPW	C. Peter Wagner
DAM	Donald A. McGavran
DOM	Division of Overseas Ministries
DWME	Division of World Mission and Evangelism
EFMA	Evangelical Foreign Missions Association
EID	Evangelism-In-Depth
EMQ	Evangelical Missions Quarterly
FH	Fred Holland
FOM	Fellowship Of Missions
FPC	F. Peter Cotterell
FTS	Fuller Theological Seminary
G/L	Gospel Light
GPA	Grade Point Average
GRE	Graduate Record Examinations
HEC	A History of the Expansion of Christianity
HRAF	Human Relations Area Files
ICG	Institute of Church Growth
IFMA	Interdenominational Foreign Mission Association
IRM	International Review of Missions

| JEO | J. Edwin Orr |
| JHE | James H. Emery |

| LMS | London Missionary Society |
| LA | Los Angeles |

MARC	Missions Advanced Research and Communication Center
m/f	microfilm
MGK	Marguerite G. Kraft
MRL	Missionary Research Library
MSS.	Manuscripts
MTI	Missionary Training Institute

| n.d. | no date |

PA	Practical Anthropology
PI	Programmed Instruction
PRB	Population Reference Bureau

RDW	Ralph D. Winter
Ref.	Reference
Rev. ed.	Revised edition

SCM	Student Christian Movement
SPCK	Society for the Promotion of Christian Knowledge
SWM	School of World Mission
SWM/ICG	School of World Mission and Institute of Church Growth

TAFTEE	The Association For Theological Education by Extension
TAP	Theological Assistance Program
TEE	Theological Education by Extension
TEF	Theological Education Fund

| UCLA | University of California, Los Angeles |
| USC | University of Southern California |

487

| Vol. | Volume |

| WCC | World Council of Churches |
| WEF | World Evangelical Fellowship |

'Church Growth': More Than a Man, a Magazine, a School, a Book

C. PETER WAGNER

C hristian evangelism, both in America and in the Third World, appears to be rounding a curve and entering a third stream. During the fifties and sixties, two streams of evangelism gained international prominence. The first was crusade evangelism, typified by Billy Graham. The second stream was saturation evangelism, which originated with the late Kenneth Strachan of Costa Rica and became a part of the American scene with Key 73.

The third stream of evangelism is called "church growth" and is related to Donald McGavran and his associates. Although Donald McGavran is a household name, so to speak, on the world's mission fields, his teaching is not widely recognized in the United States as yet. Not until the fall of 1972 did he attempt to apply his growth principles systematically to churches in America. But events since then, most recently the publication of McGavran's latest book, *How to Grow a Church* (with Win Arn; Regal Books, 1973), have catapulted the church-growth movement into prominence in the United States. Since church growth has clearly become one of the major trends of the times in the church, I would like to try to describe the movement.

McGavran decided to put the two common words "church" and "growth" together and make them a technical term when he became disgusted at the way in which certain theological and missiological liberals had redefined such terms as "missions" and "evangelism" in unbiblical ways. Back around 1955, while a missionary in India, McGavran began to use the phrase "church growth," filling it with his own meaning. He could not have had an inkling at that time that the term would gain the currency it now has. Among missiologists, one no longer has to stop to define church growth any more than he would have to define General Motors or free enterprise in the business world.

Particularly in America, however, many still have a hazy idea of the meaning of church growth. Some, for example, identify it as the particular view of one man. Donald McGavran is indeed the father of the church-growth movement, but it has become much more than McGavran. He has six close professional colleagues, more than 400 have graduated from his school, and thousands of others have identified with him through books, articles, and seminars. All these consider themselves very much a part of the church-growth movement.

Others identify church growth with one school. The Fuller Seminary School of World Mission and Institute of Church Growth is the institutional center for church-growth research, but church growth has far outgrown Fuller Seminary. Dozens of other seminaries and Bible schools in many countries of the world now list courses in church growth in their catalogs. More will do so in the future.

For some, church growth brings to mind a periodical. These people are among the 8,000 subscribers to the *Church Growth Bulletin,* which used to be virtually the only source for church-growth articles. Now almost all leading Christian periodicals are carrying church-growth material with increasing frequency.

The key book on church growth is McGavran's magnum opus, *Understanding Church Growth.* But the literature has now gone far beyond that. In my own library I have a shelf five feet long labeled "Hard Core Church Growth." Both Eerdmans and Moody have developed entire lines of church-growth publications, and the William Carey Library was established basically to publish church-growth materials.

489

Church growth, then, has become much more than a man or a school or a periodical or a book. It has become an entire school of thought that is profoundly influencing missiology and the theology of evangelism. Before looking at its distinctives, however, we would do well to glance at some central areas where church growth holds much in common with other lines of missiology and evangelism:

1. Theologically, church growth is in the conservative evangelical tradition. The typical church-growth advocate is thoroughly committed to the doctrines of the inspiration and authority of Scripture, the deity of Christ, the person and work of the Holy Spirit, the centrality of the Church, the depravity of man, heaven and hell, and the totality of the "faith once delivered to the saints" (Jude 3). A biblical theological position is the bedrock of church growth.

2. As to the Christian life, church-growth people believe that orthodox doctrine must prove itself in daily living. Evidence of the fruit of the Spirit, the pious life, personal Bible reading and prayer, love for one's neighbor, the cultural mandate, social service, and all other good and proper Christian qualities are both commended and practiced by church-growth people.

3. The church-growth school holds that men and women without Jesus Christ are eternally lost, and that soul-winning, disciple-making evangelism, and missions are a primary and continuing task of the entire Church.

4. The supernatural power of the Holy Spirit is a crucial part of the theory and practice of all church-growth people. All fully recognize that nothing is accomplished for the Kingdom of God without "power from on high" (Luke 24:49).

These four points have been characteristic of men and women of God throughout the ages. Other contemporary missiological schools of thought would claim them as well.

But the church-growth movement also has some distinctives. Again, these six distinctives are not the exclusive property of church growth. But years of experience have shown that these are the places where the rubber meets the road. They are the issues that have to be debated, even with others who hold the four points above in common with church growth. Evangelicals who disagree with the church-growth school of thought almost invariably do so on one or more of these six distinctives:

1. The proper combination of the lordship of Jesus Christ and the responsibility of man requires church growth. As our Lord, God has made his will clearly known in the Scriptures, and as his servants we do poorly if we do not pay attention. Our Lord, for example, is clearly not pleased with:

- Fishing without catching (Luke 5:4-11).
- An empty banquet table (Luke 14:15-23).
- Sowing without reaping (Matt. 13:3-9).

- A fig tree that bears no figs (Luke 13:6-9).
- Lost sheep that are not brought into the fold (Matt. 18:11-14).
- A lost coin that is sought but not found (Luke 15:8-10).
- Ripe harvests that are not reaped (Matt. 9:36-38).
- Proclamation without response (Matt. 10:14).

Or, by extension of these principles, God is not pleased with evangelistic or missionary work that does not result in church growth. In bolder terms, and contrary to some popular missionary literature, God *is* interested in results, since he is not willing that one man, woman, or child should perish (II Pet. 3:9).

2. What is the mission of the Church in the world? Church growth says that among the many good things God expects his Church to do in the world, a primary and irreplaceable task is to preach the Gospel to every creature, persuade men and women to become faithful disciples of Christ, and incorporate them as responsible members of his Church. When true disciples are made, there is church growth. But notice some refinements:

- The focus on the human responsibility in making disciples should not be overly individualized. The task is the task of the Church as a body, and individuals best function as members of the body. Goals are measured according to what is accomplished by the body as a whole.
- Numerical church membership growth is not the only task of the Church. But biblically it does have a very high priority, and God is glorified when new members are added to the Church.
- Ultimately, evangelistic effectiveness must be measured in terms of *disciples,* not merely *decisions.* Evangelistic reporting should, but rarely does, reflect this principle.

3. Clear objectives are necessary if the Church is to fulfill its mission in the world, and thus obey its Lord. God's will as to missiological and evangelistic goals can and must be discerned from Scripture, articulated in plain terms, and subsequently used to measure achievements. In view of this, there is no need for Christians to work under a shadow of doubt as to whether they can really know what God's objective is. Recourse to the "mysterious working of God's Spirit" is often a thinly disguised rationalization of evangelistic failure, couched in pious terms.

No command of Jesus is clearer in this regard than the Great Commission. Careful exegesis of Matthew 28:19, 20 reveals that God's imperative is to *make disciples*. Disciples are tangible, identifiable, countable people, and whenever a true disciple is made, church growth occurs. Objectives that deviate from or fall short of the ultimate objective of making disciples are, to the degree they do so, inferior, and in need of correction.

4. Sound, effective strategy must be developed as a means of accomplishing the biblical objectives mentioned above. Improved strategy will, other things being equal, result in more fruitful evangelistic work, and thus be more pleasing to God. Far from reflecting lack of spirituality, well-honed strategy is a mark of maturity and competence in God's work. Efficiency needs to be stressed, since resources are limited and God is unhappy when invested resources do not bring intended results. The Parable of the Talents warns us that servants who fail to use their Lord's resources productively are considered "wicked and slothful" (Matt. 25:26). Does this not apply to evangelists?

5. The social and behavioral sciences can contribute much to missionary strategy. Anthropology, sociology, psychology, and other related disciplines have made us aware, for example, of such valuable principles as:

- People movements. We now know that in many —if not most—circumstances, multi-individual interdependent conversions are the most productive vehicle for making disciples.

- The power encounter. Anthropologists have shown that a vital step in the conversion process of many peoples, particularly animists and followers of the occult, is a test of power between God and the evil spirits, known as the power encounter.

- Dynamics of innovation. Missionaries can be trained to avoid blunders as they try to introduce new ideas and practices into the culture in which they are working.

- Indigeneity. We now know that true indigeneity goes much deeper than self-supporting, self-governing, and self-propagating churches. Proper indigeneity can make the difference between a church that is effective in discipling an entire people and one that is sealed off and relatively impotent.

- Ethnotheology. A new discipline that combines the insights of anthropology with sound biblical theology is being developed with the goal of better communicating to peoples at home and abroad God's plan of salvation.

492

6. Research is essential for optimum church growth. Sound evangelistic strategy must be based on facts, not on vague hopes or wishes or promises. Church growth is skeptical of promotional material and success stories if the facts of the case are not clearly presented. Research into the dynamics of the growth of churches in all countries of the world attempts to penetrate foggy thinking and make known the true state of affairs. For example, church-growth research has led to:

• A recognition of the resistance-receptivity axis. We now know that some peoples are more receptive to the Gospel at a particular time than other peoples. This is a key church-growth principle. Resistant peoples must be neither neglected nor abandoned, but sound evangelistic strategy will concentrate available resources on receptive peoples.

• A ruthlessly objective attitude toward evangelistic methods. Methods simply cannot be "canned" in Lower Zax, for example, and exported to Mamba Bamba. Church growth diligently seeks to locate, describe, and analyze, for each time and place, the methods that God has blessed and those he has not blessed.

• A discovery of the crucial importance of structures throughout missionary history. The concept of the relation between modalities (the parish church) and sodalities (voluntary societies of Christians) is proving to be an invaluable aid to missionary strategy, particularly now that missionary societies are proliferating in the Third World.

Church growth believes that unfruitfulness is a curable disease. The remedies are diagnostic research, prescriptive treatment, and strategic care.

Three moods characterize all church-growth advocates, I have found, and these can therefore be said to be moods of the movement in general:

Obedience. Full obedience to the Word of God and the will of God is essential. No apologies at all are made for whatever unswerving obedience might involve.

Pragmatism. Church-growth people do not hesitate to use whatever means God provides to do the best possible job in reaching the goals. They are not very much interested in what *should* bring unbelievers to Christ, but they are acutely interested in what does, in fact, bring unbelievers to Christ.

Optimism. Christ said, "I will build my church and the gates of hell shall not prevail against it." There is no warrant to be gloomy in Christian work. We are ultimately on the winning side. If God be for us, who can be against us? □

CHRISTIANITY TODAY

C. Peter Wagner is associate professor of Latin American studies, Fuller School of World Mission, Pasadena, California. He has master's degrees from Fuller Seminary, Princeton Seminary, and the School of World Mission. He formerly was a missionary in South America.

REPORT OF THE CURRICULUM COMMITTEE
ON THE TRAINING OF MISSIONARIES

The administrators of the William S. Carter Symposium, held at Milligan College, Tennessee, in April 1974, appointed a committee comprising Gerald H. Anderson, Charles Forman, Linwood Barney, Tetsuano Yamamori and Alan Tippett (Convener) to examine the question of guidelines for a curriculum suitable for the training of missionaries in cross-cultural understanding.

The members of the committee corresponded briefly with each other prior to the meeting at Milligan College, and for the meeting Alvin Martin was added as a resource person.

The committee met informally on April 6 for a general discussion, Fr. Boberg being present also, with Dr. and Mrs. J. C. Hoekendijk. After the discussion, the committee decided to meet again on April 7 and draft a statement.

The committee duly met and determined on the content of the statement and suggested model guidelines. These will be formulated by the Convener - henceforth the Chairman of the Committee - and circulated to the members for feedback and approval. The statement and guidelines will be published in the *Milligan Missiogram*, the guidelines (model) being specified as tentative and calling for feedback from readers.

The committee, having only commenced its task, is now directed to continue with correspondence and data-collecting, to the end that, (1) the tentative model may be more critically examined and improved, and (2) its efforts may be co-ordinated with those of similar bodies, which our discussions have shown to be in operation.

Ultimately, it is hoped that when the model is firmed up, suitable bibliographies may be prepared and the question of the need for new textbooks be investigated. Meantime, Dr. Yamamori indicates that the working costs of the committee, correspondence and other business may be a charge against the Symposium funds at Milligan College.

495

The Statement

1. The training of cross-cultural missionaries for the changing times and conditions of the mission fields of the world in our day, requires more and more understanding and empathy. For many years the discipline of anthropology (especially such aspects as social and applied anthropology, acculturation, cultural dynamics, the phenomenology of religion and ethnolinguistics) has been inadequately utilized in the majority of educational institutions where missionaries are trained.

With the availability of this kind of education in our day, the sending forth of missionaries untrained in anthropology is no longer justifiable.

2. We recoginze that the missionary situation in the world has changed dramatically since World War II, and that the old methods need revision, and the training provided for missionaries needs to be more relevant to the new situations. This requires a re-evaluation of missionary methods and a reconsideration of fields of concentration in any missionary training curriculum.

Although many institutions are no longer training missionaries, we recognize that as long as missionaries do go forth, under whatever auspices, they need to be trained within a well-developed and relevant cross-cultural curriculum.

3. The attached model is recommended for consideration by any institution planning or adjusting its curriculum for the training of missionaries. This is a purely tentative model and only meant to suggest approximate fields of emphasis, not precise courses. It is meant to serve as a basis for discussion and not in any way to limit or control the field - merely to assure that all these emphases receive serious condideration.

It is assumed that each missionary candidate will have received his general education, together with his theological and biblical training. The fields set out in the model are related to preparation for service in Christian *cross-cultural* mission, not the home ministry, which may, or may not, overlap with this, according to the circumstances.

The model is arranged in three columns (1 to 3) representing a sequence of increasing diversification (i) for a larger faculty, or (ii) for a training program for a wider range of mission fields.

We do not say that all these subjects should be taught before the candidate leaves the institution: e.g., Language Learning might be taken in a special institution or on the field - but it should be taken somewhere.

We also assume that some attention is to be paid to the Spiritual Formation and Growth of the Missionary at whatever degree of diversification.

496

Milligan College, Tennessee
April 7, 1974

A. R. Tippett
Chairman, C.C.T.M.

1. SIMPLIFIED	2. MORE DEVELOPED	3. MOST DIVERSIFIED
1. History of Missions	History of Missions to the Reformation History of Missions since the Reformation	Expansion of the Early Church Missions – Middle Ages to Reformation History of Modern Missions & Ecumenics
2. Theology of Mission	Theology of Mission – Gospels Theology of Mission – New Testament Church	People of God in the Old Testament Theology of Mission – Gospels Theology of Mission – New Testament Church
3. Principles and Practice	Principles and Practice Indigenous Church	Principles and Practice Indigenous Church Theological Education by Extension
4. Cultural Anthropology	Cultural Anthropology Social Structure and Authority Patterns	Cultural Anthropology Social Structure and Authority Patterns Contemporary Trends in Missiology
5. Comparative Religion	Hinduism and Buddhism Islam	Hinduism and Buddhism Islam Other Eastern Religions
6. Applied Anthropology	Applied Anthropology Theory of Anthropology	Applied Anthropology Theory of Anthropology Data Collecting (Research Method)
7. Traditional Religions	Phenomenology of Traditional Religion Traditional Religious Practices & Practitioners	Phenomenology of Traditional Religion Traditional Religious Practices & Practitioners Nativistic & Revitalization Movements
8. Church Growth Case Studies	Case Studies from Africa Case Studies from Asia and Latin America	Case Studies from Africa Case Studies from Asia Case Studies from Latin America
9. Language Learning	Language Learning Language and Culture	Language Learning Language and Culture Translation
10. Missionary Internship	Missionary Internship Mission Project	Missionary Internship Mission Project Reading Courses
11. Global Awareness and World Affairs	Global Awareness and World Affairs Cultural Dynamics	Global Awareness and World Affairs Cultural Dynamics
12. Spiritual Formation and Growth of the Missionary		

RESEARCH METHOD AND THE MISSIOLOGICAL PROCESS

AT THE SCHOOL OF WORLD MISSION[1]

by

Alan R. Tippett

Research in the School of World Mission has to operate within certain missiological 'givens', which arise from the nature of the task in our day rather than from the nature of education. The school provides resources and guidance for leading nationals and experienced missionaries from all parts of the world.[2] This requires a wide range of specialized techniques, an extensive intake of worldwide information and an extremely complex pattern of operation. It cannot be otherwise if we are to be true to our name - "World Mission".

In Christian cross-cultural mission we stand between the Colonial Era, which has died suddenly, and the Post-Colonial Era which has imposed itself suddenly on a sleeping home Church. Our faculty members were pointing this out before the event twenty years ago.[3] A second 'given' is that not only are we operating in new social and political alignments and opportunities, but the character of our tools have changed. Anthropology, Sociology, Communication, Linguistics, Human Geography and other areas of of research have developed academically, both in theory and application. Missionary training and proficiency has to be related to these developments and national leaders have to be orientated to them. Furthermore missionary and national have to learn to use these insights cooperatively, because the New Era requires new kinds of relationship between national and expatriate.[4]

498

Thus for the present the SWM faculty requirement has been experience under Colonial Mission, which produced a striving for Post-Colonial Age patterns. We stand today at the most formative point of time in the history of modern missions. We could win or lose all in world mission in this very decade as far as the next century is concerned. I could almost call it a mutational point in the history of Christian mission.[5]

My assignment today is to give you a model that demonstrates what is going on in research methodology at the SWM. Whatever pattern I sketch, it cannot be a static one like an organizational chart with boxes. I turn to biology rather than to sociology or business administration - kind of flowchart, if you like - because I am dealing with a continuous process. New things are always being fed in, tested, adopted or discarded, modified, or applied in new ways. I want an organismic model[6] that gives the impression of interaction that never rests. Any missionary or any national can feed into it, either for his term among us or more permanently in what he leaves behind.

Granted this creates problems in our curriculum, for example, and we try to cover it with special seminars, projects and reading courses, both in the school and on return visits to the field during summer (690,691, 693, 695; 790, 791, 793, 795). These are needed to develop the skill of our men and the quality of their distinctly individual contributions. The tremendous range of potential our men bring to us demands this kind of flexibility; and if we seem to be rebels and fail to conform to normal educational stereotypes and classifications, it is just this very nonconformity which justifies our existence at this point of history.

The Flow-Chart of Missiology

Examine the accompanying flow-chart. It is intended to create the impression of a number of forces flowing into and through two focal points which one might call nuclear centers. At the top of the chart is situated the field of Missionary Experience. The process starts there. Every faculty member and every research associate comes here from some mission out in the world. He knows its problems, its successes and failures. He comes to us both to give something and to receive something. Thus there is fed into our nuclear centers each year a combination of new problems and new innovations.

499

The end of the process is at the bottom of the chart, where the same men go forth into the world again, either back to their fields, or into posts as Professors of Missions, or maybe Board Secretaries. They go forth with new skills and insights as applied missiologists. Now let us examine the other forces which flow into the nuclear centers where missiologists are born.

The three major disciplines from which we draw are Theology (mainly Biblical Theology), Anthropology (mainly Social, Applied, and Theoretical, Primitive Religion, Linguistics, Cultural Dynamics and Culture Change) and History; but we also draw from Sociology, Psychology, Communications, Computer Techniques, etc. In the first nuclear centre these disciplines and sub-disciplines begin to interact, and they do so within the structures and problems of cross-cultural mission, with the Gospel motivation as the driving force of that interaction. What happens is something entirely new - not a mere sum of the parts. Ethnohistory, Ethnolinguistics, Ethnopsychology, Ethnotheology - all of which are emerging as fields for special research in our school, and mostly they are recognized in the Human Relations Area Files classification.[7] Several of them have already technical journals - *Ethnohistory*, for example, being now in its twentieth year and having so established its methodology that its articles are now being applied to social problems.[8] At several of these points our faculty have engaged with their peers from secular universities, travelling to scholarly conferences at their own expense to do so. As a result of these contacts many secular anthropologists and historians are taking a new look at[9] missionary archives and records as potential data bases. The diversity of these interactions in the nuclear center lends itself to the diversity of the men who come to us, in that it permits them to be selective with the ingredients we set before them, and in which we agree to direct their research.

500   *Emerging Missiologists*

Let me mention quickly four men who have passed on to the D.Miss. degree under my mentorship. I choose these men only because, as my own men, I know them best. Each had his own unique critical path out of the missionary world and back into the world again.

Kwast had already done our MA, and wanted to dig deeper into Ethnohistory. His Anthropology was stronger than his History so I sent him back to History and insisted he do a

reading course in Historiography before starting his dissertation research. I think this detour shows up in his dissertation methodology, especially in his use of primary sources,
when he brought his anthropological skills to bear on them.
This was something new which he could not have obtained from
either discipline alone.[10]

Conley had his MA in Anthropology when he came to us.
He had served in Kalimantan and was now a Professor of Mission. Since he had left the field a large tribe of Kenyahs
had become Christian and Conley wanted to study this religious change in terms of Anthropological Theory. As no
anthropological monograph on this tribe existed his dissertation required a more-than-usually long anthropological
description of the culture pattern. There was only one way
of doing this. He returned to Kalamantan for a rather long
summer, verified his descriptions, did extensive interviewing
in the vernacular, and finished up with a "before and after"
study which no-one else in the world could have written. A-
part from being appropriate for use in secular Anthropology,[11]
it has a missiological significance of paramount importance.

From the opposite side Weerstra came to us with no
training in Anthropology, but wanted to deal with the responsiveness of Maya peasant communities to the Gospel. Apart
from his regular courses in Anthropology he devoted six
months to reading anthropological writing by Central American specialists, and eventually left here with an up-to-date
specialized knowledge of the subject which would have been
adequate for a Ph.D. In addition to this he spent a summer
in Mayan communities, interviewing and using research schedules he had set up here before he went. His field notes[12]
comprise a volume of single-spaced typescript 3" thick.

Read came to us with a MTh and a year of Church Growth
(ICG). He had a wide experience in Brazil and worked in Portuguese. The book he wrote in Eugene has been the most widely cited of all our books by sociologists.[13] He led the
CGRILA teach for which he was prepared in interviewing techniques in a two-week experimental trial in Mexico.[14] His
dissertation research occupied ten years. The appendix
comprises 4500 pages of computer printouts. He describes a
procedure for using the computer to study migration and development in Brazil, relating it to potential for church
planting. This required some specialized supervision beyond
the capacity of our faculty, so we had Dr. Tim Smith of Cal
State University, on his committee. They spent many hours
together, as he understood the use of the computer in spacial

501

diffusion studies. He told me that in this field this was all Ph.D. material in any university.[15]

These four men, from West Africa, Indonesia, Central and South America, all brought different kinds of missionary experience and had majored in different disciplines in their academic work; they came from five different denominations and used five different languages for their field research; and each added a contribution in the nuclear centers which no other person could have added, at the same time drawing from his peers. Each went out having developed his own particular gifts for more intensive application. The School of World Mission is no educational 'match factory', and probably does not fit any normal organizational chart. But we believe that God has called us together for a particular task at a particular time in history. That is what gives us our cohesion and our programs.

Notes

[1] Prepared for presentation to the United Faculty and Trustees Fuller Theological Seminary, Feb. 4, 1974.

[2] We are now in the second term this year. Up to date our mission-associates have included 40 nationals and 60 missionaries, 6 missionary educators, 3 executives and 6 special roles. These have come from 25 different denominational missions and several horizontal structures, and have operated in 38 different countries.

[3] See McGavran: "New Methods for a New Age in Missions" *International Review of Missions* xliv. 1955, 394-403; Tippett: "A Historical Survey of the Character & Training of the Fijian Ministry" 1961, prepared for the TEF Consultation on Theological Training in the Pacific, etc.

502

[4] Malinowski and Fortes saw this while it was yet in the Colonial Age. See *Methods of Study of Culture Change in Africa*, 1938 (Reptd. 1965) Ed. Malinowski, xii-xxv, 60-63.

[5] Like William Carey in the last decade of the 18th century, we stand at another all-important point of time, when new resources demand a reconsideration of what the Great Commission means to our day and generation - see Carey's *Enquiry*

Sect.I, pp. 7-13.

[6]This term is used after the manner of Wallace: see "Revitalization Movements" *American Anthropologist* 1956, 265-266, in another context.

[7]See Murdock et al: *Outline of Cultural Materials*, 1961 in the 820 categories, where the whole decade is devoted to these "ethno-" combinations.

[8]For example the leading article in the winter number of 1972 of *Ethnohistory* was devoted to Ethnohistory and contemporary social problems.

[9]In particular anthropologists interested in culture change, the acceptance and rejection of innovations, and applied anthropology are increasingly making use of missionary material. As to our faculty work in these areas, Dr. Kraft has a book on Ethnotheology ready for publication, and has had numerous articles on the subject published. See also my *Aspects of Pacific Ethnohistory*, much of which was presented at scientific and university meetings.

[10]"The Origins & Nineteenth Century Development of Protestant Christianity in West Cameroon: 1841-1886"

[11]"The Kalimantan Kenyah: A Study of Tribal Conversion in Terms of Dynamic Cultural Themes"

[12]"Maya Peasant Evangelism: Communication, Receptivity and Acceptance Factors among Maya Campesinos"

[13]*New Patterns of Church Growth in Brazil*, Read   503

[14]*Latin American Church Growth*, Read et al.

[15]"Brazil 1980: A Tool for the Evangelization of Brazil"

February 4, 1974

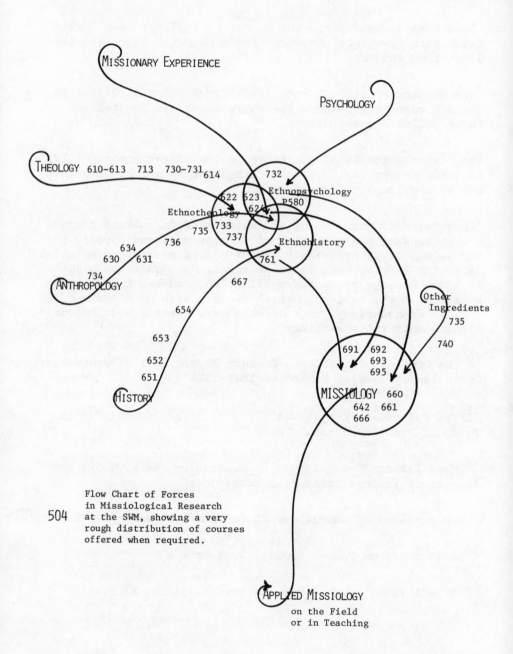

MISSIONARY EXPERIENCE

PSYCHOLOGY

THEOLOGY 610-613   713   730-731 614

732

Ethnopsychology
P580

622 623
624

Ethnotheology

735 733
737

736

634
630   631

734

ANTHROPOLOGY

Ethnohistory

761

667

654

653

652

651

HISTORY

Other
Ingredients
735

740

691   692
693
695

MISSIOLOGY   660
642   661
666

Flow Chart of Forces
in Missiological Research
at the SWM, showing a very
rough distribution of courses
offered when required.

504

APPLIED MISSIOLOGY
on the Field
or in Teaching

Seeing the task graphically

RALPH D. WINTER

Without apology, we see the entire world as the legitimate target of Christian expansion. This does not mean we envision forcing anyone to be a Christian, nor forcing anyone to change his language or his culture in order to become a Christian. This is not an institutional "triumphalism." We simply believe everyone has an equal right to knowledge of, and faith in, Jesus Christ. But if this is our goal, how are we doing?

HOW ARE WE DOING?

The first graphic clearly shows by an exact scale drawing the explosive growth of mankind during what was once predicted to be the "Christian century." The details are at the end of the article.[1] But you can tell by the unaided eye that the darkened (non-Christian) areas are getting larger, not smaller, and are bigger today than in the year 1900, and, at present rates projected, will be even larger by the end of the century. Bluntly, the number of people yet to be won in Africa and Asia has more than doubled since 1900 and will be more than tripled by the end of the century.

Ralph D. Winter is associate professor of missions at the Fuller Theological Seminary School of World Mission. He is a graduate of Caltech, Columbia University, Cornell University, and Princeton Theological Seminary. He served two terms under the National Evangelical Presbyterian Church of Guatelama as a fraternal worker of the United Presbyterian Church. He is the author of *Theological Education by Extension* and *The Twenty-Five Unbelievable Years, 1945-1969.*

505

This article is taken by permission from the January 1974 issue of EVANGELICAL MISSIONS QUARTERLY

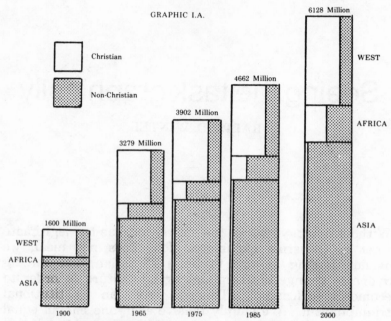

Christian

Non-Christian

6128 Million

WEST

4662 Million

AFRICA

3902 Million

3279 Million

ASIA

1600 Million

WEST

AFRICA

ASIA

1900   1965   1975   1985   2000

WORLD POPULATION GROWTH DURING THE "CHRISTIAN CENTURY"

However, first impressions may be misleading. The facts above have led some people to shout "Hopeless!" and then go on to propose that Buddhists don't really need to know Jesus Christ. (What would such people have said when there were only twelve disciples to do the task that Jesus left?) The other side of the coin is that while non-Christians in Africa and Asia have more than doubled since 1900 and will more than triple by the year 2000, the number of Christians in Africa and Asia is today *thirteen* times what it was in 1900, and by 2000 it will be 34 times as large.[2] The crucial factor is the difference in *rates* of growth. When we take *rates* of growth into account, as in the next graphic, we are not concerned simply by the fact that non-Christians are getting more numerous each year. Rather, we ask a much more important question: Just how fast are they growing? And, Is the rate of growth of the non-Christians faster than that of the Christians? What this means is that we mentally divide all the people of Africa and Asia into groups of one hundred and then ask, After one year of growth how many more than the original 100 are there?

The answer to this question is told in Graphic I.B. where

506

3

the very first pair of columns says this: "For every 100 non-Christian Africans there were 1.2 more at the end of a year (on the average, during 1900-1975), while for every 100 Christians there were 4.6 more!"[3]

For the same period we see Asian Christians growing at an average of 2.8 more each year per hundred Christians, while non-Christians grew by only 1.0 person per hundred. This, by the way, is called simple annual percentage growth. It is like interest on money in a savings account, and it is the easiest way to compare growth rates of two different groups of people.

GRAPHIC I.B.

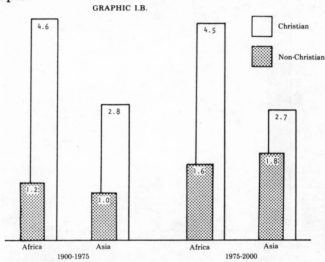

POPULATION INCREASE EACH YEAR PER HUNDRED PERSONS
(Christian growth rate exceeds that of non-Christians in both Africa and Asia
and does so during both periods—the latter based on present rates)

Note, however, that on the right half of Graphic I.B. our projections for 1975-2000 are not quite as striking a picture as on the left. During the entire first 75 years the Christians in Africa and Asia have been growing about three times as fast as non-Christians. But during 1975-2000 our estimates show the non-Christians increasing their rate of growth, and the gap between growth rates narrowing. In Asia, in particular, Christians are growing only 50 percent faster than non-Christians. The main point remains: While Graphic I.A. shows non-Christians truly exploding in sheer numbers, Graphic I.B. reveals the fact that the Christians in Africa and Asia are steadily catching up: they are on record

507

4

as growing three times as fast during the last 75 years, and will likely continue to grow at least 50 percent faster in the next 25 years. If this is true, what is the discernible impact on the over-all population?

Graphic I.C. answers this question. It shows that in 1900 non-Christians out-numbered Christians 75 to one in Asia, and 28 to one in Africa. Today the same ratio is only 22 to one in Asia and 2.5 to one in Africa! Should present growth rates merely hold (not even increase), the picture in A.D. 2000 is definitely brighter. Are we going backwards? Not exactly![4]

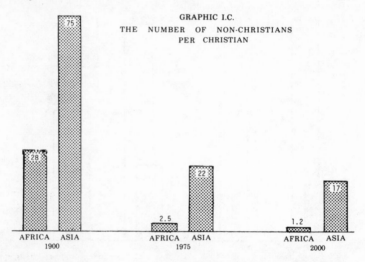

GRAPHIC I.C.

THE NUMBER OF NON-CHRISTIANS
PER CHRISTIAN

However, we must in all honesty admit that the growth picture in Asia is not what it needs to be. In order to see just what the problem is, let us take a closer look at the kind of people who are yet to be won.

WHO IS TO BE WON?

Winning people to Christ in Europe and America—in the Western world—where most people consider themselves Christians, is not a problem to be ignored. Every new generation has to be reevangelized, and hollow, nominal Christianity is a massive, urgent problem, even in the so-called mission lands, where unevangelized second and third-generation Christians are as nominal as the average citizen of the Western world. Big as this problem is, the task of winning non-Christian Asians and Africans is both far

508

5

different and far larger. This is the task often referred to as the two billion who have never heard the name of Christ. For convenience, in Graphic II.A. we break these groups of people down into cultural rather than geographic categories.[5] Immediately three groups loom large. Most missionaries and most mission boards may hope that someone else will worry about the special problem of winning Muslims, Hindus, and Chinese, since these have historically been the most resistant to the gospel. But let's face it—these groups are by far the larger part of the task we face. There are now new insights regarding the reaching of these particular "resistant" peoples. But first let us avoid a common misunderstanding.

Current gloating over the emergence of the overseas "national churches" could easily lead us to suppose that we at least have a beachhead of Christians within each of these major non-Christian blocks. This is not exactly true. All of a sudden we have a reappearance of Jewish Christians among the Jews. But there are very few "Muslim Christians" or "Muslim churches" today. (The closest thing to this is the Christian movement resulting from SUM work in the Lake Chad area in Africa.) Chinese Christians are a tiny minority, and are isolated from the bulk of the Chinese by geographic, linguistic and cultural barriers. Most of the castes of India are not represented among the Christian denominations of that land. Ninety-five percent of the Christians come from less than 5 percent of the castes: this means that 400 million middle caste peoples in India cannot join any existing church without monumental social dislocation (the kind Paul didn't think the Greeks had to undergo).

Thus, the following graphic displays three mammoth fast-growing blocks, Hindus, Muslims, Chinese, that are *mainly beyond the reach of the ordinary evangelism of Christians reaching their cultural near-neighbors.* This horrifying fact means specifically that "native missionaries using their own language" can hardly begin to do this job. Recall also that most missionaries are not focused on any one of these three blocks of humanity. Yet in 1975 in these three blocks alone there will be roughly two billion people who will constitute 83 percent of the non-Christians in Asia and Africa.

509

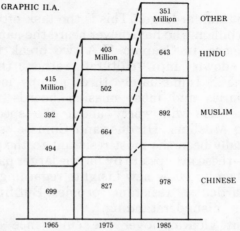

GRAPHIC II.A.

GROWTH OF NON-CHRISTIANS IN AFRICA AND ASIA

Graphic II.B goes on to show the amazing fact that the other 403 million non-Christians, who are 17 percent of the task, are the object of the attention of 38,000 missionaries who are 95 percent of the force. Meanwhile, the Hindu, Muslim, and Chinese blocks, some 1993 million people in all, are the object of the attention of only 5 percent of the missionary force. Please do not suppose that too many missionaries are devoted to the 403 million! The major lesson here is that we need to exert more effort on behalf of the bigger problem: if it is *reasonable* (and we believe it is) to send 38,000 missionaries (from all Protestant sources) to

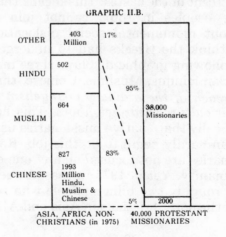

GRAPHIC II.B.

ASIA, AFRICA NON-CHRISTIANS (in 1975)

40,000 PROTESTANT MISSIONARIES

403 million people, then it is *unreasonable* to send only 2,000 to reach 1993 million. If we were to give the larger group equal effort per million, it would require 212,000 missionaries—almost 100 times as many as the 2,000 we are now sending!

But is this necessary? Yes. Can we do it? Yes. Will we do it? I don't know. We surely will not bestir ourselves if we are not convinced that it is both necessary and possible. Note in passing that the 38,000 working among the 403 million are extensively aided (and often even out-numbered) by national Christians working on an E-1 basis within those peoples. By contrast there is not any comparable internal evangelism going on at all among the 1993 million, with the possible exception, in part, of the Chinese. Surely in the Hindu middle-castes and in the Muslim world, there are virtually no internal allies. This fact greatly deepens the problem we face, and it is necessary to take a closer look at the full implications of it.

HOW "FAR AWAY" ARE THEY?

Our remarks just above lead us to spell out the problem of *cultural* distance. In Graphic III.A. we depict a typical village in India. Happily, thousands of villages in India today include Christians; nevertheless, there are still over 500,000 villages without any worshipping Christian group! Worse still, even where there is a church—note the cross—it is in most cases located in the ghetto of former "untouchables," in Telegu called *Palem.* The distance from this ghetto to the center of the village may be only half-a-mile *geographically,* but it is like 25,000 miles *culturally.* In this same sense, at least *80 percent of the non-Christians in the world today are beyond the reach of existing churches!*

Graphic III.B. portrays Acts 1:8, where Jesus uses an analysis that is not basically *geographic* distance. E-1

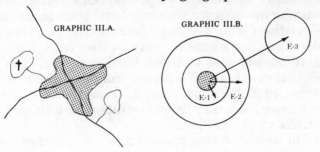

GRAPHIC III.A.

GRAPHIC III.B.

E-3

E-1   E-2

511

8

evangelism is ordinary evangelism, where you cross only the one barrier between the church and the world; and if there were no other barriers ordinary evangelism would be good enough. It would be good enough to pray that every church in the world would be warmly evangelistic in reaching out to its culturally near neighbors.

But there are other barriers. Jesus pinpointed a small community on the doorstep of the Judeans, called Samaritans with whom the Jews were not on speaking terms. They were culturally and ethnically *related* to the Jews, but their differences were significant enough to be considered an additional barrier. Call this E-2 evangelism.

Jesus then mentioned the whole rest of the world—" unto the ends of the earth"—where you don't expect any linguistic head start at all, no cultural affinity whatsoever. This is E-3 evangelism and is humanly speaking, the hardest kind.

Where there is a specific prejudice factor, the problem, whether in the E-1, E-2, or E-3 areas, may be so difficult that wise strategy will be to arrange for someòne to make the contact who is not the special object of prejudice. This is one reason why Christian witnesses *from a geographical distance* have always played so strategic a role in the expansion of Christianity down through history. In evangelism cultural distance is always more important than geographical distance, because cultural distance, whether it consists of linguistic difference or structured prejudice barriers, obstructs effective communication no matter how close the evangelist is geographically.

This is what is meant when we say that "crossing an ocean never made a missionary," or "you can go 18,000 miles but it's the last 18 inches that count." Geography is thus nearly irrelevant in such well known observations. But a brand new astonishing meaning for the same basic truth is the fact that the Christians who live next door to the Muslims in the Middle East, for example, may be the least likely to be effective missionaries to those Muslim people: it is the 18 inches that count, and if a person from afar can more easily cross that 18 inches, then so be it, it has got to be arranged. In such cases there may be little strategy in waiting for local Christians to do the job.

The full weight of this presses down on us when we recall

512

9

that the vast bulk (say 80 percent) of the non-Christian world is at the E-2 and E-3 cultural distance from every existing Christian. This fact in turn has profound implications for concrete arrangements in strategy.

WHAT WE MUST DO

In keeping with the concept of "body evangelism" we must not feel content—we can hardly feel our job is begun— unless people are brought into vital fellowship with other Christians. Once this is clear, there are four different categories of growth of the Christian movement which can usefully be distinguished, because *all four must take place.*

GRAPHIC IV

Internal Growth	Expansion Growth	Extension Growth	Bridging Growth
			E-2
			E-3
1. Spiritual growth	1. Biological growth	Church planting	Cross-cultural
2. Structural growth	2. Transfer growth		Church Planting
3. E-0 Conversion growth	3. E-1 Conversion growth		

The first broad category of growth, *internal growth,* includes three quite different processes: (1) *Structural growth*[6]—the growth of internal structure, for example, the formation of a youth group; (2) The *spiritual growth* of the church community, and (3) *E-0 conversion growth*—the confirmation, the "evangelical experience" which, through E-0 evangelism (which crosses "zero" culture barriers) transforms mere members of the church *community* into *communicant* members. This kind of evangelism is very important but not the same as E-1 evangelism, where you are working across the cultural barrier between the church and the world. Thus *internal growth* does not include expansion of the church community but does refer to anything related to the development of life and health within the church. Internal growth makes sure both new and old persons in the fellowship are edifyingly related. In Japan this has been so great a problem that a high proportion of new Christians leave by the back door within two years.

513

Expansion growth expands the local church community. Hopefully, this expansion is the result of winning people

10

from the community outside of the church. But it may also result from people coming from other congregations elsewhere. Lest these two mechanisms be confused with each other, or with a third, let us define the components of all three: (1) *Biological growth*—where an excess of births over deaths increases the size of the Christian community; (2) *Transfer growth*—an excess of believers transferring in (from other congregations) over the number transferring out, and (3) *E-1 conversion growth*—the excess of people outside the church being converted into the church over the number of those in the church who may revert to the world.

Extension growth is where new churches are planted. Few pastors have a vision for this and in certain spheres it is almost a lost art. It requires a very different set of skills from that of expansion growth; yet it involves, crucially, all the skills of internal growth and expansion growth as well. Studies have shown that a church movement that falls back on expansion growth alone—and is not able and willing to plant new congregations—is a movement whose growth rate will rapidly taper off.

Bridging growth—to the right of the heavy dotted line symbolizing cultural barriers—is that special case of extension growth where the new church being planted is made up of people who are sufficiently different from the kind of people in the mother church that they would be happier running their own church. This, according to our definitions, requires E-2 evangelism, or perhaps even E-3 evangelism. In other words, it requires cross-cultural communication in addition to all the other skills involved in the categories of internal, expansion, and extension growth.

Tough as this fourth category of growth is—it is the classical missionary task—it must be pointed out that all of our preceding charts suggest nothing less than that this task and technique is crucially necessary for the reaching of at least 80 percent of the non-Christian world in Africa and Asia. But, this *is* what we must do! Alas, how many missionaries are content to "let the nationals do it" in a social unit already penetrated, meanwhile overlooking pockets and strata in the same field which the nationals are not as able to reach as the foreign missionary! This is especially true when the "national church" unconsciously restricts the missionary to the limitations of its own

514

11

immediate vision. These sobering thoughts introduce us to our final section.

HOW CAN WE DO IT?

At this point, we could easily give up. The task seems so vast, so distant culturally, so complicated to tackle. What can possibly be the vehicle of all this special effort? Two thousand years give us only one answer: the para-church structure. There is powerful evidence that while Paul *began* at Antioch, he did not simply work out of Antioch. He apparently employed a "missionary band" structure or an "apostolic team" structure borrowed from the Pharisaic proselytizing movement, just as he borrowed the Jewish synagogue structure for his local churches. Thus then and now we see both church and mission—two separate, very different structures which must both be considered normal.

This understanding is crucial for the immense task we face. Roman Catholic orders girdled the globe for well over 200 years *after the Reformation* with essentially no Protestant competition until William Carey broke the logjam and launched the mission that catalyzed the formation of a dozen other missions in the next two decades. In the ensuing 175 years Protestants in general have never quite become used to the para-church structure.

We must become much better acquainted with the subject, however, because successful world evangelization depends almost totally on the proper relation of the para-church mission structure to the on-going churches in both the sending and receiving countries.

Taking first the relation of missions to sending churches, Graphic V.A shows four common relationships. Since we hope and pray (and plan?) for all churches everywhere to be *sending* churches, these relationships apply just as well to overseas churches and their relationship to *their own national missions*. But we'll pick that up in a moment.

GRAPHIC V.A.

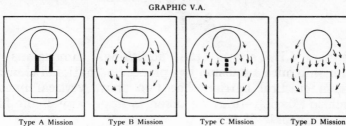

| Type A Mission | Type B Mission | Type C Mission | Type D Mission |

515

12

A *Type A Mission* is one that is (1) related to a specific church body; this is signified by the large circle; (2) administrated by that church through a board appointed by ecclesiastical processes; this is signified by the vertical bar on the left; and (3) funded by that church through a unified budget which discourages (or prevents) local churches from affecting the percentage going to the mission structure; this is signified by the vertical bar on the right and the *absence* of small arrows of relationship between the church and the mission.

A *Type B Mission* differs from Type A missions only in the elimination of the third characteristic mentioned. This type of mission raises its own support. It does not depend on a certain percentage of a church budget. Most Type A missions used to be of this kind.

A *Type C Mission*, such as the Conservative Baptist Foreign Mission Society, sustains a close relation to a church body (the Conservative Baptist Association) but neither its administration nor its budget are determined by the official processes of that church.

Type D Missions acknowledge no special relation to any specific church (although churches may choose to regard a certain Type D mission as their official expression in overseas work). All IFMA missions are of this type. By comparison, the EFMA includes all four types, and the DOM of the National Council includes mainly Type A structures.

GRAPHIC V.B.

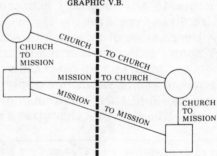

516

Graphic V.B. shows the additional dimensions of relationship once a mission has planted a "national church" across a cultural barrier. The two short vertical lines— Church-to-Mission—may be taken to imply any of the four cases in Graphic V.A.

13

Mission to Church. This relation may best be only temporary. Once a national church is able and autonomous it may choose to be related to a sister church directly rather than through a mission agency.

Church to Church. When a new national church is related directly to a sister church in a foreign land, this signifies full equality and maturity. This is why many U.S. churches have added a new office to handle these relations.

Mission to Mission. The tendency in some quarters is to phase out the older mission apparatus in favor of the church-to-church relationship. This is a profound mistake, since (as we have seen) the non-Christian world is not dwindling. Far better: encourage the national church to sponsor its own E-2 and E-3 outreach by means of its own mission initiative. This then allows the two mission structures to continue on, in relationship with each other, to complete the task of world evangelization.

If all churches are to become sending churches, they will be most effective only if they can express their energies through the mobile specific ministries carried on by dedicated mission structures. There are already more than 200 such agencies in the non-Western world. But there is still vast confusion both in the Western and non-Western world regarding the nature and destiny of the mission society. We need to be as concerned about the care and feeding of the mission structure as we are about the church structures.

Can we now "see" the task ahead? A relatively tiny trickle of missionaries from the Western world has, under God, produced over 200 million Christians in the non-Western world. Roughly half of these are in Africa, the other half in Asia. This is a significant achievement. It proves that Christianity, unlike any other religion, is truly universal. It provides an unprecedented base for what must, in the days ahead, be an unprecedentedly strong new push forward.

517

[1] *West* refers to all people of Western culture, whether in Europe, the Western hemisphere, Australia, New Zealand, South Africa, etc. For simplicity, all non-western peoples not in Africa are included here under *Asia,* such as those in Oceania, and New World aboriginals.

Graphic I.A. is drawn from the data in the following table which in turn is derived from Table IV in David Barrett's famous article "AD 2000: 350 Million Christians in Africa" in the January 1970 issue of the *International Review of Mission.* Note that he is calling *Christian* those who call themselves *Christian.*

14

This leaves Africa and Asia (as defined above) as the two large non-Christian continents. Also, since he gives world data for only the three yeas, 1900, 1965 and 2000, we have had to calculate the data for the intervening years 1975 and 1985, by using the average annual growth rate between 1965 and 2000.

Table VI.

	1900		1965		1975		1985		2000	
	NonCn	Cn	NonCn	Cn	NonCn	Cn	NonCn	Cn	NonCn	Cn
West	131	443	272	857	327	965	388	1101	500	1371
	.30 to 1		.32 to 1		.34 to 1		.35 to 1		.36 to 1	
Africa	114	4	231	75	282	116	337	181	417	351
	28.5 to 1		3.1 to 1		2.4 to 1		1.9 to 1		1.2 to 1	
Asia	896	12	1769	75	2114	98	2527	128	3297	192
	74.7 to 1		23.6 to 1		21.6 to 1		19.7 to 1		17.2 to 1	

Total Cn:	459	1007	1179	1410	1914
Total NonCn:	1241	2272	2723	3252	4214
Cn +NonCn:	1600	3279	3902	4662	6128

[2]These conclusions may be arrived at from the data in Table VI. For example, the number of African and Asian Christians in 1900 was 4 + 12 million, while today it is 116 + 98 million, or 13.375 times as great.

[3]Note that these rates are not the general biological growth rates for these areas of the world, nor are they the biological growth rates of specifically the Christian or non-Christian populations. In each case they consist of the biological rates plus (or minus) the effect of conversions from one group to the other.

[4]One of the rumors going around is simply, "The percentage of Christians in the world is getting smaller." This, it is said, is due to "the population explosion." We have seen that the percentage of Christians in Africa and Asia is markedly increasing not decreasing, despite the population explosion. Of this there is no question. How can people say that the overall number of Christians in the world is decreasing percentagewise? Easy: the great mass of Christians, nominal though they may be, has been in the Western world (defined in note #1). When Communism pulled a mass of these nominal Christians into nominal atheism there was a huge drop in the apparent number of Christians. At the same time Christians in Europe have been unable to win their children to true Christian faith. Finally, what Christians there were have decided on a zero population growth. What this does not mean, however, is that Christianity in the so-called mission lands cannot keep up with the very real population explosion in those areas of the world. There is where the crucial race is, and the presence or absence of population growth among Western Christians is not going to decide that issue.

[5]I am indebted for part of these data to the MARC office in Monrovia, California, but they must not be blamed for the guess work I have added in regard to other parts, growth rates, etc. Graphic II.B. cities 50,000 Protestant missionaries. This datum MARC offered to me in advance from their soon-to-appear *Mission Handbook: North American Protestant Ministries Overseas* (Monrovia: MARC, 1973).

[6]Alan Tippett has called this organic growth, because it involves the development of the internal structure of a social organism.

[7]Norman Cummings in a recent paper has presented this phrase as well as the underlying exegesis of the New Testament.

[8]A more extended discussion of this analysis, and many other characteristics of mission agencies, is found in a chapter entitled "Organization of Missions Today" in *Mission Handbook: North American Protestant Ministries Overseas* (Monrovia, MARC, 1973).

[9]An extended discussion of this diagram and this general subject is found in Chapter Seven, "Planting Younger Missions," in C. Peter Wagner, Editor, *Church/Mission Tensions Today* (Moody Press, 1973).

518

Five Expectations for the School of World Mission

by Donald McGavran

Fuller Seminary's School of World Mission is tied closely to the future of the whole missionary enterprise. So the five expectations I voice will begin with those for Christian mission and shift gradually to those for this School.

I. My First and Most Basic Expectation is That in the Midst of Rapid Changes the Deep Rooted Purpose of God for the Salvation of Men Will Continue.

It is not God's will that any should perish—though many will no doubt choose the broad way. Peter's great shout on the day of Pentecost will resound every day, till all have heard: "Repent and be baptized everyone of you in the name of Jesus Christ."

Paul tells us, as recorded in Romans 16:26, that "by command of the everlasting God the gospel has been revealed to bring the peoples of earth to the obedience of the faith." I expect the gospel to do that for which God has revealed it.

As the mighty Mississippi flows resistlessly south to the Gulf of Mexico, undeterred by eddies and contrary winds, so God's purpose for the salvation of men and nations through Jesus Christ continues resistlessly to disciple the nations.

Oh, some countries close to the gospel—for a few years. And some governments persecute the Church—till they fall. And some denominations go a-whoring after other gods—till Ahab dies. Midian oppresses the Hebrews—till God raises up Gideon. God's unswerving purpose will not be thwarted by ephemeral obstacles. His Word will prevail.

II. My Second Expectation Is That Today's Wide Receptivity to the Gospel Will Increase.

True, we have just passed through rough times. The rapidly changing world has required adjustments difficult to make. The political and military retreat of the West has jolted us. The treacherous attacks from within on the sanctity of the family and the authority of the Bible have damaged the Church. But grave as these and other dangers are, they must not hide from us the growing responsiveness of men and societies to Christ's call. Never have the people of God enjoyed so broad an opportunity to speak the message of eternal life. Never have as many men been as ready to become his disciples. Never have there been more winnable than there are today.

Responsiveness is caused by many factors. Let me mention three.

First is the glorious Good News itself. Nothing so attractive, so transforming, so applicable in every culture is to be found outside Christianity. No book can compare with the Bible. The Koran, the Ramayan, the Analects of Confucius, the writings of Marx and Mao—all are available in English. Go read them and you will come back to the Bible as from bran to bread.

Second is the tremendous church growth which *has* occurred in the last 200 years. For example, there are more Presbyterians in Indonesia than in America. The first church in all the world to seat 25,000 is being built in Brazil by a denomination not 25 years old. And in the United States itself, church members increased from less than a million in 1773 to over 100,000,000 in 1973.

Third, there is no viable alternative to Christianity. Hedonism? Agnosticism? Marxism? Scientism? Nihilism? All are poor indeed compared to the riches of Christ. Men see that even the poverty of Christ is greater wealth than the treasures of Egypt.

For all these reasons—and many more—I expect that *receptivity to the Gospel will steadily increase.*

III. My Third Expectation is That the School of World Mission Will Multiply the Export of Missionary Ideas.

The business of any institution of higher learning is to generate, teach, test and disseminate true ideas.

The quiet revolution spreading among many evangelical and some conciliar churches and missions has been greatly assisted by ideas developed at and exported from Fuller's School of World Mission.

This School has no administrative power in denominations and mission societies. Our influence comes solely through *ideas* taught to missionary and research associates studying here, written in articles and books, hotly debated around the world by seminars, lectures and workshops, and emphasized in a stream of publications.

We've been doing a fairly brisk export business in ideas!! Our missions professors don't have offices. They have *idea factories* and turn out a high quality product—gutty biblical theory of church growth and Christian mission. Dean Glasser has made notable contributions here. An intellectually defensible cohesive theory of missions. An anthropologically sound and sophisticated typology of evangelism. A liberating concept of the amazing cultural diversity of expanding Christianity which must be housed in the one overarching church of Jesus Christ. Have you read Dr. Kraft's fine article in the January 19, 1973 issue of *Christianity Today?* A kit of powerful research tools to dig up facts about the progress of Christianization. And when you think of historical understanding of awakenings, those bursts of divine power experienced by the Church—everyone thinks of Dr. Orr.

My third expectation is that this School of World Mission will greatly expand its research programs, multiply its research fellowships and increase production and export of life-giving, salvation-spreading ideas.

IV. My Fourth Expectation Is that Fuller's School of World Mission Will Make Many Advances, of Which I Mention only One: We Will Establish a Ph.D. in Missiology.

As increasing numbers of able men beat a path to our doors, we need to add to our fine professional doctorate, the academic degree, *doctor of philosophy in Missiology.*

We must end the intolerable situation in North America in the education of missionaries, whereby teachers cannot get a Ph.D. in Missiology. We now have the following ludicrous situation: because no man can get a Ph.D. in Missiology, a Ph.D. in education (like mine), or history, or linguistics, or anthropology is lamely accepted by American Association of Theological Schools as qualifying a man to teach *missions!*

This basic error handicaps the entire missionary enterprise. Fuller's professional degree now in operation has partially removed the handicap. Fuller's academic or research degree—yet to be instituted—will completely remove it.

Fuller has—largely through the brilliant work of Dr. Winter—organized scholars in North America interested in missions into the first American Society of Missiology. Dr. Tippett is the editor of its learned journal, titled simply *Missiology.*

This international recognition of missiology as a discipline in its own right opens the door for launching a program leading to the degree *doctor of philosophy in missiology.* I expect Fuller to march boldly through that door. Believe me, nothing would *more* enhance the influence of this School, nothing more benefit the spread of the gospel.

V. My Fifth Expectation Grows Out of a Dream.

As I taught missions in the late fifties, emphasizing church growth principles which apply in Asia, Africa and Latin America, American seminarians would say to me, "Your principles apply in this country also. Please found an *American Institute of Church Growth.*"

But, as the School of World Mission took shape, we had to devote our entire time to missions and church growth abroad. In the last six months however, due largely to Professor Wagner's initiative, it has become clear that the United States is ready for coast to coast church growth emphasis. Hundreds—perhaps thousands—of ministers, pastors and eminent laymen want church growth training.

Many experiments in church growth, now going on in the United States, should be drawn together: Kennedy's method of evangelism in Coral Ridge, Schuller's great demonstration of church growth in Garden Grove, the small group movement spreading everywhere, Campus Crusade's tremendous program of training laymen in evangelism and Graham's huge crusades so blessed of God.

The fifty to eighty million unchurched and the enormous numbers of young Christians who backslide in college and university, present memorable opportunities.

The day has dawned for a Domestic Institute of Church Growth with a faculty of church-planting ministers who are also qualified social scientists. The program will stress research in church growth in this country. Research will be done in all denominations. We'll discover why some American churches grow—and more do not. We'll teach all we discover and go out to discover more. We'll help create from coast to coast a conscience on church growth and through business-like publication disseminate information about how churches grow.

My fifth expectation is that this American Institute of Church Growth will take shape at Fuller Seminary.

These five expectations demand an adequate, well-equipped beautiful *missions building.* The magnificent site at the southern gateway to the campus has been set apart to house the whirring dynamo which is the School of World Mission. Research, teaching, publication, extension, archives, idea factories, seminar rooms, think tanks, map rooms, a global center of the vast missionary enterprise! This notable building, this beautiful symbol of the compassion of Christ, is a concrete expression of all five of my *expectations.*

I said expectations, not hopes. These are likely to happen. This is the way the land lies. This is the way history is moving. Human need demands this. This is what the Fuller Ten Year Plan, the Basic Purpose, the faculty and supporters want. In short, these expectations, I believe, lie in the will of God. As such I share them with you, my friends. ∎

ALVIN MARTIN, Missionary Educator

BORN October 25, 1919, near Magnolia, Minnesota
PARENTS Oscar and Hanna (Thu) Martin, both deceased
MARRIED Ruth Mildred Pierce, August 12, 1942
CHILDREN Daniel Lee, 1947; Keith Philip, 1949; Shirley
Ruth, 1952; Nathan Brian, 1954; Darrell John, 1961.

EDUCATION Graduate, St. Paul Bible Institute, 1942;
Graduate, Missionary Training Institute, Nyack, 1945;
Th.B., University of the State of New York, 1947;
M.A., B.D., Th.M., Winona Lake School of
Theology, 1955, 1958, and 1962;
N.Y. University and Biblical Seminary in N.Y., 1956;
The Hebrew University, Jerusalem, 1965;
The University of Judaism, Los Angeles, 1972;
D.Missiology, School of World Mission and Institute of
Church Growth, Fuller Theological Seminary, 1974.

VOCATION Ordained Minister, The Christian and Missionary
Alliance, 1944--;
Pastor, United Brethren Church, Grey Eagle, 1942-44;
Assistant Dean of Men, MTI, Nyack, 1945-47;
Christian and Missionary Alliance Missionary,
Israel, 1947-54, 1973;
Instructor, Canadian Bible College, Regina, 1956-58;
Founding Pastor of Fourth Ave. Alliance Church,
Regina, (Now Woodward Ave. Alliance), 1957-58;
President, Canadian Bible College, Regina, 1958-72;
Founding President, Canadian Theological College,
Regina, Saskatchewan, 1970-72;
Academic Dean, Summer Institute of International
Studies, 1974.
OTHER
ACTIVITIES Board of Directors, Canadian Bible College, 1958-72;
Member of Education Department, The Christian and
Missionary Alliance, 1958-72;
Vice President, Archibald Foundation, 1957-72;
Instructor of Hebrew, Chicago Graduate School of
Theology, 1969;
Founding President, Association of Canadian Bible
Colleges, 1967-68;
Member of Old Testament Translation Team, New
International Version, 1971--.

2   VITA, Alvin Martin

ASSOCIATION Evangelical Theological Society, 1958--
OR SOCIETY   National Association of Professors of Hebrew, 1959
MEMBERSHIPS American Society of Missiology, charter member, 19

HONORS &
AWARDS   Named Distinguished Alumnus of the Year, Winona
                 Lake School of Theology, 1968;
             Who's Who in Saskatchewan, 1969;
             Who's Who in the West, 1970--;
             Intercontinental Biographical Association
                 (Annual Fellow), 1971;
             International Scholars Directory, 1972;
             Men of Achievement, 1973.

THE MEANS

of world evangelization:

MISSIOLOGICAL EDUCATION

at the
Fuller School of World Mission

LATIN AMERICA

ANIMISTIC AYMARAS AND CHURCH GROWTH
Nordyke, Barclay. . . . . 3.45(2.07)
INDUSTRIALIZATION: BRAZIL'S CATALYST FOR
CHURCH GROWTH, Gates. . . . . . 1.95(1.17)
LATIN AMERICAN CHURCH GROWTH, Read,
Monterroso, Johnson, Eerdmans. . 8.95(5.37)
MAN, MILIEU, AND MISSION IN ARGENTINA,
Enns, Eerdmans. . . . . 3.95(2.37)
NEW PATTERNS OF CHURCH GROWTH IN BRAZIL
Read, Eerdmans. . . . . 2.45(1.47)
THE PROTESTANT MOVEMENT IN BOLIVIA
Wagner, WCL. . . . . 3.95(2.37)
THE ROLE OF THE FAITH MISSION: A
BRAZILIAN CASE STUDY, Edwards,
WCL. . . . . 3.45(2.07)
TINDER IN TABASCO, Bennett,
(on Mexico), Eerdmans. . . . . . 2.95(1.77)
AN URBAN STRATEGY FOR LATIN AMERICA,
Greenway, Baker . . . . 4.95(2.97)
---JUST OFF THE PRESS---
UNDERSTANDING LATIN AMERICANS, Nida,
WCL. . . . . 3.95(2.37)
BRAZIL 1980, MARC (no discount) . . 7.50(7.50)

FOREIGN LANGUAGE BOOKS

SPANISH:
AVANCE EVANGELICO EN LA AMERICA
LATINA, Read, Monterroso & Johnson,
CASA. . . . . .6.00(3.60)
LA SERPIENTE Y LA PALOMA (re: La
Iglesia Apostolica de la Fe de
Mexico), Gaxiola, WCL. . . . . .2.95(1.77)
MANUAL DEL CRECIMIENTO DE LA IGLESIA
Gerber, WCL (short discount) . . 1.25(1.00)
PRINCIPIOS DEL CRECIMIENTO DE LA IGLESIA
Weld & McGavran (A programmed
book). . . . . .3.95(2.37)
FRENCH:
EVANGELISATION ET CROISSANCE DE
L'EGLISE, Gerber, WCL (a short
discount book) . . . . .1.25(1.00)

CASSETTES

CHURCH GROWTH EYES I, McGavran . . . 3.50(2.10)
CHURCH GROWTH EYES II, McGavran. . . 3.50(2.10)
PEOPLE MOVEMENTS, McGavran . . . . . 3.50(2.10)
FIVE KINDS OF LEADERS, McGavran. . . 3.50(2.10)
WITHOUT CROSSING BARRIERS, THE CULTURAL
MOSAIC, McGavran. . . . . 3.50(2.10)
THE CRUCIAL PROBLEM IN MISSIONS,
McGavran. . . . . 3.50(2.10)
GARDEN GROVE WONDER: Schuller's Talks
to Ministers. Set of 4. (Include
$1.20 for postage and handling) 13.95(6.97)
MISSIONS AHEAD, Moffett. . . . . . . 3.50(2.10)

REFERENCE

BIBLIOGRAPHY FOR CROSS-CULTURAL
WORKERS, Tippett, WCL, cloth . . 5.95(3.57)
paper . . 3.95(2.37)
CHURCH GROWTH BULLETIN, Vols.I-V, VI-IX
McGavran, Editor, WCL . . . . . 4.95(2.97)
cloth . . 6.95(4.17)
ENCYCLOPEDIA OF MODERN CHRISTIAN MISSIONS:
THE AGENCIES, Goddard, ed.,
Gordon Conwell. . . . . .25.00(8.95)
EVANGELICAL MISSIONS QUARTERLY, FIRST
6 YEARS, in 2 vols. WCL
cloth . .14.95(8.97)
THE GOSPEL AND GRONTIER PEOPLES,
R. Pierce Beaver, ed. WCL. . . . 2.95(1.77)
THE NEW ENGLISHMAN'S GREEK CONCORDANCE
Sigram, WCL, cloth . . 9.95(5.97)
THE WORLD DIRECTORY OF MISSION-RELATED
EDUCATIONAL INSTITUTIONS, Buker &
Ward, WCL. . . . . 19.95(11.97)
---JUST OFF THE PRESS---
AN AMERICAN DIRECTORY OF SCHOOLS & COLLEGES
OFFERING MISSIONS COURSES, Schwartz,
WCL. . . . . 9.95x(2.36)
EVANGELICAL MISSIONS QUARTERLY, Vols. 7-10
WCL. . . . . 8.98(5.37)
MANUAL OF ARTICULATORY PHONETICS,
Smalley, (short discount). . . . 3.95(3.16)
MISSIONS HANDBOOK (10th ed. of
NORTH AMERICAN PROTESTANT MINISTRIES
OVERSEAS DIRECTORY, MARC (no
discount). . . . . 10.00(10.00)
WORLD DIRECTORY OF RADIO AND TELEVISION
BROADCASTING, ICB, WCL, cloth. 19.95(11.97)

OTHER

GROWTH AND LIFE IN THE LOCAL CHURCH,
Porter, WCL. . . . . 1.95(1.17)

MESSIANIC MOVEMENTS, Oosterwal, Institute
of Mennonite Studies in Edinburgh1.00(.60)

MISSIOLOGY: AN INTERNATIONAL REVIEW
(quarterly) Official organ of the
American Society of Missiology)
Yearly subscription rate. 8.00

REACH OUT (New Testament "Living"
transl), Taylor, Tyndale. . . . .2.95(1.77)

LIVING BIBLE (whole Bible paraphrased)
Taylor, Tyndale cloth . . . .9.95(5.97)

Conditions of Membership

BOOKS ON CHURCH GROWTH

BUILDING CHRISTIAN COMMUNITIES,
Clark, Ave Maria Press. . . . . . 1.50(.90)
CHURCH GROWTH AND GROUP CONVERSION
Pickett, McGavran, etc. WCL . . 2.45(1.47)
CHURCH GROWTH AND THE WORD OF GOD
Tippett, Eerdmans. . . . . 1.95(1.17)
GOD, MAN, AND CHURCH GROWTH
Tippett, ed., Eerdmans . . . . . . 7.95(4.77)
THE GROWING CONGREGATION, Benjamin,
(book & workbook), Lincoln
College Press. . . . . 3.25(1.95)
HOW CHURCHES GROW, McGavran,
Friendship. . . . . 3.50(2.10)
HOW TO START A DAUGHTER CHURCH,
Benson. . . . . .93(.60)
GOD'S WAY TO KEEP A CHURCH GOING AND
GROWING, Gerber, Regal. . . . . . 1.45(.87)
UNDERSTANDING CHURCH GROWTH,
McGavran, Eerdmans . . . . 3.95(2.37)
WHY CONSERVATIVE CHURCHES ARE GROWING,
Kelley, Harper. . . . . 6.95(5.21)
---JUST OFF THE PRESS---
A GUIDE TO CHURCH PLANTING,
Hodges, Moody. . . . . 1.50(.90)
HOW TO GROW A CHURCH,
McGavran & Arn, Regal Bks. . . . . 2.95(1.77)
HOW BIBLICAL IS THE CHURCH GROWTH MOVEMENT?
McQuilkin, Moody. . . . . 1.95(1.17)
THE INDIGENOUS CHURCH, Hodges,
Gospel Publishing House. . . . . . 2.00(1.20)
THE PLANTING AND DEVELOPMENT OF
MISSIONARY CHURCHES, Nevius,
Presby. & Ref. Pub. Co. . . . . . 1.75(1.05)

THEOLOGY OF MISSIONS

A BIBLICAL THEOLOGY OF MISSIONS,
Peters, Moody . . . . .6.95(4.17)
SHAKEN FOUNDATIONS: THEOLOGICAL
FOUNDATIONS FOR MISSION, Beyerhaus,
Zondervan . . . . .1.95(1.17)
VERDICT THEOLOGY IN MISSIONARY THEORY,
Tippett, WCL. . . . . .4.95(2.97)

POPULARIZING MISSIONS

SAY YES TO MISSION, Winter, WCL, less
than 10 only with another order .25(.15)
GIVE UP YOUR SMALL AMBITIONS, Griffiths,
Moody. . . . . .1.95(1.17)
LANGUAGE AND FAITH, Wycliffe
Bible Trans. . . . . 3.95(2.37)
THE VALIDITY OF THE CHRISTIAN
MISSION, Trueblood, Harper &
Row (25% off only) . . . . 2.95(2.36)
---JUST OFF THE PRESS---
STOP THE WORLD I WANT TO GET ON
Peter Wagner, Regal. . . . . . . .1.95(1.17)

PRACTICAL HELPS

MANUAL FOR ACCEPTED MISSIONARY CANDIDATES
Marjorie Collins, WCL. . . . . . .2.45(1.47)
MANUAL FOR MISSIONARIES ON FURLOUGH
Marjorie Collins, WCL. . . . . . .2.95(1.77)
THE MISSIONARY WIFE AND HER WORK
Joy Turner Tuggy, Moody. . . . . .3.95(2.37)
GOD'S WORD IN MAN'S LANGUAGE,
Nida, WCL. . . . . .2.95(1.77)

ASIA

ASPECTS OF PACIFIC ETHNOHISTORY,
Tippett, WCL. . . . . 3.95(2.37)
BATAK BLOOD AND PROTESTANT SOUL,
Pedersen, Eerdmans. . . . . 3.95(2.37)
A HISTORY OF CHRISTIANITY IN JAPAN,
Drummond, Eerdmans. . . . . 4.95(2.97)
AN HOUR TO THE STONE AGE, Horne,
Moody. . . . . 2.95(1.77)
LAITY MOBILIZED: REFLECTIONS ON CHURCH
GROWTH IN JAPAN AND OTHER LANDS,
Braun, Eerdmans. . . . . 3.95(2.37)
MO BRADLEY AND THAILAND, Lord,
Eerdmans . . . . 3.95(2.37)
NEW TESTAMENT FIRE IN THE PHILIPPINES
Montgomery, CGRIP. . . . . 2.50(1.50)
NOTES ON CHRISTIAN OUTREACH IN A PHILIPPINE
COMMUNITY, Mayers . . . . 1.45(.87)
PEOPLE MOVEMENTS IN SOUTHERN POLYNESIA
Tippett, Moody . . . . 6.95(4.17)
THE PHILIPPINE CHURCH: GROWTH IN A
CHANGING SOCIETY, Tuggy . . . . . 3.45(2.07)
SEEING THE CHURCH IN THE PHILIPPINES
Tuggy & Toliver, OMF. . . . . . . 2.50(1.50)
THE UNRESPONSIVE, RESISTANT OR NEGLECTED:
Liao, Moody. . . . . 2.95(1.77)
WILDFIRE: CHURCH GROWTH IN KOREA,
Shearer, Eerdmans. . . . . 2.95(1.77)
---NEW LISTINGS---
CHRISTIAN MASS MOVEMENTS IN INDIA,
Pickett. . . . . 2.50(1.50)
SINGAPORE: THE CHURCH IN THE MIDST OF
SOCIAL CHANGE, Wong. . . . . 3.95(2.37)

EUROPE

THE CHALLENGE FOR EVANGELICAL
MISSIONS TO EUROPE: A SCANDINAVIAN
CASE STUDY, Malaska. . . . . . . .2.45(1.47)
THE PROTESTANT MOVEMENT IN ITALY:
ITS PROGRESS, PROBLEMS, AND PROSPECTS,
Hedlund, WCL. . . . . .3.95(2.37)
PROTESTANTS IN MODERN SPAIN: A STRUGGLE
FOR RELIGIOUS PLURALISM,
Vought, WCL . . . . 3.45(2.07)

AFRICA

APPROACHING THE NUER OF AFRICA THROUGH
THE OLD TESTAMENT, McFall, WCL. . 1.95(1.17)
CHURCH GROWTH IN CENTRAL AND SOUTHERN
NIGERIA, Grimley, Robinson,
Eerdmans. . . . . 3.25(1.95)
CHURCH GROWTH IN SIERRA LEONE, Olson,
Eerdmans. . . . . 3.95(2.37)
THE DISCIPLING OF WEST CAMEROON:
A STUDY OF BAPTIST GROWTH,
Kwast, Eerdmans . . . . 3.45(2.07)
GOD'S IMPATIENCE IN LIBERIA
Wold, Eerdmans. . . . . 2.95(1.77) **477**
PEOPLES OF SOUTHWEST ETHIOPIA,
Tippett, WCL . . . . 3.95(2.37)
THE PLANTING OF CHURCHES IN SOUTH AFRICA
Sales, Eerdmans . . . . 3.45(2.07)
PROFILE FOR VICTORY: NEW PROPOSALS FOR
MISSIONS IN ZAMBIA, Randall, WCL. 3.95(2.37)
TONGA CHRISTIANITY, Shewmaker, WCL . 3.45(2.07)

The editor of the Church Growth Bulletin, knowing how difficult it is for missionaries around the world to know where to get Church Growth Books, their price, and what is available, is printing the following complete list of books available to Club members.

THE CHURCH GROWTH BOOK CLUB

305 Pasadena Ave., South Pasadena, California 91030, U.S.A. (213) 682-2047

All paid up subscribers to the Church Growth Bulletin have membership privileges

March Selection: Breaking the Stained Glass Barrier

On page 352 we have discussed the book selected for this month's emphasis. The book is a Harper book, and consequently the Club could not obtain it at its usual discount rate. In fact, in order to get a discount even near the usual rate, the Club has to buy 500 copies at a time. Therefore, even though this book is a valuable book for your library, it is being offered on a once-only basis. Until the 500 copies are exhausted, and only until then, will it be available. Standing order members receive theirs automatically. All others who wish this book, write immediately. The retail price is $5.95. Your price is $3.87 + 35¢ postage and handling. (Add 5% tax if you are a California resident.) Since this is the selection for March, it may be ordered by itself without the additional 50¢ charge for an order of less than 3 books if when ordering you state that it is the selection and if your letter is postmarked before May 1, 1974.

GENERAL

MISSION STRATEGY

ALL LOVES EXCELLING, Beaver,
Eerdmans . . . . 2.95(1.77)
BRIDGES OF GOD, McGavran,
Friendship . . . . 2.50(1.50)
CALL TO MISSION, Neill,
Fortress . . . . 2.50(1.50)
THE CHURCH AND CULTURES, Luzbetak,
Divine Word. . . . . 3.95(2.37)
CHURCH/MISSION TENSIONS TODAY
Wagner, ed., Moody . . . . . . 4.95(2.97)
CROSSROADS IN MISSIONS, Blaw,
Sherer, Lefever, Street,
Beaver, WCL (5 books in 1) . . 9.95(5.97)
CRUCIAL ISSUES IN MISSIONS TOMORROW
McGavran, editor, Moody. . . . 4.95(2.97)
DYNAMICS OF CHURCH GROWTH,
Picket, Abingdon   Cloth . . 2.50(1.50)
THE EVANGELICAL RESPONSE TO
BANGKOK, Winter, ed. WCL . . . 1.95(1.17)
EYE OF THE STORM THE GREAT DEBATE
IN MISSIONS, Word   Cloth . . 6.95(4.17)
FRONTIERS IN MISSION STRATEGY,
Peter Wagner, Moody   Cloth . . 4.95(2.97)
THE FUTURE OF THE CHRISTIAN WORLD
MISSION, Danker, Kang,
Eerdmans   Cloth . . 5.95(3.57)
AN INTRODUCTION TO THE SCIENCE OF
MISSIONS, Bavinck, Pres.&Ref. . 3.50(2.10)
LOOK OUT, THE PENTECOSTALS ARE
COMING, Wanger, Creation . . . . 4.95(2.97)
MESSAGE AND MISSION,
Nida, WCL . . . . 3.95(2.37)
THE MINISTRY OF THE SPIRIT,
Allen, Eerdmans. . . . . 1.95(1.17)
MISSIONARY METHODS: ST. PAUL'S
OR OUR'S? Allen, Eerdmans . . . 1.95(1.17)
MISSIONS IN THE SEVENTIES,
Boberg & Scherer, editors,
Chicago Cluster. . . . . 5.00(3.00)
MISSIONS FROM THE THIRD WORLD
Wong, editor, Church Growth Study
Center . . . . 2.95(1.77)
MISSIONS: WHICH WAY?
Beyerhaus, Zondervan . . . . . 1.95(1.17)
MOBILIZING FOR SATURATION EVANGELISM
Taylor, Coggins, EMIS. . . . . 2.95(1.77)
PROFIT FOR THE LORD
Danker, Eerdmans. . . . . . . .3.95(2.37)

THE REVOLUTIONARY MASSES AND CHRIST'S
WILL, McGavran, WCL . . . . . . .50(.30
SPONTANEOUS EXPANSION OF THE CHURCH
Allen, Eerdmans . . . . .1.95(1.17
TO APPLY THE GOSPEL, SELECTIONS FROM THE
WRITINGS OF VENN, Warren. . . .6.95(4.17
TO ADVANCE THE GOSPEL, Pierce
Beaver, Eerdmans. . . . . . . .5.95(3.50
THE WARP AND WOOF: ORGANIZING FOR
MISSION, Winter, Beaver, WCL. . .1.25(.75
WINDS OF CHANGE IN CHRISTIAN MISSIONS,
Moody   2.25(1.35

HISTORY OF MISSIONS

CAMPUS AFLAME, Orr, Regal Bks. . . .2.95(1.77
THE FLAMING TONGUE, Orr, Moody . . .4.95(2.97
A GLOBAL VIEW OF WORLD MISSIONS
Kane, Baker. . . . . 8.95(5.37
A HISTORY OF CHRISTIANITY (1500 pgs.
in 1 vol.), Latourette, Harper
& Row, short discount. . . . . 11.95x(9.45
HISTORIC PATTERNS OF CHURCH GROWTH,
Cook, Moody . . . . 1.95(1.17
THE HOLDEMAN PEOPLE: THE CHURCH OF GOD
IN CHRIST, MENNONITE, 1859-1969,
Hiebert, WCL . . . . .17.95(10.
STUDENT POWER IN WORLD EVANGELISM,
Howard, IV Press. . . . . 1.25(.
THE TWENTY-FIVE UNBELIEVABLE YEARS,
1945-1969, Winter, WCL. . . . . 1.95(1.

BIOGRAPHY

GIVE THE WINDS A MIGHTY VOICE,
THE STORY OF CHARLES E. FULLER OF
THE OLD FASHIONED REVIVAL HOUR,
Fuller, Word. . . . . .5.95(3.
DAKTAR, Viggi Olson, Moody . . . . .5.95(3.
JUSTINIAN WELZ: EARLY PROPHET OF MISSION,
Scherer, Eerdmans . . . . .2.45(1.
MO BRADLEY AND THAILAND, Lord,
Eerdmans. . . . . .3.95(2.
PHYSICIAN TO THE MAYAS, Barton,
Fortress. . . . . .5.95(3.
STRACHAN OF COSTA RICA: MISSIONARY
INSIGHTS AND STRATEGIES, Roberts,
Eerdmans. . . . . .2.95(1.
A YANKEE REFORMER IN CHILE: THE LIFE AND
WORKS OF DAVID TRUMBULL, Paul, WCL 3.95(2.

476

HURCH GROWTH
BULLETIN

INSTITUTE OF
CHURCH GROWTH

Address:
FULLER THEOLOGICAL
SEMINARY
135 N. Oakland
Pasadena, Calif. 91101

DONALD A. McGAVRAN, B.D., Ph.D.
Director

November 1973   Subscription $1 per year   Volume X No. 2

CONTENTS

ARTICLES

CLEAR THINKING ON MISSION(S)
by
Dr. Alan R. Tippett

Missions, the human organizations, must be distinguished from mission, the assignment received as a mandate from our Lord. Discussion
of one also involves the other. The validity of the church's institu-
tionalized program depends on the validity of the idea of mission,
namely, that Christ commanded his followers to bring the lost to him
for salvation.

The ethical validity of this idea is under attack from inside and
outside the church, and especially from universalists. Against evange-   475
listic (converting) missions it is popularly reasoned that Christian ex-
clusivism (Christ being claimed as the only way - John 14:6: Acts 4:12)
(1) is an affront on rational human personality, (2) is monological
proclamation in a day which demands dialogue, (3) fails to recognize
the divine in non-Christian religions, (4) is divisive and hinders ecumenicity, and (5) savors of antequated revivalism and church extension
when new forms are needed. These critics would redefine such terms as

SEND correspondence, news, and articles to the Editor, Dr. Donald McGavran, at the Institute
of Church Growth, Fuller Theological Seminary. Published bi-monthly, send subscriptions
and changes of address to the Business Manager, Norman L. Cummings, Overseas Crusades,
Inc., 265 Lytton Avenue, Palo Alto, California 94301, U.S.A. Second-class postage paid at
Palo Alto, California.

7.

CHURCH GROWTH BULLETIN, BOOK CLUB
AND AMERICAN SOCIETY OF MISSIOLOGY

ames Wong 38600 Dundee Road ngapore 3	Bill Yang 38950 1471 Wesley Ave. Pasadena, Ca. 91104	Norvald Yri 39200 P.O. Box 40 Sidamo Prov. Ethiopia
erb Works 38800 360 Patterson Court ugene, Ore. 97405	Dr. Donald Yates 39000 221 S. 6th St. Terre Haute, Ind. 48701	Helen Yu 39300 Mrs. Albert Wu 980 Summer N.E. Salem, Ore. 97301
ayland Wong 38700 524 El Camino Dr. osemead, Ca. 91770	John Yoon 39100 I.P.O. 3476 Seoul, Korea	
ed Yamamori 38900 illigan College illigan, Tenn.	Joseph Young 39150 1675 Amberwood Dr. No. 8 South Pasadena, Ca. 91030	

471

Smuts Van Rooyen   35700
5327 Sierra Vista
Riverside, Ca. 92505

William Van Tol   35800
S.U.M. Serti
Mt. View Hostel-Box 261
Jos, Nigeria

Trung Van Tot (Toke)
Evang. Ch. of Vietnam
30, Huynh Guang Tien
Saigon, Vietnam

Eino Johannes Vehanen 36000
2126 Furushiro Machi
Yatsushiro Shi
Kumamoto Ken 866
Japan

Rodney Venberg   36100
B.P. 7
Pala, Chad
Africa

Duain Vierow   36180
Box 1068 Jalan Semangat
Petaling Jaya Selangor
Malaysia

John Vigus   36200
6 Fortescue St.
E. Fremantle
Western Australia 6158

Ceferino Villegas   36250
320 Mission Rd.
Glendale, Ca. 91205

470

Janvier Voelkel   36300
Carrera 28 #46-06
Bogota 2, Colombia S.A.

Charles S. Vore   36350

Dale Vought   36400
Talia 26
Madrid 22, Spain

Abe Vreeke   36500
Mt. View C.R.C. Hostel
261 Jos
Northern Nigeria, W. Africa

C. Peter Wagner   36600
2440 Santa Rosa Ave.
Altadena, Ca. 91001

Lester Wait   36700
Overseas Crusades
265 Lytton Ave.
Palo Alto, Ca. 94301

Orlando Waltner   36800
Gen. Conf. Mennonite
Newton, Kans.

John Wang   36850
130 N. Oakland Ave.
Pasadena, Ca. 91101

Bruce Warner   36900
P.O. Box 358
Medan, Sumatera Utara
Indonesia

Hazel Watson   36990
19 7 2 Chm Uehara
Shibuya Ku
Tokyo 15 1, Japan

Leslie Watson   37000
19 7 2 Chm Uehara
Shibuya Ku
Tokyo, Japan

Hans Weerstra   37200
Lic. Eduardo Vasconcelos
Tlacolula, Oaxaca
Mexico

Wayne Weld   37300
Apartado Aereo 3041
Medellin, Colombia
South America

Edwin Wentz   37400
1269-5 Akasegawa
Akune Shi, Kagoshima Ken
899-16 Japan

Norman Wetther   37
C.B.H.M.S. Office
Box 828
Wheaton, Ill. 60187

   37
   37
Mr. & Mrs. Stanley Wick
San Cristobal de Totonic
Guatemala, C.A.

Hans Wilhelm   37
Overseas Crusades
265 Lytton Ave.
Palo Alto, Ca. 94301

Robert Willman   37
Box 153
Taichung, Taiwan
Rep. of China

Jack Wing   38
Mision Evangelico Amigos
Gracias Lempiro
Honduras, C.A.

Harry Winslow   38
Box 63
Pingtung
Taiwan, Rep. of China

Robert Winters   38
CBFMS
P.O. Box 5
Wheaton, Ill. 60187

Ruth Wintersteen   38
Box 2323
Addis Ababa
Ethiopia

Joseph Wold   38
Box 1046
Monrovia, Liberia

Thomas Wolf   38
715 S. Brady
Los Angeles, Ca. 90022

Fred Wolff   38
Las Magnolias 495
San Isidro
Lima, Peru

Stock   33000
Date Ave.
ance, Ca. 90503

Strunk   33100
a Postal 2561
00 Belo Horizonte, M.G.
il

ata Subbamma   33200
Cross Rd.
ienet, Andhra Pradesh
a

s Sunda   33300
Kimball Rd.
his, Tenn. 38111

hiro Suzuki   33350

n Swanson   33400
Lane 241
a Rd.
hung, Taiwan

on Swanson   33500
Bellevue Dr.
dale, Ca. 91205

s Tai   33600
Ford Pl. #11
lena, Ca. 91101

hiro Takami   33700
Nozuta, Machida Shi
, Japan

John Tamahori   33735
John's College
and 5, New Zealand

n Tank   33750
huan Rd., #6
n. Hualien
an. Rep. of China

Francis Van Tate   33800
Harding College
Box 615
Searcy, Ark. 72143

Lopeti Taufa   33900
Pacific Theol. College
Box 388
Suva, Fiji Islands

Jack Taylor   34000
Texas Probation Tr. Project
9821 Katy Freeway
Suite 58
Houston, Texas 77024

Samuel Taylor   34100
130 N. Oakland Ave.
Pasadena, Ca. 91101

Herman Tegenfeldt   34200
Bethel Theol. Seminary
3949 Bethel Dr.
St. Paul, Minn. 55112

John Thannickle   34300
8603 Bright Ave.
Whittier, Ca. 90608

Harold Thomas   34400
Casilla 544
La Paz, Bolivia

Clancy Thompson   34500
c/o Dr. Kilpatrick
Free Methodist Bd.
Winona Lake, Ind.

J. Donald Thomas, M.D. 34600
3700 Mayfair
Pasadena, Ca. 91107

Neil Thompson   34700
c/o Union Memorial Hospital
33rd & Calvert Sts.
Baltimore, Md. 21218

William Thompson   34800
2887 Potter St.
Eugene, Ore. 97405

Abraham Thottungal   34900
Malabra Marthoma Syrian
Christian Evang. Assoc.
Tiruvalla, Kerala
India

Ronald Thurman   35000
Jl. May. Jen. Haryono
Malang (East Java)
Indonesia

Ralph Toliver   35100
O.M.F.
237 W. School House Lane
Philadelphia, Pa. 19144

John Tooke   35150
96 N. Catalina
Pasadena, Ca. 91106

Arthur Trevor   35200
59, Nishino
Teine, Sapporo 065
Hokkaido, Japan

Philip Tsuchiya   35300
465 Ford Pl., #1
Pasadena, Ca. 91205

Leonard Tuggy   35400
320 E. Mission Rd.
Glendale, Ca. 91205

Jean Underwood   35450
784 Santa Barbara St.
Pasadena, Ca. 91101   469

John Underwood   35455
784 Santa Barbara St.
Pasadena, Ca. 91101

Paul Utley   35500
909 E. Carter
Marion, Ill. 62959

Johan Vandenburg   35600
6, Min Chuan 6 St.
Meilun Hwalien
Taiwan

Charlotte Self 30110
13521 Gershon Pl.
Santa Ana, Calif. 92705

Warren Simandle 31000
1237 A Clayton St.
San Francisco, Ca. 94114

James Sohn 32000
121-3 Rokbon Dong
Suedai Moon Ku
Seoul, Korea

Paul Selleck 30200
814 Sunset Drive
Wabash, Ind. 46902

Stewart Simpson 31100
20 Surrey St.
East Bentleigh
Victoria, Australia 3165

Dagfinn Solheim 32100
3-39 Chimorimachi
1-chome, Suma-du
Kobe 654, Japan

Roy Shearer 30300
608 S.E. 104th Ave.
Vancouver, Wa. 98664

Lalthankhum Sinate 31200

Kenneth Speer 32200
Casilla 14807
Correo 21
Santiago, Chile

J. Stanford Shewmaker 30400
Mujulanyana Village
Box 224
Livingstone, Zambia AFRICA

Alexander Sinclair 31250
Box 21102
Phoenix, Ariz. 85036

Frederick Sprunger 32300
Takao Cho, 3 Chome
25 Gaiko 24
Miyakonojo, Miyazaki Ken
Japan

Samuel Shewmaker 30500
Box 330
Choma, Zambia AFRICA

Roger Singer 31300
108 Springs Ave.
Gettysburg, Pa. 17325

Hugh Sprunger 32400
Box 165
Taichung, Taiwan 400
Rep. of China

Merlin Shields 30600
Caixa Postal 203
Goiania, Goias
Brazil

Samuel Skivington 31400
Box 1110
Makati, Rizal D-708
Philippines

Erwin Spruth 32500
New Guinea Lutheran Miss.
Wabag, New Guinea

Benjamin Shinde 30630
130 N. Oakland Ave.
Pasadena, Ca. 91101

Ebbie Smith 31500
Box 1, Kediri
Java, Indonesia

Richard Standerwick 32590
1353 Elizabeth St.
Pasadena, Ca. 91104

Harold Shock 30700

468

Elaine Smith 31600

Vernon Stanley 32600
125 S. Minnesota Ave.
Glendora, Calif. 91740

J. Timothy Shumaker 30800
c/o Rev. B. Willard
605 Curtis St.
Nogales, Ariz. 85621

Eugene Smith 31700
2823 Riverview St.
Eugene, Ore. 97403

Wayne Stephens 32700
3675 Chino Ave.
Chino, Ca. 91710

Werner Sidler 30900
Missionheim
3625 Heiligenschwendi
Switzerland

Mickey Smith 31800
c/o Christian Missy. Fellow.
P.O. Box 1189
Addis Ababa, Ethiopia

Philip Steyne 32800
R.D.2
Conestoga, Pa. 17516

Ed Silvoso 30985
350 S. Madison #207
Pasadena, Ca.

Mont Smith 31900
Northwest Christian College
11th & Altar
Eugene, Oregon 97403

Josephine Still 32900
715 S. Bradley, Apt. 17
Santa Maria, Ca. 93454

R.E. Reimer 506-52-4310
Christian & Missionary Alli.
FPO San Francisco, Ca. 96620

27400

Vernon Reimer 27500
Apartado Aereo 6557
Cali, Colombia

Herminio Reyes 27600
717 Santa Barbara, Apt. 1
Pasadena, Ca. 91101

Norman Riddle 27700
c/o 6180 Via Real
Carpinteria, Ca. 93103

Kenneth Rideout 27800
Box 881
Bangkok, Thailand

William Rife 27900
Pacific Ocean Miss. Inc.
Box 901
Guam 96910

Sang Kook Ro 28000
400 W. 122nd St.
New York, N.Y. 10027

Gordon Robinson 28100
PBM 5113
Ibadan, Nigeria

James Robinson 28150
526 S. Greenleaf
Whittier, Calif. 90602

Milton Robinson 28200
Casilla 6096
La Paz, Bolivia

Ruth Ann Robinson 28300
Casilla 6096
La Paz, Bolivia

Jack Roeda 28350
108 S. Chester Ave.
Pasadena, Ca. 91106

Paul Roland 28400
3-22 Gomen-Cho
Nishinomiya 662
Japan

Joel Romero 28500
Casilla 364
Tucaman, Argentina

Elmer Root 28600
3252 S. 182nd Pl.
Seattle, Wash. 98188

Loretta Root 28700
c/o Dr. Kilpatrick
Free Methodist Bd.
Winona Lake, Ind. 46590

Charles Ross 28800
E.C.Z., Kananga
B.P. 117
Rep. of Zaire

Shem Rubaale 28850
130 N. Oakland Ave.
Pasadena, Calif. 91101

Murray Russell 28900
461 Central Ave.
First Presby. Church
Fillmore, Ca. 93015

George Samuel 29000
P.O. No. 16
Tiruvalia
Kerala, India

Philip Sandahl 29050
1619 Las Lunas
Pasadena, Ca. 91106

Richard Sanner 29060
1509 Oxford Ave.
Pasadena, Ca. 91104

Ezra Sargunam 29100
5 Waddell Rd.
Kelpauk, Madras
Tamilnadu 600010 India

James Sauder 29200
Box 77
La Ceiba
Honduras, C.A.

Peter Savage 29300
Casilla 2475
Cochabamba, Bolivia

Sheldon Sawatsky 29400
Box 165
Taichung, Taiwan 400

David Schneider 29500
5977 Thurston Rd.
Springfield, Oregon

Mary Schneider 29600
c/o Sudan Interior Mission
Cedar Grove, N.J. 07009

Roger Schrage 29700
Gospel Light Publications
110 W. Broadway
Glendale, Ca. 91204

George Schroeder 29800
U.M.S. Box 171
Ilorin, Nigeria

467

John Schwab 29900
12-8 Narita Nishi 1-Chome
Suginami Ku, Tokyo 166
Japan

Glenn Schwartz 30000
1543 Topeka St.
Pasadena, Ca. 91104

Miriam Seger 30100
Apartado 78
Puebla, Pueblo, Mexico

Elwin Pelletier 24600
Baptist Miss., Kisoro
via Kabale
Uganda, East Africa

Taylor Pendley 24700
304 Baptist Bldg.
Dallas, Texas 75228

Edward Pentecost 24800
527 N. Madison
Pasadena, Ca. 91101

Pablo Perez 24900
3909 Swiss Ave.
Dallas, Texas 75204

Roger Perkins 25000
Caixa Postal 100
Sobradinho
Brasilia, D.F. Brazil

Lorene Persons 25100
Christ's Center
Lexington, Ky.

Dorothy Peters 25200
997 Onakazato
Fujinomiya-shi
Shizuoka-ken 418 Japan

Abraham Philip 25300
144 N. Los Robles
Pasadena, Ca. 91101

466

Thomas Philip 25400
Marukara-Maramom P.O.
Kerala, India

M. Saku Pinola 25420
1440 Elizabeth St.
Pasadena, Ca. 91104

Daryl Platt 25460
1594 E. Howard St.
Pasadena, Ca. 91104

Jim Pomayayitch 25500
Northwestern Christian College
11th & Altar
Eugene, Ore.

Paul Pomerville 25525
Assemblies of God D. For.Miss.
1445 Boonville Ave.
Springfield, Mo. 65803

Cathy Pott 25575
1612 N. Hill Ave.
Pasadena, Ca. 91104

Hank Pott 25580
1612 N. Hill Ave.
Pasadena, Ca. 91104

Ernest Poulson 25600
Singapore Bible College
9-11 Adam Rd.
Singapore 11

Melvin Pownall 25700
Northside Ch. of Christ
2130 N. Grand Ave.
Santa Ana, Ca. 92701

Douglas Priest 25800
Box 1189
Addis Ababa, Ethiopia

Marjorie Priest 25900
Box 1189
Addis Ababa, Ethiopia

Ted Profitt 26000
15631 Gaymont Dr.
La Mirada, Ca. 90638

Glenn Prunty 26100
Apartado 5273
Panama City 5-Ind. Miss. Bd.
Panama

Dorothy Raber 26200
Box 11450
Kaohsiung, Taiwan
Republic of China 800

Paul Rader 2630
Salvation Army
Intl. P.O. Box 1192
Seoul, Korea

David Rambo 2640
Canadian Theol. College
4400 4th Ave.
Regina, Sask., CANADA

Nene Ramientos 265
Philippines Crusades
Box 2557
Manila, Philippines

Max Randall 266
104 Carter Lane
Lincoln, Ill. 62656

Walter Rasch 267
Box 20, Ogoja
S.E. State
Nigeria

Herbert Ratcliff 268
Box 1245
Port of Spain
Trinidad, W. Indies

William R. Read 269
Bear Creek Presbyterian
3101 South Kipling Stree
Denver, Colorado

Albert Reasoner 270
Pres. Miss. Ch.
Caixa Postal 100
Sobradinho, Brasilia, D.
Brazil

Grady Wood Reed 271
Box 365
Livingstone, Zambia
AFRICA

Jerold Reed 272
847 Santa Barbara
Pasadena, Ca. 91101

Niles Reimer 273
American Mission
Pokwo
Gambela, Ethiopia

ldred Morehouse   21700
l Hakwuku
nogawa-ku
kohama, Japan 221

nes Morris   21800
F Bible Training Center
ayao, Chiang Rai
ailand

nard Muindi   21880
N. Oakland Ave.
adena, Ca. 91101

nes Mulkey   21900
opean Bible Institute
Alle des Chenes
60 Lamorlaye, France

ard Murphy   22000
rseas Crusades, Inc.
Lytton Ave.
o Alto, Ca. 94301

nn Musselman   22100
Carlos Gomes, 458
00 Jundiai, S.P.
zil

Robert Musser   22200
rati Hospital
. Shirati via Tarime
zania, East Africa

rles Mylander   22300
18 E. Russell St.
ttier, Ca. 90603

rge McBane   22400
ring
z Bhatti Road
ree, Pakistan

ard McFarland   22500
ernational Students, Inc.
9 E. St. N.W.
hington. D.C. 20037

l McKaughan   22600
P.A.L.
30.548
Paulo, Brazil

Peter Nanfelt   22700
Djalan H. Fachruddin 9
Djakarta
Java, Indonesia

Raymond Narusawa   22800
Caixa Postal 9841
Sao Paulo
Brazil

Justin Ndandali   22850
135 N. Oakland Ave.
Pasadena, Ca. 91101

William Needham   22900
World Vision, Inc. MARC
919 W. Huntington Dr.
Monrovia, Ca. 91016

Amirthraj Nelson   23000
10 Pico St.
Pasadena, Ca. 91105

Marlin L. Nelson   23100
World Vision of Korea
West Gate Box 44
Seoul, Korea

Bernd Neuman   23150
1787 Prince Albert Dr.
Riverside, Ca. 92507

Judy Niemeyer   23195
Zambia Christian Mission
P.O. Box 178
Ndola, Zambia   AFRICA

Larry Niemeyer   23200
Zambia Christian Mission
P.O. Box 178
Ndola, Zambia   AFRICA

Quentin Nordyke   23300
Casilla 544
La Paz, Bolivia, S.A.

Rodney Northrup   23400
Northwest Christian College
11th & Altar
Eugene, Oregon

Dennis Oliver   23500
Canadian Bible College
4400 4th Ave.
Regina, Sask., CANADA

Walter Olsen   23600
Chemin De Serez
27750 La Coutoure-Boussey
France

West Africa Mission   23700
Box 89 Blama
Sierra Leone, West Africa

Robert Orr   23800
Caixa Postal 94
89230 Sao Francisco do Sul
Santa Catarina, Brazil

Robert Palfanier   23900
Casilla 389
Bahia Blanca
Argentina

Sylvia (Huang) Pan   24000
1426 Carroll Ave.
Los Angeles, Ca. 90026

Reuben Tito Paredes   24100
3338 Sawtelle Ave. Apt. 13
Los Angeles, Ca. 90066

Millard Parrish   24200

465

Eric Parsons   24300
272 W. Grandview
Sierra Madre, Ca. 91024

Cecil Patey   24400
142 Maple St.
Gatineau
Quebec, CANADA

Stanley Peach   24500
9 Lane 309 An Tung St.
Taipei, 106, Taiwan
Rep. of China

Thomas Ledbetter 19300
c/o C.T. Ledbetter
9745 Long Pt. Rd.
Houston, Texas 77055

Hilkka Onerva Malaska 20100
Kankurinkatu 4, B.21
Helsinki, FINLAND

Charles Mellis 2085
524 N. Stanford Ave.
Fullerton, Calif. 92631

Larry Lenning 19350
1630 N. Hill St.
Pasadena, Ca. 91104

Marjorie Malm 20130
145 N. Oakland Ave.
Pasadena, Ca. 91101

Hilton Merritt 2090
1127 E. 38th Place
Tulsa, Okla. 74105

Leota Lenning 19355
1630 N. Hill St.
Pasadena, Ca. 91104

Alvin Martin 20200
373 Mission Rd.
Glendale, Ca. 91205

Clifford Michelsen 2100
B.P. 111
N'gaoundere
Cameroun, W. Africa

Barbara Lewis 19400
200 F-7/4, Street 55
Shalimar 7, Islamabad
West Pakistan

George Martindale 20300
2233 S. Hacienda Blvd.
Suite 202
Hacienda Hgts., Ca. 91745

Vern Middleton 2110
Union Biblical Seminary
Yeotmal, Maharashtra
India

David Liao 19500
2900 W. Ramona Rd. #10
Alhambra, Ca. 91803

Lili Martinsen 20400
Tamakiso 202
Nichikura cho 6-1
Ashiva-Shi 659, JAPAN

Kenneth Milhous 2120
50-100 Shimo Kawahara
Shimo Yasumatsu
Tokorozawa Shi
Saitama Ken 359, Japan

Jeannie Lockerbie 19550
G.P.O. Box 78
Chittagong
BANGLADESH

Augustus Marwieh 20500
E.N.I. Mission
P.O. Box 167
Greenville, Sinoe County
Liberia

James Mitchell 2130
Box 76
Stanley, N.C. 28164

Donald Lundquist 19600
I.B.U. Goyongo
B.P. 140, Gemena
Dem. Rep.-Congo
Kinshasa, Africa

Remat Masih 20510
130 N. Oakland
Pasadena, Ca. 91101

John Mizuki 2132
12368 Haley St.
SunValley, Ca. 91352

Gary Lutes 19700

464

Michael Mast 20600
Casilla 196
Cuidad de Formosa
Argentina

Daniel Moncivaiz
543 No. Howard Ave., #19
Montebello, Ca. 90640

Robert MacLean 19800
460 Ford Pl.
Pasadena, Ca. 91101

Edward Mathews 20700
Apartado 702
Guatemala, C.A.

Victor Monterroso 2140
Box 10250
San Jose, Costa Rica
Central America

Charles Mack 19900
Christian Miss. Fellowship
Box 26306
Lawrence, Ind. 46226

Erroll Mechem 20770
P.O. Box 233
Faribault, Minn. 55021

James Montgomery 2150
Overseas Crusades
P.O. Box 1416
Manila, Philippines

Pat Major 20000
Miss. Bungalow, Morsi
Amravati Dist.
Maharastra, India

Lynn Mefferd 20800
Sierra Leone Bible College
P.O. Box 890
Freetown, Sierra Leone

Donald Moore 2160
Calle 7A-310
Glenview Gardens
Ponce, P.R. 00731

uce Johnston   16900
A Far Eastern Div.
x 226
0 Thomson Rd.
ngapore

dney Johnston   17000
lla Bellevue-Bon Air
ute de Limonest
St. Didier-Au-Mont-D'or
ance

x Jones   17100
rst Christian Church
O. Box 215
pert, Idaho 83350

. Roy Just   17110
hor College
llsboro, Kansas 67063

to Kaiser   17200
15 Park Ave. #1
s Angeles, Ca. 90026

wrence Kamasi   17300
lan Fachruddin 9
karta, Indonesia

ns Kasdorf   17400
46 N. 3rd St.
esno, Ca. 93726

chard Kay   17500
O. Box N-924
ssau, N.P.
hamas, B.W.I.

ane Kepner   17510
3 Holt Ave.
Centro, Ca. 92243

uce Ker   17600
49 S.E. 60th Ave.
rtland, Ore. 97215

k Whang Kim   17700
9-10 Hongje-Dong
daemoon-Ku
oul, Korea

Myung Kim   17750
470 E. Washington, Apt. F
Pasadena, Ca. 91104

Samuel Kim   17800
425 N. El Molino
Pasadena, Ca. 91106

Bambi Kishi   17850
144 S. Oakland Ave.
Pasadena, Ca. 91104

Gunnar Kjaerland   17900
Norwegian Lutheran Miss.
P.O. Box 5540
Addis Ababa, Ethiopia

Henry Klassen   17985
1275 N. Chester Ave.
Pasadena, Ca. 91104

Jacob Klassen   17995
316 Mission Rd.
Glendale, Calif. 91205

John Klassen   18000
C.P. 688
Sao Paulo, S.P.
Brazil

John Klebe   18100
43 Cecil Ave.
Hillside, Bulawayo
Rhodesia

Herbert Klem   18120
1592 E. Orange Grove Blvd.
Pasadena, Ca. 91107

Esther Kniss   18200

Paul Kniss   18210

Elizabeth Knox   18400
Slessor House
145 N. Oakland Ave.
Pasadena, Ca. 91101

Mr. W. Knox   18410
Ch. of the Nazarene
6410 the Paseo
Kansas City, Mo. 64131

Charles Koch   18500
Latin American Miss.
285 Orchard Terrace
Bogota, N.J. 17603

Won Yong Koh   18600
10527 Bulcher Ave.
Granada Hills, Ca. 91340

Margaret Kraft   18650
1200 Lyndon
South Pasadena, Ca. 91030

Harold Kurtz   18700
American Mission
Box 1111
Addis Ababa, Ethiopia

Lloyd Kwast   18800
14787 Mansa Dr.
La Mirada, Ca. 90638

463

Bato Lamesa   18900
Enttoto ECMY (Lutheran Ch)
P.O. Box 30438
Addis Ababa, Ethiopia

J. Paul Landrey   19000
Sepal, Brazil
C.P. 30 548
Sao Paulo, Brazil 01 000

Peter Larson   19100
Casilla de Correo 1551
La Rioja
Argentina

Richard Lash   19200
Box 290
Pusan, Korea

Paul Herman 14400 711 Circle Dr. Santa Barbara, Calif. 93108	Roy Hoops 15300 c/o Miss. Bd. - Ch. of God P.O. Box 2498 Anderson, Ind. 46011	Hiroyasu Iwabuchi 16050 270 Madison Ave., #6 Pasadena, Calif. 91106
Paul Hetrick 14500 P.O. Box 3 Siteki, Swaziland	Nancy Hornberger 15350 Ricardo Rivera Navarrete 495 Lima, 27, Peru S.A.	Leonard Jacobsen 16100 Mission Lutherienne Fort Dauphin Madagascar
James Hill 14600 Casilla de Correo 30 SGO Del Estero R.P. Argentina	Stephen Hornberger 15355 Ricardo Rivera Navarrete 495 Lima, 27, Peru S.A.	Siegfried Jaeger 1446 Topeka St. Pasadena, Ca. 91104
D. Leslie Hill 14700 Box 94 Davao City, Philippines	Paul Hostetter 15390 2524 Lambros Drive Midland, Mich. 48640	Robert Johanson 16200 P.O. Box 2828 Fullerton, Calif. 92633
Robert Hill 14800 1601 Nabal Rd. La Habra, Calif. 90631	Tillman Houser 15400 Gen. Miss. Bd.-Free Meth. Ch. Winona Lake, Ind. 46590	Alfred Johnson 16300 Apartado 501 Barquisimeto Venezuela, S.A.
Stephen Hislop 14910 6250 Savannah Dr. Melbourne, Fla. 32901	Lois Howat 15500 Door of Life Hospital Ambo, Ethiopia	Don Johnson 16400 P.O. Box 1189 Addis Ababa, Ethiopia
J. Samuel Hofman 15000 Apartado 8, San Cristobal Sas Casas, Chiapas Mexico	James Hubbard 15600	Harmon Johnson 16500 Caixa Postal 30 548 Sao Paulo, Brazil

462

David Hoisington 15100 Miss. Aviation Fellowship P.O. Box 2828 Fullerton, Calif. 92633	J. Edwin Hudspith 15700 Thailand Baptist Miss. Fellow. Box 29 Chiengmai, Thailand	John Johnson 16600 Casilla 1334 Cuenca, Ecuador S.A.
Clifton Holland 15200 c/o Latin American Mission A.P.D.O. 10250 San Jose, Costa Rico C.A.	Kermit Hultgren 15800 American Mission Gorei, Ethiopia	Luverne Johnson 16700 Cons. Bapt. E.M.B. P.O. Box 5 Wheaton, Ill.
Ian Hollingsworth 15225 Box 2828 3519 W. Commonwealth Fullerton, Calif. 92633	Paul Hurlburt 15900 B.P. 5, Butembo, Kivu Rep. of Zaire, AFRICA	Raymond Johnson 16800 P.O. Box 5 Wheaton, Ill.
Searle Hoogshagen 15275 1521 Rock Glen, Glendale, Calif. 91205	James Hutchens 16000 1431 N. Harding Pasadena, Calif. 91104	Warren Johnson 1515B No. Oxford Pasadena, Calif. 91104

Gernot Fugmann 11700
Lutheran Mission
Box 2006
Madang, New Guinea

Robert Fuhriman 11800
405A S. Almansor
Alhambra, Calif. 91801

Ronald Fults 11900
Apdo Aereo 5969
Cali, Colombia

James Gamaliel 12000
School of World Mission
135 No. Oakland Ave.
Pasadena, Calif. 91101

Edwin P. Gant 12050
Casilla de Correo 38
Concepcion
Tucuman, Argentina

Robert Garber 12100
Box 102
Dire Dawa
Ethiopia

Alan Gates 12200
Lane 217, #15
Lin Chuan Rd.
Taichung, Taiwan 400

Manual Gaxiola 12300
Apartado 84
Mexico 1, D.F.
Mexico

Jacob Geddert 12400
Apartado Aereo 6557
Cali, Colombia

Richard Gibbs 12500
Caixa Postal 995
Campinas, Sao Paulo
Brazil, S.A.

Ray Giles 12600
Box 1189
Addis Ababa, Ethiopia

Donald Goldsmith 12700
c/o Mrs. Carl Wintersteen
2854 Piedmont Ave.
La Crescenta, Calif. 91214

Robert Gordon 12800
B.P. 1898
Rep. of Zaire, AFRICA

Herman Gray 12900
Takum Christian Hospital
c/o Mt. View Hostel
P.O. Box 261
Jos, B.P. Nigeria

Kenneth Greenlee 13000

John Grimley 13100
3 McKinley St.
Brookville, Ohio 45309

Jeanne Grover 13200
Casilla 2492
Lima, Peru

James Gustafson 13300
14 Pramuan Rd.
Bangkok, Thailand

Keith Hamilton 13400
Casilla 3615
La Paz, Bolivia

Robert Hancock 13500
2718 Hollister Terrace
Glendale Calif. 91206

Louise Hannum 13550
275 Oakland Ave.
Pasadena, Calif. 91106

Walter Hannum 13555
275 Oakland Ave.
Pasadena, Calif. 91106

Paul Hansen 13600
208 Sheriff St.
Campbellsville, Georgetown
Guyana, S.A.

Gary Hardaway 13700
Andes Evang. Mission
Cajon 514, Cochabamba
Bolivia, S.A.

Dr. Pat Harrison 13800
11 Garibaldi St.
Armidale, N.S.W. 2350
Australia

Douglas Hayward 13900
U.F.M.
Sentani, West Irian
Indonesia

Thomas Headland 13950
320 C Mission Rd.
Glendale, Calif. 91205

Mrs. Della Headley
265 N. Oakland No. 12
Pasadena, Ca. 91101

George Heckendorf 13980
C.M.A. Mission
Konkaen, Thailand

461

Roger Hedlund 14000
14311 E. Merced
Baldwin Park, Calif.

Dr. W. Joseph Hemphill
Executive Director
Nat. Sunday School Assoc.
Box 685

James Henneberger 14200
Rivadavia 2257
Olavarria, F.G.R.
Argentina

Dale Herendeen 14300
10 Beckett Place
Regina, Sask., Canada

Patrick Dickens 8750
275 No. Oakland
Pasadena, Calif. 91101

Dr. Donald Dilworth 8800
Clinica Runatacuyac
Casilla 269
Latacunga, Ecuador, S.A.

Lee Roy Donnell 8900

Patricia Donnell 9000

Cecelia Drenth 9100
610 11th St.
Redlands, Calif. 92373

James Dretke 9200
33 N. 4th St.
Alhambra, Calif. 91801

James Duren 9300
Spanish-American Area
3137 Conquista
Long Beach, Calif. 90291

460
Wayne Dye 9390
1170 Topeka St.
Pasadena, Ca. 91104

Fred Edwards 9400
2421 Clark
Venice, Calif. 90291

Philip Edwards 9420
Christian Miss. Fellowship
P.O. Box 26306
Indianapolis, Ind. 46226

9500

Eddie Eggerichs 9600
925 Webster
Wheaton, Ill. 60187

Daniel Ellis 9700
Christian Miss. Fellowship
Box 1189
Addis Ababa, Ethiopia

H. Theodore Ellis 9800
Chang Jung Boy's School
East Gate Rd.
Tainan, Taiwan

Edgar Elliston 9900
Box 1189
Addis Ababa, Ethiopia

Arno Enns 10000
Cons. Bap. For. Miss. Soc.
Box 5
Wheaton, Ill. 60187

Marlan Enns 10110
Apartado 415
Ciudad Satelite
Estado de Mexico, Mexico

Paul Enyart 10100
Apartado 8
Chiquimula, Guatemala

Dean Erickson 10200
Biblical Seminary
Apdos. Aereo 3041
Medellin, Colombia

Donald Erickson 10300
Box 127
Kenmore, N. Dak. 58746

Mrs. Donald Erickson 10400
Box 127
Kenmore, N. Dak. 58746

Edwin Erickson 10500
Bapt. Gen. Conf. Mission
P.O. Box 2323
Addis Ababa, Ethiopia

Roger Erickson 106
675 Santa Barbara
Pasadena, Calif. 91101

Abram Esau 107
E.F.M.C. Kajiji
B.P. 4341 Kinshasa 11
Rep. Demucratique de Con

Judy Eslick 108
Wycliffe Bible Translato
219 W. Walnut, Box 1960
Santa Ana, Calif. 92702

Percy T. Espinoza 109

Melvin Evans 110
San Fernando Ch. of Chr
1226 Glenoaks Blvd.
San Fernando, Calif.

Wilson Ferreira 111
Caixa Postal 133
Campinas, S.P.
Brazil

Mrs. Carmel Field 112
Assemblies of God En. M
1445 Boonville
Springfield, Mo. 65802

John Fleming 11
c/o Thomas Stebbins
Box 923
Saigon, Vietnam

Benjamin Ford 114
San Juan Mission
P.O. Box 720
Farmington, N. Mex. 874

Tom Fort 11
Rt. 1, Box 7
Yamhill, Oregon 97148

Andrew Friend 11
C.P. 4, Salazar
Mozambique, AFRICA

ert Chapman   6200
istian Missy. Fellowship
. Box 26306
rence. Ind. 46226

o Him Chiong   6300
R. Regente St.
ondo, Manila
lippines

ren Christianson   6400
Ford Place #9
adena, Calif. 91101

Hian Chua   6500
S 27, Marylebone Rd.
don, N.W.I. 5Jr.
land

1 Chung   6600
3Ka, Choongjungro,
aimoonku, Seoul Theol. Sem.
ul, Korea

Leon Clymore   6700
S. Chambers, #23
remore, Ok. 74017

id Cochran   6750

ce Colson   6800
02 Walnut St.
ita Calif.   90717

shall Combs   6900
thwest Christian Coll.
h and Alter Sts.
ene, Oregon

ene W. Congdon   7000
o 17, San Cristobal
Casas, Chipas
ico

es Conklin   7090
03 Van Ness
rance, Calif. 90504

William Conley   7100
St. Paul Bible College
Bible College, Minn. 55373

William Conrad   7200
Apartado 3977
San Jose, Costa Rica
Central America

Clyde Cook   7210
Biola College
La Mirada, Calif. 90639

Norman Cook   7300
Overseas Crusades
265 Litton Ave.
Palo Alto, Calif.

James Cooper   7350
139 W. Cypress
Monrovia, Calif.   91016

Gary Copeland   7400
Marin Covenant Church
25 Mitchell Blvd.
San Rafael, Calif. 94903

Gollapalli Cornelius   7500
Hindustan Bible Institute
2 Madavakkam Tank Rd., Kilpauk
Madras 10, India

Emmett D. Cox   7700
Bd. of Missions
407 U.B. Bldg.
Huntington, Ind. 46750

Howard Crowl   7720
320 F Mission Rd.
Glendale, Calif. 91205

Norman Cummings   7800
Overseas Crusades
265 Lytton Ave.
Palo Alto, Calif. 94301

Robert Cunville   7820
135 N. Oakland Ave.
Pasadena, Ca. 91101

Michael Curry   7900
55 Hurlbut #15
Pasadena, Calif. 91105

Graham Cyster   7980
1612 N. Hill St.
Pasadena, Calif. 91104

K.C. Daniel   8000
Kurumanasseril House
Payipad P.O. Vos Haripad
Kerala State, So. India

Ramescandra Dass   8100
135 N. Oakland Ave.
Pasadena, Calif. 91101

Frank Daugherity   8200
285 S. Hudson, #19
Pasadena, Calif.   91106

Linnell Davis   8300
A.I.C. Mbooni
P.O. Kikima, Machakos
Kenya, East Africa

459

Ray Davis   8400
P.O. Box 21010
Nairobi, Kenya

Keith Dawson   8500
S.I.L. B.P. 8857
Abidjan-Cocody
Ivory Coast

Charles Derr   8600
Apdo. Aereo 190
Sincelejo, Columbia

Jacob Deshazer   8700
c/o Dr. Kilpatrick
Free Methodist Bd.
Winona Lake, Ind.

Keith Bentson 3100
Liniers 930
Temperley (Bs.As.)
Argentina

Bert Block 3200
8556 Wentworth
Sunland, Calif. 91040

Clarence Boehm 3300
1521 Rock Glen Ave.
Glendale, Calif. 91205

Ernest Boehr 3400
P.O. Box 60
Miaoli, Taiwan
Rep. of China

Harvey Boese 3500
P.O. Box 1
Korat, Thailand

Robert Bolton 3600
313 Mission Rd.
Glendale, Calif. 91205

Miss Ladell Bones 3700
Evang. Alliance Miss.
Mission School, Tachira
San Cristobal, Venezuela

458
Paul Boschman 3800
Box 370
Rosthenn. Sask.
Canada

Rolla Bradley 3900
c/o Baptist Mission
0 Jung Dong 201-5
Taejon. 300, Korea

Malcolm Bradshaw 4000
895 Sacketts Ford Road
Ivyland, Pa. 18974

John K. Branner 4100
151 Jen Yi St.
Kaohsuing 800
Taiwan, Rep. of China

Eugene Braun 4200
Centro de Motivacion
Y Asesoria
Carrion 1359
Quito, Ecuador S.A.

Neil H. Braun 4300
2317 Broadway
Bellingham, Wash. 98225

William D. Braun 4400
c/o Latin American Mission
Costa Rica

Don Bray 4410
Wesleyan Mission, Box 489
Mt. Hagen, W.H.D.
Papua, New Guinea

Wendell St. Broom 4500
Box 8040 Station Acc
Abilene, Texas 79601

David R. Brougham 4600
Jl. Besar Ijen 79
Malang, Java Timur
Indonesia

Keith Brown 4700
Overseas Crusades
265 Lytton Ave.
Palo Alto, Calif. 94301

Elden Buck 4800
Memorial Chapel, Kwajalein
Marshall Islands - Box 1711
APO San Francisco 96555

Allan Buckman 4900
P.M.B. 101
Ogoja, S.E. State
Nigeria

Herman Buehler 5000
Liebenzell Miss. of USA, Inc.
Schooley's Mt. N.J. 07870

Harry D. Burke 5100
Apartado 21-983
Mexico 21, D.F.

Donald Burns 5200
Casilla 5080
Quito, Ecuador

Charles O. Butler 5300
Apartado 6424
Panama 5, R. de Panama

Ray Canfield 5400
Parcelamento El Florida
Morales, Izabel
Guatamala, C.A.

Mrs. D.L. Carr 5500
P.O. Box 3
Hsi Lo, Taiwan
Rep. of China

E. Earl Carver 5600
P.O. Box 1112
Caguas, Puerto Rico 00625

Lew Cass 5700
Kotak Pos 15
Salatiga, Jateng
Indonesia

Eun Soo Chae 5800
1300 E. Covina Hills Rd.
Covina, Calif.

Victor Chamberlin 5900
3514 Kenora Dr.
Spring Valley, Calif. 9207

Wilson Chan 5980
Kreyssler Hall, #33
130 N. Oakland Ave.
Pasadena, Calif.

Tom Chandler 6000
Overseas Crusades, Inc.
P.O. Box 56 KBT
Jakarta, Indonesia

Joseph Chang 6
718 South Marengo
Pasadena, Calif. 91101

arl Ackland 100
rthwest Christian Coll.
th and Alter Sts.
gene, Oregon

rry Acton 200
. of Miss. - Cumberland
Pres. Church
O. Box 4149
mphis, Tenn. 38104

. Imotemjin Aier 290
35 N. Oakland Ave.
asadena, Ca. 91101

d Ailanjian 300
70 Catherine Rd.
tadena, Calif. 91001

Frank Alexander 400
julanyana Village
O. Box 172
vingstone, Zambia AFRICA

colyn Alexander 490
3 Highland Ave.
rovia, Calif. 91016

. Merton J. Alexander 500
3 Highland Ave.
rovia, Calif. 91016

red Allin 600
P.O. Box 111
Forest
Hermon, Calif. 95041

Alliston 700
thwest Christian Coll.
h and Alter Sts.
ene, Oregon

rles F. Altig 800

ard Altig 900
W. 48th
g Beach, Calif. 90805

Albert Alsop 910
2330 E. Del Mar Blvd.
Pasadena. Calif. 91107

Eleanor Anderson 1000
93 Fu Teh Rd.
Hsin Kang. Chiayi Hsien
Taiwan. Rep. of China

Loren Anderson 1100
Instituto Biblico Quiche
San Cristobal, Toto
Guatamala, C.A.

William Anderson
Makarere College
Box 7062
Kampala, Uganda

Egbert W. Andrews 1300
P.O. Box 5-53
Kaohsiung, Taiwan
Rep. of China

Paul Ariga 1400
6-5, 3 Chome
Tsurumaki-cho
Setagaya-Ku, Tokyo JAPAN

Joseph Arthur 1500
309 Mission Rd.
Glendale, Calif. 91205

Cecil Ashley 1600
Caixa Postal 11 922
Sao Paulo 10, E.S.P.
Brazil, S. America

Raymond Aspinall 1700
Ayacuche 1858
Rosarie, Pcia Santa Fe
Argentina, S. America

John Astleford 1800
Friends Mission
Apartado 8, Chiquimula
Guatemala, C.A.

Allen Avery Jr. 1900
P.O. Box 172
Livingstone, Zambia AFRICA

James E. Baker 2000
Assemblies of God
1445 Boonville Ave.
Springfield, Mo.

Bruce W. Baillie 2100
1025 E. Lomita
Glendale, Calif. 91205

Paul Balisky 2200
SIM, P.O. Bonga
Kaffa, Ethiopia

Yesu Bandela 2300
99 S. Grand Oaks
Pasadena, Calif. 91107

Dr. David Barrett 2400
Unit of Research
P.O. Box 230
Nairobi, Kenya AFRICA

Elwood R. Bartlett 2500
Mulungwishi
Sac Prive Lubumbashi
Rep. du Congo

Ronald Beech 2600
Box 14
Baquio City
Philippines

457

William Bengtson 2700
Las Magnolias 495
San Isidro
Lima 27 Peru

Charles Bennett 2800
Box 2828
Fullerton, Calif. 92633

Mary Bensick 2900
1496 E. Howard
Pasadena, Ca. 91104

Stanley Benson 3000

Paul Hostetter 15390	Hazel Watson 36990	John Yoon 391C
Pakistan	Japan	Korea Evan. Inter-Miss. A▮
Ref. Ch.	S. Bapt.	Hong Kong
73	67/68	71/72
Judy Niemeyer 23190	Charles S. Vore 36350	Norvald Yri 392C
Zambia	Guatemala	Ethiopia
Ch. of Christ	Friends	Norwegian Evan. Luth.
71/72	73	71/72/73

Johan Vandenberg Taiwan Gen. Conf. Menn. 68/69	35600	Lester Wait Taiwan Overseas Crusades, Inc. 72	36700	Jack Wing Honduras Friends 72	38000
Smuts Van Rooyen South Africa SDA	35700	Orlando Waltner Gen. Conf. Menn.	36800	Harry Winslow Taiwan Free Meth. 69/70	38100
William Van Tol Sudan United Miss. (Chr. Ref. Bd.) 70/71	35800	Bruce Warner Indonesia U. Meth. Ch. 66/67, 71/72	36900	Ruth Wintersteen Ethiopia Bapt. G.C. 67/68	38200
Truong Van Tot (Toke) Vietnam CMA 70/71	35900	Leslie Watson Japan S. Bapt. 67/68	37000	Joseph Wold Liberia LCA 70/71	38300
Eino Johannes Vehanen Japan LCA 69/70	36000	Hans Weerstra Mexico Chr. Ref. FMB 70/71/72	37200	Thomas Wolf Spain S. Bapt. 67/68/69	38400
Rodney Venberg Chad L. Breth. of Am. 69/70	36100	Wayne Weld Colombia Evan. Covenant Ch. 67/68, 72/73	37300	Fred Wolff Peru LCA 70/71	38500
John Vigus Bolivia AEM 69/70	36200	Edwin Wentz Japan LCA 68/69	37400	James Wong Singapore Anglican 71/72	38600
Janvier Voekel Colombia LAM 70/71	36300	Norman Wetther Guam C.B.H.M.S. 66/67	37500	Herb Works Ch. of Christ-USA 72/73	38700
Dale Vought TEAM Spain 72/73	36400	Mr.&Mrs. Stanley Wick Guatemala COEMAR (UP) 68/69	37600 37700	Wayland Wong Hong Kong Evan. Free Ch. 68/69	38800
Abe Vreeke Nigeria Ch. Ref. Bd. 70/71	36500	Hans Wilhelm Brazil Overseas Crusades 65/66	37800	Ted Yamamori 61/62	38900
C. Peter Wagner Bolivia Andes Evan. Miss. 67/68	36600	Robert Willman Taiwan TEAM 71/72	37900	Dr. Donald Yates	39000

455

Hugh Sprunger Taiwan Gen. Conf. Menn. 71/72	32300	Allen Swanson Taiwan LCA 67/68	33400	Donald Thomas, M.D. Zambia Ch. of Christ 71/72	345

Hugh Sprunger 32300
Taiwan
Gen. Conf. Menn.
71/72

Allen Swanson 33400
Taiwan
LCA
67/68

Donald Thomas, M.D. 345
Zambia
Ch. of Christ
71/72

Frederick Sprunger 32400
Japan
Gen. Conf. Menn.
69/70

Gordon Swanson 33500
Philippines
C & MA
67/68

William Thompson 346

Erwin Spruth 32500
New Guinea
LCMS
69/70

James Tai 33600
Taiwan
Campus Crusade
72/73/74

Clancy Thompson 347
Free Meth. Bd.

Vernon Stanley 32600
Zaire
Am. Bapt.
72

Toshihiro Takami 33700
Japan
UCC-Japan
68/69

Neil Thompson 348
Thailand
Ch. of Christ
71/72

Wayne Stephens 32700
Vietnam
C. of Christ
72/73

Francis Van Tate 33800
Kenya
Ch. of Christ
69/70

Abraham Thottungal 349
India
Marthoma
66/67

Philip Steyne 32800
South Africa
TEAM
72/73/74

Jack Taylor 33900

Ronald Thurman 350
Indonesia
Campus Crusade
68/69

Josephine Still 32900
Honduras
Friends
68/69

Vernon Tank 34000
Taiwan
Mustard Seed, Inc.
67/68

Ralph Toliver 351
O.M.F.
Philippines
67/68

454

Fred Stock 33000
W. Pakistan
COEMAR
67/68

Lopeti Taufa 34100
Fiji Islands
Free Wesleyan Ch. of Tonga
67/68

Arthur Trevor 352
Japan
O.M.F.
71/72

Leon Strunk 33100
Brazil

69/70

Herman Tegenfeldt 34200
Burma
Baptist G.C.
71/72

Philip Tsuchiya 353
Japan

72/73

Venkata Subbamma 33200
India
LCA

John Thannickle 34300
India
Assem. of God
72/73/74

Leonard Tuggy 354
Philippines
CBFMS
67/68, 73/74

James Sunda 33300

Harold Thomas 34400
Bolivia-Friends
69-73

Paul Utley 355
U. Meth. Ch.
69/70

ra Sargunam dia erseas Crusades /73	29100	Charlotte Self Pakistan Presby. 73	30110	Lalthankhum Sinate 31200 India Indo-Burma Pioneer Miss. 67/68	
mes Sauder nduras stern Menn. Bd. /71	29200	Paul Selleck 66/67	30200	Roger Singer 31300 Hong Kong LCA 67/68	
ter Savage livia des Evang. Miss. /68	29300	Roy Shearer Korea U. Pres. USA 67/68, 71/72	30300	Samuel Skivington 31400 Philippines CBFMS 69/70	
eldon Sawatzky iwan n. Menn. Bd. /70	29400	Stanford Shewmaker Zambia Ch. of Christ 66/67/68/69	30400	Eugene Smith 31500 Brazil CMF 68/69	
vid Schneider	29500	Samuel Shewmaker Zambia Ch. of Christ 71/72	30500	Mrs. Della Headley 31600 Ethiopia Presby. 71/72	
y Schneider	29600	Merlin Shields Brazil 62	30600	Ebbie Smith 31700 Indonesia Ch. of Christ 69/70	
er Schrage azil hany Fellowship '73	29700	Harold Shock Hong Kong ABFMS 66/67	30700	Mont Smith 31800	
rge Schroeder eria sionary Ch. 73	29800	Timothy Shumaker Mexico Gen. Miss. Bd. 71/72	30800	Elaine Smith 31900	453
n Schwab an	29900	Werner Sidler Ethiopia Missionsheim 73	30900	James Sohn 32000 Korea U. Meth. Ch. 72/73	
nn Schwartz bia th. in Christ 72/73	30000	Warren Simandle Brazil Young Life 67/68/69	31000	Dagfinn Solheim 32100 Japan Norwegian Luth. Mis. 71/72	
iam Seger ico 69/70	30100	Stewart Simpson India Plymouth Breth. 72/73	31100	Kenneth Speer 32200 Chile Ch. of Christ 66/67	

Douglas Priest Ethiopia ICG	25800	William Read Brazil U. Pres. Ch. USA 65/66, 71/72/73	26900	Sang Kook Ro Korea Presby. 71/72/73	28000
Marjorie Priest Ethiopia ICG	25900	Albert Reasoner Brazil Pres. Miss Ch. 66/67	27000	Gordon Robinson Nigeria Nigerian Bapt. 66/67	28100
Ted Profitt CBA 70/71	26000	Grady Wood Reed Zambia Ch. of Christ 70/71	27100	Milton Robinson Bolivia Methodist 73	28200
Glenn Prunty Panama Ind. Miss. Bd. 69/70	26100	Jerald Reed Ecuador Evang. Covenant 68/69	27200	Ruth Ann Robinson Methodist Bolivia 73	28300
Dorothy Raber Taiwan Free Meth. 70/71/72	26200	Niles Reimer Ethiopia American Mission 65/66	27300	Paul Roland Japan Norwegian Evan. Luth. Fr. Ch. 71/72	28400
Paul Rader Korea The Savation Army 71/72/73	26300	Reginald Reimer Vietnam C & MA 70/71/72	27500	Joel Romero Argentina CBFMS 69/70	28500
David Rambo Philippines CMA 67/68	26400	Vernon Reimer Columbia Menn. Breth. 66/67	27500	Elmer Root India Free Meth. 62	28600

452

Nene Ramientos Philippines Overseas Crusades 71	26500	Herminio Reyes Philippines C & MA 72/73	27600	Loretta Root India Free Meth. 62	28700
Max Randall Zambia Ch. of Christ 66/67	26600	Norman Riddle Zaire A.B.F.M.S. 69/70	27700	Charles Ross Zaire Presbyterian 66/67, 71/72	28800
Walter Rasch Nigeria Lutheran 72/73	26700	Kenneth Rideout Thailand C & MA 72/73	27800	Murray Russell Presby. 66/67	28900
Herbert Ratcliff Trinidad Nazarene, 71/72	26800	William Rife Guam Pacific Ocean Miss, 68/69	27900	George Samuel India Marthoma Syrian Ch. 70/71/72/73	29000

Howard McFarland	22500	Walter Olsen France CBFMS 70/71	23600	Taylor Pendley Bapt. Gen. Conv. 69/70	24700
Paul McKaughan Brazil S.E.P.A.L. 66/67	22600	Gilbert Olsen Sierra Leone Evang. U.B. 65/66, 68/69	23700	Edward Pentecost Mexico Phia. Col. of Bible 71/72/73	24800
Peter Nanfelt Indonesia C & MA 71/72	22700	Robert Orr Brazil Christ. Nat. Evan. Comm. 69/70	23800	Pablo Perez Mexico Presbyterian 71/72/73	24900
Raymond Narusawa Brazil Japanese Evan. Miss. Soc. 69/70	22800	Robert Palfenier Argentina Evan. Union S. America 69/70	23900	Roger Perkings Brazil	25000
William Needham World Vision 69/70	22900	Sylvia (Huang) Pan 72/73	24000	Lorene Persons 70/71	25100
Amirthraj Nelson India 71/72/73/74	23000	Reuben Tito Paredes Peru Peruvian Evang. Ch. 71/72	24100	Dorothy Peters Japan FEGC 69/70	25200
Marlin Nelson Korea World Vision 66/67	23100	Millard Parrish	24200	Abraham Philips India Mar Thoma 72/73/74	25300
Larry Niemeyer Zambia Ch. of Christ 70/71	23200	Eric Parsons FEBC 67/68	24300	Thomas Philip India Syrian Orthodox 71/72	25400
Quentin Nordyke Bolivia Friends 70/71/72	23300	Cecil Patey 67/68	24400	Jim Pomayayitch	25500
Rodney Northrup	23400	Stanley Peach Taiwan CBFMS 63	24500	Ernest Poulson Singapore Miss. Enterprise, Inc. 69/70	25600
Dennis Oliver Canada C& MA 71/72/73	23500	Elwin Pelletier Uganda	24800	Melvin Pownall Ch. of Christ 70/71, 72/73	25700

451

Barbar Lewis 19400 West Pakistan Presb yterian 71/72	Augustus Marwieh 20500 Liberia Chr. Nationals' Evang. Comm. 71/72	Victor Monterroso 21400 Costa Rica Latin American Mission 65/66, 70/71, 72/73
David Liao 19500 Taiwan Overseas Crusade 66/67/68/69	Ramat Masih 20510 Pakistan 73	James Montgomery 21500 Philippines Overseas Crusades 64
Donald Lundquist 19600 Zaire ECC 65/66	Michael Mast 20600 Argentina Mennonite 71/72	Donald Moore 21600 Puerto Rico S. Bapt. 71/72
Gary Lutes 19700 Costa Rica Ch. of Christ 66/67	Edward Mathews 20700 Guatemala Ch. of Christ 69/70	Mildred Morehouse 21700 Japan FEGC 70/71
Robert MacLean 19800 Indonesia Ch. of Christ 71/72/73/74	Lynn Mefferd 20800 Sierra Leone United Breth. in Christ 71/72	James Morris 21800 Thailand OMF 71/72
Charles Mack 19900 Ch. of Christ	Hilton Merritt 20900 Ch. of Christ 66/67	James Mulkey 21900 France Campus Crusade 67/68
450 Pat Major India CBFMS 65/66	Clifford Michelsen 21000 Cameroun ALC 68/69	Edward Murphy 22000 Brazil Overseas Crusades 65/66, 70/71/72
Hilkka Onerva Malaska 20100 Finland Nazarene 69/70	Vern Middleton 21100 India Fellship Bapt. Miss.	Glenn Musselman 22100 Brazil Menn. Bd-Elkhart 69/70
Alvin Martin 20200 Israel C & MA 72/73/74	Kenneth Milhous 21200 Japan Bapt. G.C. 71/72	Dr. Robert Musser 22200 Tanzania Brethren in Christ 72
George Martindale 20300 63/64/65	James Mitchell 21300 Mexico Assoc. Ref. Pres-For Miss. 69/70	Charles Mylander 22300 Bolivia Friends 70/71
Lili Martinsen 20400 Japan Luth. Free Ch.-Norway, 71/72	Daniel Moncivaiz 21310 Mexico Foursquare 73	George McBane 22400 Pakistan Assoc. Ref. Pres. Miss. 70/71

Alfred Johnson 16300 Venezuela WEC 66/67	Lawrence Kamasi 17300 Indonesia CMA 71/72/73	Won Yong Koh 18300 Korea Korean Presby. Ch. 69/70, 71/72, 72/73
Don Johnson 16400 Ethiopia CMF 64	Hans Kasdorf 17400 Brazil Menn. Brethren 72/73/74	Paul Kniss 18400
Harmon Johnson 16500 Brazil Indo. A. of God 65/66, 67/68, 68/69	Richard Kay 17500 Bahamas, B.W.I. Island Miss. Soc. 70/71/72	Esther Kniss 18500
John Johnson 16600 Ecuador World Miss. Prayer League 66/67	Duane Kepner 17510 Mexico MGF 72	Mr. W. Knox 18600 Ch. of the Nazarene
Laverne Johnson 16700 Con. Bapt. E.M.B.	Bruce Ker 17600	Harold Kurtz 18700 Ethiopia COEMAR American Mission 65/66
Raymond Johnson 16800	Duk Whang Kim 17700 Korea Methodist 70/71	Lloyd Kwast 18800 Cameroom NAm. Baptist 67/68, 71/72
Bruce Johnston 16900 Singapore Seventh-Day Adventist 71	Samuel Kim 17800 Korea Presby. Ch. of Korea 72/73/74	Bato Lamesa 18900 Ethiopia Lutheran Ch. 73
Rodney Johnston 17000 France TEAM 70/71	Gunnar Kjaerland 17900 Ethiopia Norwegian Luth. Miss. 70/71	J. Paul Landrey 19000 Brazil Overseas Crusade 66/67
Rex Jones 17100 Ethiopia CMF 70/71	John Klassen 18000 Rhodesia	Peter Larson 19100 Argentina Baptist 72/73
Dr. Roy Just 17110 Menn. Brethren 72/73	John Klebe 18100 Rhodesia	Richard Lash 19200 Korea Christian Ch. 67/68
Otto Kaiser 17200 Sq. Gospel 73/74	Charles Koch 18200 Colombia Latin American Miss. 69/70	Thomas Ledbetter 19300 Brazil Christian Ch. 67/68

449

John Grimley 13100
Nigeria
Ch. of the Brethren
62/63

Jeanne Grover 13200
Peru
WBT
65/66

James Gustafson 13300
Thailand
ECC
69/70

Keith Hamilton 13400
Bolivia

Robert Hancock 13500
Indonesia
SDA
72/73

Paul Hansen 13600
Guyana
LCA
71/72

Gary Hardaway 13700
Bolivia & Philippines
Overseas Crusade
69/70

448

Dr. Pat Harrison 13800
Australia

Douglas Hayward 13900
West Irian
UFM
71/72

Roger Hedlund 14000
Italy
CBFMS
69/70/71/72/73

Dr. Joseph Hemphill 14100

70/71

James Henneberger 14200
Argentina
LCA
67/68

Dale Herendeen 14300
Viet Nam
C & MA
71/72/73

Paul Herman
14400
Episcopal
72/73

Paul Hetrick 14500
Swaziland
Nazarene
71/72

James Hill 14600
Argentina
Bapt. Gen. Conf.
68/69

Leslie Hill 14700
Philippines
S. Bapt.
72/73

Robert Hill 14800
Cen. Afr. Republic
Brethren Ch.
68/69

George Hackendorf 14900
Thailand
C & MA
64

Samuel Hofman 15000
Mexico
Ref. Ch. in Amer.
70/71

David Hoisington 15100
Indonesia
MAF
72

Clifton Holland 15200
Costa Rico
Latin American Mission
67/68/69/70/71

Roy Hoops 15300
Kenya
Ch. of God
70/71

Tillman Houser 15400
Rhodesia
Free Methodist Ch.
69/70

Lois Howat 15500
Ethiopia
Bapt. Gen. Conf.
68/70

James Hubbard 15600
Church of God
66/67

Edwin Hudspith 15700
Thailand
ABFMS
65/66

Kermit Hultgren 15800
Ethiopia
UPUSA
70/71

Paul Hurlburt 15900
Zaire
CBFMS
66/67

James Hutchens 16000
Israel
Independent
72/73/74

Leonard Jacobsen 16100
Madagascar
ALC
66/67/68

Siegfried Jaeger 16110
Japan
Liebenzell
73/74

Robert Johanson 16200
Indonesia
MAF
72/73

heodore Ellis aiwan anadian Presby. Mis. 8/69	9800	Percy Espinoza Church of Christ	10900	James Gamaliel India I. Evang. Luth. Miss. 66/67	12000
dgar Elliston thiopia MF 7/68	9900	Melvin Evans Zambia Ch. of Christ 69/70/71	11000	Robert Garber Ethiopia Menn.-Eastern Board 69/70	12100
rno Enns rgentina BFMS 6/67	10000	Wilson Ferreira Brazil Presby. C. of Brazil 67/68/69	11100	Alan Gates Taiwan CBFMS 65/66, 70/71	12200
aul Enyart uatemala riends 9/70	10100	Mrs. Carmel Field Assemblies of God 69	11200	Manuel Gaxiola Mexico Apostolic 68/69	12300
ean Erickson olumbia CC 8/69	10300	John Fleming Vietnam	11300	Jacob Geddert Columbia Menn. Breth. 68/69	12400
onald Erickson olivia orld Mission Prayer League 0/71	10300	Benjamin Ford Navajo Indian Episcopal 66/67	11400	Richard Gibbs Brazil CBFMS 66/67	12500
rs. Donald Erickson olivia MPL 0/71	10400	Tom Fort Zambia Ch. of Christ 71/72	11500	Ray Giles Ethiopia CMF 67/68	12600
dwin Erickson thiopia aptist Gen. Conference 6/67, 71, 72	10500	Andrew Friend South Africa TEAM 69/70	11600	Donald Goldsmith Brazil Bapt. Gen. Conf. 66/67	12700
oger Erickson thiopia aptist. Gen. Conf. 6/67	10600	Gernot Fugmann New Guinea Lutheran 68/69	11700	Robert Gordon Haiti MAF 70/71	12800
bram Esau aire enn. Breth. 1/72	10700	Robert Fuhriman Japan Campus Crusade 72/73	11800	Herman Gray Nigeria Chr. Ref. B. of F. M. 66/67	12900
udy Eslick ndia ycliffe 5/66	10800	Donald Fults Columbia Overseas Crusades 69/70	11900	Kenneth Greenlee Ch. of Christ 68	13000

447

Cyril Simkins

THE MEANS

of world evangelization:

MISSIOLOGICAL EDUCATION

at the
Fuller School of World Mission

edited by Alvin Martin